EFFICIENCY AND INPUT-OUTPUT ANALYSES

Theory and Applications

EFFICIENCY AND INPUT-OUTPUT ANALYSES

Theory and Applications

Thijs ten Raa

Utrecht School of Economics, The Netherlands

World Scientific

NEW JERSEY • LONDON • SINGAPORE • BEIJING • SHANGHAI • HONG KONG • TAIPEI • CHENNAI • TOKYO

Published by

World Scientific Publishing Co. Pte. Ltd.
5 Toh Tuck Link, Singapore 596224
USA office: 27 Warren Street, Suite 401-402, Hackensack, NJ 07601
UK office: 57 Shelton Street, Covent Garden, London WC2H 9HE

Library of Congress Cataloging-in-Publication Data
Names: ten Raa, Thijs, author.
Title: Efficiency and input-output analyses : theory and applications /
Thijs ten Raa, Utrecht School of Economics, The Netherlands.
Description: New Jersey : World Scientific, 2021. | Includes bibliographical references and index.
Identifiers: LCCN 2020056885 | ISBN 9789811231230 (hardcover) |
ISBN 9789811233296 (ebook) | ISBN 9789811233302 (ebook other)
Subjects: LCSH: Input-output analysis. | Economics, Mathematical.
Classification: LCC HB142 .R323 2021 | DDC 339.2/3--dc23
LC record available at https://lccn.loc.gov/2020056885

British Library Cataloguing-in-Publication Data
A catalogue record for this book is available from the British Library.

For any available supplementary material, please visit
https://www.worldscientific.com/worldscibooks/10.1142/12131#t=suppl

Desk Editors: Aanand Jayaraman/Lum Pui Yee

Typeset by Stallion Press
Email: enquiries@stallionpress.com

After his *Input-Output Economics: Theory and Applications*, Thijs ten Raa has extended his research to efficiency analysis. He has contributed to the microeconomic theory of performance measurement, has made applications to industries, national economies and international trade, and has written on the history of economic thought. Twenty-five new papers, published over the last decade, are now collected and interrelated by an introduction, amounting to a unification of theory and applications in efficiency and input-output analyses.

About the Author

Thijs ten Raa is Lecturer and Researcher at the Utrecht School of Economics and has been affiliated with New York, Erasmus and Tilburg Universities. He has published a dozen books and numerous articles in professional journals. He chaired the economics committee of the Netherlands Organization for the Advancement of Research (NWO). He shared the Wassily Leontief Centennial Medal with Professors Klein and Solow. He is fellow of the International Input-Output Association.

Contents

Introduction

In the last decade, I have tried to merge efficiency analysis and input-output analysis. As one hopes with such an endeavor, this project has been fruitful to both branches of economic science. My papers of the last decade, collected in this volume, witness this mutual development.

Let me characterize the two subfields of economics I have studied. Efficiency analysis studies the relative performance of firms within an industry or a national economy, possibly across countries. The basic approach is to represent firms by their input-output vectors. The scatter diagram of all these input-output vectors is a subset of the production possibility set of the industry (or the economy). A firm is represented by a point in the scatter diagram, and its proximity to the boundary of the production possibility set measures the efficiency of the firm. An issue is in which direction one should measure the distance between the firm, represented by its input-output vector, and the production possibility set frontier? My take is that the direction should be determined by the consumers' wants. More precisely, my take is that efficiency analysis should be grounded in the concept of Pareto efficiency, as articulated by Debreu. This, however, requires a general equilibrium framework, and that is where input-output analysis enters the investigation.

As alluded to, the benefit of a synthesis between efficiency analysis and input-output analysis is a two-way street. Input-output analysis — the study of the interrelations between industries, the indirect effects of consumption and production activities — also has some open issues and, therefore, has scope for improvement. Perhaps the best-known issue is the input-output analytic assumption of complementarities of inputs. Industries are characterized by their aggregate input and output vectors and an issue is which form of aggregation is appropriate? The main approaches are the so-called commodity model and the industry model, but there are numerous issues. What are input-output coefficients; what is their relationship to the production possibility set? Economic theory needs to sort this out. Another issue is the identification of key sectors, e.g. in development economics. Input-output analysis identifies them by measures of indirect effects. I find this procedure flawed; it better be replaced by something based on efficiency measures.

My idea to commingle efficiency and input-output analyses is quite simple. Efficiency analysts measure relative performance, relative to the best practice, a firm or collection of firms on the production possibility frontier. More precisely, efficiency is relative productivity, where the latter is essentially output per "unit" of input. On the other hand, input-output analysts study input per "unit" of output. I thought, hey, aren't they chasing the same animal? Isn't the concept of the one the inverse of the other? The answer is basically yes, and this insight will help resolve open issues in either branch of economic science.

In the first chapter of this volume, I ground my analyses in Debreu's efficiency framework. The title of the paper is "Debreu's coefficient of resource utilization, the Solow residual, and TFP: The connection by Leontief preferences". I interrelate the various productivity and efficiency measures in a concise manner, even in a single equation. As a byproduct, I expose some defects of competing measures in the literature.

The second chapter, written jointly with Victoria Shestalova, sets up a general framework for total factor productivity analysis (TFP). The title of the paper is "The Solow residual, Domar aggregation, and inefficiency: A synthesis of TFP measures". The chapter synthesizes alternative TFP measures.

The first half of the book focuses on efficiency analysis. The third chapter contributes to this field by developing the theory of benchmarking. This paper, "Benchmarking and industry performance", is the scientific consolidation of my book *The Economics of Benchmarking* (Palgrave Macmillan, 2009) on which Financial Times contributor John Kay quipped "Many people in business talk about benchmarking. This book provides techniques that actually enable you to do it". I establish a firm connection between efficiency and competitive markets.

The fourth chapter, "Performance measurement in an input-output framework", shows how my ideas pertain to input-output analysis. It is a short theoretical piece, a prelude to the huge application in Chapter 5, written jointly with Antonio Amores: The efficiency analysis of the Andalusian economy.

Environmental economics is perhaps the most important topic on the interface of efficiency and input-output analyses. Due to market failures, inefficiencies abound and many economists, particularly input-output economists, wrongly think that the only solution to the problem is technical change. In Chapter 6, Victoria Shestalova and I lay out a general framework for environmental analysis, grounded in the national accounts, and show how environmental objectives can be achieved by reallocating production. In the sequel, Chapter 7, we extend the analysis to stochastics, providing confidence intervals.

While most economists understand IO stands for industrial organization, some think it means input-output. No worries, I synthesize the two in Chapter 8, "Efficiency measures for industrial organization". I show how my benchmarking theory can be used to measure how well (or poorly) industries are organized. Industrial organization is an important branch of economic theory and I provide it with an explicit definition and measure.

The next four papers provide a more neoclassical approach to efficiency analysis. In Chapter 9, "Monopoly, Pareto and Ramsey mark-ups", I analyze different pricing rules encountered in industrial organization. Monopoly prices are known to be inefficiently high, but the mark-ups (relative to competitive prices) are thought to have optimal proportions. This is known to be true for independent demands with constant elasticities, but I show that the result breaks down the moment one departs from this simple case.

The other three neoclassical papers are connected. In Chapter 10, "Consumer surplus and CES demand", I find the formula for consumer surplus of an important class of demand functions, namely those based on constant elasticity of substitution utility functions. This formula fills a gap in the literature. However, consumer surplus has not so good a reputation as a welfare measure. It is considered an approximate measure, whereas other measures are deemed exact: the so-called compensating and equivalent variations. In Chapter 11, I investigate this issue for a class of demand functions encompassing CES demands and conclude that this point of view, however widely spread, is incorrect. Consumer surplus deserves a better reputation and in Chapter 12, "The consumer's index", I advocate a variant as a good welfare measure.

The efficiency analysis part of the book culminates in a review of measures in Chapter 13, "Performance: The output/input ratio". This chapter, 13, is taken from the recent Handbook of Economic Performance Analysis, edited jointly with Bill Greene.

The next part of the present volume focuses on input-output analysis. The first two chapters, 14 and 15, written jointly with Amar Sahoo, analyze the efficiencies of the formal and informal sectors of the Indian economy, and also of the entire Indian economy, using general equilibrium analysis.

The next three chapters, 16–18, written jointly with José Rueda-Cantuche, investigate the construction of input-output coefficients from a theoretical perspective. Alternative constructs co-exist and we have tested the two most popular ones.

Chapter 19, "The use-make framework and the derivation of functional forms in production theory", bridges the models of production used in neoclassical economics and input-output analysis. I show how the stuff I learned in studying efficiency analysis is useful in input-output analysis and, conversely, how use-make tables may serve as an organizing framework not only for national accounting but also for economic theory.

Chapter 20, "Linkages, fields of influence and key sectors", criticizes prominent input-output concepts on the basis of efficiency and other theoretical considerations. The concepts better be replaced by new ones and I hope the challenge will be taken up.

The volume concludes with two chapters on trade and three on the history of economic thought.

Chapter 21, "Professor Jones's re-appraisal of Heckscher–Ohlin trade flows", takes on Professor Jones's questioning of Leontief's procedure to test if a country's trade pattern is according to the Heckscher–Ohlin theory of factor abundance. In a Heckscher–Ohlin framework, he shows that the country with the higher capital/labor endowment ratio may export a relatively labor-intensive commodity, whereas its import-competing sector is more capital-intensive. In other words, Leontief's such finding of the United States's economy does not invalidate the Heckscher–Ohlin theory. However, I argue that imports which drive domestic producers out of the market should enter the calculation and show that this observation resurrects Leontief's procedure. Moreover, I shed some light on the paradox that American exports are more labor-intensive than the imports.

Chapter 22, "Facets of innovation and stages of development", relates the components of productivity growth, technical change and efficiency change, to the stages of development. The latter component is more important to developing economies. Empirical studies confirm that R&D is more potent in developed economies and that competition and free trade spur development.

Chapters 23–25, of which the last two have been written jointly with William Baumol, place the works of Wassily Leontief and Anne Carter in perspective, in the context of the history of economic thought.

Last, but not least, it is a great pleasure to acknowledge the crucial and pleasant collaboration with my co-authors. Thank you, Antonio Amores, José Rueda-Cantuche, Amar Sahoo and Victoria Shestalova. And Will Baumol co-authored the last two chapters: may his memory be a blessing.

Chapter 1

Debreu's Coefficient of Resource Utilization, the Solow Residual, and TFP: The Connection by Leontief Preferences*

Thijs ten Raa

Department of Economics, Tilburg University, Tilburg, The Netherlands

tenraa@uvt.nl

Abstract. Debreu's coefficient of resource utilization is freed from individual data requirements. The procedure is shown to be equivalent to the imposition of Leontief preferences. The rate of growth of the modified Debreu coefficient and the Solow residual are shown to add up to TFP growth. This decomposition is the neoclassical counterpart to the frontier analytic decomposition of productivity growth into technical change and efficiency change. The terms can now be broken down by sector as well as by factor input.

Keywords: Efficiency, Productivity, Debreu's Coefficient, Solow Residual

JEL-codes: D24, O47

*Reprinted from *Journal of Productivity Analysis*, **30**, 191–199, 2008, with permission from Springer Nature.

1. Introduction

Total factor productivity (TFP) may grow by more efficient utilization of resources or by technical change. Debreu (1951) measured the utilization of resources and Solow (1957) measured technical change, but their models are remote. Solow's model is macro-economic and assumes perfect competition, while Debreu's model is micro-economic and assumes no technical change. In this paper I show how the measures of Debreu and Solow can be commingled into TFP. I take Debreu's model as point of departure, because it is quite general and, therefore, accommodating. The drawback of Debreu's coefficient of resource utilization, however, is that it hinges on individual preferences data. I will free his coefficient from this prohibitive data requirement, by making Debreu's concept of a 'better' commodity set independent of the specifics of individual preferences. The procedure will be shown to be equivalent to the adoption of Leontief preferences, confirming Diewert's (1983) idea that such preferences remove misallocations between consumers as a source of inefficiency. The consequent coefficient of resource utilization yields a more conservative estimate of inefficiency than Debreu's coefficient resource of utilization. As a bonus, the procedure makes the measure of inefficiency a function of total consumption only, not the individual breakdown. This paves the way for macro-economic applications and Solow residual analysis. The Solow residual is generalized to Debreu's setting.

Neoclassical economics encounters some refreshing competition from frontier analysis. See Nishimizu and Page (1982), Färe, Grosskopf, Norris and Zhang (1994), Färe and Grosskopf (1996), Kumar and Russell (2002) and the references given there. This literature provides a useful decomposition of productivity growth into technical change and efficiency change. I take the idea into the neoclassical general equilibrium realm. The connection is at a rather abstract level, for the mechanisms behind efficiency change are different in frontier analysis and neoclassical economics. Frontier analysis captures technological catch-up with the leader and the choice of inputs in terms of costs. Neoclassical analysis captures potential reallocations of resources between sectors. This type of efficiency change is harder to detect. Frontier analytic inefficiency is exposed by the gap with the best practice, a conceptually straightforward concept. Neoclassical inefficiency, however, not only comprises gaps with production possibility frontiers, but also hidden misallocations. A nice exposition is Debreu (1951) and Diewert (2001) discusses the reduction of TFP. A contribution of my paper is that it shows how the tools of frontier analysis, particularly the input- and output-distance functions, can be applied to the measurement of allocative efficiency.

The pieces of the puzzle fit pleasingly well. More precisely, in this paper I show that total factor productivity growth is the sum of technical change and efficiency change, where the former is the (generalized) Solow residual and the latter is the rate of growth of the modified coefficient of resource utilization.

2. The Debreu Coefficient of Resource Utilization

Debreu (1951) measures the inefficiency of the allocation of resources in an economy by calculating how much less resources could attain the same level of satisfaction to the consumers. I will review his so-called coefficient of resource utilization.

The economy comprises m consumers with preference relationships $\succsim_i$ and observed consumption vectors $\mathbf{x}_i^0 \in \mathbb{R}^l$ $(i = 1, \ldots, m)$, where l is the number of commodities. $Y \subset \mathbb{R}^l$ is the set of possible input vectors (*net* quantities of commodities consumed by the whole production sector during the period considered), including the observed one, $\mathbf{y}^0$. A combination of consumption vectors and an input vector is *feasible* if the total sum — the economy-wide *net* consumption — does not exceed the vector of *utilizable physical resources*, $\mathbf{z}^0 \in \mathbb{R}^l$.[1] Vector $\mathbf{z}^0$ is assumed to be at least equal to the sum of the observed consumption and input vectors, ensuring the feasibility of the latter.

[1]For example, if the last commodity, l, represents labor, and this is the only nonproduced commodity, then $\mathbf{z}^0 = Ne_l$, where N is the labor force and e_l the l-th unit vector.

The set of net consumption vectors that are at least as good as the observed ones is

$$\mathcal{B} = \left\{\sum \mathbf{x}_i | \mathbf{x}_i \succsim_i \mathbf{x}_i^0, \ i = 1, \ldots, m\right\} + Y \tag{1}$$

The symbol $\mathcal{B}$ stands for 'better' set. The minimal resources required to attain the same levels of satisfaction that come with $\mathbf{x}_i^0$ belong to $\mathcal{B}^{\min}$, the South-western edge or subset of elements $\mathbf{z}$ that are minimal with respect to $\geqq$.[2] Assume that preferences are convex and continuous, and that production possibilities form a convex and closed set, then the separating hyperplane theorem yields a supporting price vector $\mathbf{p(z)} > \mathbf{0}$ such that $\mathbf{z}' \in \mathcal{B}$ implies $\mathbf{p(z)} \cdot \mathbf{z}' \geqq \mathbf{p(z)} \cdot \mathbf{z}$.[3] The *Debreu coefficient of resource utilization* is defined by

$$\rho = \max_{\mathbf{z}}\{\mathbf{p(z)} \cdot \mathbf{z}/\mathbf{p(z)} \cdot \mathbf{z}^0 | \mathbf{z} \in \mathcal{B}^{\min}\} \tag{2}$$

Coefficient ρ measures the distance from the set of minimally required physical resources, $\mathbf{z} \in \mathcal{B}^{\min}$, to the utilizable physical resources, $\mathbf{z}^0$, in the metric of the supporting prices (which indicate welfare indeed). Debreu (1951, p. 284) shows that the distance or the max in (2) is attained by[4]

$$\mathbf{z} = \rho \mathbf{z}^0 \in \mathcal{B}^{\min} \tag{3}$$

[2] By convention, this vector inequality holds if it holds for all components.

[3] $\mathbf{p} > \mathbf{0}$ means that all components are positive. The prices are positive because of the min-superscript in $\mathbf{z} \in \mathcal{B}^{\min}$ and the fact that $\mathbf{z}$ is the *only* point in common to $\mathcal{B}$ and $\{\mathbf{z}'|\mathbf{z}' \leqq \mathbf{z}\}$; hence $\mathbf{p}$ may be chosen such that $\mathbf{p} \cdot \mathbf{z}' < \mathbf{p} \cdot \mathbf{z}$ for $\mathbf{z}' \leqq \mathbf{z}$ (except $\mathbf{z}' = \mathbf{z}$). This argument requires no monotonicity and Debreu (1951) does not assume it indeed. An example is an exchange economy ($Y = \{0\}$) with one consumer and two commodities of which the quantities are nonnegative. Let $\mathbf{x} \succsim \mathbf{x}'$ if $(2 - x_1)^2 \leqq (2 - x_1')^2$. Let $\mathbf{x}^0 = \mathbf{z}^0 = (3 \ 1)$. Then $\mathcal{B}^{\min} = \{\mathbf{x}|\mathbf{x} \succsim \mathbf{x}^0\}^{\min} = \{\mathbf{x}|1 \leqq x_1 \leqq 3\}^{\min} = \{(1 \ 0)\}$. In this point, any positive price vector renders $\mathcal{B} = \{\mathbf{x}|1 \leqq x_1 \leqq 3\}$ more expensive.

[4] There are two, related caveats in Debreu's (1951) analysis: $\mathbf{z} = \rho\mathbf{z}^0 \in \mathcal{B}^{\min}$ need not exist and ρ may not be unique if the separating price vector is not unique. Consider again the exchange economy ($Y = \{0\}$) with one consumer and two commodities. Let $\mathbf{x} \succsim \mathbf{x}'$ if $\min(x_1, x_2) \geqq \min(x_1', x_2')$. Let $\mathbf{x}^0 = (1 \ 1)$ and $\mathbf{z}^0 = (1 \ 2)$. Then $\mathcal{B}^{\min} = \{\mathbf{x}|\mathbf{x} \succsim \mathbf{x}^0\}^{\min} = \{\mathbf{x}|\mathbf{x} \geqq (1 \ 1)\}^{\min} = \{(1 \ 1)\}$ contains no $\rho\mathbf{z}^0 = \rho(1 \ 2)$. What is the coefficient of resource utilization? In this case, any $\mathbf{p} > \mathbf{0}$ separates $\mathcal{B} = \{\mathbf{x}|\mathbf{x} \geqq (1 \ 1)\}$ and $\{\mathbf{z}'|\mathbf{z}' \leqq (1 \ 1)\}$; hence (2) yields $\rho = \mathbf{p} \cdot (1 \ 1)/\mathbf{p} \cdot (1 \ 2) = (p_1 + p_2)/(p_1 + 2p_2)$, a number between 0.5

In other words, the Debreu coefficient of resource utilization is the smallest fraction of the actually available resources that would permit the achievement of the levels of satisfaction that come with $\mathbf{x}_i^0$. Coefficient ρ is a number between zero and one, the latter indicating full efficiency. In modern terminology, this result means that ρ is the *input-distance function*, determined by the program

$$\rho = \min_r \left\{ r \middle| \sum \mathbf{x}_i + \mathbf{y} \leqq r\mathbf{z}^0, \mathbf{x}_i \succsim_i \mathbf{x}_i^0, \mathbf{y} \in Y \right\} \tag{4}$$

There is also an output-distance function, but that one is opaque. The measurement of satisfaction is in terms of utility, an ordinal concept that generally admits no aggregation over consumers.

3. The Farrell Efficiency Measure

Following ten Raa (2007), let me clear up some confusion on the relationship between Debreu and Farrell's efficiency measures. Farrell (1957) decomposes efficiency in technical efficiency and allocative efficiency. He notes the similarity between his technical efficiency and the Debreu coefficient of resource utilization. Indeed, both the Farrell technical efficiency measure and the Debreu coefficient of resource utilization are defined through proportionate input contractions. The analogy is sheer formality, but confusing at a conceptual level. It suggests that Farrell takes the Debreu coefficient, augments it, and thus constructs a more encompassing overall measure. It is the other way round; the sway of the Debreu coefficient is far greater than that of Farrell's measure. Particularly Farrell's allocative efficiency measure is a partial (dis)equilibrium concept, conditioned on prices. It takes

and 1. To resolve the multiplicity, we may address the efficiency problem in primal space. The preference relationship is represented by utility $\min(x_1, x_2)$. Subject to feasibility constraint $\mathbf{x} \leqq \mathbf{z}^0 = (1\ 2)$, the maximum utility is 1. This is attained by $\mathbf{x}^0 = (1\ 1)$. Hence the allocation is optimal. Following Debreu's (1951, p. 275) introduction, $\rho = 1$. This implies that $\mathbf{p} = (1\ 0)$. Indeed, this is the supporting price system of the second welfare theorem. However, it is not positive.

If the minimal $\rho\mathbf{z}^0$ belongs to $\mathcal{B}^{\min}$, then the prices in (2) are positive and the coefficient ρ generated by (4) solves (2), following Debreu (1951, p. 284). If the minimal $\rho\mathbf{z}^0$ does not belong to $\mathcal{B}^{\min}$, the prices in (2) are only nonnegative, but the coefficient ρ generated by (4) still solves (2).

into account the cost reduction attainable by changing the mix of the inputs, given the prices of the latter. The Debreu coefficient, however, is a general (dis)equilibrium concept. It measures the technical and allocative inefficiency in the economy given only its fundamentals: resources, technology, and preferences. Prices are derived and enter the definition of the Debreu coefficient, see (2). Debreu (1951) then *proves* that the coefficient can be freed from these prices, by equation (3) or non-linear program (4). Prices remain implicit, however. They support the better set in the point of minimally required physical resources. The Debreu coefficient measures technical and allocative inefficiency, both in production and consumption, solving the formidable difficulty involved in assessing prices, referred to by Charnes, Cooper, and Rhodes (1978, p. 438). Farrell refrains from this, restricting himself to technical efficiency and price-conditioned allocative efficiency.

The formal analogy between the Debreu coefficient and the Farrell measure of technical efficiency prompted Zieschang (1984) to coin the phrase "Debreu-Farrell measure of efficiency," a term picked up by Chakravarty (1992) and Grifell-Tatjé, Lovell and Pastor (1998). This practice is confusing. Debreu's coefficient of resource allocation encompasses both Farrell's technical efficiency and his allocative efficiency measures, and frees the latter from prices. On top of this, Debreu's coefficient captures consumers' inefficiencies. The confusion persists. Färe, Grosskopf and Zelenyuk (2002) speak of the "Debreu-Farrell measure of technical efficiency." A recent review of Farrell's contribution states

> "(Debreu) worked only from the resource cost side, defining his coefficient as the ratio between minimised resource costs of obtaining a given consumption bundle and actual costs, for given prices and a proportional contraction of resources." Førsund and Sarafoglou (2002), footnote 4.

However, Debreu (1951) calculates the resource costs *not* of a given consumption bundle, but of an (intelligently chosen) Pareto equivalent allocation. (And the prices are not given, but support the allocation.) It is true, however, that the Debreu measure would become applicable if the aggregated consumption bundle can be considered given. The next section shows that this pragmatic approach is doable. The approach is exact if preferences are Leontief, as the subsequent section will prove.

4. Absent Individual Data: The Debreu-Diewert Coefficient of Resource Utilization

Following Debreu (1951) a simple symbol $\mathcal{B}$ has been used to denote the 'better set.' Definition (1) reveals, however, that the set depends on the observed consumption vectors and on preferences. The informational requirements involved are prohibitive. To overcome this problem, I will define a version of the Debreu coefficient, namely the *Debreu-Diewert coefficient of resource utilization*, ρ^*. Only in the next section it will transpire why I choose this name.

I want that the notion of 'better' set is independent of the specifics of preferences. For this purpose, all I assume is that preferences are weakly monotonic in the sense that they belong to

$$\mathcal{M} = \{\succsim |(\mathbf{x}' \geqq \mathbf{x}) \text{ implies } (\mathbf{x}' \succsim \mathbf{x})\} \tag{5}$$

I now define the tight better set as the intersection of all better sets over $\mathcal{M}$:

$$\mathcal{B}^* = \cap \left\{ \sum \mathbf{x}_i | \mathbf{x}_i \succsim \mathbf{x}_i^0, \ i = 1, \ldots, m \right\} + Y \tag{6}$$

The replacement of the better set, $\mathcal{B}$, by the tight better set, $\mathcal{B}^*$, implies that definition (2) produces the Debreu-Diewert coefficient ρ^* instead of the Debreu coefficient ρ. A comparison between these two coefficients is obtained by rewriting program (4):

$$\rho^* = \min_r \left\{ r | \sum \mathbf{x}_i + \mathbf{y} \leq r\mathbf{z}^0, \mathbf{x}_i \succsim \mathbf{x}_i^0 \text{ for all } \succsim \in \mathcal{M}, \mathbf{y} \in Y \right\} \tag{7}$$

The constraint set of (7) is contained in the one of (4); hence the solution to program (4) must be sharper:

$$\rho \leqq \rho^* \tag{8}$$

In other words, use of the Debreu-Diewert coefficient will overestimate efficiency hence underestimate inefficiency. Debreu's (1951) measure of inefficiency reflects scope for reallocation of resources between consumers with different tastes and, therefore, is quite high; the flipside of this observation is that the Debreu coefficient is relatively low. Figure 1 illustrates.

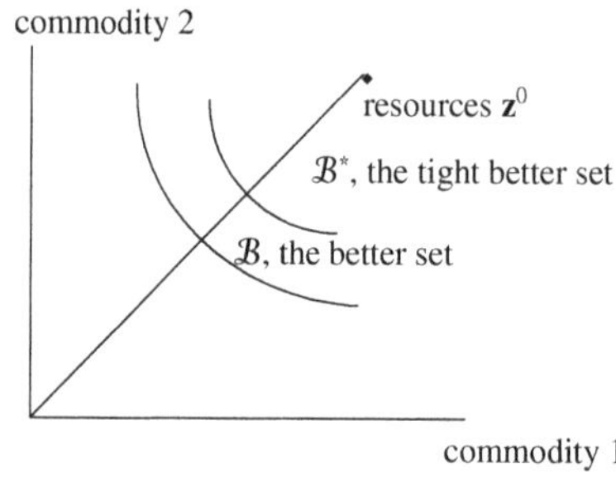

Fig. 1. Half the resources suffice to make consumers at least as well off. Two-thirds of the resources are needed to produce the total consumption vector. The Debreu coefficient of resource utilization is 1/2 and the Debreu-Diewert coefficient is 2/3.

5. The Debreu-Diewert Coefficient and Leontief Preferences

I can be a bit more specific about the Debreu-Diewert coefficient of resource utilization. I will show that it is generated by Leontief preferences. As I noted in the introduction, Diewert (1983) first had the idea that such preferences remove misallocations between consumers as a source of inefficiency. This explains the name giving.

Leontief preferences $\succsim(\mathbf{a})$ with nonnegative bliss point $\mathbf{a} \in \mathbb{R}^l_+$ are defined for nonnegative consumption vectors by $\mathbf{x}' \succsim(\mathbf{a})\mathbf{x}$ if $\min x'_k/a_k \geqq \min x_k/a_k$ where the minimum is taken over commodities $k = 1, \ldots, l$. The minima exist if $\mathbf{a}$ is nonzero, which I assume.[5] The following lemma shows that the tight better set is obtained by imposing Leontief preferences on all individuals. Notice, however, that the preferences feature the observed individual consumption baskets as bliss points and, therefore, differ.

Lemma $\mathcal{B}^* = \{\sum \mathbf{x}_i | \mathbf{x}_i \succsim (\mathbf{x}_i^0)\mathbf{x}_i^0,\ i = 1, \ldots, m\} + Y = \{\mathbf{x} | \mathbf{x} \geqq \sum \mathbf{x}_i^0\} + Y$.

[5]Situations like labor supply are covered by letting the commodity be leisure time. Division by zero is assumed to yield infinity.

Proof: Using the fact $\succsim(\mathbf{x}_i^0) \in \mathcal{M}$, I have that the first term of $\mathcal{B}^*$ in (6), $\cap\{\sum \mathbf{x}_i | \mathbf{x}_i \succsim_i \mathbf{x}_i^0, i = 1, \ldots, m\} \subset \{\sum \mathbf{x}_i | \mathbf{x}_i \succsim (\mathbf{x}_i^0)\mathbf{x}_i^0, i = 1, \ldots, m\} = \{\sum \mathbf{x}_i | \mathbf{x}_i \geqq \mathbf{x}_i^0\} = \{\mathbf{x} | \mathbf{x} \geqq \sum \mathbf{x}_i^0\} \subset \cap\{\sum \mathbf{x}_i | \mathbf{x}_i \succsim_i \mathbf{x}_i^0, i = 1, \ldots, m\}$, which is itself. The last inclusion is shown as follows. For $\mathbf{x} \geqq \sum \mathbf{x}_i^0$, allocate the surplus in any nonnegative way, for example by putting $\mathbf{x}_1 = \mathbf{x}_1^0 + \mathbf{x} - \sum \mathbf{x}_i^0$, $\mathbf{x}_2 = \mathbf{x}_2^0, \ldots, \mathbf{x}_m = \mathbf{x}_m^0$, then $\mathbf{x}_i \succsim_i \mathbf{x}_i^0$ for all $\succsim_i \in \mathcal{M}$. □

The first equality in the Lemma implies that if the consumers have Leontief preferences, then the Debreu coefficient reduces to the Debreu-Diewert coefficient. The second equality in the Lemma, $\{\sum \mathbf{x}_i | \mathbf{x}_i \geqq \mathbf{x}_i^0\} = \{\mathbf{x} | \mathbf{x} \geqq \sum \mathbf{x}_i^0\}$, is a perfect aggregation result. Aggregated consumption is monotonic if and only if individual consumptions are. One might say that if preferences are Leontief with varying bliss points (according to the observed consumption baskets), there is a social welfare function. The better set, $\mathcal{B}$, is freed from preferences, $\succsim_i$, as well as from individual consumption baskets, $\mathbf{x}_i^0$. The tight better set, $\mathcal{B}^*$, depends only on the *total consumption vector*, $\sum \mathbf{x}_i^0$. This modification facilitates measurement of the coefficient of resource utilization. In fact, the tightening creates the option to determine the degree of efficiency in terms of outputs, resurrecting the output-distance function.

Corollary. *Assume that the total consumption vector $\sum \mathbf{x}_i^0$ is nonnegative and nonzero. Assume that the production set Y features the impossibility to produce something from nothing and constant returns to scale. Then $\gamma = 1/\rho^*$ transforms the input-distance function program (7) into the output distance function program*

$$\gamma = \max\left\{c | c \sum \mathbf{x}_i^0 + \mathbf{y} \leqq \mathbf{z}^0, \mathbf{y} \in Y\right\}$$

Proof: By the Lemma, program (7) can be rewritten as

$$\rho^* = \min\left\{r | \sum \mathbf{x}_i + \mathbf{y} \leqq r\mathbf{z}^0, \mathbf{x}_i \succsim (\mathbf{x}_i^0)\mathbf{x}_i^0,\ i = 1, \ldots, m,\ \mathbf{y} \in Y\right\}$$

or

$$\rho^* = \min\left\{r | \mathbf{x} + \mathbf{y} \leqq r\mathbf{z}^0, \mathbf{x} \geqq \sum \mathbf{x}_i^0,\ \mathbf{y} \in Y\right\}$$

This can be simplified further to

$$\rho^* = \min\left\{r \middle| \sum \mathbf{x}_i^0 + \mathbf{y} \leqq r\mathbf{z}^0,\ \mathbf{y} \in Y\right\}$$

The solution is positive. (Otherwise input vector $\mathbf{y} \leqq -\sum \mathbf{x}_i^0 \leqq 0$, but not equal to zero, would produce something from nothing.) The transformation is completed by multiplication by $c = 1/r$ and a change of variable ($c\mathbf{y}$ to $\mathbf{y}$), using constant returns to scale. □

The output-distance function program informs us by which factor the total consumption vector can be expanded, given the resources.

6. Application to National Accounts

The Corollary shows that under constant returns to scale the inverse of the Debreu-Diewert coefficient of resource utilization is the expansion factor of the economy, γ. ten Raa (2005) calculates γ for the Canadian economy, defines $1 - 1/\gamma$ as inefficiency, and decomposes the latter into productive inefficiency, allocative inefficiency, and trade inefficiency. It follows that ten Raa's (2005) measure of inefficiency is $1-\rho^*$. In view of inequality (8), this measure of inefficiency underestimates Debreu's (1951) degree of inefficiency, $1 - \rho$. Debreu (1951) finds more scope for efficiency gains as marginal rates of substitution may be equalized across consumers. The Debreu-Diewert coefficient does not take into account this source of inefficiency.

ten Raa and Mohnen (2002) and ten Raa (2005) divide the commodities between produced goods and factor inputs, respectively. Use table $\mathbf{U}$ is a table depicting the use of goods by sectors and make table $\mathbf{V}$ is a table depicting the outputs of the sectors in terms of goods. $\mathbf{U} - \mathbf{V}^\top$ is the net input table; its dimension is that of goods by sectors.[6] $\mathbf{L}$ is the factor input table; its dimension is factor inputs by sectors. An element of $\mathbf{y} \in Y$ has components $(\mathbf{U} - \mathbf{V}^\top)\mathbf{s}$ and $\mathbf{Ls}$, and Y is defined by letting the allocation vector $\mathbf{s} \geqq 0$. Similarly, $\sum \mathbf{x}_i^0$ has components $\mathbf{f}$ and $\mathbf{0}$, where $\mathbf{f}$ is the vector of final goods consumption, while $\mathbf{z}^0$ has components $\mathbf{0}$ and $\mathbf{N}$, where $\mathbf{N}$ is

[6]Superscript $^\top$ denotes transposition. The use and make are of opposite dimension in the System of National Accounts (ten Raa, 2005).

the vector of factor endowments, and $\mathbf{z}$ has components $\mathbf{0}$ and $\mathbf{Ls}$. The output-distance function program of the Corollary becomes

$$\gamma = \max_{c,\mathbf{s}}\{c|c\mathbf{f} + (\mathbf{U} - \mathbf{V}^{\top})\mathbf{s} \leqq \mathbf{0}, \mathbf{Ls} \geqq \mathbf{N}, \mathbf{s} \geqq \mathbf{0}\} \tag{9}$$

The solution to this program yields the potential standard of living, relative to the observed one.[7] The shadow prices of the second constraint yield the factor productivities.

The standard interpretation of a sector is that of an industry, but conceptually it is possible to disaggregate it into firms, for example by using the reported data. Then program (9) will select for each industry best practice firms, which transform the industry inputs into potential industry output, in the sense of Johansen (1972).

7. Relationship with the Solow Residual

This section is the centerpiece of the paper. The Debreu-Diewert coefficient of resources and a generalized Solow residual are tied up into total factor productivity growth. What is productivity?

An economy transforms physical resources into final consumption by means of production. The ratio of consumption to the resources is called the *productivity* of the economy. A multi-input and output measure is the Malmquist index proposed by Caves, Christensen, and Diewert (1982). Productivity may grow because the production possibility set increases or because resources are better utilized. Productivity growth equals the sum of technical change and efficiency

[7]Of course, any positive coefficient may be entered in the objective function and this is commendable, to scale the price level. As is, by the main theorem of linear programming, the factor input shadow prices fulfill $\mathbf{w} \cdot \mathbf{N} = \gamma$. Since γ is of the order one but $\mathbf{N}$ of the order millions, $\mathbf{w}$ will be tiny. A handy objective function is $\mathbf{e} \cdot \mathbf{f}c$, where $\mathbf{e}$ is the unit vector with all components one. The dual constraints then show that $\mathbf{p} \cdot \mathbf{f} = \mathbf{e} \cdot \mathbf{f}$ and $\mathbf{w} \cdot \mathbf{N} = \mathbf{p} \cdot \gamma\mathbf{f}$. In other words, the product prices are normalized at unity and the factor input prices fulfill the potential national income identity. The proof is as follows. Multiplication of the dual constraint associated with variable $\mathbf{s}$, by $\mathbf{s}$, yields $\mathbf{p} \cdot (\mathbf{U} - \mathbf{V}^{\top})\mathbf{s} + \mathbf{w} \cdot \mathbf{Ls} = 0$. Replace the two terms using the two respective constraints of program (14): $-\mathbf{p} \cdot \gamma\mathbf{f} + \mathbf{w} \cdot \mathbf{N} = 0$, where (priced) inequalities are binding according to the phenomenon of complementary slackness. The product price normalization follows by the main theorem of linear programming or $\mathbf{w} \cdot \mathbf{N} = \mathbf{e} \cdot \mathbf{f}\gamma$.

change. Technical change is the shift of the production possibility frontier and efficiency change is the increase in the coefficient of resource utilization. The two add to productivity growth according to Nishimizu and Page (1982), Färe, Grosskopf, Norris, and Zhang (1994), and ten Raa and Mohnen (2002). I will now uncover the relationship at the level of generality of the Debreu model.

The point of departure is the Debreu-Diewert coefficient of resource utilization (ρ^*), determined by program (7) or, using the Lemma,[8]

$$\rho^* = \min\left\{r | \sum \mathbf{x}_i^0 + \mathbf{y} \leqq r\mathbf{z}^0, \ \mathbf{y} \in Y\right\} \tag{10}$$

Assuming free disposal, input may be added to $\mathbf{y} \in Y$ until the constraint is binding:

$$\sum \mathbf{x}_i^0 + \mathbf{y} = \rho^* \mathbf{z}^0 \tag{11}$$

This is the material balance.

Let $\mathbf{p}$ support the tight better set defined in (5), $\mathcal{B}^*$, in the sense introduced before (2).[9] According to the phenomenon of complementary slackness, non-linear program (10) yields[10]

$$\mathbf{p} \cdot \sum \mathbf{x}_i^0 = \rho^* \ \mathbf{p} \cdot \mathbf{z}^0 - \mathbf{p} \cdot \mathbf{y} \tag{12}$$

This is the identity between national product and national income; it holds even when there is no free disposal and, therefore, the material balance, (11), is not fulfilled. The national product is on the left hand side and on the right hand side is factor income plus profit. (Remember, $\mathbf{y}$ is net input, hence $-\mathbf{y}$ is net output.) All this is at the optimum allocation ($\sum \mathbf{x}_i^0, \mathbf{y}, \rho^* \mathbf{z}^0$) and supporting (or competitive) prices $\mathbf{p}$, not the actual allocation ($\sum \mathbf{x}_i^0, \mathbf{y}^0, \mathbf{z}^0$) and prices.

The economy transforms resources $\mathbf{z}^0$ into consumption $\sum \mathbf{x}_i^0$. The ratio of the latter to the former constitutes the level of total factor productivity. Since the objects are vectors, they must weighed by prices, for which $\mathbf{p}$ is employed. The *level* of total factor productivity

[8] See the proof of the Corollary.

[9] Footnote 4 shows that the supporting prices are not necessarily positive.

[10] The nonlinearity is due to production set Y.

is thus $\mathbf{p}\cdot\sum\mathbf{x}_i^0/\mathbf{p}\cdot\mathbf{z}^0$. If there are constant returns to scale, profit is zero, and, by equation (12):

$$\mathbf{p}\cdot\sum\mathbf{x}_i^0/\mathbf{p}\cdot\mathbf{z}^0=\rho^* \tag{13}$$

This equation shows that the level of total factor productivity is equal to the Debreu-Diewert coefficient of resource utilization.

Another interesting connection is the following. Let all variables vary with time and let d denote a time derivative. *Total factor productivity growth* is the rate of growth of the level of total factor productivity at *fixed* price weights:[11]

$$TFP=\mathbf{p}\cdot d\sum\mathbf{x}_i^0/\mathbf{p}\cdot\sum\mathbf{x}_i^0-\mathbf{p}\cdot d\mathbf{z}^0/\mathbf{p}\cdot\mathbf{z}^0 \tag{14}$$

The following proposition shows that *TFP* is the sum of the Solow residual, generalized to Debreu's framework, and the rate of growth of the Debreu-Diewert coefficient. The *generalized Solow residual* is defined by

$$SR=-\mathbf{p}\cdot d\mathbf{y}/\mathbf{p}\cdot\sum\mathbf{x}_i^0 \tag{15}$$

This expression features the change in optimal net output, $-\mathbf{y}$, and will be shown to be a generalized Solow residual indeed, evaluated at the frontier. The demonstration is in the next section, where the residual will be shown to measure the shift of the production possibility function.

Proposition. *Under constant returns to scale,* $TFP=SR+d\rho^*/\rho^*$.

Proof: Under constant returns to scale equation (13) holds. Substitution in equation (14) yields $TFP=[\mathbf{p}\cdot d\sum\mathbf{x}_i^0-\rho^*\mathbf{p}\cdot d\mathbf{z}^0]/\mathbf{p}\cdot\sum\mathbf{x}_i^0$. Substitution of the material balance, (11), and the product rule yield $TFP=[-\mathbf{p}\cdot d\mathbf{y}+\mathbf{p}\cdot\mathbf{z}^0 d\rho^*]/\mathbf{p}\cdot\sum\mathbf{x}_i^0$. Substitution of equations (13) and (15) yields the posted formula. □

The first *TFP* term, *SR*, reflects *technical change.* The second *TFP* term, $d\rho^*/\rho^*$, is the rate of growth of the Debreu-Diewert coefficient of resource utilization and, therefore, represents *efficiency change.*

[11]Warning: I use *TFP* for TFP growth. No symbol is needed for the level of TFP.

8. The Solow Residual

Solow (1957) divides commodities between a single output and factor inputs. Denoting the latter by a vector $\mathbf{l}$, the producible output is $F(\mathbf{l}, t) - s$, where $F(\cdot, t)$ is the production function at time t (presumed quasi-concave) and s is slack.[12] A net input vector $\mathbf{y} \in Y$ has components $-F(\mathbf{l}, t) + s$ and $\mathbf{l}$, respectively. The production possibility set Y is obtained by letting $\mathbf{l} \geqq \mathbf{0}$ and $s \geqq 0$. The vector of available resources, $\mathbf{z}^0$, has components 0 and $\mathbf{l}^0$, respectively. Let ρ^* be the Debreu-Diewert coefficient of resource utilization and $\mathbf{y}$ be the optimal net input vector, which solve efficiency program (10), then $\mathbf{y}$ has components $-F(\mathbf{l}, t)$ and $\mathbf{l} = \rho^* \mathbf{l}^0$. The first or product component of the material balance, (11), reads

$$\left(\sum \mathbf{x}_i^0\right)_1 - F(\mathbf{l}, t) = \rho^* 0 = 0 \tag{16}$$

The other or factor components read

$$0 + \mathbf{l} = \rho^* \mathbf{l}^0 \tag{17}$$

An intuitive interpretation of the Debreu-Diewert coefficient of resource utilization, ρ^*, is in terms of actual output, $F(\mathbf{l}^0, t) - s^0$, where $F(\mathbf{l}^0, t)$ is potential output and s^0 is observed slack. Actual output could also be generated by optimal factor input $\mathbf{l}$ (with no slack). It follows that the actual/potential output ratio is $F(\mathbf{l}, t)/F(\mathbf{l}^0, t)$. By equation (17), this is ρ^* if the production has constant returns to scale. *The Debreu-Diewert coefficient is the ratio of actual to potential output.*

As is well known, the solution $\mathbf{y}$ is supported by price vector $(1\ \mathbf{w}) = (1\ \partial_{\mathbf{l}} F(\mathbf{l}, t))$ where ∂ denotes partial derivatives (with respect to $\mathbf{l}$ in this case) or marginal productivities.[13] I will now evaluate $SR = -\mathbf{p} \cdot d\mathbf{y} / \mathbf{p} \cdot \sum \mathbf{x}_i^0$ of definition (15) for this special setting. The numerator reduces to

$$-\mathbf{p} \cdot d\mathbf{y} = dF(\mathbf{l}, t) - \mathbf{w} d\mathbf{l} \tag{18}$$

and the denominator is, in view of the first terms of (16) and (17),

$$\mathbf{p} \cdot \sum \mathbf{x}_i^0 = \left(\sum \mathbf{x}_i^0\right)_1 + 0 = F(\mathbf{l}, t) \tag{19}$$

[12] Slack scalar s should not be confused with allocation vector $\mathbf{s}$ of section 5.
[13] If $F(\cdot, t)$ is not differentiable, a subgradient will do.

using (16). Hence the quotient is

$$\begin{aligned} SR &= -\mathbf{p}\cdot d\mathbf{y}/\mathbf{p}\cdot \sum \mathbf{x}_i^0 \\ &= dF(\mathbf{l},t)/F(\mathbf{l},t) - \sum_k [w_k l_k/F(\mathbf{l},t)]dl_k/l_k \end{aligned} \tag{20}$$

The expression on the right hand side is, indeed, the residual between the output growth rate and the input growth rates, where value shares weight the latter. The shares add up if the production function has constant returns to scale, by Euler's theorem. The input prices are competitive marginal productivities, which are high in the sense that they leave no room for profit. The use of lower, observed prices, will bias upward expression (20).

The main point of Solow (1957) was that the residual measures technical change, a result that is easily verified. By equation (18), $-\mathbf{p}\cdot d\mathbf{y} = dF(\mathbf{l},t) - \partial_1 F(\mathbf{l},t)d\mathbf{l}$. But by total differentiation, $dF(\mathbf{l},t) = \partial_1 F(\mathbf{l},t)d\mathbf{l} + \partial_t F(\mathbf{l},t)$. Hence $SR = -\mathbf{p}\cdot d\mathbf{y}/\mathbf{p}\cdot\sum \mathbf{x}_i^0$ of definition (15) has a numerator $\partial_t F$ and we obtain, using equation (19),

$$SR = -\mathbf{p}\cdot d\mathbf{y}/\mathbf{p}\cdot \sum \mathbf{x}_i^0 = \partial_t F(\mathbf{l},t)/F(\mathbf{l},t) \tag{21}$$

The Solow residual measures the relative shift of the production function indeed.

Residual expression (20) can be generalized to multi-products. Then the output growth term is an output-value share weighted expression. Intermediate products can also be accommodated; this will be detailed in the next section. All are encompassed by definition (15): $SR = -\mathbf{p}\cdot d\mathbf{y}/\mathbf{p}\cdot\sum \mathbf{x}_i^0$, where $-\mathbf{y}$ is resource minimizing net output and $\sum \mathbf{x}_i^0$ is observed total consumption.

For constant returns to scale, the minimization of resources subject to total consumption — see program (10) — amounts to a maximization of consumption subject to available resources — program (9). As was shown there, this merely involves a change of variable from $\mathbf{y}$ to $c\mathbf{y}$ and a replacement of $\sum \mathbf{x}_i^0$ by $c\sum \mathbf{x}_i^0$. The expansion factors c in the numerator and in the denominator of the generalized Solow residual, $SR = -\mathbf{p}\cdot d\mathbf{y}/\mathbf{p}\cdot\sum \mathbf{x}_i^0$, cancel and its expression may therefore be reinterpreted in terms *maximal* consumption and sustaining optimal net output. The maximum consumption vector has the same proportions as the observed consumption vector. The prices in the generalized Solow residual are not affected at all, because of the constant returns to scale.

9. Productivity and Efficiency Decompositions

There are two further decompositions of total factor productivity growth than in technical change and efficiency change. The first decomposition is in factor productivity growth rates; it sounds dull, but is not achieved in frontier analysis. The second decomposition is by input-output sector.

The decomposition by *factor* is standard neoclassical analysis, at least for the Solow residual. Assume constant returns to scale, then $\mathbf{p}\cdot\mathbf{y} = 0$ and the generalized Solow residual becomes

$$SR = -\mathbf{p}\cdot d\mathbf{y}/\mathbf{p}\cdot\sum \mathbf{x}_i^0 = d\mathbf{p}\cdot\mathbf{y}/\mathbf{p}\cdot\sum \mathbf{x}_i^0 \tag{22}$$

Remember, $\mathbf{y}$ is the vector of net inputs. $\mathbf{p}$ is the vector of shadow prices or marginal productivities. Equation (22) imputes the technical change term of total factor productivity to the various inputs. It is very general. It reduces to the more familiar Jorgenson and Griliches (1967) form in the Solow world with a macro-economic production function, introduced in the previous section. There $\mathbf{y}$ has components $-F(\mathbf{l}, t)$ and $\mathbf{l}$, and $\mathbf{p} = (1\ \mathbf{w}) = (1\ \partial_1 F(\mathbf{l}, t))$. Hence the numerator of the generalized Solow residual (22) reduces to $d\cdot\mathbf{py} = d\mathbf{w}\cdot\mathbf{l}$, while the denominator is $F(\mathbf{l}, t)$ by equation (19).

It follows that the Solow residual becomes

$$SR = -\mathbf{p}\cdot d\mathbf{y}/\mathbf{p}\cdot\sum \mathbf{x}_i^0 = \sum_k [w_k l_k/F(\mathbf{l}, t)]\, dw_k/w_k \tag{23}$$

The expression on the right hand side is the growth rate of the factor productivity, with components weighted by their value shares. The input prices are competitive marginal productivities, which are high in the sense that they leave no room for profit. The use of lower, observed prices, will bias downward expression (23), unlike expression (20), which was biased upward in this case. The (primal) expression (20) and the (dual) expression (23) thus provide inconsistent estimates when no competitive prices are used.

The inclusion of efficiency change amounts to proportional increases of the factor productivity growth rates. By Debreu's equation (3), the minimally required physical resources, $\mathbf{z}$, are proportional to the utilizable physical resources, $\mathbf{z}^0$.[14] In the world of Solow this proportionality is between minimal factor inputs $\mathbf{l}$ and observed factor inputs $\mathbf{l}^0$, see equation (16), or $\rho^* = l_k/l_k^0$, all k. Hence the efficiency change term of *TFP* reads, assuming constant returns to scale,

$$\begin{aligned} d\rho^*/\rho^* &= \sum_k [w_k l_k/F(\mathbf{1},t)] d\rho^*/\rho^* \\ &= \sum_k [w_k l_k/F(\mathbf{1},t)](dl_k/l_k - dl_k^0/l_k^0) \end{aligned} \tag{24}$$

Substituting expressions (23) and (24) into the Proposition (section 7), all TFP-growth is now decomposed in terms of factor contributions:

$$TFP = \sum_k [w_k l_k/F(\mathbf{1},t)](dw_k/w_k + dl_k/l_k - dl_k^0/l_k^0) \tag{25}$$

The leading term measures factor productivity growth and the remainder the factor utilization growth. For each factor, the value share of the factor weights the sum of the two growth measures.

The generalized Solow residual is decomposed by *sector* by adding the structure of section 6. What follows is an activity variant of Hulten's (1978) analysis. In section 6, the net input vector $\mathbf{y}$ sustaining maximal consumption has components $(\mathbf{U} - \mathbf{V}^\top)\mathbf{s}$ and $\mathbf{Ls}$, where $\mathbf{U}$ is a table depicting the use of goods by sectors, $\mathbf{V}$ a table depicting the outputs of the sectors in terms of goods, $\mathbf{L}$ the factor input table, and allocation vector $\mathbf{s} \geqq 0$. Similarly, $\sum \mathbf{x}_i^0$ has components $\mathbf{f}$ and $\mathbf{0}$, where $\mathbf{f}$ is the vector of final goods consumption. The maximal consumption is $\gamma\mathbf{f}$, which we enter in the denominator, as discussed at the end of the last section. The respective prices are denoted $\mathbf{p}$ and $\mathbf{w}$, respectively; these are the shadow prices of program (9). The

[14] See the disclaimer in footnote 4 though.

generalized Solow residual thus becomes

$$SR = -\{\mathbf{p} \cdot d[(\mathbf{U} - \mathbf{V}^\top)\mathbf{s}] + \mathbf{w} \cdot d(\mathbf{L}\mathbf{s})\}/\mathbf{p} \cdot (\gamma \mathbf{f}) \tag{26}$$

The shadow prices fulfill the dual constraint,

$$\mathbf{p}^\top(\mathbf{U} - \mathbf{V}^\top) + \mathbf{w} \cdot \mathbf{L} - \boldsymbol{\sigma}^\top = \mathbf{0} \tag{27}$$

where $\boldsymbol{\sigma}$ is the shadow price of $\mathbf{s} \geqq 0$. The product rule and substitution of equation (27) into expression (26) reduce the generalized Solow residual to

$$SR = -[\mathbf{p}^\top d(\mathbf{U} - \mathbf{V}^\top) \cdot \mathbf{s} + \mathbf{w}^\top d\mathbf{L} \cdot \mathbf{s} + \boldsymbol{\sigma}^\top d\mathbf{s}]/\mathbf{p} \cdot (\gamma \mathbf{f}) \tag{28}$$

By the phenomenon of complementary slackness,

$$\boldsymbol{\sigma} \cdot \mathbf{s} = 0 \tag{29}$$

expression (28) becomes

$$\begin{aligned} SR = {} & (\mathbf{p}^\top d\mathbf{V}^\top - \mathbf{p}^\top d\mathbf{U} - \mathbf{w}^\top d\mathbf{L} + d\sigma) \\ & \times (diag\, \mathbf{V}\mathbf{p})^{-1} (diag\, \mathbf{V}\mathbf{p})\mathbf{s}/\mathbf{p} \cdot (\gamma \mathbf{f}) \end{aligned} \tag{30}$$

Here $(\mathbf{p}^\top d\mathbf{V}^\top - \mathbf{p}^\top d\mathbf{U} - \mathbf{w}^\top d\mathbf{L} + d\boldsymbol{\sigma})(diag\, \mathbf{V}\mathbf{p})^{-1}$ is the row vector of sectoral Solow residuals, while $(diag\ \mathbf{V}\mathbf{p})\mathbf{s}/\mathbf{p} \cdot (\gamma \mathbf{f})$ is the vector of Domar weights, which add to the gross output/net output ratio of the economy, a number greater than one.[15]

To include sectoral efficiency changes, recall from section 6 that the optimal (sustaining maximal consumption) and utilizable resources have only factor components, namely $\mathbf{L}\mathbf{s}$ and $\mathbf{N}$, respectively. Application of the phenomenon of complementary slackness and the main theorem of linear programming to (9) yields $\mathbf{w}^\top \mathbf{L}\mathbf{s} = \mathbf{w} \cdot \mathbf{N} = \gamma$. According to the Corollary, ρ^* is the inverse of this expression. It follows that the efficiency term of *TFP* becomes, substituting in the denominator $\mathbf{w}^\top \mathbf{L}\mathbf{s} = \mathbf{p}^\top(\mathbf{V}^\top - \mathbf{U})\mathbf{s} = \mathbf{p} \cdot (\gamma \mathbf{f})$ by equations

[15]This number is also called the Domar ratio. For any vector $\mathbf{x}$, *diag* $\mathbf{x}$ denotes the diagonal matrix with $\mathbf{x}$ on the diagonal.

(27), (29), and material balance (9),[16]

$$
\begin{aligned}
d\rho^*/\rho^* &= -d(\mathbf{w}^\top \mathbf{Ls})/(\mathbf{w}^\top \mathbf{Ls}) \\
&= -\sum_j [d(\mathbf{w}\cdot \mathbf{l}_{\cdot j} s_j)/(\mathbf{p}\cdot \mathbf{v}_j s_j)]\cdot(\mathbf{p}\cdot \mathbf{v}_j\cdot s_j)/\mathbf{p}\cdot(\gamma \mathbf{f}) \quad (31)
\end{aligned}
$$

where the summation is over sectors. The efficiency growth is a Domar weighted average of optimal factor input reduction growth rates.

A further specification is that of *input-output analysis*, where $\mathbf{U}$ and $\mathbf{V}$ are square matrices, $\mathbf{V}^\top \mathbf{s}$ is denoted $\mathbf{q}$, the vector of (optimal) gross outputs, and $\mathbf{A} = \mathbf{U}(\mathbf{V}^\top)^{-1}$ and $\mathbf{F} = \mathbf{L}(\mathbf{V}^\top)^{-1}$ are the matrices of (intermediate and factor) input coefficients. Expression (26) for the generalized Solow residual becomes

$$
SR = -\{\mathbf{p}\cdot d[(\mathbf{A}-\mathbf{I})\mathbf{q}] + \mathbf{w}\cdot d(\mathbf{Fq})\}/\mathbf{p}\cdot(\gamma \mathbf{f}) \quad (32)
$$

and price equation (27) reads

$$
\mathbf{p}^\top(\mathbf{A}-\mathbf{I}) + \mathbf{w}^\top \mathbf{F} - (\mathbf{V}^{-1}\boldsymbol{\sigma})^\top = \mathbf{0} \quad (33)
$$

Assume $\mathbf{s} > \mathbf{0}$.[17] As shadow prices are nonnegative, equation (29) sets the last term of equation (33) zero:

$$
\mathbf{p}^\top(\mathbf{A}-\mathbf{I}) + \mathbf{w}^\top \mathbf{F} = \mathbf{0} \quad (34)
$$

This permits the following rewrite of the generalized Solow residual, (32):

$$
SR = -(\mathbf{p}^\top d\mathbf{A} + \mathbf{w}^\top d\mathbf{F})(diag\ \mathbf{p})^{-1}(diag\ \mathbf{p})\mathbf{q}/\mathbf{p}\cdot(\gamma \mathbf{f}) \quad (35)
$$

[16] According to program (9), the material balance is an inequality. However, the premultiplication by the price vector eliminates the slack, by the phenomenon of complementary slackness. Alternatively, the material balance may be transformed to an equality in the same way that equation (11) was derived from program (10), assuming free disposal. Vectors $\mathbf{l}_{\cdot j}$ ($\mathbf{v}_j$) denotes the j-th column (row) of matrix $\mathbf{L}$ ($\mathbf{V}$).

[17] Well known sufficient conditions are $\mathbf{f} > \mathbf{0}$ and $\mathbf{A}$ has nonnegative Leontief inverse. For details see ten Raa (2005), chapter 2.

This is essentially formula (12) of Wolff (1994).[18] The first half of this expression, $-(\mathbf{p}^\top d\mathbf{A} + \mathbf{w}^\top d\mathbf{F})(diag\ \mathbf{p})^{-1}$, is the row vector of sectoral Solow residuals and the remainder, $(diag\ \mathbf{p})\mathbf{q}/\mathbf{p}\cdot(\gamma\mathbf{f})$, is the vector of Domar weights, which add to the gross output/net output ratio of the economy, a number greater than one.[19] Expression (35) details the right hand side of equation (21): The generalized Solow residual measures the shift of the production function by means of reductions in intermediate and factor input coefficients.

The inclusion of sectoral efficiency changes is analogous to equation (31), obtained by substitution of $\mathbf{Ls} = \mathbf{Fq}$, equation (34), and material balance $(\mathbf{I} - \mathbf{A})\mathbf{q} = \gamma\mathbf{f}$:[20]

$$\begin{aligned} d\rho^*/\rho^* &= -d(\mathbf{w}^\top\mathbf{Fq})/(\mathbf{w}^\top\mathbf{Fq}) = -d[\mathbf{p}^\top(\mathbf{I} - \mathbf{A})\mathbf{q})]/\mathbf{p}\cdot(\gamma\mathbf{f}) \\ &= -\sum_k \{d[(p_k - \mathbf{p}\cdot\mathbf{a}_k)q_k]/p_k q_k\}\cdot(p_k q_k)/\mathbf{p}\cdot(\gamma\mathbf{f}) \qquad (36) \end{aligned}$$

where the summation is over commodities. The efficiency growth is a Domar weighted average of optimal factor input or value-added reduction growth rates.

10. Conclusion

In this paper I have interrelated the Debreu coefficient of resource utilization, the Solow residual, and total factor productivity growth. Freed from individual data requirements, the Debreu coefficient's growth rate and the Solow residual sum to TFP growth. The procedure is equivalent to the imposition of Leontief preferences. The decomposition is the neoclassical counterpart to the decomposition

[18] Wolff (1994) substitutes observed values for gross output $\mathbf{q}$ and final goods consumption $\gamma\mathbf{f}$, which are optimal. However, since gross output and final goods consumption are linked by the same Leontief inverse, $\mathbf{q}$ is obtained by inflating observed gross output by γ. As this factor cancels against the one in the denominator, the difference is immaterial.

[19] The input-output disaggregation, (35), is slightly different than the activity analytic one, (30), as sectors are now defined in terms of products, but the totals are the same. This wedge disappears when secondary products are absent (in the sense that output table $\mathbf{V}$ is diagonal).

[20] See footnote 16.

of productivity growth into technical change and efficiency change made in frontier analysis and admits breakdowns by factor input as well as by sector.

Acknowledgment

This paper is an offspring of the workshop *Alternative measures of Total Factor Productivity growth* held on 13 September 2002 at the Department of Econometrics and Operations Research of Tilburg University and co-sponsored by the Netherlands Organization for Scientific Research (grant 460-02-031-A). I gratefully acknowledge comments from Victoria Shestalova, Erwin Diewert, Rolf Färe, other participants of the Aggregation, Efficiency and Measurement Conference held on 23–25 May 2003 at the Department of Economics of University of California, Riverside, two anonymous referees and an anonymous associate editor.

References

Caves, D. W., L. R. Christensen and W. Erwin Diewert. (1982). The economic theory of index numbers and the measurement of input, output, and productivity. *Econometrica*, **50**(6), 1393–1414.

Chakravarty, S. R. (1992). Efficiency and concentration. *Journal of Productivity Analysis*, **3**, 249–255.

Charnes, A., W. W. Cooper and E. Rhodes (1978). Measuring the efficiency of decision making units. *European Journal of Operational Research*, **2**, 419–444.

Debreu, G. (1951). The coefficient of resource utilization. *Econometrica*, **19**(3), 273–292.

Diewert, W. E. (1983). The measurement of waste within the production sector of an open economy. *Scandinavian Journal of Economics*, **85**(2), 159–179.

Diewert, W. E. (2001). Which (Old) ideas on productivity measurement are ready to use? In *New Developments in Productivity Analysis*, Eds. Hulten C. R., E. R. Dean and M. J. Harper, Chicago: University of Chicago Press, pp. 85–101.

Färe, R. and S. Grosskopf. (1996). Productivity and intermediate products: A frontier approach. *Economics Letters*, **50**, 65–70.

Färe, R., S. Grosskopf, M. Norris and Z. Zhang. (1994). Productivity growth, technical progress, and efficiency change in industrialized countries. *American Economic Review*, **84**(1), 66–83.

Färe, R., S. Grosskopf and V. Zelenyuk (2002). Finding common ground: Efficiency indices. UPEG Working Paper 0305, presented at the North American Productivity Workshop at Union College, Schenectady, NY.

Farrell, M. J. (1957). The measurement of productive efficiency. *Journal of the Royal Statistical Society, Series A*, **120**(III), 253–281.

Førsund, F. R. and N. Sarafoglou. (2002). On the origins of data envelopment analysis. *Journal of Productivity Analysis*, **17**, 23–40.

Grifell-Tatjé, E., C. A. K. Lovell and J. T. Pastor. (1998). A Quasi-Malmquist productivity index. *Journal of Productivity Analysis*, **10**(1), 7–20.

Hulten, C. R. (1978). Growth accounting with intermediate inputs. *Review of Economic Studies*, **45**(3), 511–518.

Johansen, L. (1972). *Production Functions*, Amsterdam: North-Holland.

Jorgenson, D. W. and Z. Griliches. (1967). The explanation of productivity change. *Review of Economic Studies*, **34**(3), 308–350.

Kumar, S. and R. Robert Russell. (2002). Technological change, technological catch-up, and capital deepening: Relative contributions to growth and convergence. *American Economic Review*, **92**(3), 527–548.

Nishimizu, M. and J. M. Page, Jr. (1982). Total factor productivity growth, technological progress and technical efficiency change: Dimensions of productivity change in Yugoslavia. *Economic Journal*, **92**, 920–936.

ten Raa, Th. (2005). *The Economics of Input-Output Analysis*, Cambridge University Press, Cambridge.

ten Raa, Th. (2007). Don't aggregate efficiency but disaggregate inefficiency. In *Aggregation, Efficiency, and Measurement*, Eds. Färe, R., S. Grosskopf and D. Primont, Heidelberg: Springer, pp. 145–151.

ten Raa, Th. and P. Mohnen. (2002). Neoclassical growth accounting and frontier analysis: A synthesis. *Journal of Productivity Analysis*, **18**, 11–128.

Solow, R. M. (1957). Technical change and the aggregate production function. *Review of Economics and Statistics*, **39**(3), 312–320.

Wolff, E. N. (1994). Productivity measurement within an input-output framework. *Regional Science and Urban Economics*, **24**(1), 75–92.

Zieschang, K. D. (1984). An extended Farrell technical efficiency measure. *Journal of Economic Theory*, **33**(2), 387–396.

Chapter 2

The Solow Residual, Domar Aggregation, and Inefficiency: A Synthesis of TFP Measures*

Thijs ten Raa[†] and Victoria Shestalova[‡]

[†] *Department of Economics, Tilburg University, Tilburg, The Netherlands*
tenraa@uvt.nl

[‡] *Netherlands Bureau for Economic Policy Analysis, The Hague, The Netherlands*

Abstract. We consolidate and interrelate the four main approaches to the measurement and decomposition of total factor productivity growth, namely Solow's residual analysis, the index number approach, Data Envelopment Analysis, and Domar aggregation. Two new results link the general technology TFP growth measure to the industry Solow residuals and inefficiency.

Keywords: TFP Solow Residual, Index Numbers, Data Envelopment Analysis, Input–Output Analysis, Domar Aggregation, Malmquist Index

JEL-codes: D24, O47

1. Introduction

This paper presents a general framework that encompasses and interrelates the four main approaches to the measurement of total factor productivity (TFP)-growth: (1) Solow's aggregate production

*Reprinted from *Journal of Productivity Analysis* **36**, 71–77, 2011, with permission from Springer Nature.

function model, (2) Index Numbers, (3) Data Envelopment Analysis (DEA), and (4) the Domar aggregation approach, which is associated with Input–Output (I–O) analysis. Our consolidating framework serves two purposes. It is a vehicle to review the different approaches to productivity measurement in the literature. Moreover, it is a breeding ground for new results. In particular, two propositions (3 and 4) link the general technology TFP growth measure to the industry Solow residuals and inefficiency.

A conceptual difference between these approaches is the treatment of prices. Traditional productivity indices use observed prices and rest on the assumption that the observed prices are competitive, so that factors are paid their marginal products. Under this assumption observed value shares are indeed the appropriate weights for the aggregation of the factor productivities into TFP. In the parametric literature adjustments are made for mark-ups and returns to scale (Diewert and Fox 2008). Frontier approaches, particularly DEA, make no behavioral assumption. Its TFP-growth measure, the so-called Malmquist index, is based on production statistics only and the value shares are generated by the shadow prices of the linear program that determines the production possibility frontier. The I–O analytical frame-work is on either side of the fence. As is well known, it accounts for intersectoral linkages and yields a TFP measure that is conceptually close to the macro-economic Solow residual; see, e.g., Wolff (1994). However, I–O can accommodate the shadow prices from a general equilibrium model, which moves its TFP-growth measure close to the DEA's (ten Raa 2008). Since shadow prices reflect marginal product values at the optimum, their use in computation does not conflict with the assumption of competitive pricing required by methods operating with observed prices. Hence, it is possible to reunite both these methodologies in one framework, capable of working with either of these prices.

Another difference lies in the assumption of optimizing behavior. The assumption provides economic justification to index numbers such as Törnqvist and Fisher's, but has the drawback that it bars inefficiencies. The TFP-growth measure arising in DEA makes no such assumption and has the capacity to ascribe TFP growth to not only technical change but also efficiency change. In order to incorporate this attractive feature, we must relax the assumption of optimizing behavior.

The framework consists of (1) the technology, which in some cases is defined by means of a linear program; (2) data on inputs, net outputs, and either observed or shadow prices; and (3) rather general behavioral assumptions, such as the assumption on prices to reflect marginal products. The latter assumption is weaker that the assumption of profit maximizing behavior and allows for inefficiency. As a result, similarly to DEA, TFP growth includes both technical change and efficiency change. The former represents a shift of the production frontier and resembles the Solow residual as defined under the assumption of optimizing behavior, and the latter corresponds to a movement towards the frontier.

A novelty of this paper is the consolidation of all the four main alternative TFP-growth measures in a common theoretical framework. Although the economic literature contains excellent review articles on productivity indices, such as Diewert (1992) and Diewert and Nakamura (2003), to our knowledge this paper is the first to encompass all four main measures, including interrelating DEA efficiency measurement and Domar aggregation.

2. General Framework

The measurement of TFP involves data, technological assumptions and possibly behavioral assumptions. We begin describing each of them in turn and define the concept of TFP growth that we use throughout this paper.

- **Data.** We assume that for each point of time t we observe of firms (industries or economies) the factor inputs x and the (net) outputs y, column vectors of different dimensions. We denote the prices of the outputs and the inputs by row vectors p and w, respectively. The prices can be either data or shadow prices of a maximization problem used to estimate technology.
- **Technology.** In each point of time the production possibility set is a subset in the commodity space of nonnegative factor inputs and unsigned net outputs, denoted by $P^t = \{(x, y) : \Phi(x, y, t) \leq 0\}$. The frontier is given by $\Phi(x, y, t) = 0$. We assume Φ to be continuous, piece-wise differentiable and convex in (x, y). A simple example, $\Phi(x, y, t) = y - tx$, illustrates why marginal products

will be given by $-\partial\Phi/\partial x$ and the shift of the production function by $-\partial\Phi/\partial t$, both including a minus sign. We assume that the data are possible in the sense that all $(x(t), y(t))$ belong to P^t.

- **Behavioral assumptions.** If observed prices are used, they are assumed to reflect the marginal products on the production frontier. This assumption is weaker than those of cost minimization or profit maximization. In particular, productive and allocative inefficiencies are admitted. It should be mentioned that if price data are not used, shadow prices may fill the gap and will automatically reflect marginal products.
- **Definition of TFP.** TFP growth $\hat{T}$ is defined as the (Solow) residual between the output and input growth rates, expressed by Divisia indices:

$$\hat{T} = \sum \beta_j \hat{y}_j - \sum \alpha_i \hat{x}_i; \quad \alpha_i = w_i x_i / wx,$$
$$\beta_j = p_j y_j / py, \tag{1}$$

Here the symbol $\hat{}$ denotes the growth rate of a variable, for example, $\hat{y}_j = \frac{dy_j}{dt}/y_j$. The weights in Eq. (1) may come from external value share data or from endogenous calculations. The distinction delineates the alternative approaches reviewed in this paper.

The first proposition shows that under rather general assumptions the Solow residual (1) can be decomposed into technical change and efficiency change. The first term measures the shift of the frontier by the partial derivative of the production frontier with respect to time. The second term measures the movement in the distance to the frontier.

It is convenient to use input distance functions, as defined in DEA.[1] More precisely, for (non)frontier observations we have $\Phi(x, y, t)(<) = 0$ and we contract input x by a factor D so that y remains just producible from input Dx. By construction, for any producible (x, y) at time t there is $0 \leq D(x, y, t) \leq 1$ such that

$$\Phi[D(x, y, t)x, y, t] = 0. \tag{2}$$

[1]The results would carry through for an output orientation. Propositions 1, 3 and 4 will assume constant returns to scale, under which the two approaches are equivalent. Proposition 2 can be modified in the obvious way.

Following Debreu (1951) distance function D is here defined by

$$D(x, y, t) = \min\{\theta : (\theta_x, y) \in P^t\}. \tag{3}$$

Proposition 1: *Under constant returns to scale — meaning Φ is linearly homogeneous in (x, y) — and if prices reflect marginal products — meaning all $\frac{\rho_j}{w_i} = -\frac{\partial\Phi/\partial y_j}{\partial\Phi/\partial x_i}$ — TFP growth decomposes into technical change and efficiency change: $\hat{T} = \frac{-\partial\Phi/\partial t}{\sum\{\partial\Phi/\partial y_j\}y_j} + \hat{D}$.*

Proof: Differentiate Eq. (2) totally with respect to time:

$$\sum \frac{\partial\Phi}{\partial x_j}\left(D\frac{dx_j}{dt} + \frac{dD}{dt}x_j\right) + \sum \frac{\partial\Phi}{\partial y_j}\frac{\partial y_j}{dt} + \frac{\partial\Phi}{\partial t} = 0. \tag{4}$$

Rearrange the terms in Eq. (4):

$$\sum \frac{\partial\Phi}{\partial y_j}\frac{\partial y_j}{dt} + \sum \frac{\partial\Phi}{\partial x_j}\frac{\partial x_j}{dt}D = -\frac{\partial\Phi}{\partial t} - \sum \frac{\partial\Phi}{\partial x_j}x_j\frac{dD}{dt}. \tag{5}$$

The derivatives of Φ in Eq. (5) are evaluated in the associated frontier point $(D(x, y, t)x, y, t)$. Here, by linear homogeneity, Euler's equation holds as follows: $\sum(\partial\Phi/\partial y_j)y_j = -\sum(\partial/\partial x_j)(Dx_j)$ Use either side of this equation to divide the terms in Eq. (5):

$$\begin{aligned}
&\frac{\sum(\partial\Phi/\partial y_j)\,\partial y_j/dt}{\sum(\partial\Phi/\partial y_j)\,y_j} - \frac{\sum(\partial\Phi/\partial x_j)\,\partial x_j/dt}{\sum(\partial\Phi/\partial x_j)\,x_j} \\
&\quad = \frac{-\partial\Phi/\partial t}{\sum(\partial\Phi/\partial y_j)\,y_j} + \frac{1}{D}\frac{dD}{dt}.
\end{aligned} \tag{6}$$

By assumption vectors (p, w) and $(\partial\Phi/\partial y) - \partial\Phi/\partial x$ are collinear, so that $\partial\Phi/\partial y$ and $-\partial\Phi/\partial x$ on the left hand side of Eq. (6) may be replaced by p and w, respectively. This turns the left hand side into $\hat{T}$, defined by (1). □

The assumption of constant returns to scale can be dispensed. This would yield a third TFP component, namely a scale effect.

Following Färe and Grosskopf (2004), the leading, technical change term in Eq. (6) can also be expressed in the distance function and we shall do so for the two main representations of TFP growth, DEA and Domar aggregation. The next proposition shows the underpinning. It features free input disposability, which is defined by the condition that $(x, y) \in P^t$, $z \geq 0$ implies $(\mathrm{x} + z, y) \in P^t$.

Proposition 2: *Under free input disposability,*

$$P^t = \{(x, y) : 1 - 1/D(x, y, t) \leq 0\}.$$

Proof: If $(x, y) \in P^t$, then, by definition of D, $0 \leq D(x, y, t) \leq 1$, and, therefore, $1 - 1/D(x, y, t) \leq 0$. Hence $(x, y) \in \{(x, y) : 1 - 1/D(x, y, t) \leq 0\}$. Conversely, if the latter holds, $0 \leq D(x, y, t) \leq 1$, and, therefore, $z = [1 - D(x, y, t)]x \geq 0$. By definition of D, $(D(x, y, t)x, y) \in P^t$. By free input disposability, $(D(x, y, t)x + z, y) = (x, y) \in P^t$.

The upshot of this proposition is that we may reparametrize the production possibility set using $1 - 1/D$ instead of Φ. In particular, we will differentiate D instead of Φ when measuring technical change. □

3. Approaches to the Measurement of TFP Growth

In this section we show how our framework encompasses the main measures of TFP growth and review the relevant literatures.

3.1. *Solow residual*

Solow (1957) analyzed a macro-economic model with one output and two inputs, capital and labor, interrelated by a production function, F. This situation can be derived from our framework by imposing a particular form on Φ, namely $\Phi(K, L, Y, t) = Y - F(K, L, t)$, and assuming no slack in production and proportionality between prices and marginal products. These assumptions were made by Solow (1957), imply production efficiency, $D = 1$ hence $\hat{D} = 0$, and reduce Proposition 1 to $\hat{T} = \frac{\partial F}{\partial t}/F$. This replicates Solow's result that TFP growth measures the shift of the aggregate production function under the assumptions.

3.2. *Index numbers*

Since our point of departure, definition (1), is the Divisia index, other conventional indices are encompassed. In discrete time, Christensen and Jorgenson (1970) approximate the Divisia index by the Törnqvist index,

$$\sum_j \sum_j \frac{1}{2}(\beta_j^t + \beta_j^{t+1}) + (\ln y_j^{t+1} - \ln y_j^t) - \sum_i \frac{1}{2}(\alpha_j^t + \alpha_j^{t+1}) \times (\ln x_j^{t+1} - \ln x_j^t), \tag{7}$$

and Diewert (1976) by the Fisher index,

$$\frac{1}{2}\left(\ln\frac{p^t y^{t+1}}{p^t y^t} + \ln\frac{p^{t+1} y^{t+1}}{p^{t+1} y^t}\right) - \frac{1}{2}\left(\ln\frac{w^t x^{t+1}}{w^t x^t} + \ln\frac{w^{t+1} x^{t+1}}{w^{t+1} x^t}\right) \tag{8}$$

These indices require observable price information. As in Sect. 3.1, we assume that there is no slack and that the prices reflect marginal products. This reduces TFP growth to technical change. Under the stronger assumption of price-taking profit maximization Diewert has shown that both indices are exact for certain functional forms. The Törnqvist index (7) is exact for the translog production function and, therefore, Diewert (1976) calls it the translog index. The Fisher index (8) is exact for a rather flexible functional form (a second order approximation to an arbitrary twice continuously differentiable aggregator function), a property Diewert (1976, p.117) calls 'superlative.'[2] Although the Törnqvist and Fisher productivity indices are exact for different production functions, most practical time-series applications yield similar numerical values; see Black *et al.* (2003). Diewert and Nakamura (2003) interrelate the physical and financial concepts of TFP growth for these indices, as well as for the Malmquist index, which we cover in Sect. 3.3.

---

[2]More specifically, Diewert (1992) proves that under certain parameter restrictions, the Fischer productivity index is exact for a time-dependent revenue function of the following form $r^t(p, x) = \sigma_t(p^\top Apx^\top Cx + \alpha^\top p\beta^t xp^\top \beta^t x)^{1/2}$, $A = A^\top$, $C = C^\top$, $t = 0, 1$, where σ_t is a positive number, A, C, and B^t are parameter matrices, and α^t and β^t are parameter vectors.

3.3. *Data envelopment analysis*

In DEA technology Φ is constructed by the piece-wise linear envelopment of the available observations on inputs and outputs. Under constant returns to scale, the production possibility set represents a convex hull. There is no need to impose behavioral assumptions; DEA does not require them. The data requirement is reduced to outputs and inputs; DEA does not use the observed prices but shadow prices that reflect marginal values on the production frontier.

Because DEA subscribes to definition (3) of the distance function, Proposition 2 applies under free input disposability and we may use $\Phi = 1 - 1/D$ Consequently $\frac{\partial\Phi/\partial t}{\partial\Phi/\partial y_j} = \frac{\partial D/\partial t}{\partial D/\partial y_j}$ and, therefore, the technical change term in Proposition 1 becomes $\frac{-\partial D/\partial t}{\sum(\partial D/\partial y_j)y_j}$, the movement in the distance function D. Now by construction of the distance function, $\Phi(xD(x,y,t),y,t) = 0$ or, invoking constant returns to scale, $\Phi(x,y/D(x,y,t),t) = 0$. Differentiation with respect to y yields $\partial\Phi/\partial y \cdot [1/D - (y \cdot \partial D/\partial y)/D^2] = 0$. Hence, $(\partial D/\partial y_j)y_j = D$; and therefore the technical change is reduced to $\frac{\partial D(x,y,t)}{D\partial t}$.

Substituting the latter in Eq. 6 and using the differentiation rules yield:

$$\begin{aligned}\hat{T} &= \frac{dD(x,y,t)}{Ddt} - \frac{\partial D(x,y,t)}{D\partial t}\\ &= \frac{\partial \ln D(x,y,t)}{\partial x}\frac{dx}{dt} + \frac{\partial \ln D(x,y,t)}{\partial y}\frac{dy}{dt}\end{aligned} \tag{9}$$

In discrete time, the right hand side of this expression is approximated as $\ln D(x^{t+1},y^{t+1},\cdot) - \ln D(x^t,y^t,\cdot) = \ln\frac{D(x^{t+1},y^{t+1},\cdot)}{D(x^t,y^t,\cdot)}$. Evaluating this expression at t and $t+1$, taking the average of the two logarithms and exponentiating, one obtains the standard expression of Malmquist productivity index:

$$\left[\frac{D(x^{t+1},\ y^{t+1},t)}{D(x^t,y^t,t)}\frac{D(x^{t+1},\ y^{t+1},t+1)}{D(x^t,y^t,t+1)}\right]^{1/2}. \tag{10}$$

The decomposition of Malmquist index into technical change and efficiency change is well known; see Färe *et al.* (1989, 1996). If we assume inefficiency away, the efficiency change term drops out and the Malmquist index features only the technical change component.

This component corresponds to technical change as defined by Solow under the assumptions of no slack and inputs paid by marginal products. The explicit price information in the expression of the Solow residual is replaced by the implicit shadow price information, derived from the shape of the frontier; see Coelli and Rao (2001).

Two important results from the DEA literature provide a link between the Malmquist index and two other TFP growth indices, namely, Törnqvist and Fisher indices. First, Caves *et al.* (1982) have shown that the Malmquist index becomes a Törnqvist productivity index (7) provided that the distance functions are of translog form with identical second order coefficients, and that the prices are those supporting cost minimization and profit maximization. Second, Färe and Grosskopf (1992) proved that under the assumption of profit maximizing behavior the Malmquist index is approximately equal to the Fisher productivity index (8). In both cases the assumption that prices support cost minimizing and profit maximizing behavior is crucial. Balk (1998) reviews comprehensively, including non-constant returns to scale.

3.4. *Domar aggregation*

In a multi-sectoral economy, aggregate TFP growth can be represented as a combination of industry productivity growths, the Domar (1961) aggregation. In this section we show how the Domar aggregation can be derived from our framework. For this purpose we use a functional form of U which reflects the I–O model of Leontief (1936) and assume no production slack and zero profits. No production slack is weaker than the assumption of optimizing behavior that underlies many TFP models. In addition to production slack there may be allocative inefficiencies, but these do not occur in Leontief's model.

I–O analysis is based on the gross outputs z_j (of industry $j, j = 1, \ldots, n$), interindustry transactions z_{kj} (the quantity of the intermediate input industry k supplies to industry j, at price p_k) and factor inputs x_{ij} (the quantity of factor input i utilized in the production of industry j, at price w_i). Letting e be the unit vector (all components equal to one), and introducing obvious vector and matrix notations, the utilized inputs are given by vector Xe and the net supply is given by $z - Ze$. The utilized inputs cannot exceed the available resources of the economy, given by vector x, and the net product supply must at least be the final demand vector, given by vector y. Hence the feasibility constraints are $Xe \leq x$ and $z - Ze \geq y$. In I–O analysis technology is represented by the input coefficients $a_{kj} = z_{kj}/z_j$ and $b_{ij} = x_{ij}/z_j$. With obvious matrix notation, (x, y) belongs to the I–O production possibility set if for some gross output vector $z \geq 0$ the feasibility constraints are fulfilled, $Bz \leq x$ and $z - Az \geq y$ The distance function of the I–O model is given by the following program: $D(x, y, t) = \min \theta$ subject to:

$$[I - A(t)]z \geq y, B(t)z \leq \theta x, z \geq 0. \tag{11}$$

By Proposition 1, technical change is measured by $\frac{-\partial\Phi/\partial t}{\sum(\partial\Phi/\partial y_j)y_j}$. The following proposition provides the relation between this expression and the well known Domar aggregation (Wolff 1994), linking the general technology TFP growth measure to the industry Solow residuals under the assumption of technically efficient production.

Proposition 3: *In the I–O model technical change* $\frac{-\partial\Phi/\partial t}{\sum(\partial\Phi/\partial y_j)y_j}$ *is measured by the Domar weighted sum of industry Solow residuals,* $\hat{T} = \sum \hat{\tau}_j p_j z_j / py$, *where* $\hat{\tau}_j = -\sum_k \frac{p_k z_{kj}}{p_j z_j} \hat{a}_{kj} - \sum_i \frac{w_i x_{ij}}{p_j z_j} \hat{b}_{ij}$, *and prices and production levels are the shadow prices and the optimal production levels of program* (11).

Proof: Technology function Φ can be given by $\Phi(x, y, t) = \max\{B(t)[I - A(t)]^{-1}y - x\}$ where the maximum is taken with respect to factor input components. Here the distance function has been derived from the production possibility set. Because inputs are freely disposable in model (11), by Proposition 2 we may use $\Phi = 1 - 1/D$ and, as in Sect. 3.3, technical change is measured by $\frac{-\partial D/\partial t}{\sum(\partial D/\partial y_j)y_j}$. By program (11) the partials of the distance function with respect to output components are equal to the sensitivity of objective θ with respect to the first bound components, hence its Lagrange multipliers: $\partial D/\partial y_j = p_j$ The partials of the distance function with respect to time are determined by the sensitivity of the objective with respect to constraint coefficients. As shown in ten Raa (2005), Eq. 4.33, the derivative of $\max_q aq$: $C(t)q \leq b$ equals $-\lambda \frac{dC}{dt} q$, where λ is the row vector of Lagrange multipliers and q the optimum. Because in the present situation,

$q = \left[\begin{smallmatrix}\theta \\ z\end{smallmatrix}\right]$, $a = (-1\ 0)$, $\lambda = (p\ w\ \alpha)$ and $C(t) = \begin{bmatrix} 0 & A(t)-I \\ -x & B(t) \\ 0 & -I \end{bmatrix}$, the partial derivative of maximization objective $-\theta$ with respect to time equals $-(p\ w\ \alpha)\begin{bmatrix} 0 & dA/dt \\ 0 & dB/dt \\ 0 & 0 \end{bmatrix}\left[\begin{smallmatrix}\theta \\ z\end{smallmatrix}\right] = -(pdA/dt + wdB/dt)\,z$. It follows that $\frac{-\partial D/\partial t}{\sum(\partial D/\partial y_j)y_j} = \frac{-(pdA/dt+wdB/dt)z}{\sum p_j y_j}$. The numerator features $p\frac{dA}{dt}z = p_k\frac{da_{kj}}{dt}z_j = p_k\left(\frac{da_{kj}}{dt}/a_{kj}\right)a_{kj}z_j = p_k\hat{a}_{kj}z_{kj}$ and, similarly, $w\frac{dB}{dt}z = w_i\hat{b}_{ij}z_{ij}$. Therefore we obtain the Domar aggregation expression for technical change in this model:

$$\frac{-\partial\Phi/\partial t}{\sum(\partial\Phi/\partial y_j)y_j} = \sum \hat{\tau}_j p_j z_j/py,$$

$$\hat{\tau}_j = -\sum_k \frac{p_k z_{kj}}{p_j z_j}\hat{a}_{kj} - \sum_i \frac{w_i x_{ij}}{p_j z_j}\hat{b}_{ij}, \tag{12}$$

in which z_{ij} and x_{ij} correspond to the optimal production levels, and p_k and w_i are shadow prices. □

Since Proposition 3 has been proved for optimal production levels and shadow prices, it remains to show that under the additional assumptions of no slack and zero profits — stated at the beginning of this section — the use of this formula is also justified at observed prices and production levels.

The first assumption, no slack in production, means that the observed primary input x and net output y satisfy $\Phi(x, y, t) = \max\{B(t)[I - A(t)]^{-1}y - x\} = 0$, and therefore it is impossible to produce more y with less x. This follows that the primary input uses are at their frontier levels and sufficient to just produce net output y. Given a fixed proportion technology in production, the intermediate production must satisfy $z - Az = y$. Hence, we cannot increase y by their reallocation. Hence, the observed inputs and outputs can be used in Eq. (12) instead of those from the linear program. The assumption that there is no slack implies also that the efficiency change term, $\frac{1}{D}\frac{dD}{dt}$, equals to zero and the TFP growth is fully expressed by (12).

The other assumption, that industry profits are zero, reads:

$$p_j z_j = \sum_k p_k z_{kj} + \sum_i w_i x_{ij}, \quad \text{where } i, j, k = 1, \ldots, n. \tag{13}$$

As long as Eq. (13) holds, the industry TFP growth in the Domar aggregation expression can be represented both in terms of output and input growth levels and in terms of the growth of technical coefficients $\hat{\tau}_j = -\sum_k \frac{p_k z_{kj}}{p_j z_j}\hat{a}_{kj} - \sum_i \frac{w_i x_{ij}}{p_j z_j}\hat{b}_{ij} = \hat{z}_j - \left(\sum_k p_k z_{kj}\hat{z}_{kj} + \sum_i w_i x_{ij}\hat{x}_{ij}\right) / (p_j z_j)$. Shadow prices satisfy the zero profit conditions by complementary slackness, but we need to impose the requirement of zero profits in order to justify the use of the observed prices instead of shadow prices.

4. Synthesis of Domar Aggregation and DEA

In this section we establish a relationship between DEA and Domar aggregation. The principal difference between the two lies in the data requirements and the behavioral assumptions. As we do not impose general restrictions on these factors, there is scope for synthesis. Our approach is to allow slack in the structural approach and to replace the observed prices by shadow prices. The obtained measure of TFP is based on the fundamentals of the economy, namely technology and preferences. The model draws from ten Raa and Mohnen (2001, 2002) and Shestalova (2001), but replaces their utility based output distance function by the input distance function used in this paper and, for simplicity, takes the one-country closed economy variant. Employing the distance function program (11) and combining Propositions 1 and 3, we obtain the next proposition, which allows technical inefficiency in the I–O model and shows how to measure it as well as technical progress.

Proposition 4: *Model* (11) *yields* $\hat{T} = \sum \hat{\tau}_j p_j z_j / py + \hat{D}$, *in which the first term is evaluated at shadow prices and optimal output levels.*

Proposition 4 intermingles the Domar approach with the DEA decomposition in technical and efficiency changes, where the technical change term is expressed in the Domar aggregation form (12) taken at shadow prices and optimal production levels from the linear program (11). While in DEA the potential for efficiency is determined by cross-sectional or intertemporal best practices, in this combined model the available production technology is represented by the observed technical coefficients and inefficiency stems from the suboptimal allocation of production within the system, or from underutilization of resources in industries.[3]

In the case of an open economy, international trade represents another source of TFP growth. An extension of the above model to the case of an open economy allows us to incorporate the effect of change in the terms-of-trade. This effect has been considered by ten Raa and Mohnen (2001, 2002) for the case of a small open economy, and by Shestalova (2001) for the case three large open economies. See also Diewert and Morrison (1986) on the effect of international trade on productivity.

5. Conclusion

The paper offers a common framework which links the main approaches to the measurement of TFP growth rates, namely, the original approach by Solow (1957), conventional TFP growth indices such as Fisher and Törnqvist indices, the structural Domar aggregation approach, and Data Envelopment Analysis. We have introduced a general framework that consolidates these approaches.

For all the main well known TFP growth indices, we review the main results established in the literature concerning the conditions under which these indices yield equivalent (or close) TFP growth measures. The condition of optimizing behavior appears to be crucial in this respect. This condition, which lends theoretical support to the conventional Divisia, Törnqvist or Fisher indices, while not required in the case of Malmquist indices, explains the main conceptual difference between the conventional index numbers and the DEA-based Malmquist indices. This allows the Malmquist indices to incorporate the effect of efficiency change which is neglected by the other indices.

Our framework augments the standard production function with an efficiency term (which is similar to the efficiency term that arises

[3]Strictly speaking, DEA can incorporate other types of inefficiencies as well (for example, non-radial DEA models can account for the presence of a slack). However, we will not discuss those in this particular application, since the standard Malmquist indices based on DEA with constant returns to scale, which are typically used for the TFP measurement, do not consider them.

in DEA) and yields the TFP growth measure which is conceptually close to the Malmquist index. The measure encompasses both technical change and efficiency change. The framework interrelates the DEA approach with the other approaches. In particular, we show that in a multi-sectoral economy, the technical change component takes the Domar aggregation form known from the structural, I–O approach. Similarly to DEA, technical change is measured at shadow prices and production levels resulting from the linear program, and not at observable prices and production levels; and the efficiency is interpreted as the potential for boosting the production to reach the production possibility frontier. However, while in DEA the potential is determined by the observable best practice (possibly achieved by other market participants), in the augmented I–O model it comes from improving allocations of production factors within a multi-sectoral economy.

Acknowledgments

We are grateful to four anonymous referees and an Associate Editor for extremely careful comments. This paper is an offspring of the workshop Alternative measures of total factor productivity growth held on 13 September 2002 at the Department of Econometrics and Operations Research of Tilburg University and co-sponsored by the Netherlands Organization for Scientific Research (Grant 460-02-031-A).

Open Access

References

Balk, B. M. (1998). *Industrial Price, Quantity and Productivity Indices, the Micro-Economic Theory and an Application*, Boston: Kluwer Academic Publishers.

Black, M., M. Guy and N. McLellan. (2003). Productivity in New Zealand 1988 to 2002. WP 03/06, New Zealand Treasury.

Caves, D. W., L. R. Christensen and W. E. Diewert. (1982). The economic theory of index numbers and the measurement of input, output and productivity. *Econometrica*, **50**(6), 1393–1414.

Christensen, L. R. and R. W. Jorgenson. (1970). U.S. real product and real factor input, 1929–1967. *Review of Income and Wealth*, **16**, 19–50.

Coelli, T. and D. S. Prasada Rao. (2001). Implicit value shares in Malmquist TFP index numbers. CEPA Working Paper No. 4/2001, University of New England, Armidale.

Debreu, G. (1951). The coefficient of resource utilization. *Econometrica*, **19**(3), 273–292.

Diewert, W. E. (1976). Exact and superlative index numbers. *Journal of Econometrics*, **4**, 115–146.

Diewert, W. E. (1992). Fisher ideal output, input and productivity indexes revisited. *Journal of Productivity Analysis*, **3**, 211–248.

Diewert, W. E. and K. J. Fox. (2008). On the estimation of returns to scale, technical progress and monopolistic markups. *Journal of Econometrics*, **145**(1–2), 174–193.

Diewert, W. E. and C. Morrison. (1986). Adjusting output and productivity indexes for changes in terms of trade. *The Economic Journal*, **96**, 659–679.

Diewert, W. E. and A. Nakamura. (2003). Index number concepts, measures and decompositions of productivity growth. *Journal of Productivity Analysis*, **19**, 127–159.

Domar, E. D. (1961). On the measurement of technological change. *The Economic Journal*, **LXXI**, 709–729.

Färe, R. and S. Grosskopf. (1992). Malmquist indexes and fisher ideal indexes. *The Economic Journal*, **102**(410), 158–160.

Färe, R. and S. Grosskopf. (1996). *Intertemporal Production Frontiers: With Dynamic DEA*, Boston: Kluwer Academic Publishers.

Färe, R. and S. Grosskopf. (2004). *New Directions: Efficiency and Productivity*, Boston: Kluwer Academic Publishers.

Faŕe, R., S. Grosskopf, B. Lindgren and P. Roos. (1989). Productivity development in Swedish hospitals: A Malmquist output index approach. Discussion Paper No. 89-3, Southern Illinois University, Illinois.

Leontief, W. (1936). Quantitative input and output relations in the economic system of the United States. *The Review of Economics and Statistics*, **18**(3), 105–125.

Shestalova, V. (2001). General equilibrium analysis of international TFP growth rates. *Economic Systems Research*, **13**(4), 391–402.

Solow, R. M. (1957). Technical change and the aggregate production function. *The Review of Economics and Statistics*, **39**(3), 312–320.

ten Raa, T. (2005). *The Economics of Input–Output Analysis*. Cambridge: Cambridge University Press.

ten Raa, T. and P. Mohnen. (2002). Neoclassical growth accounting and frontier analysis: A synthesis. *Journal of Productivity Analysis*, **18**(2), 111–128.

ten Raa, T. and P. Mohnen. (2001). The location of comparative advantages on the basis of fundamentals only. *Economic Systems Research*, **13**(1), 93–108.

ten Raa, T. (2008). Debreu's coefficient of resource utilization, the Solow residual, and TFP: The connection by Leontief preferences. *Journal of Productivity Analysis*, **30**, 191–199.

Wolff, E. N. (1994). Productivity measurement within an input–output framework. *Regional Science and Urban Economics*, **24**(1), 75–92.

Chapter 3

Benchmarking and Industry Performance*

Thijs ten Raa

Department of Economics, Tilburg University, Tilburg, The Netherlands
tenraa@uvt.nl

Abstract. In this paper I interrelate productivity analysis and the theory of industrial organization. A proposition proves that an industrial organization is efficient if and only if it is supportable in the entry-proofness sense. Industrial performance is decomposed in efficiency and technical change terms as well as an industrial organization component. The performance measure is shown to be consistent with the Solow residual and Malmquist productivity indices for its components are provided.

Keywords: Scope (dis)economies, Industrial Organization, Efficiency, Aggregation, Productivity

JEL-codes: L10, D24, O47

1. Introduction

In this paper I define benchmarking through a function that maps two arguments, namely the object to be benchmarked — a firm, represented by the pair of its input vector and its output vector — and the backdrop against which it is benchmarked — the industry — into a scalar, namely the efficiency of the firm. The mapping summarizes

*Reprinted from *Journal of Productivity Analysis*, **36**, 285–292, 2011, with permission from Springer Nature.

a program that identifies the best practice technologies or *benchmarks* for the firm. The performance of a firm will be measured by its output/input ratio or productivity — a concept that I will connect explicitly to the aforementioned efficiency function. Aggregate performance may rise more than firm performance scores suggest, if resources are better allocated between firms. The excess is the industrial organization effect.

Debreu (1951) recognized imperfections in economic organization as a source of aggregate inefficiency and Diewert (1983) analyzed them for open economies, focusing on price distortions. I operationalize these ideas in an activity analytic framework, but without using external price information (such as the world prices an open economy faces), as Nesterenko and Zelenyuk (2007) do. Another novelty is that my theory of benchmarking extends my interrelationship of two value-based performance measures — Diewert's (1981) price index measurement and Solow's (1957) residual analysis — from the back-of-the-envelope calculation for production functions (ten Raa 2005) to the activity framework.

There is more to the performance of a composite such as an industry than micro or firm performance and composition effects. Blackorby and Russell (1999) and Briec *et al.* (2003) have shown that things do not add up except under restrictive conditions. Bartelsman and Doms' (2000, p. 571) understanding that "Aggregated productivity can be computed as the share-weighted average of individual productivity" is not exactly right. Indeed, Briec *et al.* (2003, Proposition 5) and Färe and Grosskopf (2004, p. 108) noticed a bias, ten Raa (2005) related it to the departure of the industrial efficiency condition that marginal productivities are equalized, and Balk (2009) shows that in a growth accounting setting with independent disaggregated price and quantity information differential price changes add a term to aggregate productivity change. I now proceed to interpret the bias as an industrial organization inefficiency measure.

A main contribution of this paper is the interrelation of productivity analysis and the theory of industrial organization. A proposition proves that an industrial organization is efficient (in the sense of productivity analysis) if and only if it is supportable in Sharkey and Telser's (1978) sense of being entry-proof.

The closest framework is that of Li and Ng (1995), who distinguish technical efficiency, allocatively efficiency and reallocative efficiency;

the latter corresponds to my measure of industrial organization efficiency. They measure all efficiencies using the shadow prices of the efficiency program of the industry as a whole, while I employ the individual firm shadow prices for the micro efficiencies and show that departures between the two signal organizational inefficiency.

2. Benchmarking: Price Analysis

Denote firm i's input vector by $x^i \neq 0$ and its output vector by $y^i \neq 0, i = 1, \ldots, I$.[1] Input vectors have a common dimension, output vectors have a common dimension, and these two dimensions may differ (some positive integers). For example, inputs can be labor, capital, and land, while outputs may be numerous goods and services. Some commodities can be both input and output. An industrial organization can be represented by the allocation $(x^i, y^i)_{i=1,\ldots,I}$, which is denoted briefly by (X, Y). If $I = 1$, the industrial organization is a monopoly; if $I = 2$, it is a duopoly. If Y is a diagonal matrix, we have monopolistic competition. If X is a row vector, we have an input price taking industry, for which inputs can be aggregated to 'cost'. The efficiency of a firm is determined by benchmarking its structure $(x^i y^i)$ against the industrial organization (X, Y). This is a comparison between the firm's actual output level and the best practice output level achievable with its available input vector, just as Farrell's (1957) productive efficiency measurement technique and Shephard's (1970) output distance function. The idea is to reallocate the input, x^i, over all the activities $j = 1, \ldots, I$, and to run the latter with intensities θ_j, as to inflate the output, y^i, by an expansion factor $1/\varepsilon$:[2]

$$\max_{\varepsilon,\theta_j \geq 0} 1/\varepsilon : \sum \theta_j x^j \leq x^i, \quad y^i/\varepsilon \leq \sum \theta_j y^j \tag{1}$$

[1] All I need are firms' input and output data. This simplicity has a price: I miss performance failures on the demand side. However, a theoretical underpinning of this supply side approach is given in ten Raa (2008), where it is demonstrated that my supply side efficiency measure is conservative (in the sense of underestimating full inefficiency) and sharp (attained by certain demand functions).

[2] I do not surround the objective and constraints by the set symbol $\{.\}$. I omit $j = 1, \ldots, I$ under the summation model, following the Einstein summation convention.

Program (1) assumes that activities $(x^i y^i)$ can be run with constant returns to scale and that inputs and outputs are freely disposable.[3] Let ε^i optimize primal program (1). The expanded y^i/ε^i is the potential output of firm i, using the best practice technologies. ε^i is a number between 0 and 1 which indicates the firm efficiency for firm i. The best practice firms or benchmarks relevant to firm i are signaled by $\theta_j > 0$ in program (1).

Denote the shadow prices of the constraints in (1) by w^i and p^i, for the inputs and outputs, respectively; these solve the dual program:[4]

$$\min_{p,w\geq 0} wx^i : py^j \leq wx^j, py^i = 1, \quad \text{all } j \tag{2}$$

This dual program is essentially the original tack to Data Envelopment Analysis, taken by Charnes *et al.* (1978).[5] The connection between efficiency and valuations — a central theme in this paper — is made by the main theorem of linear programming. According to this theorem the primal and dual programs have equal solution values:

$$1/\varepsilon^i = w^i x^i \tag{3}$$

Substituting the price normalization constraint of program (2) in Eq. (3), the efficiency of firm i becomes:

$$\varepsilon^i = p^i y^i / w^i x^i \tag{4}$$

This result establishes a connection between benchmarking and price index measurement. The efficiency is the ratio of the value of output to the value of input at shadow prices. Georgescu-Roegen

[3] An obvious extension of this paper will be the generalization to variable returns to scale, but this comes with integer problems (known in the theory of contestable markets) that obscure the relationship between the contestability and the efficiency of an industry revealed and measured in the present paper. In other words, that generalization better be relegated to a separate paper. Under constant returns to scale output and input based benchmarking procedures are equivalent. The program is linear in the nonnegative variables $1/\varepsilon, \theta_j$.

[4] The price normalization constraint features no slack, because the non-negativity constraint for $1/\varepsilon$ is non-binding (as $1/\varepsilon = 1$ is feasible by choice of $\theta_i = 1$ and $\theta_j = 0, j \neq i$).

[5] Under the alternative scheme of input contraction, the dual would maximize the value of output.

(1951) called it return to the dollar in a more complicated framework, involving investment and not necessarily shadow prices. Under constant returns to scale the ratio should equal unity for profit maximizers. A perhaps surprising feature is that the ratio is evaluated at private prices, because the potential output of firm i has idiosyncratic commodity proportions and because of the presence of multiple inputs. For example, if the output mix of a firm is relatively intensive in terms of some input, the shadow price of that input will be high.

We now apply the apparatus to the efficiency of the industry. The definition goes back to Farrell (1957) and Førsund and Hjalmarsson (1979), who call it structural efficiency. Related, Johansen (1972) defines potential industry output as a function of total input. Following Färe and Grosskopf's (2004) extension, the idea is to reallocate the combined inputs of all firms, industry input $x = \sum x^i$, as to inflate the aggregate output vector, $y = \sum y^i$, by an expansion factor $1/\varepsilon$. Under constant returns to scale the industry technology is the cone spanned by the firm technologies, which is the same technology as the reference technology in the firm efficiency program (1). Hence the only modification to the latter is the replacement of firm resources and output target by industry resources x and output target y:

$$\max_{\varepsilon,\theta_j \geq 0} 1/\varepsilon \ : \sum \theta_j x^j \leq x, \ y/\varepsilon \ \leq \sum \theta_j y^j \tag{5}$$

Let ε solve program (5). It is a number between 0 and 1 which indicates the industry efficiency. The best practice firms or benchmarks relevant to the industry are signaled by $\theta_j > 0$ in program (5). Denote the shadow prices of the constraints in program (5) by w and p, for the inputs and outputs, respectively; these industry prices solve the dual program:[6]

$$\min_{p',w' \geq 0} w'x : p'y^j \leq w'x^j, \ p'y = 1, \ \text{all } j \tag{6}$$

Analogous to Eq. (3), potential output increases by the following factor:

$$1/\varepsilon = wx \tag{7}$$

[6]I prime the variables in the program to avoid confusion with the simple notation for the optimal values.

Analogous to Eq. (4), industry efficiency becomes:[7]

$$\varepsilon = py/wx. \tag{8}$$

3. Industrial Organization: An Efficiency Measure

Extending Briec *et al.* (2003, Proposition 5), Färe and Zelenyuk (2003, formula 2.12) and Färe and Grosskopf (2004, p. 108), Proposition 1 establishes a one-sided relationship between the efficiencies of the firms and the efficiency of the industry.

Proposition 1: *Industry efficiency is less than the market share weighted harmonic mean of the firm efficiencies:* $\varepsilon \leq 1/\sum \frac{s^i}{\varepsilon^i}$, *where* $s^i = py^i/py$ *are the market shares evaluated at the prices determined by dual program* (6).

Proof: In the dual program (2), consider the socially optimal prices p/py^i and w/py^i (which need not be privately optimal). The denominator has been chosen as to fulfil the price normalization constraint in program (2) and the inequality constraint carries over from program (6). In short, these prices are feasible with respect to program (2). But by their suboptimality (in this private minimization program), $(w/py^i)x^i \geq w^i x^i$ or $wx^i \geq py^i w^i x^i = py^i/\varepsilon^i$, using Eq. (3). Summing and invoking Eq. (7) and the price normalization constraint of (6), we obtain $1/\varepsilon = wx = w\sum x^i \geq \sum py^i/\varepsilon^i = \sum s^i/\varepsilon^i$. Inverting, industry efficiency becomes $\leq 1/\sum \frac{s^i}{\varepsilon^i}$.

Extending Briec *et al.* (2003, p. 259), the next proposition shows that the gap is zero if and only if the private prices of the firms coincide. The sufficiency part is reminiscent of Koopmans (1957) result that the industry profit function equals the sum of the firm profit functions. Proposition 2 will be used later to show that an industrial organization is efficient if and only if it features price competition and free entry.

Recall the formal model: Firms are represented by nonzero input-output activities $(x^i, y^i), i = 1, \ldots, I$ which can be run with constant

[7]Since prices are in the numerator and the denominator of formula (8), the price normalization in (6) is a wash: it yields no effect.

returns to scale and free disposability. Given these data program (1) determines the firm efficiencies ε^i — with private shadow prices generated by dual program (2) — and program (5) determines industry efficiency ε — and the dual of latter is used to define the market shares as in Proposition 1. □

Proposition 2: *The industry efficiency equals the market share weighted harmonic mean of the firm efficiencies if and only if all relative private price vectors match.*

Proof: The private prices p^i and w^i solve program (2). Rescale them by letting them solve $\min_{p,w \geq 0} wx^i : py^j \leq wx^j py = 1$, all j (normalizing against y instead of y^i). If the relative price vectors are equal, i.e. (p^i, w^i) are collinear, then, by the now common normalization constraint, (p^i, w^i) are equal, say (p, w). I claim these prices solve program (6). Feasibility carries over from any of the rescaled linear programs. Suppose the prices are not optimal. Then there would be a superior (p^*, w^*) with $p^*y^j \leq w^*x^j, p^*y = 1$ and $w^*x < wx$. Hence $w^*x^i < wx^i$ for some i. This contradicts that (p, w) solves the rescaled dual program of that firm i. Since (p, w) are also privately optimal, the inequalities in the Proof of Proposition 1 are binding. The bindingness of the last of these inequalities equates industry efficiency with the harmonic mean of the firm efficiencies. Conversely, if this equality holds, the inequalities in the Proof of Proposition 1 are binding. Hence p/py^i and w/py^i are privately optimal. These private prices are collinear. □

Remark: There may be corner/multiple solutions. For example, If two firms each produce one unit of output with one unit of labor and one unit of capital, then $(X, Y) = (x^i, y^i)_{i=1,2} = (((1,1),1),((1,1),1))$ and the private input price vectors are (w_1, w_2) with nonnegative w_1, w_2 summing to unity. The industry prices are the same, with the same multiplicity. When there is multiplicity, the relative price vectors are sets and Proposition 2 shows that if these sets are equal industry efficiency equals mean firm efficiency (and vice versa). I am grateful to a sharp referee for letting me complete this point.

The reason that industry efficiency is generally less than mean firm efficiency is that the industrial organization is suboptimal. It is a form of allocative inefficiency. Firms better be split or merged, specialize or diversify. This will be discussed after the defining industrial organization efficiency. The optimal industrial organization is determined by the benchmarks in program (5). Suboptimality is signalled by a distortion between private and social prices (Proposition 2). The efficiency of the industrial organization can thus be measured by the ratio of the industry efficiency to the mean firm efficiency, or, using Proposition 1:

Definition 1: The efficiency of an industrial organization, (X, Y), equals $\varepsilon^{\mathrm{IO}} = \varepsilon \sum s^i/\varepsilon^i$, where s^i are the market shares evaluated at the prices determined by dual program (6).

Definition 1 frees Nesterenko and Zelenyuk (2007)'s definition of group revenue reallocative efficiency from its price dependence. By Proposition 1 the efficiency of an industrial organization is a number between 0 and 1, with the latter value representing full efficiency according to Proposition 2. Bogetoft and Wang (2005) explore the potential efficiency gains of a better industrial organization, including what they call the harmony effect. Five simple examples show the measurability.

Examples

1. Consider an industry with equally efficient firms: $\varepsilon^i = \bar{\varepsilon}$. Then by Proposition 1, $\varepsilon \leq 1/\sum \frac{s^i}{\varepsilon^i} = \bar{\varepsilon}$. Hence industry efficiency is less than firm efficiency. The efficiency of the industrial organization is $\varepsilon^{\mathrm{IO}} = \varepsilon/\bar{\varepsilon}$.
2. Consider an industry that produces a single good from labor and capital. Three firms each produce one unit of output. Firm 1 uses just one unit of labor, firm 2 uses just one unit of capital, and firm 3 uses 1/3 units of both inputs. Since firm 1 has labor only, the technologies of firms 2 and 3 (which employ capital) are of no use. There is no potential increase of its output. The same conclusion holds for firm 2. Firm 3 could reallocate its labor and capital to the technologies employed by firms 1 and 2, respectively, but its output would go down from 1 to 2/3. Hence no firm has scope for an increase in output. All potential outputs are equal to the observed outputs and, therefore, all firms are 100% efficient. The industry, however, is not efficient. If firms 1 and 2 would merge and

adopt the technology of firm 3, the new firm would be three times as big as firm 3, hence produce three units of output, which is one more than they produce using their own technologies. Potential output is four units (instead of three), so that the expansion factor is 4/3 and, therefore, the industry efficiency is 3/4 or only 75%. The efficiency of the industrial organization is $75/100 = 0.75$ or 75%. The industry would do better if the two specialized firms would merge. The shadow prices differ indeed. The shadow input price of firm 1 is (1, 2). (Under this price firms 1 and 3 break even.) The shadow input price of firm 2 is (2, 1).

3. It is straightforward to construct an example where the industry would do better if a firm were split: Simply substitute diseconomies of scope for the economies of scope in Example 2, by letting firm 3 use 2/3 units of both inputs (instead of the 1/3 in Example 2).
4. Add a fourth firm to Example 2, with the same inputs as firm 3, but only 1/2 a unit of output. Clearly, firm 4 could produce a full unit of output (adopting the technology of firm 3). Its efficiency is 50%. In the present example, the outputs are 1, 1, 1, 0.5. The market shares are 2/7, 2/7, 2/7, 1/7. The firm efficiencies are 100%, 100%, 100%, 50%. The harmonic mean is $1/\sum s^i/\varepsilon^i = 1/(\frac{2/7}{1.00} + \frac{2/7}{1.00} + \frac{2/7}{1.00} + \frac{1/7}{0.50})$ or 87.5%. For the industry potential output is three for firms 1 and 2 jointly (see Example 2) and one for firms 3 and 4 each, hence five in total (instead of three and a half), so that the expansion factor is 5/3.5 and, therefore, the industry efficiency is 3.5/5 or only 70%. The efficiency of the industrial organization is $70/87.5 = 0.8$ or 80%.
5. Example 2 may also be varied as to have the price variation on the output side. Consider an industry that produces goods and services from a single input. Three firms each use one unit of input. Firm 1 produces one unit of the good, firm 2 produces one unit of the service, and firm 3 produces 2/3 units of either output. By the price normalization constraint in program (2), firm 1 has a good price of 1. The input price is 1. The service price must render the other two activities unprofitable, hence be in the interval $[0, 1/2]$. For firm 2 the output prices are opposite.

Analogous to Nesterenko and Zelenyuk's (2007, Proposition 1) revenue property, an immediate consequence of Definition 1 is the following.

Proposition 3: *Industry efficiency is the product of (market share weighted harmonic) mean firm efficiency and the efficiency of the industrial organization.*

Proposition 3 will enable us to refine the decomposition of productivity growth in technical change and efficiency change in the next section, but first I make an observation on the connection between the efficiency and the supportability of an industrial organization in a contestable market. In a contestable market, a potential entrant can tap the incumbents' technology and the entry costs are zero; see Baumol *et al.* (1982). Their solution concept is that of a sustainable industrial organization. The definition of sustainability involves demand conditions, but a simple, necessary condition is Sharkey and Telser's (1978) supportability, and that is all I need.

Definition 2: An industrial organization (X, Y) is supportable by price vector (p, w) if the latter renders every incumbent firm profitable $(wx^i \leq py^i)$, but any potential entrant unprofitable. $(\sum \theta_j x^j \leq x^e, y^e \leq \sum \theta_j y^j, \theta_j \geq 0 \Rightarrow wx^e \geq py^e)$.

The next result connects the benchmark industrial organization involving price competition plus free entry with efficient outcomes. In fact, Proposition 4 articulates the Baumol and Fischer (1978, p. 461) intuition that "it would be highly surprising if there were not a rough correspondence between the most economical market form and what actually occurs" and extends Baumol *et al.* (1982) proposition that in a sustainable industry configuration total industry cost must be minimized. In Proposition 4 full industrial organization efficiency means $\varepsilon^{\mathrm{IO}} = 1$ (Definition 1) and full firms efficiencies that the solutions to all programs (1) are $\varepsilon^i = 1$.

Proposition 4: *An industrial organization is supportable if and only if it is fully efficient and comprises fully efficient firms.*

Proof: Let me first prove the only if part, which is known, at least for given input prices. So let the industrial organization be supportable by (p, w). I claim that the normalized supporting prices p/py^i

and w/py^i solve the dual program of an incumbent firm, (2). For this purpose, take $\theta_j = 1$ and $\theta_k = 0$, k $\neq$ j in Definition 2. Then $x^j \leq x^e, y^e \leq y^i \Rightarrow wx^e \geq py^e$. In particular, $wx^j \geq py^j$. (In fact, the inequality is binding by the first condition in Definition 2.) This shows that the first constraint in (2) is met. The second constraint is met by the normalization by py^i. The value of the objective function in (2) must be at least $wx^i \geq py^i$ according to the first constraint in (2) with $j = i$. By the first condition in Definition 2 this lower bound py^i is not exceeded by wx^i of Definition 2, which renders the latter optimal in (2).

By Eq. (4), firm i is fully efficient. Moreover, since the relative prices solving dual program (2) are common to all incumbent firms, Proposition 2 applies and the industry efficiency is also 1. Substituting these findings in Definition 1, it follows that the industrial organization must be fully efficient.

To prove the converse, consider a fully efficient industrial organization comprising fully efficient firms. By Proposition 2, there is a common price vector (p, w) such that p/py^i and w/py^i are privately optimal. I claim that (p, w) supports the industrial organization. By Eq. (4), $wx^i = py^i$. Let $\sum \theta_j x^j \leq x^e$ and $y^e \leq \sum \theta_j y^j, \theta_j \geq 0$. Then $wx^e \geq w \sum \theta_j x^j \geq p \sum \theta_j y^j \geq py^e$, where the middle inequality holds term by term in view of the constraints in program (2) that characterizes the privately optimal prices. □

4. Recovery of the Solow Residual

Performance will be measured by the Solow (1957) residual, the difference between the output and input growth rates. Both growth rates are share-weighted expressions, using competitive valuations. In a noncompetitive environment the residual captures not only technical but also efficiency change. Since the latter concept is defined by the price-free benchmarking program (1), a little work has to be done to make the connection. Introduce time by subscripting inputs and outputs, as well as the derived constructs, using the symbol t. Firm i has input and output vectors x_t^i *and* $y_t^i, i = 1, \ldots, I$. By benchmarking, y_t^i/ε_t^i is derived, the potential output of firm i. Its efficiency is indicated by ε_t^i, a number between 0 and 1. As a percentage, efficiency change is:[8]

$$EC_t^i = \frac{d}{dt}\varepsilon_t^i/\varepsilon_t^i \tag{9}$$

Technical change manifests itself as a shift of the production possibility frontier. At each point of time, the frontier is determined by the industrial organization (x_t, y_t). Program (1) determines the efficiency of firm i as a function of (x_t^i, y_t^i) and (X_t, Y_t), say $\varepsilon_t^i = e(x_t^i, y_t^i, X_t, Y_t)$. Now the program that determines the efficiency of the industry, (5), has precisely the same structure as that for the firms (the only difference is that the pair of total input and output vectors replace the role of a firm's pair), hence the same mapping e governs the relationship between the data and industry efficiency: $\varepsilon_t = e(x_t, y_t, X_t, Y_t)$. Mapping e has two arguments, the input-output pair that is benchmarked, (x_t^i, y_t^i) in case of the firm, and the industry constellation that determines the frontier, (X_t, Y_t). Denote the row vectors of the two respective partial derivatives of the mapping by e_1 and e_2. By total differentiation, the efficiency change of firm i is:

$$\begin{aligned}
&\frac{de}{dt}(x_t^i, y_t^i, X_t, Y_t)/e(x_t^i, y_t^i, X_t, Y_t)\\
&\quad = \mathrm{e}_1(x_t^i, y_t^i, X_t, Y_t)\frac{d}{dt}(x_t^i, y_t^i)/e(x_t^i, y_t^i, X_t, Y_t)\\
&\qquad + \mathrm{e}_2(x_t^i, y_t^i, X_t, Y_t)\frac{d}{dt}(X_t, Y_t)/e(x_t^i, y_t^i, X_t, Y_t)
\end{aligned} \tag{10}$$

The measurement of technical change involves a sign issue. If firm i stays put — $(x_t^i y_t^i)$ = constant — but potential output increases, there must be technical progress. Now an increase in potential output, $1/\varepsilon_t^i$, is equivalent to a decrease in efficiency, ε_t^i. Hence a negative partial derivative with respect to the second argument — which captures the external effect — indicates technical progress. Indeed, if a firm is fixed, but it becomes less efficient, it must be that the

[8]The efficiency is the solution value to linear program (1), where the data, the inputs and outputs of the firms, appear in the constraint coefficients and bounds. The sensitivity with respect to the bounds is given by the shadow prices (Jansen *et al.* 1997). The differentiability need not be in the limited sense of functions but must be generalized (Rockafellar, 1980). The sensitivity with respect to the constraint coefficients is differentiable (Freund, 1985).

benchmarks have moved out. In short, technical change is measured by:

$$TC_t^i = -e_2(x_t^i, y_t^i, X_t, Y_t)\frac{d}{dt}(X_t, Y_t)/e(x_t^i, y_t^i, X_t, Y_t) \tag{11}$$

Productivity growth of firm i ought to be defined irrespective the shift of the production possibility frontier. Productivity growth is defined by the effect of its own inputs and outputs on the efficiency performance of the firm:

$$PG_t^i = e_1(x_t^i, y_t^i, X_t, Y_t)\frac{d}{dt}(x_t^i, y_t^i)/e(x_t^i, y_t^i, X_t, Y_t) \tag{12}$$

This definition of productivity growth is essentially the Solow residual, but because of its generality (the own effect of a firm on its efficiency, keeping the environment constant) this must be demonstrated. Now Solow (1957) defined his residual (applied to firm i) by $p_t^i \frac{d}{dt} y_t^i / p_t^i y_t^i - w_t^i \frac{d}{dt} x_t^i / w_t^i x_t^i$. His prices are implicit in the partial derivatives of my efficiency function. Proposition 5 makes it explicit, proving that expression (12) equals the Solow residual.

Proposition 5: *Productivity growth is measured by the Solow residual:* $PG_t^i = p_t^i \frac{d}{dt} y_t^i / p_t^i y_t^i - w_t^i \frac{d}{dt} x_t^i / w_t^i x_t^i$.

Proof: The proof is by duality analysis. Mapping e's first (sub)argument, x_t^i, lists the bound in program (1). The partial derivative of the objective value, $1/\varepsilon_t^i$, with respect to this bound is the shadow price w_t^i. By the chain rule, $\frac{-1}{\varepsilon_t^{i2}} \frac{\partial \varepsilon_t^i}{\partial x_t^i} = w_t^i$. Mapping e's next (sub)argument, y_t^i, is a coefficient in program (1). Setting up the Lagrangian function and application of the envelop theorem yields that the partial derivative of the objective value, $1/\varepsilon_t^i$, with respect to coefficient y_t^i is $-p_t^i(1/\varepsilon_t^i)$. By the chain rule, $\frac{-1}{\varepsilon_t^{i2}} \frac{\partial \varepsilon_t^i}{\partial y_t^i} = -p_t^i(1/\varepsilon_t^i)$. Substituting these in expression (12), we obtain $PG_t^i = \frac{(-w_t^i \varepsilon_t^{i2}, p_t^i \varepsilon_t^i)\frac{d}{dt}(x_t^i, y_t^i)}{\varepsilon_t^i} = \frac{p_t^i \frac{d}{dt} y_t^i - \varepsilon_t^i w_t^i \frac{d}{dt} x_t^i}{p_t^i y_t^i} = \frac{p_t^i \frac{d}{dt} y_t^i}{p_t^i y_t^i} - w_t^i \frac{d}{dt} x_t^i / w_t^i x_t^i$, by the price normalization constraint of program (2) and Eq. (4). □

Summarizing, efficiency change is defined by (9), technical change by (11), productivity growth by (12), and the former two sum to the latter by Eq. (10), yielding Eq. (13):

$$PG_t^i = EC_t^i + TC_t^i \tag{13}$$

Things look only slightly different at the level of the industry. Now industry input and output, (x_t, y_t), are benchmarked against the frontier. The productivity growth of the industry is:

$$PG_t = e_1(x_t, y_t, X_t, Y_t)\frac{d}{dt}(x_t, y_t)/e(x_t, y_t, X_t, Y_t) \tag{14}$$

This expression is basically a summation of the firm productivity growth rates, (12), with the modification that private shadow prices have been replaced by social values.[9] The price difference constitutes a wedge which is precisely the aggregation bias uncovered by ten Raa (2005). I will now explain the role of industrial organization in the performance measure of productivity. Inspired by Caves *et al.* (1982), Faïe *et al.* (1994) define the Malmquist productivity index by

$$\begin{aligned} M_t^i &= \sqrt{\frac{e(x_{t+1}^i, y_{t+1}^i, X_t, Y_t)}{e(x_t^i, y_t^i, X_t, Y_t)} \cdot \frac{e(x_{t+1}^i, y_{t+1}^i, X_{t+1}, Y_{t+1})}{e(x_t^i, y_t^i, X_{t+1}, Y_{t+1})}} \\ &= \frac{e(x_{t+1}^i, y_{t+1}^i, X_{t+1}, Y_{t+1})}{e(x_t^i, y_t^i, X_t, Y_t)} \\ &\quad \times \sqrt{\frac{e(x_t^i, y_t^i, X_t, Y_t)}{e(x_t^i, y_t^i, X_{t+1}, Y_{t+1})} \cdot \frac{e(x_{t+1}^i, y_{t+1}^i, X_t, Y_t)}{e(x_{t+1}^i, y_{t+1}^i, X_{t+1}, Y_{t+1})}} \end{aligned} \tag{15}$$

where the second line decomposes it in efficiency change and technical change. Similar to the firm index (15) the industry Malmquist productivity index is:

$$M_t = \sqrt{\frac{e(x_{t+1}, y_{t+1}, X_t, Y_t)}{e(x_t, y_t, X_t, Y_t)} \cdot \frac{e(x_{t+1}, y_{t+1}, X_{t+1}, Y_{t+1})}{e(x_t, y_t, X_{t+1}, Y_{t+1})}} \tag{16}$$

Proposition 6: *The Malmquist productivity index aggregates the change in the efficiency of the industrial organization, firm efficiency*

[9] Indeed, if the private and social prices would match, $PG_t = e_1(x_t, y_t, X_t, Y_t) \sum \frac{\frac{d}{dt}(x_t^i, y_t^i)}{e(x_t, y_t, X_t, Y_t)} = \sum PG_t^i e(x_t^i, y_t^i, X_t, Y_t)/e(x_t, y_t, X_t, Y_t)$.

changes, and technical change:

$$M_t = \frac{\varepsilon_{t+1}^{\text{IO}}}{\varepsilon_t^{\text{IO}}} \cdot \frac{\sum s_t^i / e(x_t^i, y_t^i, X_t, Y_t)}{\sum s_{t+1}^i / e(x_{t+1}^i, y_{t+1}^i, X_{t+1}, Y_{t+1})} \cdot \\ \times \sqrt{\frac{e(x_t, y_t, X_t, Y_t)}{e(x_t, y_t, X_{t+1}, Y_{t+1})} \cdot \frac{e(x_{t+1}, y_{t+1}, X_t, Y_t)}{e(x_{t+1}, y_{t+1}, X_{t+1}, Y_{t+1})}}$$

Proposition 6 decomposes productivity growth in technical change and efficiency change and disaggregates the latter to the level of firms. This disaggregation involves a bias, which is accounted for by the industrial organization effect. The first quotient measures the change in the efficiency of the industrial organization. Firm efficiencies are aggregated in the second quotient by the market share weighted harmonic mean and market shares are evaluated at the shadow prices of the industry efficiency program (5). The square root measures technical change.[10]

Proof: Apply the second line of formula (15) to the industry and substitute, using Definition 1, $e(x_t, y_t, X_t, Y_t) = \varepsilon_t^{\text{IO}} / \sum s_t^i / e(x_t^i, y_t^i, X_t, Y_t)$ and similar for $e(x_{t+1}, y_{t+1}, X_t, Y_t)$. □

5. Illustration

Consider the Japanese banks ($i = 1, \ldots, I = 136$) over a five year period ($t = 1992, \ldots, 1996$).[11] There are three inputs (labor, capital, and funds from customers) and two outputs (loans and other investments). Formally we have a panel of inputs and outputs, (x_t^i, y_t^i). For the four transitions between periods Thanh Le Phuoc has computed the dynamic performance measure of productivity growth,

[10]Because Malmquist productivity indices are ratios near 1 (a growth rate of 1% is an index of 1.01), we essentially have the sum of the three effects. Proposition 6 frees Zelenyuk (2006)'s analysis from its price dependence and the assumption of the Law of One Price.

[11]Fukuyama and Weber (2002) kindly made available their data. The data were obtained by extracting Nikkei's data tape of bank financial statements. Six banks had missing data and were excluded. These were Akita Akebono, Bank of Tokyo, Hanwa, Hyogo, Midori, and Taiheiyo.

Table 1. The three contributions to the performance of the Japanese banking industry.

Period	Industrial organization (%)	Firms efficiency (%)	Technical change (%)	Total productivity (%)
1992–1993	0.07	−0.51	0.52	0.08
1993–1994	0.57	0.31	−0.58	0.29
1994–1995	−0.45	0.35	1.28	1.18
1995–1996	0.23	0.70	2.19	3.15
Total, annualized	0.11	0.21	0.85	1.17

and, applying Proposition 3, its decomposition in the industrial organization effect, firms efficiency change and technical change. The results are in Table 1.[12]

The last column of Table 1 shows that total productivity was initially stuck (0.08% growth in the period 1992–1993) but climbed strongly (to 3.15% in the period 1995–1996); on average it grew 1.17%. The bottom row decomposes this figure in technical change, efficiency change and the industrial organization effect. As usual, technical change is the most important source of productivity growth, contributing 0.85% per year. As is known from the growth accounting literature, technical change can be negative — see the second period. This means that the best practices were worse than in the year before. This phenomenon is natural in mining, but less so in banking.

Tulkens and Vanden Eeckaut (1995) redefine the frontier in terms of current and past practices; this technique would force technical change nonnegative and reduce efficiency change. Efficiency change can be negative — see the first period — but on average it augments technical change (0.85%) with a quarter (0.21%). Industrial organization is the third contributor to productivity growth, half the size of efficiency change. Thus, on average, the industrial organization of

[12]When Malmquist indices and its components are properly reported as fractions of the order 1, the product of the components equals total productivity growth. When reported as percentages, the components sum to total factor productivity growth, up to a first order Taylor approximation. This and rounding errors explain why not all row figures add.

Japanese banking improved in the 1990s, but as for firms's efficiency it can go up and down.

6. Conclusion

An industry may perform better, in the sense of productivity growth, by technical progress or by efficiency change. Both sources of growth have been decomposed in firm contributions, but the aggregation is known to be imperfect. The bias reflects the inefficiency of the industrial organization. This paper offers measures for the latter.

Acknowledgments

Author completed the paper at Bar-Ilan University and NYU Polytechnic Institute and the Berkley Center for Entrepreneurship and Innovation at the Stern School of Business. I am also grateful to Shawna Grosskopf and Sverre Kittelsen for literature references, and two referees for detailed comments.

Open Access

References

Balk, B. M. (2009). Measuring and relating aggregate and subaggregate productivity change without neoclassical assumptions. Discussion Paper 09026, Statistics Netherlands.

Bartelsman, E. J. and M. Doms. (2000). Understanding productivity: Lessons from longitudinal microdata. *Journal of Economic Literature*, **38**(3), 569–594.

Baumol, W. J. and D. Fischer. (1978). Cost-minimizing number of firms and determination of industry structure. *Quarterly Journal of Economics*, **92**(3), 439–468.

Baumol, W. J., J. C. Panzar and R. D. Willig. (1982). *Contestable Markets and the Theory of Industry Structure*, New York: Harcourt Brace Jovanovich.

Blackorby, C. and R. R. Russell. (1999). Aggregation of efficiency indices. *Journal of Productivity Analysis*, **12**(1), 5–20.

Bogetoft, P. and D. Wang. (2005). Estimating the potential gains from mergers. *Journal of Productivity Analysis*, **23**(2), 145–171.

Briec, W., B. Dervaux and H. Leleu. (2003). Aggregation of directional distance functions and industrial efficiency. *Journal of Economics*, **79**(3), 237–261.

Caves, D. W., L. R. Christensen and W. E. Diewert. (1982). The economic theory of index numbers and the measurement of input, output and productivity. *Econometrica*, **50**(6), 1393–1414.

Charnes, A., W. W. Cooper and E. Rhodes. (1978). Measuring the efficiency of decision making units. *European Journal of Operational Research*, **2**(6), 429–444.

Debreu, G. (1951). The coefficient of resource utilization. *Econometrica*, **19**(3), 273–292.

Diewert, W. E. (1981). The economic theory of index numbers. In *Essays in the Theory and Measurement of Consumer Behaviour in Honour of Sir Richard Stone*, Ed. Deaton, A., London: Cambridge University Press, pp. 163–208.

Diewert, W. E. (1983). The measurement of waste within the production sector of an open economy. *Scandinavian Journal of Economics*, **85**(2), 159–179.

Färe, R. and S. Grosskopf. (2004). *New Directions: Efficiency and Productivity*, Boston: Kluwer Academic Publishers.

Färe, R. and V. Zelenyuk. (2003). On aggregate Farrell efficiencies. *European Journal of Operational Research*, **146**, 615–620.

Färe, R., S. Grosskopf, B. Lindgren and P. Roos. (1994). Productivity development in Swedish hospitals: A Malmquist output index approach. In *Data Envelopment Analysis: Theory, Methodology and Applications*, Eds. Charnes, A., W. Cooper, A. Y. Lewin and L. M. Seiford, Boston: Kluwer Academic Publishers, pp. 253–272.

Farrell, M. J. (1957). The measurement of production efficiency. *Journal of the Royal Statistical Society Series A*, **120**, 253–278.

Førsund, F. R. and L. Hjalmarsson. (1979). Generalised Farrell measures of efficiency: An application to milk processing in Swedish dairy plants. *The Economic Journal*, **89**, 294–315.

Freund, R. M. (1985). Postoptimal analysis of a linear program under simultaneous changes in matrix coefficients. *Math Program Study*, **24**, 1–13.

Fukuyama, H. and W. L. Weber. (2002). Estimating output allocative efficiency and productivity change: Application to Japanese banks. *European Journal of Operational Research*, **137**, 177–190.

Georgescu-Roegen, N. (1951). The aggregate linear production function and its applications to von Neumann's economic model. In *Activity Analysis of Production and Allocation*, Ed. Koopmans, T., New York: Wiley, pp. 98–115.

Jansen, B., J. J. de Jong, C. Roos and T. Terlaky. (1997). Sensitivity analysis in linear programming: Just be careful! *European Journal of Operational Research*, **101**, 15–28.

Johansen, L. (1972). *Production Functions,* Amsterdam: North-Holland.

Koopmans, T. C. (1957). *Three Essays on the State of Economic Science*, New York: McGraw-Hill.

Li, S. K. and Y. C. Ng. (1995). Measuring the productive efficiency of a group of firms. *International Advances in Economic Research*, **1**(4), 377–390.

Nesterenko, V. and V. Zelenyuk. (2007). Measuring potential gains from reallocation of resources. *Journal of Productivity Analysis*, **28**(1–2), 107–116.

Rockafellar, R. T. (1980). Generalized directional derivatives and subgradients of nonconvex functions. *Canadian Journal of Mathematics*, **32**(2), 257–280.

Sharkey, W. W. and L. G. Telser. (1978). Supportable cost functions for the multiproduct firm. *Journal of Economic Theory*, **18**, 23–27.

Shephard, R. W. (1970). *Theory of Cost and Production Functions*, Princeton: Princeton University Press.

Solow, R. M. (1957). Technical change and the aggregate production function. *Review of Economics and Statistics*, **39**(3), 312–320.

ten Raa, T. (2005). Aggregation of productivity indices: The allocative efficiency correction. *Journal of Productivity Analysis*, **24**(2), 203–209.

ten Raa, T. (2008). Debreu's coefficient of resource utilization, the Solow residual, and TFP: The connection by Leontief preferences. *Journal of Productivity Analysis*, **30**, 191–199.

Tulkens, H. and P. Vanden Eeckaut. (1995). Non-parametric efficiency, progress and regress measure for panel data: Methodological aspects. *European Journal of Operational Research*, **80**, 474–499.

Zelenyuk, V. (2006). Aggregation of Malmquist productivity indexes. *European Journal of Operational Research*, **174**, 1076–1086.

Chapter 4

Performance Measurement in an Input-Output Framework*

Thijs ten Raa

Department of Economics, Tilburg University, Tilburg, The Netherlands

tenraa@uvt.nl

Abstract. This paper fruitfully combines two complementary theories: performance measurement and input-output analysis. Our point of departure is the theory of the consumer, who maximizes utility subject to a budget constraint. His well-being can be measured by the change in the consumption bundle, valued at constant prices. Input output analysis is invoked to impute the change in this bundle to technical change, a terms-of-trade effect and two types of efficiency change. The analysis is extended to environmental economics.

Keywords: Performance Measurement, Growth Accounting, Terms of Trade, Environmental Constraint

JEL-codes: C67, O47, Q56

1. Introduction

In this paper I bring to fruition the neoclassical measurement of performance change in an input-output framework. Some pitfalls are avoided. First, market prices need not be perfectly competitive and, more generally, the observed allocation of resources may be inefficient. Solow's ascription of TFP-growth to technical change holds in

*Reprinted from *Journal of Economic Structures*, **1**, Article number: 2, 2012, with permission from Springer Nature.

an idyllic neoclassical world where resources are rewarded according to their marginal productivities, but not beyond. Market power, managerial slacks and other sources of inefficiency abound and we must factor in their variations to properly account for performance changes. Since these conditions differ between industries, an input output framework seems promising.

The strategy of this paper is the following. I find it reasonable to assume that households are price takers. This point of departure is quite powerful, because the first order condition of the problem of the consumer, which equates the marginal rates of substitution to the price ratios, reveal that prices measure marginal utilities (up to an uninteresting multiplicative constant, the marginal utility of money) *even* when those prices are distorted. So I measure changes in the level of well-being of consumers by tracking final consumption. Then I use input-output analysis to decompose that bill of final goods and services. It may increase due to reductions in input coefficients, Solow's technical change, but obviously for other reasons as well. This paper sorts it out.

2. Utility Based Performance Measurement

In general equilibrium analysis — of which input-output is an important instance — consumers have initial endowments, including their labor skills. Some consumers are better off than others, i.e. have bigger endowments, and this translates into greater budget sets, hence opportunities. If, however, we assume away income effects in their utility functions — as is the case for constant elasticity of substitution (including Cobb-Douglas and Leontief) utility functions, then the relationship between the percentage rate of change in utility and in consumption is independent of the level of well being.

Formally, a consumer maximizes $U(x)$ subject to $px \leq p\omega$, where x is a consumption vector, ω the initial endowment, p the price (row) vector, and U the utility function. I assume U is linearly homogeneous (no income effects). Exogenous to the consumer are p and ω (price taking behavior). How does the consumer respond to change? Well, that's determined by the envelope theorem, according to which the change in the objective value is given by the *partial* derivatives of the objective function with respect to the exogenous parameters.

(The point of the theorem is that the change in the endogenous parameter, consumption, may be ignored.) Since the envelope theorem is formulated for free maximization problems, we must first handle the constraint. This is done in the usual way by setting up the Lagrangian function, $U(x) + \lambda(p\omega - px)$, and maximizing that.

Change the parameters: dp and $d\omega$. By the envelope theorem dU is determined by the partial derivatives with respect p and ω. The first effect is $\lambda(\omega - x)dp$; the consumer is better of his resources are priced higher and worse off if his consumption bundle is priced higher. The second effect is $\lambda p d\omega$; the consumer is better off if he is better endowed. In total $dU = \lambda dp(\omega - x) + \lambda p d\omega$. This can be simplified. (For simplicity I assume, quite realistically, that the budget constraint is binding, but otherwise the simplification still holds by the phenomenon of complimentary slackness, $\lambda = 0$.) Differentiating the budget equation, $p(\omega - x) = 0$, we obtain $dp(\omega - x) + pd\omega - pdx = 0$. Substituting, $dU = \lambda pdx$. The well-being of the consumer is assessed by tracking consumption. An immediate and well known consequence is that the vector of marginal utilities is $U' = \lambda p$.

Here the Lagrange multiplier is the marginal utility of income, but the no income effects assumption gets rid of it. Formally, linear homogeneity means $U(\theta x) = \theta U(x)$. Differentiating with respect to (positive) θ, using the chain rule, $U'(x)x = U(x)$. (This is Euler's theorem.) The (percentage) rate of change of utility becomes now $dU/U = \lambda pdx/U'(x)x = \lambda pdx = pdx/px$. If we have two consumers, then their rates of change are pdx^1/px^1 and pdx^2/px^2. Defining x as the total consumption bundle, the weighted average is $(px^1/px)pdx^1/px^1 + (px^2/px)pdx^2/px^2 = pdx/px$. In other words, pdx/px is a robust measure for tracking utility.

Performance, however, is the latter per unit of endowment, hence as a growth rate performance is measured by subtracting the change in endowment from the change in consumption: $(pdx - pd\omega)/px$.

3. Embedding Performance Measurement in the Input-Output Framework

I assume that utility is a function of the consumption of the produced commodities. This neglects the utility of leisure time, but is not bad if labor is supplied in elastically (e.g. when overall utility is a Cobb-Douglas function of commodity consumption utility and leisure). I also identify household consumption with domestic final demand, i.e. incorporating investment. This has been given a theoretical foundation by Weitzman (1976). Net output $y = x + z + s$, where z is net exports and s is slack (output not allocated to intermediate demand, domestic final demand or exports, i.e. inventory investment). The initial endowment does not enter this equation. I assume that the initial endowment consists of (currently) no produced factors, capital K and labor L. This dichotomy between produced and no produced commodities is handled by reserving the last two dimensions for capital and labor, with prices r and w. With a slight abuse of notation I reserve p for the price (row) vector of the produced goods and services-the price vector of Section 2 becoming $(p\,w\,r)$. The performance measure becomes $(pdx - rdK - wdL)/px$.

If there is no slack ($s = 0$) and balance of payments ($pz = 0$) then consumption x may be replaced by net output y in the performance measure and we recognize the Solow residual. I will not make these neoclassical assumptions. I will use, however, the balance equations, for gross output $q = Aq+y$, and for the factor inputs $K = kq+K$ and $L = lq+\lambda$. Input-output coefficients populate matrix A (intermediate inputs) and row vectors k and l (factor inputs). K and λ represent idle capital and labor. (Product slack s was already accounted for in net output y.) Substitution turns performance $((pdx - rdK - wdL)/px)$ into $[pd(q - Aq - z - s) - rd(kq + K) - wd(lq + \lambda)]/px$. Applying the product rule to Aq, Kq and lq, and rearranging numerator of this performance measure is decomposed into four parts:

(i) $-(pdA + rdk + wdl)q$
(ii) $-pdz$
(iii) $(p - pA - rk - wl)dq$
(iv) $(-pds + rdK + wd\lambda)$.

All have to be divided by px. The first term measures the reductions in the input coefficients, i.e. *technical change*. Because we multiply with gross output components and divide by the main component of net output, this is a weighted average of industrial Solow residuals, with the weight summing to the gross/net output ratio of the economy (Domar aggregation, ten Raa 2006). The second term measures the value in the change in the net imports, $-z$, i.e. the *terms-of-trade-effect*. It is straightforward to understand this. If the balance of payments does not change, pz constant, then $pdz = (dp)z$, which measures the improvement in the prices of the net exports. The third term measures the reallocation of output in terms of profitability, i.e. *allocative efficiency change*. The fourth term measures the reduction of slack in the utilization of goods and services, capital and labor, i.e. *X-efficiency change* (Comanor and Leibenstein 1969).

A perfectly competitive economy shows only the first two effects, technical change and the terms-of-trade effect. Indeed, the trade sector can be considered an industry where the exports are the inputs and the imports are the outputs. An improvement in the terms of trade is a reduction of the exports required per unit of imports, just like a reduction of the input coefficients in the regular industries. Solow (1957) analyzed a closed perfectly competitive economy and discovered that the residual (now called Solow residual) measures technical change. The role of the term-of-trade has been in the air for long and was articulated by ten Raa and Mohnen (2002). They also relate the broad decomposition into technical change and efficiency change to the operations research/productivity literature. The further decomposition into X-efficiency and allocative efficiency has been studied in the same literature, but in micro contexts. This paper encompasses all, using an input-output framework of the economy.

I have not assumed that the prices are equilibrium prices. Even when prices are distorted, they point the way to the greatest increase of utility, by the first order condition of the problem of the consumer, and that's all we needed. Things get different when one wants to assess the *level* of efficiency. This is matter of determining how much better off the consumers could be. There are several ways to find the Pareto frontier. A natural one — particularly when assuming linearly homogeneous utility functions — is to find alternative allocations that maximize the utility levels with a common multiplicative factor, subject to the balances. Then the prices are the shadow prices to the latter constraints. This methodology is particularly helpful when markets are incomplete, prices are missing.

4. The Environmental Extension

The classical example of missing prices is that for externalities, such as pollution. Elsewhere I (2008) have argued that a conservative way to estimate the inefficiency involved is to assume Leontief preferences. I have also shown that, then, the problem to determine inefficiency is solved by maximizing the level of consumption subject to the balance constraints. Denote that level by u, where the observed level corresponds to $u = 1$. Hence u is the expansion factor for consumption. For example, if u can be 1.25, then consumption could be 25% higher and, therefore, it is only at 80% of its potential. We say that the economy is 20% inefficient. The constraints are $Aq + xu + z \leq q$, $kq \leq K$, $lq \leq L$, $pz \leq pz^o$. Here the variables are q, u, z, pz^o is the observed trade balance, at world prices. Maximizing u, the shadow prices to the produced balance constraint can be seen to be proportional to p (ten Raa 2006). The shadow prices to the next two constraints are denoted r and w. Bring in emission coefficients, organized in row vector m, and a policy level M of maximum emission. That is equivalent to adding a constraint $mq \leq M$. Denote the shadow price by t, then the dual constraint becomes $p \leq pA + rk + wl + tm$, with slack indicating that the output of a product must be zero. These shadow prices are competitive prices, sustaining the efficient allocation, and reflect the cost of pollution, which is equal to the Pigovian tax.

Performance growth accounting a la Section 3 is straightforward, because formally pollution is equivalent to the addition of a third resource.

5. Conclusion

The reconciliation of performance measurement and input-output analysis is mutually beneficial. The input-output framework facilitates economy-wide performance measurement, including a quantification of the terms-of-trade effect and a decomposition of efficiency change in allocative and X-efficiency changes, even down to the level of industry. Conversely, performance measurement makes input-output analysis richer. The doctor not only knows how the parts of the body interact, but also how healthy the patient is.

Competing Interests

The author declares that he has no competing interests.

References

Comanor, W. S. and H. Leibenstein. (1969). Allocative efficiency, X-efficiency and the measurement of welfare losses. *Economica*, **26**, 304–309.

Solow, R. (1957). Technical change and the aggregate production function. *The Review of Economics and Statistics*, **39**(3), 312–320.

ten Raa, T. (2006). *The Economics of Input-Output Analysis,* Cambridge: Cambridge University Press.

ten Raa, T. (2008). Debreu's coefficient of resource utilization, the Solow residual, and TFP: The connection by Leontief preferences. *Journal of Productivity Analysis*, **30**, 191–199.

ten Raa, T. and P. Mohnen. (2002). Neoclassical growth accounting and frontier analysis: A synthesis. *Journal of Productivity Analysis*, **18**(2), 111–128.

Weitzman, M. L. (1976). On the welfare significance of national product in a dynamic economy. *Quarterly Journal of Economics*, **90**, 156–162.

Chapter 5

Firm Efficiency, Industry Performance and the Economy: Three-Way Decomposition with an Application to Andalusia*

Antonio F. Amores[†,‡,¶] and Thijs ten Raa[‡]

[†]*Department of Economics, Pablo de Olavide University, Quantitative Methods and Economics History Ctra. Utrera Km. 1, 41013 Sevilla, Spain*
afamoher@upo.es

[‡]*Department of Economics, Tilburg University, Tilburg, The Netherlands*
tenraa@uvt.nl

Abstract. An economy may perform better because the firms become more efficient, the industries are better organized, or the allocation between industries is improved. In this paper we extend the literature on the measurement of industry efficiency (a decomposition in firm contributions and an organizational effect) to a third level, namely that of the economy. The huge task of interrelating the performance of an economy to industrial firm data is accomplished for Andalusia.

*Reprinted from *Journal of Productivity Analysis*, **42**, 25–34, 2014, with permission from Springer Nature.

¶Corresponding author.

Keywords: Input-Output, Industrial Organization, Comparative Advantage, Allocative Efficiency, Efficiency Decomposition

JEL-codes: L10, D24, O47

1. Introduction

Inefficiencies abound at the micro, meso and macro levels of the economy. Firms do not apply best-practices; industries may be organized suboptimally — with too many or too few firms — and the resources of the economy may be misallocated between industries. These concerns are the subject of the theory of the firm, industrial organization, and macro-economics, but are rarely connected. There are two reasons of this shortcoming. First, in the theoretical literature the focus of efficiency analysis is on the aggregation issue. Two levels are distinguished and there are more gains to be made than at the lower level: gains to trade in a system of regions or gains to reorganization in an industry. In this paper we extend the analysis to more levels. Second, modern economies comprise many industries and very many firms and it is a daunting task to express their performance in terms of the micro data. This paper makes a first attempt.

In the next section, we review a measure for the industrial organization efficiency. In section 3, we propose an inclusion of the industrial specialization efficiency in the economy. In section 4, the economy-wide efficiency is analyzed and decomposed. An application is presented in section 5. The paper ends with some conclusions. Three appendices with a demonstration and data details and procedures are provided, along with a supplementary spreadsheet file containing detailed results.

2. Review of Organization Efficiency

Following ten Raa (2011) the organization efficiency of an industry is analyzed by determining the output gain attainable from a reallocation of resources between the firms. We maintain ten Raa's implicit assumption that not only inputs but also outputs must have fixed proportions at the level of the firm, but not at the level of the industry. Industries produce their own products (primary outputs) and the products of other industries (secondary outputs). In the organization efficiency calculation we expand the own or primary output of an industry without requiring that secondary output increases at the same rate. This more flexible approach admits potential efficiency gains within industries which would be missed if ten Raa's (2011) output proportionality were maintained at the industry level. This flexibility at the industry level is consistent with the assumption of fixed proportions at the firm level, as is well understood ever since Houthakker (1956).

Denote the input and output vectors of firm i in industry k by x_{ik} and y_{ik}, $i \in I_k; k \in K$, where I_k is the set of the firms of the industry k and K is the set of the industries in the economy. e is a unitary vector of suitable dimension. The firm efficiency, ε_{ik}, is the solution to the following linear program:

$$\max_{\varepsilon_{ik},\lambda_{jk}\geq 0} e^{\top} y_{ik}/\varepsilon_{ik} : \sum_{j\in I_k} \lambda_{jk}x_{jk} \leq x_{ik}, \sum_{j\in I_k} \lambda_{jk}y_{jk} \geq y_{ik}/\varepsilon_{ik} \quad (1)$$

Expression (1) is a linear program in efficiency variable $1/\varepsilon_{ik}$ and allocation variables λ_{ik}. It includes a multiplicative constant in the objective function that will merely normalize the price variables in the dual program. Because a feasible solution to (1) is a reproduction of firm ik (by putting $\lambda_{ik} = 1$ and all other weights 0) the efficiency score ranges between 0 and 1. This is a Data Envelopment Analysis (DEA) model with Constant Returns to Scale and Output orientation (DEA CRS-O).[1] The dual program associated with (1) is:

$$\min_{p_{ik},w_{ik}\geq 0} w_{ik}x_{ik} : p_{ik}y_{jk} \leq w_{ik}x_{jk}, p_{ik}y_{ik} = e^{\top} y_{ik}, j \in I_k, k \in K \quad (2)$$

where dual variables w_{ik} and p_{ik} are the shadow prices of the constraints of (1).

[1]Details and complete DEA descriptions may be found in specific books such as Charnes *et al.* (1995) or Cooper *et al.* (2000). We included constant $e^{\top} y_{ik}$ (which is total production of firm i of industry k, $^{\top}$ is transposition) in the objective function; this monotonic transformation will prove useful for the price normalization.

The efficiency of industry k, ε_k, is the solution to the next program:

$$\max_{\lambda_{jk}\geq 0,\varepsilon_k} e^T \sum_{i\in I_k} y_{ik}/\varepsilon_k : \sum_{j\in I_k} \lambda_{jk}x_{jk} \leq \sum_{i\in I_k} x_{ik}, \sum_{j\in I_k} \lambda_{jk}\breve{y}_{jk}$$
$$\geq \sum_{i\in I_k} \breve{y}_{ik}, \sum_{j\in Ik} \lambda_{jk}\hat{y}_{jk} \geq \sum_{i\in I_k} \hat{y}_{ik}/\varepsilon_k \tag{3}$$

where ε_k is again a number between 0 and 1, because a feasible solution is a reproduction of all firms in the industry. Superscript ˆdenotes the primary output of industry k. Superscript ˇdenote the secondary outputs.[2] This notation will also be used for their prices. The idea is to reallocate the industry inputs, as to maximize k-specific output, inflating it by the expansion factor $1/\varepsilon_k$. Non-specific aggregate output, $\sum_{i\in I_k} \breve{y}_{ik}$, may also be expanded, but not necessarily in the same proportion. Since it remains at least the same, our expansion model is

[2]In national accounts statistics, firms are classified within industries following national or international classifications (NAICS in US, Canada and Mexico; NACE in the EU: ISIC in the UN) according to its primary output. However, firms usually produce also other commodities than its primary output (secondary ones) taking advantage of idle resources, i.e. a milk producing farm, whose primary output is producing milk for a diary products firms can also make home-made cheese to sell in a small shop and even provide rural tourism services with idle spaces and labor-force. Formally $\hat{y}_{jk}$ is the kth component of vector y and $\breve{y}_{jk}$ is the vector comprising all other components. Industry and commodity classifications usually match at the most common aggregation levels. i.e. NACE (Nomenclature of Activities of the European Union) matches CPA (Classification of Products by Activity) up to two digits level (breakdown in 89 industries/products): NACE: 01 Crop and animal production, hunting and related service activities CPA: 01 Products of agriculture, hunting and related services. Then, the primary product of industry k is the product k. The difference among outputs made in (3) is conceptually different from that made by Lozano and Villa (2004) in their 'hybrid' centrally planned DEA models. In the present paper, the difference is made on the basis of the consideration of specific industrial output. On the other hand, the difference in Lozano and Villa (2004) among inputs in output-oriented models is based whether on being centrally planned or not. At first, one could think that both approaches are some how related, since we 'plan' to expand only the specific industrial output. However, it is to be highlighted that we include the difference among primary and secondary outputs on the oriented side of the model, this is, the output side, while these authors differentiate between both types of inputs (not outputs) on output oriented models and vice versa.

radial respect to the primary industry output, but non-radial respect to the rest of them. Li and Cheng (1997) call ε_k the structural efficiency of industry k when all outputs are expanded. They observe that a source of structural inefficiency is that individual production units may have suboptimal output mixes. Their individual production units are the Chinese provinces. We accommodate this freedom to change the output mix at the level of industry.

The basic idea in (3) is that the demand for products is fulfilled by the industries producing them as primary outputs and secondary outputs are produced as by-products, i.e. negative inputs; using idle resources. The primary outputs of industries are maximized, but not the secondary ones. It is a more flexible approach than ten Raa (2011) because the feasible set of equation (3) is larger, as demonstrated in Appendix 1. The distinction between primary and secondary outputs and the focus on the former in assessing efficiency facilitates industries to focus on their comparative advantages.

The dual program of (3) is:

$$\min_{p_k, w_k \geq 0} w_k \sum_{i \in I_k} x_{ik} - \breve{p}_k \sum_{i \in I_k} \breve{y}_{ik} :$$

$$p_k y_{jk} \leq w_k x_{jk}, \hat{p}_k \sum_{i \in I_k} \hat{y}_{ik} = e^\top \sum_{i \in I_k} y_{ik}, j \in I_k \tag{4}$$

where the dual variables w_k and p_k are the shadow prices of the constraints of (3).

ten Raa (2011) defined industrial organization efficiency of the industry k, ε_k^o as the gap between the efficiency of the industry, ε_k, and the weighed harmonic average of the efficiencies of the firms in the industry k, H_k:[3]

$$\varepsilon_k^o \cdot H_k = \varepsilon_k; \varepsilon_k^o / \sum_{i \in I_k} \frac{s_{ik}}{\varepsilon_{ik}} = \varepsilon_k$$

[3]In the averaging procedure described in (5), the weighted harmonic mean is used because it is the most suitable procedure for averaging productivities or performances, Casas Sánchez and Santos Peña (1996, pp. 78–81). Indeed, according to Proposition 1 of ten Raa (2011) the harmonic mean of disaggregated efficiencies is an upper bound for aggregated efficiency.

Consequently:

$$\varepsilon_k^o = \varepsilon_k \cdot \sum_{i \in I_k} \frac{s_{ik}}{\varepsilon_{ik}} \tag{5}$$

where ε_k is the ensemble efficiency determined by program (3), ε_{ik} are the efficiency scores of each firm determined by the set of programs (1) and s_{ik} are the revenue shares of each observed firm evaluated at the prices determined by dual program (4). These prices may be multiple, with possibly multiple market shares, but this multiplicity does not affect the values of the firm efficiency scores and the industry efficiency score, which are defined independent of prices. Even the condition for full industrial organization efficiency (namely equality between firm shadow prices and the industry shadow prices) holds under shadow price multiplicity; see the Remark following Proposition 2 in ten Raa (2011).

3. Industrial Specialization Efficiency

ten Raa and Mohnen (2002, 2008) analyze the reallocation of factors between industries to decompose Total Productivity Growth. ten Raa and Mohnen (2008) showed the interest of further decompose efficiency so as to consider the contribution of firms to it. The details are shown in the next section. With regard to the interpretation of efficiency measures, Shestalova (2002) further stated that the difference between augmented IOA (input-output analysis) and DEA lies on the interpretation of the frontier. The potential output is determined by the best practices (DEA at industry level) or alternatively, by the reallocation of inefficiently allocated resources among industries (IOA in a multi-sectoral economy). To the best of our knowledge, the present paper is the first to simultaneously track the inefficiencies of the firms, the industries and the economy.

Industry efficiency is calculated with model (3) instead of a DEA-O CRS model. Then, we will work at the level of sectors ($k \in K$), by pooling the vector of inputs and outputs within the firms of each industry k. The efficiency of the economy, ε, is obtained by

$$\max_{\lambda_h \geq 0, \varepsilon} e^\top \sum_{k \in K} \sum_{i \in I_k} y_{ik}/\varepsilon : \sum_{h \in K} \sum_{j \in I_h} \lambda_{jh} x_{jh}$$
$$\leq \sum_{k \in K} \sum_{i \in I_h} x_{ik}, \sum_{h \in K} \sum_{j \in I_h} \lambda_{hj} y_{jh} \geq \sum_{k \in K} \sum_{i \in I_h} y_{ik}/\varepsilon \tag{6}$$

The dual program of (6), which variables w and p are the shadow prices of the constraints of the primal program, is:

$$\min_{p,w\geq 0} w \sum_{k\in K}\sum_{i\in I_k} x_{ik} : py_{jh} \leq wx_{jh}, p\sum_{h\in K}\sum_{j\in I_k} y_{jh}$$
$$= e^T \sum_{h\in K}\sum_{j\in I_h} y_{jh}, j\in I_k, h\in K \tag{7}$$

where the dual variables w and p are the shadow prices of the constraints of (6). Again by the main theorem of linear programming: $e^T \sum_{k\in K}\sum_{i\in I_h} y_{ik}/\varepsilon = w\sum_{k\in K}\sum_{i\in I_k} x_{ik}$.

The idea of (6–7) is to compute the efficiency when the maximum output is reached letting the reallocation of inputs among industries, not only within industry. This estimates the efficiency of all the firms of all the industries (the whole economy) by comparing observed output with the maximum output reachable if there are no barriers to the flow of inputs across firms and industries. Such maximum is the output that could be produced by the most efficient industries using the resources of non-efficient industries, i.e.: "how much textile could be produced using the economic resources devoted to agriculture inputs" instead of "how much textile could be produced using the physical inputs of agriculture" or "how much textile could be produced with the agriculture best-practice technique", which is impossible.

It is to be highlighted that in equations (6–7), the benchmarks are the best practices (firms) of the whole economy: The intensities in equation (6), λ_{jh}, are per firm and there is an activity constraint for each firm in the second set of constraints of equation (7). Intensities and activity constraints by industries would account for the best 'industry-average' practices, instead of the absolute best practices of the economy, not drawing the real production possibility frontier, but an average observed production. It is the same difference highlighted by ten Raa (2007), when discussing the difference between traditionally computed IO (input-output) technical coefficients and technical coefficients obtained from best practices.

Analogous to (5), industrial specialization efficiency, ε^s, is:

$$\varepsilon^s = \varepsilon \sum_{k\in K} \frac{S_k}{\varepsilon_k} \tag{8}$$

where ε is the ensemble efficiency (whole economy efficiency) determined by program (6), ε_k are the efficiency scores of each industry determined by the set of programs (3) and s_k are the revenue shares of each industry evaluated at the prices determined by dual program (7). The prices underlying these market shares may differ between industries and these differences signal industrial specialization inefficiency according to Proposition 2 of ten Raa (2011).

This ε^s accounts for, somehow, a matter of opportunity cost of the re-specialization of the output mix of the economy: the opportunity cost of producing a suboptimal output mix instead of the optimal one; this is, the cost in efficiency losses because of the wasting inputs in the production of inefficient commodities instead of in the most efficient ones (re-specialization of the output mix of the economy). This reflects the cost of the barriers to the mobility of inputs across industries: Some inputs are easy to mobilize (raw materials) because for a next season, a company can just stop buying it. Others may need training (labor force) or adaptation (capital investments). It may be impossible to take advantage of some of them and the only choice may be to wait till its depreciation (capital) or retirement (labor force).

4. Efficiency of the Economy: Three Way Decomposition

We are ready to present a single measure for the economy efficiency. Standard DEA techniques require a reference set and, therefore, are not applicable. Our measure, ε, will be derived internally. We build the efficiency measurement from the lowest level (firm) to the highest one (the whole economy) by a nesting decomposition of different efficiency measurements to isolate the effects at each level. Substituting (5) in (8) and reordering:

$$\varepsilon = \frac{\varepsilon^s}{\sum\limits_{k \in K} \dfrac{s_k}{\dfrac{\varepsilon_k^0}{\sum\limits_{i \in I_k} s_{ik}/\varepsilon_{ik}}}} \tag{9}$$

where ε^s is the industrial specialization efficiency calculated by (8), ε_k^o is the Organizational Efficiency of industry k, determined by (5),

ε_{ik} are the efficiency scores of each firm determined by the set of programs (1), and s_{ik} and s_k are the revenue shares of each firm and each industry respectively, evaluated at the prices determined by dual programs (4) and (7).

At least theoretically the decomposition can be extended with an international/interregional level, bringing in the principle of comparative advantage, but this step requires comparable micro-data at an international level.

5. Application to the Andalusian Economy

Appendix 2 provides details about the database and computation and Appendix 3 shows the classification of industries/commodities. Table 1 summarizes the results of equations 1, 3 and 5 : k is the industry code, ε_k is the industry k efficiency, ε_k^o is the organization efficiency of industry k and H_k is the firm's efficiency weighed harmonic average of firms of industry k. $\#_k$ is the number of firms within industry k.

The industries whose firms are technically inefficient could perform 1–H_k percentage points better by copying best — industry — practices. The industries whose firms may work better, ranging from 60% to 12% potential average improvement, are: Restaurants, bars and catering; Legal and Accounting services; Other services to firms; Wholesale trade; Advertising; Sale of motor vehicles and retail sale automotive fuel; Land Transport; Maintenance and repair of motor vehicles; Building completion; Architectural and engineering activities and related technical consultancy.

The industries whose organization is inefficient could perform $H_k - \varepsilon_k$ percentage points better by exploiting economies or diseconomies of scope. Ranging from 79% to 36% of potential improvement, the industries with the worst organization are: Architectural and engineering activities and related technical consultancy; Real estate activities; Retail trade; Wholesale trade; Other services to firms; Supporting and auxiliary transport activities; Sale of motor vehicles and retail sale automotive fuel; Restaurants, bars and catering; Land transport; and Renting of machinery and equipment. Most of them are typically composed by small-sized firms.

Table 1. Industry efficiencies: Industry, organizational, firms mean.

k	ε_k	ε_k^o	H_k	$\#_k$	k	ε_k	ε_k^o	H_k	$\#_k$
01	1	1	1	1	44	0.88	0.90	0.98	101
02	1	1	1	1	45	1	1	1	5
03	1	1	1	1	46	1	1	1	1
04	1	1	1	1	47	1.00	1.00	1.00	39
05	1	1	1	1	48	0.97	0.97	1.00	85
06	1	1	1	1	49	0.80	0.84	0.96	1574
07	1	1	1	8	50	0.57	0.66	0.87	1610
08	1	1	1	2	51	0.44	0.52	0.85	1468
09	0.81	0.81	1.00	135	52	0.68	0.78	0.86	946
10	0.92	0.92	1.00	167	53	0.16	0.21	0.75	5933
11	1.00	1.00	1	28	54	0.31	0.31	0.98	8887
12	0.99	0.99	1	41	55	0.69	0.75	0.93	673
13	0.99	0.99	1	43	56	0.00	0.00	0.40	2399
14	1.00	1.00	1.00	42	57	0.46	0.54	0.85	1995
15	1	1	1	4	58	1.00	1.00	1.00	19
16	1	1	1	5	59	0.53	0.55	0.97	966
17	0.80	0.81	0.99	559	60	0.97	0.98	1.00	417
18	0.89	0.89	1	82	61	1	1	1	1
19	1.00	1.00	1	22	62	1	1	1	1
20	0.92	0.92	1.00	113	63	0.75	0.80	0.94	332
21	0.72	0.75	0.96	200	64	0.28	0.28	1.00	808
22	0.90	0.91	0.99	117	65	0.59	0.62	0.95	480
23	0.81	0.82	0.98	254	66	0.57	0.62	0.92	292
24	0.97	0.97	1.00	53	67	0.92	0.93	0.99	65
25	0.90	0.91	0.99	202	68	0.21	0.39	0.55	1390
26	1	1	1	3	69	0.09	0.10	0.88	794
27	1.00	1.00	1	44	70	0.51	0.66	0.77	199
28	0.99	0.99	1.00	68	71	0.81	0.82	0.98	146
29	0.92	0.92	1.00	122	72	0.58	0.63	0.93	336
30	0.89	0.90	0.99	341	73	0.08	0.14	0.60	901
31	0.88	0.88	1.00	117	74	1	1	1	1
32	0.92	0.92	0.99	183	75	1	1	1	1
33	1.00	1.00	1.00	37	76	1	1	1	1
34	0.75	0.78	0.96	695	77	1	1	1	1
35	0.88	0.88	1.00	268	78	0.92	0.92	1.00	155
36	1.00	1.00	1	13	79	0.98	0.98	1	72
37	0.89	0.89	0.99	86	80	0.85	0.85	1.00	101
38	1	1	1	23	81	0.80	0.80	1.00	201
39	0.98	0.98	1.00	59	82	0.98	0.98	1.00	44

(*Continued*)

Table 1. (*Continued*)

k	ε_k	ε_k^o	H_k	$\#_k$	k	ε_k	ε_k^o	H_k	$\#_k$
40	0.99	0.99	1.00	60	83	0.86	0.87	0.98	231
41	0.79	0.79	1.00	89	84	0.68	0.69	0.99	571
42	1	1	1	21	85	0.92	0.93	0.99	272
43	0.78	0.82	0.95	445	86	1	1	1	1

Key: ε_k: Efficiency of the industry k, eq. 3; ε_k^o: Organization Efficiency of the industry k, eq. 5; $\#_K$: # firms in industry k; H_k: Mean Efficiency of firms in industry k, eq. 1; 1.00: Rounded when reducing decimals but smaller than 1.

On the other hand, 29 industries[4] are fully efficient. Another 22 industries could improve as much as 10% of their performance by a better industrial organization.

In order to improve the industrial organization in the industries with the worst organization (previously mentioned in the paragraph above) the resources suboptimally allocated to specialized firms may be better reallocated and merged with the resources of optimal firms. On the other hand, the resources suboptimally allocated to diversified firms would be better split and distributed among optimal firms. Suboptimality is signalled by the mismatch of firms' marginal productivities (prices that solve equation 2) and the industrial marginal productivities (prices that solves equation 4).

The marginal productivities of inputs for the firms of each industry are expressed in the sheet W of the supplementary spreadsheet file, as results in equation (2). Analogously, the industries' marginal productivities, as results in equation (4), can be seen at the end of the same sheet W. The same structure applies in sheet P of the supplementary file.

The resources of the firms with marginal productivities lower than the correspondent industrial prices are over-allocated resources. They would be better reallocated to the firms with higher marginal

[4]Note that 22 of them are industries with a single observation (see $\#_k$ in Table 1), which are efficient by definition, and consequently such industries are also efficient. See Appendix 2 for further details.

productivities. This kind of information can be useful, for example, to identify candidates for merges.

Table 2 summarizes the results of equations 3, 6 and 8: ε is the efficiency of the whole economy, ε^s is the specialization efficiency of the economy and H is the industries' efficiency weighed harmonic average. # is the number of industries. The overall inefficiency of the economy is 32%. Formula (8) decomposes this figure in 10.5% specialization inefficiency and 24% industry inefficiency. (The figures do not add because of the nonlinearity in the formula.)

As far as the specialization of the economy is inefficient, then, it can be improved by changing the output mix. Formula (8) implies that if the specialization were optimal ($\hat{\varepsilon}^s = 1$), the hypothetical economy efficiency, $\hat{\varepsilon}$, would be equal to the average industry efficiency:

$$\hat{\varepsilon} = \frac{\hat{\varepsilon}^s}{\sum_{k \in K} \frac{s_k}{\varepsilon_k}} = \hat{\varepsilon}^s \cdot H = 1 \cdot 0.76 = 0.76$$

Thus, the economy could do better in around 8 percentage points ($\hat{\varepsilon} - \varepsilon = 0.76 - 0.68 \approx 0.08$), applying the 'best-practices in the economy' and consequently changing its output mix in order to improve the commodity specialization. By contrast, applying the 'industrial best-practices', as in equations (3–4), it would improve the efficiency of the industries by the reallocation resources to the best industrial organization of each industry, but without a change in the firms' specialization.

Suboptimality is signalled by the mismatch among the industrial's marginal productivities (prices that solve equation 4) and the whole economy marginal productivities (prices that solve equation 7).

Table 2. Economy efficiencies: Economy, specialization and industrial mean.

ε	ε^s	H	#
0.679254	0.895355	0.758642	86

Key: ε: Efficiency of the economy, eq. 7; ε^s: Specialization Efficiency, eq. 8; #: # of industries in the economy; H: Mean Efficiency of the industries in the economy, eq. 3.

The capital and labor productivities sustaining the economy-wide efficiency (equation 7) are reported in Table 3. Analogously, the industrial marginal productivities, (equation 4), can be seen in Table 4.

The industrial resources with marginal productivities lower than their economy counterpart are over-allocated resources. They would be better relocated to industries with higher marginal productivities. This kind of information can be useful, for example, to identify for which industries project-financing policies are more profitable in front of those industries where the capital is redundant (capital resources reallocation). Analogously, it signals where the allocation of human resources is more efficient (labour reallocation), identifying in which industries and what kind of the retraining policies would be suitable to help in the change of the output mix of the economy.

The industry in which the capital presents the highest marginal productivity is, by far, Architectural and engineering activities and related technical consultancy, followed by other service to firms; Manufacture of grain mill, starches and starch products; Real estate activities; and Insurance and pension funding. The fact that some of them are closely related to the building industry (architectural activities and real estate) is logical, as far as the data correspond to the year 2000, the beginning of the real estate bubble, whose blast has had a large impact in Spain. However, none of them is exactly building, but just related activities. This implies that the main gains in real estate and related activities were not in the building industry but in the related activities. This shows a path for building companies in Andalusia after the real estate blast: related activities. Actually, it is what many of them have done: offshoring of activities related to building. Civil engineering has suffered the blast in a lesser extent. Then, the Spanish building corporations have disembarked in international projects using the architects and engineers of

Table 3. Economy marginal productivities of Capital and Labour (Equation 7).

Capital	Labour
0.16	0.20

Table 4. Industrial marginal productivities of Capital and Labour (Equation 4).

k	Capital	Labour	k	Capital	Labour	k	Capital	Labour
01	0.00	0.00	30	*1.26*	*0.62*	59	*1.30*	*66.27*
02	0.00	0.00	31	*1.80*	*0.65*	60	*1.53*	*31.81*
03	0.00	0.00	32	*1.73*	*0.58*	61	0.00	0.00
04	0.00	0.00	33	0.00	*0.32*	62	*12.89*	0.00
05	0.00	0.00	34	*4.09*	*0.55*	63	*3.45*	*28.87*
06	0.00	0.00	35	*0.70*	*0.64*	64	*14.62*	*313.66*
07	*3.35*	0.00	36	*4.07*	*0.21*	65	*1.43*	*39.45*
08	0.00	0.00	37	0.00	*1.76*	66	*0.64*	*29.54*
09	*3.11*	*0.53*	38	0.00	0.00	67	*1.78*	*31.10*
10	*0.45*	*0.46*	39	*5.30*	*0.41*	68	0.00	*155.86*
11	0.00	0.14	40	*0.17*	*0.39*	69	*169.85*	*55.06*
12	*1.23*	0.07	41	0.00	*0.69*	70	*2.67*	*34.44*
13	*0.76*	0.12	42	0.08	0.07	71	0.00	*22.25*
14	0.00	0.14	43	*0.94*	*0.49*	72	*2.84*	*17.04*
15	*19.95*	*0.72*	44	*2.53*	*0.68*	73	*40.99*	*109.25*
16	0.00	0.00	45	*4.98*	0.00	74	0.00	0.00
17	0.00	*0.43*	46	0.00	0.00	75	0.00	*37.00*
18	0.00	*0.20*	47	0.00	0.00	76	0.00	0.00
19	0.00	0.00	48	*0.62*	*0.31*	77	0.00	0.00
20	*2.41*	*0.36*	49	*0.46*	*29.79*	78	*2.19*	*31.78*
21	*1.40*	*0.44*	50	*3.00*	*25.83*	79	0.00	0.00
22	*4.57*	*0.49*	51	0.00	*0.95*	80	0.00	*10.02*
23	*0.34*	*0.70*	52	*2.88*	*20.08*	81	0.00	*20.18*
24	*1.66*	*0.94*	53	0.00	*4.88*	82	*8.95*	*7.29*
25	*1.22*	*0.35*	54	0.00	*0.45*	83	0.00	*12.33*
26	0.00	0.00	55	*0.69*	*22.28*	84	0.00	*148.63*
27	*0.54*	*0.52*	56	0.00	*529167.01*	85	*1.62*	*13.37*
28	*0.33*	*0.36*	57	0.00	*128.44*	86	0.00	*4.65*
29	*2.72*	*0.94*	58	*4.78*	*6.95*			

Key: Italics script: Value higher than the correspondent of Table 3.
Roman script: Value lower than the correspondent of Table 3.

their headquarters and locally hiring bricklayers by their subsidiaries. Thus, they have re-orientated their production by increasing their 'exports' of Architectural and engineering activities and consultancy and by using their 'excess' of capital underused for building, by investing in other countries, then out of our accountancy.

Analogously, the industry in which labour is the most profitable is, by large, Restaurants, bars and catering; far followed by real estate activities; Legal and Accounting services; Other entertainment, cultural and sport activities; Land Transport; and Other services to firms. Some of them are very related to Tourism (Restaurants, bars and catering; Real estate activities; Other entertainment, cultural and sport activities and Land Transport), one of the main industries in Andalusia, which represents[5] during the reference year (2000) 13.1% of regional GDP and 10.8% of the employment. The main tourism-related industry (Hotels) is not included and it is the industry which has most largely suffered the crisis. This is because of two factors: a demand totally dependant on tourism and small chances to reorient its activity in the short term due to its large physical capital investments. On the other hand, the physical investments of Restaurants, bars and catering; Real estate activities; Other entertainment, cultural and sport activities and Land Transport are quite smaller and have a more diverse demand made not only by tourists but also by locals.

The industrial outputs with industry-specific prices lower than competitive prices (economy counterpart) are inefficient. Those industries would be better producing outputs with higher industrial prices. i.e.: The industry of water transport would do better producing more "other services to firms" instead of "forestry and related activities" (cells BW39334 vs. G39334 in the sheet P of the supplementary spreadsheet file). The industry of Other entertainment, cultural and sport activities would do better by producing (in this order) Manufacture and distribution of gas and gaseous fuels through mains; Hotels; camping sites and other provision of short-stay accommodation; Market Social services; Market education; Manufacture of prepared animal feeds; Production, processing and preserving of meat and meat products; Other manufacturing; Growing of vegetables and horticultural specialties; Real estate activities; Cinema, radio and television; and Advertising. However, it is probable that the production of these products is not separable since some of them can be secondary products of the main activity. A joint study of such targets suggests that this industry would do better in producing more educational farms and rural tourism services that involve many of the suggested targets (Hotels; camping sites and other provision of

[5]Exceltur (2005).

short-stay accommodation; Market Social services; Market education; Manufacture of prepared animal feeds; Production, processing and preserving of meat and meat products; Other manufacturing; Growing of vegetables and horticultural specialties; Real estate activities).

The industries that present a price for their specific output lower than the competitive economy counterpart, do produce no other output. This rule holds for any industry except for the industry of products of refining petroleum which would do better if they produce more real estate services than its main output (cells BN39302 vs. AB39302 in the sheet P of the supplementary spreadsheet file) or the industries of Manufacture of gas, distribution of gaseous fuels through mains; and Collection, purification and distribution of water. However, such commodities are produced by natural monopolies, which are, by definition, the furthest industries from the competitive equilibrium — which is the main assumption of this model. The results show that the most efficient commodities are trade (retail trade of manufactured products and wholesale trade of services), real estate activities, and other services to firms.

The signalling of trade suggests that the direct sale of manufacturers (retail shops in factories) and the wholesale trade of services are profitable. By contrast, the latter is usually devoted to retail trade to firms, instead of to the wholesale trade. Besides, the signalling of the real estate activities is logical, as far as the data are from the year 2000 (at the beginning of the real estate bubble). Finally, the positive signal of the services to firm is expectable in a developed economy where outsourcing is a main trend.

The fact that we have only a single observation for some industries (see Appendix 2 for details) looks to be related to the fact that for such industries no change in the output mix is suggested.

6. Conclusion

An economy may perform better, in the sense of productivity growth, by technical progress or by efficiency change. The latter source of growth has been decomposed in industry and firm contributions, but the aggregation is known to be imperfect. The bias in the aggregation of the efficiencies of the firms and industries reflects the allocative inefficiency in an economy.

Efficiency gains could arise from three sources, namely firms, industrial organization and commodity specialization: Inefficient firms could replicate best-practices. At least two thirds of the industries could improve their efficiency more than 10 percentage points by industrial reorganization. Finally, the economy could improve its performance 8 percentage points by a change in its output mix.

Inefficient firms may analyze their peers and redesign the production process reallocating the budget to the proper resources and demanding them similar results to those of their peers. The industries whose firms can improve the most are those with the lowest average efficiency: Restaurants, bars and catering; Legal and Accounting services; Other services to firms; Wholesale trade; Advertising; Sale of motor vehicles and retail sale automotive fuel; Land Transport; Maintenance and repair of motor vehicles; Building completion; Architectural and engineering activities and related technical consultancy. Anyhow, a detailed study firm by firm is more informative than the study of industrial averages.

The reallocation of the resources of each industry involves corporate finance to improve industrial organization and enhance economies of scope. The industries that can improve their organization the most are those with the lowest organization efficiency: Architectural and engineering activities and related technical consultancy; Real estate activities; Retail trade; Wholesale trade; Other service to firms; Supporting and auxiliary transport activities; Sale of motor vehicles and retail sale automotive fuel; Restaurants, bars and catering; Land transport; and Renting of machinery and equipment. The change in the output mix involves the reallocation of the resources along the whole economy (beyond industries distinction). For that, changes in the activity of the firms of suboptimal oriented industries are needed and resistances need to be overcome.

The results show that the production of trade (retail trade of manufactured products and wholesale trade of services), real estate activities, and other services to firms is more efficient. The use of capital is the most efficient in real estate while the use of labour is the most efficient in tourism.

Appendix 1: Proof

We demonstrate that the feasible set of equation (3) is larger or equal than the feasible set of the industry model presented in ten Raa (2011). The latter is characterized by the pair of constraints $\sum_{j\in I_k} \lambda_{jk}x_{jk} \leq \sum_{i\in I_k} x_{ik}, \sum_{j\in I_k} \lambda_{jk}y_{jk} \geq \sum_{i\in I_k} y_{ik}/\varepsilon_k$. In equation (3) the first constraint is copied, as is the k-th component of the second constraint. The other components, $\sum_{j\in I_k} \lambda_{jk}\check{y}_{jk} \geq \sum_{i\in I_k} \check{y}_{ik}/\varepsilon_k$, are replaced by $\sum_{j\in I_k} \lambda_{jk}\check{y}_{jk} \geq \sum_{i\in I_k} \check{y}_{ik}$. Because ε_k is an efficiency score between zero and one, this replacement is a relaxation.

Appendix 2: Data and Computation Details

The IEA (Instituto de Estadística de Andalucía — Regional Statistical Office of Andalusia) provided the cross-section inputs and outputs establishment data. These data were used for the elaboration of the Input–Output Andalusian Framework 2000 — MIOAN00 (IEA, 2006), which is the input–output table for Andalusia, based on the European System of Accounts (ESA-95) published by EUROSTAT (1996). IEA publishes two use tables, which differ by valuation. One is valued at purchasers' prices and the other at basic prices, which is the same as the former but excluding trade and transport margins and net commodity taxes (see Viet, 1994, p. 28). Trade and transport margins needs simply be reallocated from the commodities where they are included, at purchasers' values, to the use matrix rows of trade and transport services. The make table is published exclusively at basic prices. The United Nations System of National Accounts (SNA) recommends basic values; production costs of goods and services are measured before they are conveyed to the market for consumption so that the effects of tax and subsidy policies as well as of differences in types of economic transactions are isolated. Valuations are in basic prices. ten Raa and Rueda-Cantuche (2007) detail the procedure, including the assumed equality of margins and net commodity taxes between establishments in a given industry, consuming a given commodity.

There is a single capital type and a single labour type. Data for each establishment is obtained from capital consumption and total equivalent employees figures in the IO dataset. The capital endowment and the total labour force are the sum across establishments of their capital consumption and total equivalent employees figures.

Sales and purchases were classified into 86 commodities, then 88 inputs (86 commodities and 2 factor inputs: capital and labour) and 86 outputs were considered for 39,272 observations: 39,258 obtained by IEA from specific surveys done to build MIOAN00 while the other 14 observations represent data of sectors which data are obtained by IEA from different statistical sources when building MIOAN00, instead of by specifically surveying establishments: The list of this latter group of sectors is presented in Table A1.

We do not claim that the data were measured without error. Particularly, basic prices building follow some usual assumptions. For a sensitivity analysis we refer to ten Raa (2005).

The results have been computed using a specifically designed and optimized GAMS v21.6 code that uses Cplex Solver. It has taken 10 hours to run it on a laptop with a processor Pentium Centrino Duo 1.66 Ghz with 32-bits architecture and 2 Gb RAM.

Table A1. Industries not surveyed for MIOAN00.

k	Industry
01	Growing of vegetables and horticultural specialties
02	Growing of Vineyard and Olive
03	Other agricultural products and services
04	Livestock and Hunting
05	Forestry and related service activities
06	Fishing
46	Manufacture of electricity
61	Financial intermediation
62	Insurance and pension funding
74	Public administration and defence; compulsory social security
75	Non-market education
76	Market education
77	Non-market Health and veterinary activities
86	Activities of households as employers of domestic staff

Source: IEA (2006).

Appendix 3: Industry/Commodity Classification

Table A2. Industry classification in MIOAN00.

k	Industry
01	Growing of vegetables and horticultural specialties
02	Growing of Vineyard and Olive
03	Other agricultural products and services
04	Livestock and Hunting
05	Forestry and related service activities
06	Fishing
07	Energy products
08	Mining of metal ores
09	Mining of non metal ores and non energy ores
10	Production, processing and preserving of meat and meat products
11	Processing and preserving of fish and fish products
12	Processing and preserving of fruit and vegetables
13	Manufacture of vegetable and animal oils and fats
14	Manufacture of dairy products
15	Manufacture of grain mill, starches and starch products
16	Manufacture of prepared animal feeds
17	Manufacture of other food and tobacco products
18	Distilling, rectifying and blending of spirits; ethyl alcohol production
19	Manufacture of beer, soft drinks; production of mineral waters
20	Preparation and spinning of textile fibres; weaving of textiles
21	Manufacture of wearing apparel, dressing of fur
22	Dyeing of fur; manufacture of articles of fur
23	Manufacture of products of wood; cork (exc. Furniture)
24	Manufacture of paper and paper products
25	Products of publishing of books, forms and other publications
26	Manufacture of refined petroleum products
27	Manufacture of basic chemicals, inclusive agrichemicals
28	Manufacture of other chemical products n.e.c.
29	Manufacture of rubber and plastic materials
30	Manufacture of cement, lime and plaster
31	Manufacture of non-refractory clay and ceramic products
32	Stone and glass products
33	Metallurgy products
34	Manufacture of metal products
35	Manufacture of machinery and equipment
36	Manufacture of office, accounting and computing machinery
37	Manufacture other electrical equipment n.e.c.
38	Manufacture of electronic, tv, radio and communications equipment and apparatus

Table A2. (*Continued*)

k	Industry
39	Manufacture of medical and surgical equipment and optics and precision equipment
40	Manufacture of motor vehicles, trailers and semi-trailers
41	Building and repairing of ships and boats
42	Manufacture of other transport equipment n.e.c.
43	Manufacture of furniture
44	Other manufacturing n.e.c.
45	Recycling products
46	Manufacture of electricity
47	Manufacture of gas; distribution of gaseous fuels through mains
48	Collection, purification and distribution of water
49	Building and civil engineering
50	Building completion
51	Sale of motor vehicles and retail sale automotive fuel
52	Maintenance and repair of motor vehicles
53	Wholesale trade
54	Retail trade, except of motor vehicles and motorcycles; repair of personal and household goods
55	Hotels; camping sites and other provision of short-stay accommodation
56	Restaurants, bars and catering
57	Transport via railways and other land transport, inclusive pipeline
58	Sea and coastal water and air transport
59	Supporting and auxiliary transport activities
60	Post and telecommunications
61	Financial intermediation
62	Insurance and pension funding
63	Activities auxiliary to financial intermediation
64	Real estate activities
65	Renting of machinery and equipment
66	Hardware, software consultancy and supply, data processing and data base activities
67	Research and Development Services
68	Legal and Accounting services
69	Architectural and engineering activities and related technical consultancy
70	Advertising
71	Private security and investigation services
72	Manufacture cleaning activities
73	Other service to firms n.e.c.

(*Continued*)

Table A2. (*Continued*)

k	Industry
74	Public administration and defence; compulsory social security
75	Non-market education
76	Market education
77	Non-market Health and veterinary activities
78	Market Health and veterinary activities
79	Non-market Social services
80	Market Social services
81	Sewage and refuse disposal
82	Activities of organizations
83	Cinema, radio and television
84	Other entertainment, cultural and sport activities n.e.c.
85	Other personal services
86	Activities of households as employers of domestic staff

Source: IEA (2006).

Acknowledgments

Firstly, we thank Jose M. Rueda-Cantuche (IPTS-Joint Research Center EU & Pablo de Olavide University) for his essential help in building the database. We also thank the feedback from: Mikuláš Luptáčik (WU Vienna University of Economics and Business) during the 24th EURO Conference held in Lisbon, July 12th, 2010; Jan Oosterhaven, Erik Dietzenbacher and Bart Los (Groningen University), Geoffrey Hewings (REAL-University of Illinois) and Tobias Kronenberg (Forschungszentrum Jülich) during the 4th Spanish Input-Output Conference held in Madrid, September 2011. Additionally, the first author thanks Thanh Le Phuoc (University of Maastricht & MERIT) and very specially to Michael R. Bussiek (GAMS Corp.) for their precious cooperation in constructing the computational model; Mònica Serrano (University of Barcelona) and Michael C. Ferris (University of Wisconsin at Madison) for his help in early calculations. He also thanks Center for hospitality and the financial support of Junta de Andalucía (Regional Government of Andalusia, Spain) and Pablo de Olavide University. We are grateful to two anonymous referees and an associate editor for critical comments that prompted many changes.

References

Casas Sánchez, J. M. and J. Santos Peñas. (1996). *Introducción a la Estadística para Economía y Administración y Dirección de Empresas*, Ed. Centro de Estudios Ramón Areces, S.A., Madrid.

Charnes, A., Cooper, W. W., Lewin, A. and Seiford, L. (1995). *Data Envelopment Analysis: Theory, Methodology and Applications*. Kluwer Academic Publishers, Dordrecht, Netherlands.

Cooper, W. W., Seiford, L. M. and Tone, K. (2000). *Data Envelopment Analysis: A Comprehensive Text with Models, Application, References and DEA-Solver Software*. Kluwer Academic Publisher, Boston.

Exceltur. (2005). *Impactur Andalucía 2005*, Exceltur, Madrid.

Houthakker, H. (1956). The Pareto distribution and the Cobb-Douglas production function in activity analysis. *The Review of Economic Studies*, **23**(1), 27–31.

IEA: Instituto de Estadística de Andalucía — Andalusian Statistical Office. (2006). *Marco Input-Output de Andalucía 2000 — MIOAN00*, Sevilla.

Lozano, S. and G. Villa. (2004). Centralized resource allocation using data envelopment analysis. *Journal of Productivity Analysis*, **22**, 143–161.

Shestalova, V. (2002). Essays in productivity and efficiency. Dissertation, Center, Tilburg University, Tilburg, The Netherlands.

ten Raa, Th. (2007). The extraction of technical coefficients from input and output data. *Economic Systems Research*, **19**(4), 453–459.

ten Raa, Th. (2011). Benchmarking and industry performance. *Journal of Productivity Analysis*, **36**, 285–292.

ten Raa, Th. (2005). *The Economics of Input-Output Analysis*, Cambridge: Cambridge University Press.

ten Raa, Th. and P. Mohnen. (2008). Competition and performance: The different roles of capital and labor. *Journal of Economic Behavior and Organization*, **3**(4), 573–584.

ten Raa, Th. and J. Rueda-Cantuche. (2007). Stochastic analysis of input-output multipliers on the basis of use and make matrices. *Review of Income and Wealth*, **53**, 318–334.

ten Raa, Th. and P. Mohnen. (2002). Neoclassical growth accounting and frontier analysis. *Journal of Productivity Analysis*, **18**, 111–128.

Viet, V. (1994). Practices in input–output table compilation. *Regional Science and Urban Economics*, **24**, 27–54.

Chapter 6

Supply-Use Framework for International Environmental Policy Analysis*

Thijs ten Raa[†] and Victoria Shestalova[‡]

[†]*Department of Economics, Tilburg University, Tilburg, The Netherlands*
tenraa@uvt.nl

[‡]*Netherlands Bureau for Economic Policy Analysis, The Hague, The Netherlands*

Abstract. The technical variation between countries in the production of goods and services, in terms of not only input coefficients, but also emission coefficients, creates scope for international trade to reduce environmental pressures. For this purpose we extend the theory of trade and the environment as to accommodate technical variation between countries in production and emissions. We use and steer close to the extended input and output tables, which include emission data. By treating environmental standards analogous to capital and labor capacity constraints, the aggregation problem for economic and environmental measures gets the same format as the well-understood aggregation problem for labor and capital. In a pilot application we determine the gains to free trade in products and emission permits.

Keywords: Environmental Input–output Accounts, Environmental Policy, Multi-economy Systems, International Trade

JEL-codes: Q56, Q51, F18, D57, D58

*Reprinted from *Economic Systems Research*, **27**, 77–94, 2015, with permission from Taylor & Francis.

1. Introduction

Climate change presses for environmental policy analysis (IPCC, 2001). The recent economic literature stresses the importance of technical change for curbing emissions, and proposes policies that can achieve it (Nordhaus, 2007; Stern, 2007; Acemoglu *et al.*, 2012). Technical change (such as energy intensity reductions) takes place primarily in production, but also in consumption. While technical change that will facilitate massive implementation of clean technologies (such as electric cars) is still 'on the way', reallocation of production can alleviate environmental pressure in the short and middle run. Policy assessment studies confirm that environmental policies are more successful if incentives to innovate are combined with incentives to reallocate (e.g. the policy analysis for the energy sector by Fischer and Newell, 2008). Efficient allocation of production activities may aid the realization of international environmental policy targets, such as stipulated in the Kyoto Protocol (United Nations, 1997) and the EU climate and energy package (2009).[1]

To enhance environmental policy research, large efforts have been undertaken to create environmentally extended input–output accounts, facilitating policy analyses at international and interregional levels. This paper contributes a model for a direct, economic analysis of the environmentally extended tables. We integrate the complementarity approach to equilibrium (Ferris and Pang, 1997) and the input–output framework for economic and environmental accounts (Leontief, 1970), this results in a simple general equilibrium model, ready-to-use for practitioners. Unlike the existing multi-country general equilibrium analyses of environmental policy evaluations, such as GEM-E3 for the EU (Capros *et al.*, 1999; Proost and Van Regemorter, 2004), our model directly extends input–output accounts of production and emissions, without the need to introduce

[1]An anonymous referee observed that by promoting minimal adverse effects on international trade and impacts on the rest of the world the Kyoto Protocol potentially bars efficient allocations. (S)he finds this no issue with our paper. Indeed, we show how member states can redirect mutual trade to reduce emissions, without changing net trade with the rest of the world. Among other targets, the EU package specifies a reduction target on greenhouse emissions of 20%. For more information, see: http://ec.europa.eu/clima/policies/package/index_en.htm.

proxies of the latter based on energy consumption. We intend to find an environmentally beneficial allocation of trade flows under different policy scenarios.

The simultaneous determination of economic and environmental comparative advantages requires a general equilibrium analysis that combines resource and environmental constraints with production and pollution coefficients and final demand patterns. The complementarity problem, a mathematical tool to solve big general equilibrium models (Ferris and Pang, 1997), is particularly useful for modern supply-use frameworks, where the number of techniques may be different than the number of products, contrary to classical input–output analysis. The complementarity problem will select the techniques. The availability of extended input and output tables, including emission data, makes it possible to fully integrate regulatory environmental constraints into the model in the same vein as the constraints on the traditional primary inputs, capital and labour. By treating environmental standards analogous to capital and labor capacity constraints, the aggregation problem for economic and environmental measures gets the same format as the well-understood aggregation problem for labor and capital in the theory of international trade. For example, when environmental constraints are tightened, new techniques may be selected. The tighter constraints will increase the cost of pollution (either by taxes or by higher prices for emission rights, depending on the institutional framework) and render new clean technologies profitable.

A subtle but important methodological issue remains. In our view, the economy is not necessarily in equilibrium. In fact, the gap between an observed allocation and the equilibrium is informative of its inefficiency. The advantage of equilibrium analysis is that by the endogeneity of prices and quantities it facilitates valuation of the trade-off between narrowly defined economic performance (GDP) and environmental scores. Our results measure the relationship between environmental measures and equilibrium performance. The benchmark equilibrium corresponds to but is not identical with the observed allocation, as allocative inefficiencies are removed. Strictly speaking our results on the connection between environmental policies and economic performance may be used as predictions of actual outcomes only if the allocative inefficiency remains the same. A full disequilibrium analysis would not have this limitation, but be sensitive to the model specification.

In Section 2 we review the relating literature and explain our contribution in more detail. In Section 3, we specify the supply-use framework, associate the general equilibrium model, and relate the specification to the linear programming approach. In Section 4 we explain how to account environmental policies, opening the road to environmental policy analysis. We offer an illustration of this method for an Institute for Prospective Technological Studies (IPTS) data set in Section 5. The last section concludes.

2. Literature Review and Contribution

To enhance environmental policy research at the European level, large efforts have been undertaken to create the environmentally extended input–output (EE-I–O) accounts for Europe (IPTS, 2006).[2] Eurostat (2011) has launched several projects to combine individual country supply and use tables (SUTs), extend them with emission data, and to create consolidated EU27 tables. The EXIOPOL[3] — project founded by the European Commission has integrated research efforts of institutions from different member states to set up a detailed EE-I–O data base, EXIOBASE (Tukker *et al.*, 2009; 2013). This new data base will facilitate the estimation of environmental impacts and of external costs of different industries, final consumption activities and resource consumption for countries in the EU. On top of this the harmonized world input–output database has been created, including links to detailed socio-economic and environmental satellite accounts (Dietzenbacher *et al.*, 2013). These new databases will facilitate not only national applications, such as multiplier analysis of demand-pull effects and the assignment of emissions to production and consumption activities, but also international analyses, e.g. of environmental footprints.

[2]The Institute for Prospective Technological Studies, Seville, Spain is one of the eight Research Institutes of the European Commission.

[3]The abbreviation EXIOPOL refers to 'a new environmental accounting framework using externality data and input–output tools for policy analysis'. It encompasses the IPTS accounts.

Introducing the special ESR issue on carbon foot printing, Wiedmann (2009a, p. 176) stresses that 'input–output analysis can contribute substantially if not decisively, to the practice of carbon foot printing at all levels'. Minx *et al.* (2009) present examples of multiregional input–output (MRIO) applications in different areas. Input–output analysis can be used for the screening of sectoral and corporate carbon footprints (Huang *et al.*, 2009) as well as for the accounting for greenhouse gas emissions from a consumption perspective. Wiedmann (2009b) reviews recent MRIO models for consumption-based emission and resource accounting, providing examples of such analyses. Employing a fully coupled MRIO model for consumption-based accounting of CO_2 emissions, Davis and Caldeira (2010) show that, in 2004, 23% of global CO_2 emissions were traded internationally, primarily as exports from emerging markets to consumers of developed economies. Wilting and Vringer (2009) compare the outcomes of consumption-based and production-based approaches, going into their policy applications in environmental policies. Considering evidence from the UK on how policy evolved around consumption-based accounting, Wiedmann and Barrett (2013) conclude that environmentally extended MRIO models are capable of generating specific policy relevant information. Our paper adds to this literature by illustrating how the model could be used to gain insight in the allocation of competitive and environmental pressure under different policy scenarios.

Two recent papers should also be mentioned. Turner *et al.* (2012) find that the analysis of policy effects on economic and environmental trade balances requires a more flexible non-input–output model and introduce a degree of substitutability in the production and consumption functions. However, we show, perhaps surprisingly, that the input–output model does feature substitutability, through interregional reallocations and flexible general equilibrium prices. Douglas and Nishioka (2012) take into account the diversity in input and emission coefficients to explain trade and the distribution of emissions, and find that differences in emissions intensity do not play a significant factor in determining patterns of trade. In our view the reason is that the emissions are not priced. We show how this can be done and would impact the pattern of trade.

The originality and usefulness of our model is that it shows how equilibrium allocations and prices (including of emissions) can be determined using the input and output data only, without augmenting specific — hence sensitive — computable general equilibrium model features. This distinction is similar to that of classical models vis-a-vis neoclassical models. Classical economics assumes constant returns to scale and is capable to explain the production structure and the distribution between factors on the basis of the supply side. If returns to scale vary, demand determines the local input coefficients and distribution; neoclassical economics shows the simultaneous determination of the allocation and prices. Since the models of international trade and pollution feature constant returns to scale, it is a challenge to analyze the issues with classical means, using only the input–output structure, and this paper accomplishes it.

We present a direct, economic analysis of the environmentally extended tables. We integrate the complementarity approach to equilibrium Ferris and Pang (1997) and the input–output framework for economic and environmental accounts Leontief (1970), this results in a simple general equilibrium model, ready-to-use for practitioners. Unlike the existing multi-country general equilibrium analyses of environmental policy evaluations, such as GEM-E3 for the EU (Capros *et al.*, 1999; Proost and Van Regemorter, 2004), our model directly extends input–output accounts of production and emissions, without the need to introduce proxies of the latter based on energy consumption. We intend to find an environmentally beneficial allocation of trade flows under different policy scenarios. This aim is close to Duchin (2005), but her concept of comparative advantage is flawed by price dependency. A baseline is assumed for the factor prices, which is subsequently augmented with shortage premiums. The location of comparative advantages and the total factor commodity prices depend on the exogenous baseline and, therefore, are not determined by differences in resource abundance or technology.

The technical variation between countries in the production of goods and services, in terms of not only input coefficients, but also emission coefficients, creates scope for international trade to reduce environmental pressures. Copeland and Taylor (2005) have developed a neoclassical model to assess the environmental effects of trade, particularly on the developing world. In their view the developed world has a comparative advantage in capital intensive production — which is more polluting — but stricter environmental regulations drive pollution to havens in the developing world.

Promoting free trade strengthens the first force and, therefore, is in the interest of the environment, particularly in the developing world. However, this argument hinges on the Heckscher–Ohlin hypothesis that factor abundance drives trade, assuming that all countries have access to state-of-the-art technology. It breaks down when developed economies have superior technology, particularly in terms of emissions.

Related, this neoclassical model is too stringent for empirical estimation. Copeland and Taylor (2005) make a short-cut by regressing emissions on capital–labor ratios and trade and confirm their theory that trade is good to the environment, but others arrive at opposite conclusions. Peters *et al.* (2011) find that between 1990 and 2008 the net emission transfers via international trade from developing to developed countries more than offset the Kyoto Protocol emission reductions and suggest that the effect of trade was detrimental. However, their result does not preclude that less trade would yield higher emissions.

For a proper analysis of the role of technology in trade and environmental policy the composition of trade is at least as important as the volume of trade. By mapping comparative advantages in production and emissions, environmental reallocation policy can be designed to reduce global pollution (Copeland and Taylor, 2005). This challenge is taken up now using the supply-use accounting framework and showing how pollution regulations can be allocated efficiently. A pilot application to three countries demonstrates the feasibility of our methodology.

Recently input–output and general equilibrium analyses have moved closer. Shestalova (2001), ten Raa and Mohnen (2001, 2002), ten Raa and Pan (2005) and ten Raa and Shestalova (2011) analyzed trade flows with a linear program that maximizes the levels of domestic final demands. This paper closes the gap entirely by constructing the supply and demand functions which are implicit in the input and output tables of economies and determining the equilibrium prices that match supply and demand. We provide an economic theoretic foundation to the linear programming approach by showing its equivalence with the equilibrium analysis. We also demonstrate that the complementarity problem approach to supply-use accounts facilitates environmental analysis of large international economic systems.

3. Base Model

3.1. *Input–Output Accounts*

Building bricks of the national accounts of an economy (we use this terminology even when an economy is a region) are the SUTs, **V** and **U**, respectively. The columns of these tables display the respective outputs and inputs of the industries. Industries may produce varieties of products, and the varieties may overlap, as is the case in national accounts. The dimension of a supply or use table is product by industry, where 'industry' stands for activity. In a micro framework it would be a reporting accounting unit, say a firm, while in a macro framework it would be an aggregate of firms. Aggregation involves loss of information and is possible but not necessary to run our model.[4] Moreover, new technologies can be analyzed in the activity framework by augmenting columns. Running a model at a more disaggregated level (capturing technology differences between firms) would bring scope for pollution reductions within national industries in addition to the opportunities due to international trade. Since we ignore these domestic reallocations, our analysis is conservative.

The dimensions may vary across economies. This is best appreciated in the context of micro data, where 'industries' are firms. Some economies have more firms than others and the product dimensions may differ as well, but tradable commodities have the same dimension across economies, even when they are not produced in some economies, such as wine. Interregional balances are expressed in product units of tradable commodities and there is no need to harmonize industry classifications (ten Raa, 1995). If, however, the industry classifications are uniform and match the commodity classification, then one can post multiply the SUTs by the inverse supply table and use gross outputs instead of activity levels as the allocation variable. In this case the supply use framework is equivalent to the (commodity) technology-based input–output model.

Subtraction of use from supply defines the net output table of an economy: $\mathbf{V} - \mathbf{U}$. Summation of net output across industries, which

[4]Although the theory does not require aggregation, it may still be handy to do it in practical applications, as otherwise the dimension of the model becomes very large.

is achieved by post-multiplication of $\mathbf{V} - \mathbf{U}$ with the unit vector $\mathbf{e}$ (of which all entries are equal to 1), defines final demand. This vector depicts the national product by product. Summing across products, which is achieved by pre-multiplication with the unit row vector, defines value-added, at least if the data are in current values. This row vector depicts the national income by industry. Since the sum of row totals equals the sum of column totals, we hereby confirm the macro-economic identity between national product and national income.

3.2. *Supply Functions*

The use and make tables, augmented with the factor input tables, describe the production technology and allow us to define the supply function for each industry. The first industry (corresponding to the first column of the SUTs) produces outputs, $\mathbf{v}_{\cdot 1}$, from intermediate inputs, $\mathbf{u}_{\cdot 1}$, and factor inputs, capital and labor, K_1 and L_1, respectively. Assuming constant returns to scale, it is also possible to produce output $\mathbf{v}_{\cdot 1}s_1$ from the inputs $\mathbf{u}_{\cdot 1}s_1$, $K_1 s_1$ and $L_1 s_1$, where $s_1 \geq 0$ represents the activity level. For example, if $s_1 = 1.1$, activity 1 is operated at a 10% higher level than observed. Assuming free disposal, it is possible to produce less output with more input. The assumption of constant returns to scale is typical in neoclassical growth accounting. Firms do not meet this assumption, but in competitive economies they must operate at minimum average cost and the industry output varies the number of firms. This mechanism of entry and exit yields constant returns to scale at the level of the industry. Burnside (1996) and Basu and Fernald (1997) estimated the returns to scale for the US manufacturing industries and conclude that the most robust evidence suggests the typical industry displays constant returns.

We now set up the supply function of industry 1. Denote the product prices by row vector $\mathbf{p}$, the rental rate of capital in this industry by r_1, and the economy-wide wage rate by w. We assume that capital is immobile but labor is mobile between industries.[5] Value-added

[5]In other words, we assume capital is industry specific (machines and equipment installed for the production of given commodities). We also assume that neither

equals $\mathbf{p}(\mathbf{v}_{.1} - \mathbf{u}_{.1})s_1$, factor costs are $(r_1K_1 + wL_1)s_1$, and the difference is profit. If the prices are such that value-added exceeds factor costs, the profit maximizing activity level would be infinite. If value-added equals factor costs, the profit maximizing activity level would be any. If value-added is less than factor costs, the profit maximizing activity level would be zero. The assumption of profit maximization is typical in economic models and reasonable in a static setting adopted here.[6] This completes the verbal description of the supply function and we will now spell it out.

The first case (where value-added exceeds factor costs and an infinite activity level is most profitable) is inconsistent with equilibrium on the factor markets (where supply is finite) and can be ruled out. Hence, $\mathbf{p}(\mathbf{v}_{\cdot 1} - \mathbf{u}_{\cdot 1}) \leq r_1K_1 + wL_1$. The second and third cases can be summarized by the condition that $\mathbf{p}(\mathbf{v}_{\cdot 1} - \mathbf{u}_{\cdot 1}) < r_1K_1 + wL_1$ implies $s_1 = 0$. All this can be consolidated by the following condition:

$$s_1 \geq 0, r_1K_1 + wL_1 - \mathbf{p}(\mathbf{v}_{\cdot 1} - \mathbf{u}_{\cdot 1}) \geq 0,$$
$$[rK_1 + wL_1 - \mathbf{p}(\mathbf{v}_{\cdot 1} - \mathbf{u}_{\cdot 1})]s_1 = 0. \tag{1}$$

According to this condition, profits are non positive, and if they are negative, the activity level will be zero. This, indeed, describes what profit maximizing producers would undertake. They avoid activities which would incur losses.

Condition 1 states that there is *complementarity* between activity level s_1 and the value of the *loss function* $r_1K_1 + wL_1 - \text{p}(\mathbf{v}_{\cdot 1} - \mathbf{u}_{\cdot 1})$ meaning that if one of the inequalities in 1 has slack (the entity is positive) the other has no slack (the entity is zero). We have the same for the other industries: $[r_2K_2 + wL_2 - \text{p}(\mathbf{v}_{\cdot 2} - \mathbf{u}_{\cdot 2})]s_2 = 0$, and so on. By nonnegativity of the constituent factors, all these products are zero if and only if their sum is zero: $[r_1K_1 + wL_1 - \text{p}(\mathbf{v}_{\cdot 1} - \mathbf{u}_{\cdot 1})]s_1 + [r_2K_2 + wL_2 - \text{p}(\mathbf{v}_{\cdot 2} - \mathbf{u}_{\cdot 2})]s_2 + \cdots = 0$, or, using matrix notation (row vector $\mathbf{r}$, diagonal matrix $\mathbf{K}$, row vector $\mathbf{L}$ and column vector $\mathbf{s}$), $[\mathbf{rK}+w\mathbf{L} - \mathbf{p}(\mathbf{V} - \mathbf{U})]\mathbf{s} = 0$. This equality means that vectors $\mathbf{rK}+w\mathbf{L} - \mathbf{p}(\mathbf{V} - \mathbf{U})$ and s are *orthogonal*; this condition is denoted by $\mathbf{s}\perp[\mathbf{rK}+w\mathbf{L} - \mathbf{p}(\mathbf{V} - \mathbf{U})]$. Summarizing, the extension

capital nor labor moves between countries, a classical assumption in international trade, which is reasonable in the short run.

[6]However, in a dynamic setting, it may not necessarily hold in each period.

of supply condition 1 to all industries of the economy can succinctly be written as the following complementarity condition:

$$\mathbf{0} \leq \mathbf{s} \perp (\mathbf{rK} + w\mathbf{L} + \mathbf{pU} - \mathbf{pV}) \geq 0. \tag{2}$$

This expression is shorthand for three equations, nonnegativity of activities, nonpositivity of profits, and their mutual orthogonality. A consequence of the orthogonality is the national income identity:

$$\mathbf{p}(\mathbf{V} - \mathbf{U})\mathbf{s} = (\mathbf{rK} + w\mathbf{L})\mathbf{s} \tag{3}$$

3.3. *Demand Functions*

The supply functions of the industries take care not only of the products supplied, but also of intermediate demand. Industry 1 demands product quantities listed in vector $\mathbf{u}_{\cdot 1}\, s_1$ and likewise for the other industries. What remains is final demand. This consists of domestic final demand (private and public consumption and investment) and net exports (exports minus imports). Let us first look at the SUTs. Observed net output equals $(\mathbf{V} - \mathbf{U})\mathbf{e}$, where $\mathbf{e}$ is the unit vector. It comprises domestic final demand, vector $\mathbf{f}$, plus net exports, the residual $(\mathbf{V} - \mathbf{U})\mathbf{e} - \mathbf{f}$. Throughout this paper we treat trade as the residual between net output and domestic final demand, eliminating trade variables using the material balances of the economies.

How are consumption and trade reformulated for arbitrary prices, $\mathbf{p}$, $\mathbf{r}$ and w? We assume that domestic final demand can be represented by Leontief preferences. This conservative approach steers demand close to what is observed. Moreover, ten Raa (2008) provides a theoretical underpinning by showing that absent consumers demand information (taking intersections over all possible household preferences) this representation delineates the set of preferred consumption bundles, hence demand. It follows that domestic final demand is determined by the maximization of expansion factor c in vector $\mathbf{f}c$. It is constrained by the budget.

International trade theory assumes balance of payments between imports and exports. Then the budget for domestic final demand is equal to national income. In equilibrium analysis the budget is determined by the income derived from the available resources, $\boldsymbol{\kappa}\mathbf{Ke}$ and $\lambda\mathbf{Le}$, where factors $\boldsymbol{\kappa}$ (a diagonal matrix) and λ include idle capital and labor; for example, if the capital utilization rate is 82%

in industry 1, then $K_1 = \frac{1}{.82} = 1.22$. Indeed, consumers decide on the basis of prices, not the producers' actions, $\mathbf{s}$, and their demands, $\mathbf{Ks}$ and $\mathbf{Ls}$ for final inputs. However, in reality countries run a trade deficit or surplus, allowing them to consume more or less. We preserve this imbalance — which can be rationalized in a dynamic setting with intertemporal capital markets — by assuming that any net imports vector with the same value as the observed net imports vector is in the budget. Hence the budget is $(\mathbf{r}\kappa\mathbf{K} + w\lambda\mathbf{L})\mathbf{e} + \mathbf{p}[\mathbf{f} - (\mathbf{V} - \mathbf{U})\mathbf{e}]$, where $\mathbf{f} - (\mathbf{V} - \mathbf{U})\mathbf{e}$ is the observed net import vector and its value is the allowed debt, to cofund domestic consumption. Equating consumption expenditure to the budget, we obtain that the level of consumption is determined by the equation $\mathbf{pf}c = (\mathbf{r}\kappa\mathbf{K} + w\lambda\mathbf{L})\mathbf{e} + \mathbf{p}[\mathbf{f} - (\mathbf{V} - \mathbf{U})\mathbf{e}]$. This is the *expenditure–income identity.*

To treat demand symmetrically with supply, we replace the expenditure–income identity by a complementarity condition:

$$0 \leq c \perp \mathbf{pf}c - (\mathbf{r}\boldsymbol{\kappa}\boldsymbol{K} + w\lambda\mathbf{L})e - \mathbf{p}[\mathbf{f} - (\mathbf{V} - \mathbf{U})\mathbf{e}] \geq 0 \qquad (4)$$

In expression 4 expenditure $\mathbf{pf}c$ may seem to exceed income, but then the complementarity condition pushes c back to zero. As industries transform factor and produced inputs into products and condition 2 shows complementarity between their activity levels and the loss function (the difference between the values of the inputs and the outputs), the domestic final demand sectors transform a consumption bundle (the input) into factor services (the output). The loss function is the difference between the value of the input (expenditure) and the output (income). The expenditure–income identity is thus cast in the complementarity framework, which will admit easy solution. Another advantage is that expression 4 accommodates the situation where the budget for consumption is negative because of an overwhelming obligation to export (the value of the net exports exceed factor income). Direct application of the expenditure–income identity would produce a negative value for consumption, which is impossible, while the complementarity condition correctly equates it to zero.[7] Although this analysis rules out consumption substitutabilities, it does not require a representative consumer. As ten Raa (2008)

[7]This kind of situation can be observed only if the observed prices are extremely distorted–deviating from the cost structure like condition 2 — and some economy

has shown, this model is the reduced form of an economy with many consumers who have Leontief preferences (possibly idiosyncratic) and it provides a lower efficiency bound for more general economies. This completes the representation of the supply and demand functions.

3.4. *Equilibrium Prices*

The next step is to equate supply with demand by choice of the prices. Prices are determined by interregional markets. We must index the economies.[8] The data of an economy are its use and supply tables, the factor employment row vectors and utilization rates, and its domestic final demand vector. Formally, an *economy* i is the septuple $\mathbf{K}^i, \boldsymbol{\kappa}^i, \boldsymbol{L}^i, \lambda^i, \boldsymbol{U}^i, \boldsymbol{V}^i, \boldsymbol{f}^i$ of capital and labor employment vectors and utilization rates, use and supply tables, and domestic final demand vector. These data are nonnegative and the capacity factors (the inverse capacity utilization rates given by the second and fourth components) are greater than or equal to one. For each economy the capital or labor employment vector is positive and domestic final demand is nonzero. The first component of an economy is a diagonal matrix (dimension the number of industries in economy i), the second a scalar, the third a row vector (dimension the number of industries in economy i, but can be generalized to a matrix when there are different types of labor, as in ten Raa and Pan, 2005), the fourth a scalar, the fifth and the sixth are product by industry tables and the seventh is a product vector. Unlike for industries, we impose

not only subsidizes other economies in real terms (exporting big quantities), but also nominally (charging too low prices, not covering production costs), a practice not observed in competitive economies. Incidentally, the accommodation of a negative budget is a two-way street in the sense that there is deviation from the expenditure–income identity if *and only* if income is negative. The proof of this statement is simple. If there is deviation, then the loss function in condition 4 is positive and, by condition 4, consumption c is zero. Hence expenditure $\mathbf{pf}c$ is zero, and it is the remaining part of the loss function that is positive: $-(\mathbf{r}\boldsymbol{\kappa}K+w\lambda\mathbf{L})\mathbf{e}-\mathbf{p}[\mathbf{f}-(\mathbf{V}-\mathbf{U})\mathbf{e}]>0$. Multiplying through by -1 we conclude that income must be negative. Positive income will be fully spent, reflecting monotonicity of the preferences.

[8]Strictly speaking we should have done it at the outset, but the analysis thus far holds for any of the economies and it would have been superfluous to carry the index i of a typical economy.

the same number of products on each economy, by admitting zero rows across the use and make tables and domestic final demand of an economy. The corresponding product will remain absent from such an economy.

First we model the factor markets. The equilibrium rates of return on capital equate demand, $\mathbf{K}^i\mathbf{s}^i$, with supply, $\boldsymbol{\kappa}^i\mathbf{K}^i\mathbf{e}$. The latter is assumed to be inelastic.[9] Hence the capital market is represented by the complementarity condition that supply covers demand and excess supply means the price is zero:

$$\mathbf{0} \leq \mathbf{r}^i \perp \mathbf{K}^i(\boldsymbol{\kappa}^i\mathbf{e} - \mathbf{s}^i) \geq \mathbf{0}. \tag{5}$$

The labor market of an economy is modeled in the same vein. Analogous to condition 5 we have the following condition 6:

$$0 \leq w^i \perp \mathbf{L}^i(\lambda^i\mathbf{e} - \mathbf{s}^i) \geq 0. \tag{6}$$

Equations 5 and 6 treat capital and labor as being immobile between economies. This condition can be altered as well. We will do so explicitly for the environmental stock constraints, which will be modeled analogous to that of capital and labor. Turn to the tradable products markets. We need no bilateral trade information. For each economy net exports are the difference between net output and domestic final demand, $(\boldsymbol{V}^i - \boldsymbol{U}^i)\boldsymbol{s}^i - \boldsymbol{f}^i c_i$. If all economies are encompassed, as in world models, the net export vectors sum to zero. Otherwise there is a rest of the world, and we preserve the aggregate net exports to the rest of the world, allowing for free trade between the economies considered. To compute equilibrium, we need *no* information on the distribution of exports and imports of economy i between intra-regional trade (i.e. to or from the other economies considered) and trade with the rest of the world (i.e. with the economies not considered). Equilibrium product prices equate aggregate net exports to zero (for a world model) or to the observed aggregate net exports to the rest of the world (for multiregional models which do not cover the entire world). Aggregate net exports, $\sum[(\boldsymbol{V}^i - \boldsymbol{U}^i)\boldsymbol{s}^i - \boldsymbol{f}^i c_i]$, may exceed zero or the observed aggregate net exports to the rest of the world, $\sum[(\boldsymbol{V}^i - \boldsymbol{U}^i)\boldsymbol{e} - \boldsymbol{f}^i]$, but products for which there is such excess

[9] It would require an intertemporal model to analyze its response to prices through the process of investment.

supply must be free (carry a zero price). This is written succinctly by the following complementarity condition:

$$\mathbf{0} \leq \mathbf{p} \perp \sum [(\mathbf{V}^i - \mathbf{U}^i)(\mathbf{s}^i - \mathbf{e}) - \mathbf{f}^i(c_i - 1)] \geq 0 \qquad (7)$$

The pair of nonnegativity inequalities in condition 7 implies that each term in the inner product of the price row vector and the excess supply vector is zero. Hence each product in excess supply is free. It is easy to accommodate nontradable products in the model. Such products are treated as being differentiated by economy and their material balances are not pooled across economies. For example, if product 1 is nontradable, then $[(\mathbf{V}^i - \mathbf{U}^i)\mathbf{e} - \mathbf{f}^i]_1 = 0$ and the first component of the complementarity condition 7, $p_1 \perp \sum [(\mathbf{V}^i - \mathbf{U}^i)(\mathbf{s}^i - \mathbf{e}) - \mathbf{f}^i(c_i - 1)]_1$, is replaced by $0 \leq p_1^i \perp [(\mathbf{V}^i - \mathbf{U}^i)\mathbf{s}^i - \mathbf{f}^i c_i]_1 \geq 0$, for all i. In our general equilibrium analysis all prices are endogenous, in fact the shadow prices associated with the supply–demand inequalities. Tariffs can be modeled similarly as the shadow prices of restrictions to free trade, but we focus on the interplay between trade and the environment rather than political–economy protections.

3.5. *The Connection with Linear Programming*

In the linear programming approach the levels of final demand, c_i, are maximized subject to mutual proportions, $c_i = \gamma_i c_1$ (with $\gamma_1 = 1$). For each set of weights (γ_i) the linear program maximizes c_1 subject to the material and factor balances, which are the right-hand side constraints in 5–7. The first order condition of this linear program is condition 2 plus a price normalization constraint. The weights are adjusted as to meet the balance of payment constraints, which are given by the expenditure–income constraints or complementarity condition 4. It follows that a solution of the adjustment process of linear programs fulfills the equations of the present equilibrium model. Conversely a solution to the equilibrium model fulfills the material, factor and balance of payment constraints of the limit linear program.

To establish full equivalence it remains to show that a solution to the equilibrium model maximizes the levels of final demand. This is done by adaptation of Debreu's (1951) proof of the first welfare theorem, who argues that demand is such that superior commodity bundles must be more expensive and that the latter property implies the violation of some material feasibility constraint. Suppose greater levels of consumption c_i' than the equilibrium levels would be possible. Then for each economy, by Equation 4, $\mathbf{pf}^i c_i' - (\mathbf{r}^i \boldsymbol{\kappa}^i \mathbf{K}^i + w^i \lambda^i \mathbf{L}^i)\mathbf{e} - \mathbf{p}[\mathbf{f}^i - (\mathbf{V}^i - \mathbf{U}^i)\mathbf{e}] > 0$, provided that $\mathbf{pf}^i > 0$, for which a reasonable, sufficient condition is $\mathbf{f}_i > 0$ (meaning that every component is positive). Summing these inequalities over economies and substituting condition 7 for the leading term, $\sum \mathbf{pf}^i c_i'$, $\sum\{\mathbf{p}[(\mathbf{V}^i - \mathbf{U}^i)(\mathbf{s}^i - \mathbf{e}) + \mathbf{f}^i] - (\mathbf{r}^i \boldsymbol{\kappa}^i \mathbf{K}^i + w^i \lambda^i \mathbf{L}^i)\mathbf{e} - \mathbf{p}[\mathbf{f}^i - (\mathbf{v}^i - \mathbf{U}^i)\mathbf{e}]\} = \sum[\mathbf{p}(\mathbf{V}^i - \mathbf{U}^i)\mathbf{s}^i - (\mathbf{r}^i \boldsymbol{\kappa}^i \mathbf{K}^i + w^i \lambda^i \mathbf{L}^i)\mathbf{e}] > 0$. Substituting the macro identities 3, one for each economy, $\sum (\mathbf{r}^i \boldsymbol{\kappa}^i \mathbf{K}^i + w^i \lambda^i \mathbf{L}^i)(\mathbf{s}^i - \mathbf{e}) > 0$. Hence some $\mathbf{K}^i(\mathbf{s}^i - \mathbf{e})$ or $L^i(\mathbf{s}^i - \mathbf{e})$ must be positive, in violation of the factor balances of the linear program, which are the right-hand side constraints in Equations 5 and 6.

4. Extension to Environmental Policies

4.1. *Environmental Policy Restrictions*

The simplest way to incorporate environmental constraints in equilibrium analysis is to treat the environment, or at least the part that may be damaged, as a resource, just like capital or labor. In addition to a capital employment matrix and a labor employment row vector, $\mathbf{K}^i$ and $\mathbf{L}^i$, respectively, we have an environment employment vector $\mathbf{M}^i$, which records the damage to the environment by industry.

Typically the elements are emissions. The total emission in economy i is $\mathbf{M}^i\mathbf{e}$. Different types of environmental damages can be extended by extending $\mathbf{M}^i$ to a matrix. Invoking the assumption of constant returns to scale, an increase in each industry's activity results in a proportional increase of both the output and the emissions produced by the industry.

Environmental policies can be modeled by means of alternative constraints on emissions. Therefore, emissions enter our model both as a (negative) output produced together with the industrial output and as an endowment factor constrained by environmental policy. If the damage to the environment may not exceed a fraction μ^i of the observed level in economy i (a vector in case of different types of damages), the constraints are given by the second inequalities in conditions 8, one for each economy.

$$0 \leq t^i \bot \mathbf{M}^i(\mu^i \mathbf{e} - \mathbf{s}^i) \geq 0. \tag{8}$$

The prices t^i in conditions 8 are analogous to the prices of labor and capital and thus measure the marginal economic value of relaxing the environmental constraint. If it is high in say economy 1 and low in say economy 2, then the marginal benefit of allowing one more unit of pollution in economy 1 would be greater than the marginal cost of restricting pollution by one unit in economy 2. In other words, it would be beneficial to shift pollution from the economy with a low environmental price (economy 2) to the economy with a high environmental price. An international market for emission rights would bring about such a reallocation. Speculators would buy emission rights where they are inexpensive and resell them where they are expensive. Formally this amounts to a replacement of the national environmental conditions 8, by the international condition:

$$0 \leq t \bot \sum \mathbf{M}^i(\mu^i \mathbf{e} - \mathbf{s}^i) \geq 0. \tag{9}$$

The development of the model generates ever higher levels of efficiency and, therefore, can be applied to assess the allocative inefficiencies in the observed economies, both nationally and internationally. First we have is the transition of the observed economies, $(\mathbf{K}^i, \boldsymbol{\kappa}^i, \mathbf{L}^i, \lambda^i, \mathbf{M}^i, \mu^i, \mathbf{U}^i, \mathbf{V}^i, \mathbf{f}^i)$, to their competitive counterparts, $(\mathbf{K}^i \hat{\mathbf{s}}^i, \mathbf{e}, \mathbf{L}^i \hat{\mathbf{s}}^i, \mathbf{1}, \mathbf{M}^i \hat{\mathbf{s}}^i, \mathbf{1}, \mathbf{U}^i \hat{\mathbf{s}}^i, \mathbf{V}^i \hat{\mathbf{s}}^i, \mathbf{f}^i c_i)$. Here $\mathbf{s}^i$ and c_i are the equilibrium values of the model comprising Equation 2 (and similar for all other industries, in all economies), Equation 4 (for each economy and with the environmental proceeds added to the factor income), and Equations 5–8 (for all i). A hat denotes placement of on the diagonal of a matrix. This first transition reallocates activities within and between economies according to the principle of comparative advantage in production. The gains to free trade are reflected in the consumption levels, c_i. The elimination of the allocative inefficiencies also accommodates the meeting of tighter environmental constraints, $\mu_i < 1$.

The second transition comes with the replacement of the system of national environmental conditions 8 by the single, international condition 9. Since the constraint in the latter is more lax from an economic point of view (the feasible set of allocations gets bigger when constraints are pooled), but not from an environmental perspective (the total use of the environment remains the same), further efficiency gains are made and reflected in even higher consumption levels. A fine example of this transition is the clean development mechanism (CDM) of the Kyoto Protocol (1997). The CDM permits firms of economies where emission reductions are costly, particularly the developed economies, to contribute to reductions elsewhere, in economies where they are relatively cheap, notably developing countries.

In the short run emission caps or tradable permits are not available in all countries. The model can handle situations where only a subset of countries implements environmental policies by modifying the constraints 8 or 9. In particular, if only a subset of countries have an emission cap with tradable permits, such as in the case of the Kyoto Protocol, condition 8 should include only the restrictions on the participating countries, and no restrictions on the other countries. Similarly, the case of tradeable permits in a subset of countries can be accommodated by modifying condition 9 to remove the terms corresponding to nonparticipating countries. In the same vein, the formulae for the environmental conditions can be modified for the situation in which there are different policies (with different emission caps and/or permits) in different subsets of countries. Thus, the model can also serve for the analysis of regional policies, for example EU-ETS or the Australian and New Zealand carbon market.

4.2. *The Full Model*

Either model, with the environmental constraints separate or pooled, can be summarized by the general complementarity problem:

$$\mathbf{0} \leq \mathbf{z} \perp \boldsymbol{\Phi}(\mathbf{z}) \geq \mathbf{0}. \tag{10}$$

Vector $\mathbf{z} = ((\mathbf{s}^i, c_i, \mathbf{r}^i, w^i, t^i)_{i=1,\dots,I}; \mathbf{p})$ lists the components of all variables. Here I is the number of economies. The emission prices t^i are replaced by a single scalar t preceding $\mathbf{p}$ if the national environmental conditions 8 are pooled into the international condition 9. Vector $\boldsymbol{\Phi}(\mathbf{z})$ lists the respective loss functions and complementarity problem 10 can be presented piecemeal because it is equivalent to $\mathbf{0} \leq \mathbf{z}^1 \perp \boldsymbol{\Phi}^1(\mathbf{z}^1) \geq \mathbf{0}, \mathbf{0} \leq \mathbf{z}^2 \perp \boldsymbol{\Phi}^2(\mathbf{z}^2) \geq 0$ for any partition of the variables and the function, $\mathbf{z} = (\mathbf{z}^1, \mathbf{z}^2)$ and $\boldsymbol{\Phi} = (\boldsymbol{\Phi}^1, \boldsymbol{\Phi}^2)$. The expressions for the loss functions were derived earlier and can be found in Equations 2 and 4 (with the environmental proceeds added to the factor income), Equations 5, 6,[10] 8 or alternatively 9, and 7. For the case of national pollution caps we have

$$0 \le \mathbf{s}^i \perp (\mathbf{r}^i\mathbf{K}^i + w^i\mathbf{L}^i + t^i\mathbf{M}^i + \mathbf{p}\mathbf{U}^i - \mathbf{p}\mathbf{V}^i) \ge \mathbf{0}, \quad i = 1, \ldots, I,$$

$$0 \le c_i \perp \mathbf{p}\mathbf{f}^i c_i - (\mathbf{r}^i\mathbf{K}^i + w^i\mathbf{L}^i + t^i\mu^i\mathbf{M}^i)\mathbf{e} - \mathbf{p}[\mathbf{f}^i - (\mathbf{V}^i - \mathbf{U}^i)\mathbf{e}] \ge 0, \quad i = 1, \ldots, I,$$

$$0 \le \mathbf{r}^i \perp \mathbf{K}^i(\boldsymbol{\kappa}^i\mathbf{e} - \mathbf{s}^i) \ge \mathbf{0}, \quad i = 1, \ldots, I,$$

$$0 \le w^i \perp \mathbf{L}^i(\lambda^i\mathbf{e} - \mathbf{s}^i) \ge 0, \quad i = 1, \ldots, I,$$

$$0 \le t^i \perp \mathbf{M}^i(\mu^i\mathbf{e} - \mathbf{s}^i) \ge 0, \quad i = 1, \ldots, I,$$

$$0 \le \mathbf{p} \perp \sum [(\mathbf{V}^i - \mathbf{U}^i)(\mathbf{s}^i - \mathbf{e}) - \mathbf{f}^i(c_i - 1)] \ge \mathbf{0} \tag{11}$$

For tradable permits not only the last component in Equation 11 but also the next to last is subjected to summation, employing $\sum \mathbf{M^i}(\mu^i\mathbf{e} - \mathbf{s}^i)$ of Equation 9 instead, and a common scalar t replaces t^i in the second component. Then the trade surplus includes the amount of trade in permits.

5. Illustration

We demonstrate the applicability of the model in a simple example, featuring three developed economies, namely Belgium, Denmark and Spain. This admittedly odd combination serves a pilot study because their data sets have been completed and made available to us. The main purpose of the paper is to exposit how (environmental) input–output accounts can be used for general equilibrium analysis of environmental policies and the extension to an interregional model of all EU member states is straightforward once comprehensive member states data become available. For the sake of simplicity, we restrict our attention to the main greenhouse gas, CO_2, which accounts for about 80% of greenhouse pollution of the EU-15 (Gielen and Kram, 1998). We first describe the data and then compare the model outcomes under alternative environmental policy assumptions. The case

[10]Here, we present the formulation with immobile factor inputs; however, as explained earlier, this assumption can be easily altered.

of no environmental policy will serve as the benchmark for the cases of national emission caps and an international emission cap with tradable permits. Our simple model will prove capable of producing similar insights as those in other, more complicated models, but again, the purpose of the exercise is only to illustrate the applicability of the model.

5.1. *Data*

The data, provided to us by the IPTS, are based on the national and environmental accounts of each country, published by Eurostat for the year 2000. The use and supply tables, **U** and **V**, incorporate 59 products and industries. The tables are expressed in producer prices. The supply tables of the Eurostat are published in producer prices, while the use tables were estimated by the IPTS. For Denmark the data have been converted into euro's using the average exchange rate of 2000.[11] We treat the commodities with negligible values of the observed net export as non-tradable.[12] The trade with the rest of the world has been held fixed at the observed level.

Labor data (number of employed persons) originate from the EU KLEMS data. Labor unemployment rates in 2000 were: Belgium 6.9%; Denmark 4.3% and Spain 11.1% (Eurostat, 2010). These percentages represent 'unemployed persons as a percentage of the labor force, where the labor force is the total number of people employed and unemployed'. The total private capital stock in each country comes from the Kiel Institute of the World Economy's Database on Capital Stocks in OECD countries. As usual, capital employment data are a bottleneck. Since no detailed capital employment data were available by industry (in our industry classification), capital employment has been allocated across industries proportionally to

[11]Since we consider the aggregated production technology for each industry, the analysis does not account for within industry reallocations and environmental improvements.

[12]In this application, nontradable commodities are: secondary metals, water, sewerage, transportation, real estate, education, healthcare, public services, services of membership organization and private households, and other services.

Table 1. Effect of environment policy targets on expansion factors.

	Spain	Denmark	Belgium
Kyoto targets	+15%	−21%	−7.5%
Emission limits μ	0.85	0.79	0.86
Scenarios			
(a) Unrestricted	1.049	1.133	1.115
(b) National caps	0.878	0.945	1.119
(c) International permits trade	0.903	1.015	1.094
(d) Spain opts out	1.058	1.144	1.067

the industrial gross operating surpluses, assuming capacity utilization rates around 0.82, in accordance with the EU average utilization rates for that period World Bank (2010).

The environmental impact data come from the database of the IPTS that builds upon the environmental accounts published by the Eurostat. We focus on CO_2-emissions and assume the policy parameters, emission limits μ^i, to reflect the respective Kyoto targets on the reduction of greenhouse gas emissions.[13] The original Kyoto targets (−7.5% for Belgium and −21% for Denmark, and +15% for Spain) specify the percentage of the emission reduction compared to the level of 1990, while our data corresponds to 2000. Therefore, we have transformed them by the following formula: $\mu_{2000} = \mu_{1990}/(1+g)$, in which the superscripts refer to the two base years, and g denotes the change in the CO_2 emission level between these years. The data on g are derived from EEA (2002): 7.7% for Belgium, −0.4% for Denmark and 34.9% for Spain. Plugging these values into the 1990–2000 transformation formula above yields the values of μ^i reported in Table 1. Because the initial level of emissions in Spain in 1990 was low,

[13]The Kyoto targets cover emissions of the six main greenhouse gases, namely: Carbon dioxide (CO_2); Methane (CH_4); Nitrous oxide (N_2O); Hydrofluorocarbons (HFCs); Perfluorocarbons (PFCs) and Sulphur hexafluoride (SF_6). The total value of greenhouse gas emissions is constructed as a weighted average of each gas emissions with global-warming potentials as weights. The targets specify the percentage of reductions of the total emission level to be achieved in the period 2008–2012 compared to the level of 1990. In addition to these national caps, there is the EU trading scheme currently covering only CO_2 emissions of major installations. Not all industries are covered by the EU emission trading scheme.

therefore, Spain was not required to decrease the level and the value of the Kyoto target was positive for Spain. However, after the rapid increase of emissions in the period 1990–2000, surpassing the target, Spain faces a relatively stringent constraint in 2000.

5.2. *Results*

Table 1 shows the resulting expansion factors under four scenarios: (a) no environmental constraint (our benchmark), (b) national caps on CO_2, (c) international trade in CO_2 permits under a common cap and (d) when one national cap is removed. It is a comparison between scenarios (a) and (b) highlights the trade-off between the strength of the pollution caps and the resulting equilibrium consumption. While without emission caps, the model results in the expansion of consumption in all the three economies, this is no longer the case under environmental constraints. Interestingly, the expansion factor for Belgium increases. This phenomenon is explained by the shadow prices of CO_2 emissions in the three countries, which are 1.52 for Belgium, 1.58 for Denmark and 2.36 for Spain. The minimum price in Belgium reveals a low environmental cost, which attracts production.

Scenario (c) mimics international trade in permits. The expansion factors of Denmark and Spain increase, while the expansion factor of Belgium decreases compared to the national scenario (b). Free trade in emission permits reallocates production between countries and changes industry outputs and prices. This terms-of-trade effect may be unfavorable. The shadow prices of CO_2 emissions under (b) and (c) support this explanation. The maximum price in Spain means that the (environmental) cost of production is high in Spain, harming its terms of trade under (b), contrary to Belgium. In scenario (c), free trade in emission permits relieves the constraint on Spain and the situation reverses.

The final scenario (d), suggested by a referee, analyzes the Pollution Haven Hypothesis by letting an economy opt out. The suggested economy is the one with the highest growth in emissions, Spain. The scenario is hypothetical, because Spain is part of the EU trading scheme, but demonstrates how our model can handle this issue. We maintain the assumption that the other two countries adhere to the national caps under scenario (b). The theory predicts that the

Table 2. Industry expansion factors for Spain (ES), Denmark (DK) and Belgium (BE) in the scenarios (a) unrestricted, (b) national caps, (c) international permits trade and (d) Spain opts out.

	(a)			(b)			(c)			(d)		
Scenario:	ES	DK	BE	ES	DK	BE	ES	DK	BE	ES	DK	BE
Agric., forestry and fishing	1.2	0.2	1.2	1.0	1.2	0.1	1.1	1.2	0.0	1.2	0.2	1.2
Mining and quarrying	1.0	1.2	1.2	0.6	0.7	1.2	0.6	1.0	1.2	1.0	1.2	1.2
Food, beverages and tobacco	1.2	0.2	1.2	0.7	1.2	1.2	1.1	0.1	1.2	1.2	0.2	1.2
Textiles, wearing apparel	1.1	0.0	1.2	1.0	1.2	0.6	1.0	1.2	0.7	1.2	0.0	1.0
Wood, pulp and publishing	1.0	1.0	1.2	0.8	1.0	1.2	0.8	1.0	1.2	1.0	0.8	1.2
Non-metallic mineral prod.	1.2	1.2	0.9	0.8	1.2	1.0	1.1	1.2	0.4	1.2	1.2	0.9
Metal products	1.0	1.2	1.2	1.0	1.2	0.6	1.0	1.2	0.6	1.1	1.2	0.9
Machinery	1.0	1.2	1.2	0.8	1.2	1.1	0.9	1.2	1.1	1.0	1.2	1.2
Electricity, gas and water	1.0	1.2	1.2	0.9	0.5	1.2	1.0	0.1	1.2	1.1	0.7	1.1
Construction	1.2	1.2	0.4	0.8	1.2	1.2	0.8	1.2	1.2	1.2	1.2	0.4
Trade, hotels and restaurants	1.2	1.0	0.8	1.0	1.0	0.7	1.1	1.0	0.7	1.2	1.1	0.8
Transport, post and telecom.	1.1	0.9	1.2	0.9	1.2	1.0	1.1	1.1	0.7	1.1	0.9	1.1
Financial services	1.2	1.1	0.8	1.0	0.3	1.2	1.1	0.3	1.2	1.2	0.5	1.2
Other business services	1.0	1.1	1.2	0.8	1.1	1.1	0.9	1.1	1.1	1.0	1.1	1.1
Other services	1.0	1.1	1.1	0.9	1.0	1.1	0.9	1.1	1.0	1.1	1.1	1.0

removal of one-country cap will improve this country welfare, but it can either improve or worsen the welfare in other countries. Indeed, we observe that the expansion factor of Spain is now the highest of all the scenarios, however, the situation differs in the other two economics: Denmark gains, while Belgium, with its emission cost, looses.

Table 2 shows the 15 aggregated industry activity levels. Comparison between scenarios (a) and (b) reveals that the introduction of national caps will reallocate the most polluting industry, 'electricity, gas, water', from Denmark and Spain to Belgium. Production of the next most polluting industries, 'metal products' and 'non-metallic products', will also reduce substantially under scenario (b), with only Denmark maintaining the same expansion level. Our assumption that capital is immobile between industries solves the problem of corner solutions frequently encountered in input–output models, the tendency of linear models to yield specialization in production. Zero activity is still obtained for 'textile and wearing apparel' in

Denmark under scenario (a), suggesting that absent environmental policies Denmark could gain from reducing that industry. However, since this industry is relatively clean, pollution caps render it competitive under scenario (b).

The tradability of permits increase total output, through more specialization according to comparative advantages. Denmark, with its coal plants, would reduce electricity production. Finally, Spain's opting out would boost it output and increase the shadow prices of emissions in the other economies, weaken their industries to different extents and prompting further reallocations.

6. Conclusion

The complementarity problem approach to supply-use accounts traces reallocations in response to environmental policies in multi-country systems, such as the EU. Environmental regulatory constraints are incorporated in the same vein as primary input constraints and the approach — which combines the strength of general equilibrium analysis and linear programming — determines the economic and environmental gains to free trade in products and emission permits.

Acknowledgments

The authors are grateful to Bart Los and two anonymous referees for their comments.

References

Acemoglu, D., P. Aghion, L. Bursztyn and D. Hemous. (2012). The environment and directed technical change. *American Economic Review*, **102**, 131–166.

Basu, S. and J. Fernald. (1997). Returns to scale in U.S. production: Estimates and implications. *Journal of Political Economy*, **105**, 249–283.

Burnside, C. (1996). Production function regressions, returns to scale, and externalities. *Journal of Monetary Economics*, **37**, 177–201.

Capros, P., P. Georgakopoulos, D. Van Regemorter, S. Proost, T. Schmit, H. Koschel, C. Conrad and E. Vouyoukas. (1999). *Climate Change*

Strategies 2: The Macro-economic Cost and Benefit of Reducing Greenhouse Gas Emissions in the EU, Heidelberg: Physica Verlag, 224.

Copeland, B. R. and M. S. Taylor. (2005). *Trade and the Environment: Theory and Evidence,* Princeton: Princeton University Press.

Davis, S. J. and K. Caldeira. (2010). Consumption-based accounting of CO*2* emissions. *Proceedings of the National Academy of Sciences*, **107**, 5687–5692.

Debreu, G. (1951). The coefficient of resource utilization. *Econometrica*, **19**, 273–292.

Dietzenbacher, E., B. Los, R. Stehrer, M. Timmer and G. de Vries. (2013). The construction of world input–output tables in the WIOD project. *Economic Systems Research*, **25**, 71–98.

Douglas, S. and S. Nishioka. (2012). International differences in emissions intensity and emissions content of global trade. *Journal of Development Economics*, **99**, 415–427.

Duchin, F. (2005). A world trade model based on comparative advantage with m regions, n goods, and k factors. *Economic Systems Research*, **17**, 141–162.

EEA (European Environment Agency). (2002). Annual European Community Greenhouse Gas Inventory 1990–2000 and Inventory Report 2002, European Environment Agency, Copenhagen.

Eurostat. (2010). Unemployment Statistics. http://epp.eurostat.ec.europa.eu/tgm/table.do?tab=table&init=1&language=en&pcode=tsiem110&plugin=1.

Eurostat. (2011). Creating Consolidated and Aggregated EU27 Supply, Use and Input–Output Tables, Adding Environmental Extensions (Air Emissions), and Conducting Leontief-type Modelling to Approximate Carbon and Other 'Footprints' of EU27 Consumption for 2000 to 2006, Luxemburg, Eurostat. http://epp.eurostat.ec.europa.eu/portal/page/portal/environmental_accounts/documents/eeSUIOT%20TechDoc%20final%20060411.pdf.

Ferris, M. C. and J. S. Pang. (1997). Engineering and economic applications of complementarity problems. *SIAM Review*, **39**, 669–713.

Fischer, C. and R. G. Newell. (2008). Environmental and technology policies for climate mitigation. *Journal of Environmental Economics and Management*, **55**, 142–162.

Huang, Y. A., M. Lenzen, C. L. Weber, J. Murray and H. S. Matthews. (2009). The role of input–output analysis for screening of corporate footprints. *Economic Systems Research*, **21**, 217–242.

Gielen, D. and T. Kram. (1998). The role of non-CO_2 greenhouse gases in meeting Kyoto targets. *Proceedings of the OECD Workshop Economic*

Modelling of Climate Change, OECD, Paris, 17–18 September. Available at http://www.oecd.org/dev/1923119.pdf.

IPCC (Intergovernmental Panel on Climate Change). (2001). *Third Assessment Report*, Climate Change: The Scientific Basis.

IPTS (Institute for Prospective Technological Studies). (2006). Environmentally Extended Input–Output Tables and Models for Europe, Seville, Spain.

Leontief, W. (1970). Environmental repercussions and the economic structure — an input–output approach. *Review of Economics and Statistics*, **52**, 262–271.

Minx, J. C., T. Wiedmann, R. Wood, G. P. Peters, M. Lenzen, A. Owen, K. Scott, J. Barrett, K. Hubacek, G. Baiocchi, A. Paul, E. Dawkins, J. Briggs, D. Guan, S. Suh and F. Ackerman. (2009). Input–output analysis and carbon footprinting: An overview of applications. *Economic Systems Research*, **21**, 187–216.

Nordhaus, W. D. (2007). A review of the stern review on the economics of global warming. *Journal of Economic Literature*, **45**, 686–702.

Peters, G. P., J. C. Minx, C. L. Weberd and O. Edenhofer. (2011). Growth in emission transfers via international trade from 1990 to 2008. *Proceedings of the National Academy of Sciences*, **108**, 8903–8908.

Proost, S. and D. Van Regemorter. (2004). Climate change policy in European countries and its effects on industry. *Mitigation and Adaptation Strategies for Global Change*, **9**, 453–473.

ten Raa, T. (1995). Commodity and sector classifications in linked systems of national accounts. In *Social Statistics, National Accounts and Economic Analysis, Annali di Statistica*, Ed. Giovannini, E., Serie X, 6, pp. 31–36.

ten Raa, T. (2008). Debreu's coefficient of resource utilization, the Solow residual, and TFP: The connection by Leontief's preferences. *Journal of Productivity Analysis*, **30**, 191–199.

ten Raa, T. and P. Mohnen. (2001). The location of comparative advantages on the basis of fundamentals only. *Economic Systems Research*, **13**, 93–108.

ten Raa, T. and P. Mohnen. (2002). Neoclassical growth accounting and frontier analysis: A synthesis. *Journal of Productivity Analysis*, **18**, 111–128.

ten Raa, T. and H. Pan. (2005). Competitive pressures on China: Income inequality and migration. *Regional Science and Urban Economics*, **35**, 671–699.

ten Raa, T. and V. Shestalova. (2011). The Solow residual, Domar aggregation, and inefficiency: A synthesis of TFP measures. *Journal of Productivity Analysis*, **36**, 71–77.

Shestalova, V. (2001). General equilibrium analysis of international TFP growth rates. *Economic Systems Research*, **13**, 391–404.

Stern, N. (2007). *The Stern Review on the Economics of Climate Change*, New York: Cambridge University Press.

Tukker, A. and E. Dietzenbacher. (2013). Introduction to global multiregional input–output frameworks: An introduction and outlook. *Economic Systems Research*, **25**, 1–19.

Tukker, A., E. Poliakov, R. Heijungs, T. Hawkins, F. Neuwahl, J.M. Rueda-Cantuche, S. Giljum, S. Moll, J. Oosterhaven and M. Bouwmeester. (2009). Towards a global multi-regional environmentally extended input–output database. *Ecological Economics*, **68**, 1929–1937.

Tukker, A., A. de Koning, R. Wood, T. Hawkins, S. Lutter, J. Acosta, J. M. Rueda Cantuche, M. Bouwmeester, J. Oosterhaven, T. Drosdowski and J. Kuenen. (2013). EXIOPOL — Development and illustrative analyses of a detailed global MR EE SUT/IOT. *Economic Systems Research*, **25**, 50–70.

Turner, K., M. Gilmartin, P. G. McGregor and J. K. Swales. (2012). An integrated IO and CGE approach to analysing changes in environmental trade balances. *Papers in Regional Science*, **91**, 161–180.

United Nations. (1997). Kyoto Protocol to the United Nations Framework Convention on Climate Change (UNFCCC).

Wiedmann, T. (2009a). Editorial: Carbon footprint and input–output analysis — An introduction. *Economic Systems Research*, **21**, 175–186.

Wiedmann, T. (2009b). A review of recent multi-region input–output models used for consumption-based emission and resource accounting. *Ecological Economics*, **69**, 211–222.

Wiedmann, T. and J. Barrett. (2013). Policy-relevant applications of environmentally extended MRIO databases — Experiences from the UK. *Economic Systems Research*, **25**, 143–156.

Wilting H. C. and K. Vringer. (2009). Carbon and land use accounting from a producer and a consumer perspective — An empirical examination covering the world. *Economic Systems Research*, **21**, 291–310.

World Bank. (2010). Weekly Global Economic Brief of the Development Prospects Group, **43**, 1 April 2010.

Chapter 7

Complementarity in Input–Output Analysis and Stochastics*

Thijs ten Raa[†] and Victoria Shestalova[‡]

[†]*Department of Economics, Tilburg University, Tilburg, The Netherlands*
tenraa@uvt.nl

[‡]*Netherlands Bureau for Economic Policy Analysis, The Hague, The Netherlands*

Abstract. The complementarity between the quantity and value systems of input–output analysis is shown to be the basis of the complementarity problem approach to computable general equilibrium. The numerical superiority of the latter to the linear programming approach facilitates stochastic analysis of input–output scenarios. For the example where Kyoto targets are underachieved to uncertain degrees, confidence intervals are derived for the associated consumption reductions.

Keywords: Complementarity Problem, Stochastic Input–Output Analysis

1. Introduction

ten Raa and Shestalova (2014) use the complementarity problem to determine the equilibrium prices and quantities for mutually trading economies. The purpose of this sequel paper is twofold. First, we

*Reprinted from *Economic Systems Research*, **27**, 95–100, 2015, with permission from Taylor & Francis.

provide an input–output foundation to this approach. The complementarity between the quantity and value systems of input–output analysis naturally suggests itself as a basis of the complementarity problem approach to computable general equilibrium and we show that this works out indeed. Second, we demonstrate that the complementarity problem approach makes possible stochastic input–output analysis. In standard models, equilibrium is determined using a fixed point algorithm, either in commodity space or in utility space. In the first case, prices are adjusted as to equate commodity supply and demand. The second case exploits the welfare theorems (by which equilibria are efficient). It constructs a social welfare function, determines the efficient allocation and the supporting prices, compares the values of the consumption bundles to the values of the endowments, and adjusts the weights in the social welfare function as to equate the two values for each type of consumer. The welfare approach is more indirect, but numerically more efficient, because the dimension is lower; for example, in international trade models, the dimension is the number of countries or regions, which is smaller than the number of commodities — the 28 documented Chinese provinces with 50 industry input–output accounts each could thus be analysed by ten Raa and Pan (2005), in particular the effects of competitive markets on income inequality. The nonlinear complementarity problem routine of GAMS (Ferris and Munson, 2000) further reduces the time to solve big economic models, from minutes to milliseconds, and this observation suggests Monte Carlo analysis of big input–output systems. The approach is useful for applied modellers, whose analyses and reports could benefit from the additional insights concerning the sensitivity of the modelling outcomes to the measurement of emissions and environmental damages.

2. Complementarity in Input–Output

The input–output model rests on the duality between prices and quantities and has been criticized for analysing the two independently. In a recent book, however, Bródy (2005) uses the duality to connect prices and quantities in a symmetric way. We apply his idea that excess supply reduces price and excess cost reduces output, not by setting up differential equations, but by introducing complementarity. Allowing for slack, the quantity system is $(\mathbf{I}-\mathbf{A})\mathbf{x} \geq \mathbf{y}$, where $\mathbf{x} \geq \mathbf{0}$ and $\mathbf{y}$ are the gross and net output commodity vectors (n-dimensional) and $\mathbf{A}$ is the input–output coefficients matrix, and the value system is $\mathbf{p}(\mathbf{I}-\mathbf{A})\mathbf{x} \leq \mathbf{v}$, where $\mathbf{p} \geq \mathbf{0}$ and $\mathbf{v}$ are the price and factor cost row vectors. If a commodity is in excess supply (strict inequality in a component of the quantity system), the price of that commodity will be zero: $[(\mathbf{I}-\mathbf{A})\mathbf{x}]_i > y_i \Rightarrow p_i = 0$ $(i = 1, \ldots, n)$, that is, *complementarity* between the slacks in the supply and the price inequalities. This is equivalent to $p_i\ [(\mathbf{I}-\mathbf{A})\mathbf{x}-\mathbf{y}]_i = 0$ $(i = 1, \ldots, n)$ and, because a sum of nonnegative terms is zero if and only if each term is nonzero, to the single equation $\mathbf{p}[(\mathbf{I}-\mathbf{A})\mathbf{x}-\mathbf{y}] = 0$, that is, *orthogonality* of price and excess supply. The complementarity between the quantity system and prices is succinctly written as $0 \leq p \perp (\mathbf{I}-\mathbf{A})\mathbf{x}-\mathbf{y} \geq \mathbf{0}$.

Similarly, if a commodity incurs a loss (strict inequality in a component of the value system), the supply of that commodity will be zero, that is, complementarity between the slacks in the loss and output inequalities, $\mathbf{0} \leq \mathbf{x} \perp \mathbf{v}-\mathbf{p}(\mathbf{I}-\mathbf{A}) \geq \mathbf{0}$. The pair of orthogonality conditions implies $\mathbf{py} = \mathbf{vx}$, which is the identity between national product and national income. If prices $\mathbf{p}$ and quantities $\mathbf{x}$ are positive, the material and financial balances hold, $(\mathbf{I}-\mathbf{A})\mathbf{x} = \mathbf{y}$ and $\mathbf{p}(\mathbf{I}-\mathbf{A}) = \mathbf{v}$. Many input–output economists analyse these two equations in isolation — to derive gross output from net output and to derive price from factor cost — but in equilibrium analysis, the price and quantity systems interact. In the commodity market, the price and quantity variables are $\mathbf{p}$ and $\mathbf{x}$. In the factor market, the price and quantity variables are w (wage) and c (consumption level).[1] Consumption is $\mathbf{y} = \mathbf{f}c$, where $\mathbf{f}$ represents the proportions of consumption. The factor suppliers (households) have the following pair of complementarities. Excess factor supply N means a zero price $w : 0 \leq w \perp N - \mathbf{lx} \geq 0$, where $\mathbf{l}$ is the row vector of factor input coefficients, so that factor costs are $\mathbf{v} = \mathbf{wl}$. And a negative budget means zero consumption: $0 \leq c \perp \mathbf{pf}c - wN \geq 0$.

[1]More factors will be entered below. The implicit assumption of the use of consumption level to measure utility is that the latter is a Leontief, fixed-proportions function.

The variables are quantities and prices $\mathbf{z} = (\mathbf{x}, c, w, \mathbf{p})$ and they are complementary to losses in production and consumption and to excess supplies of factor inputs and outputs $\mathbf{\Phi}(\mathbf{z}) = (w\mathbf{l} - \mathbf{p}(\mathbf{I} - \mathbf{A}), \mathbf{pf}c - wN, N - \mathbf{lx}, (\mathbf{I} - \mathbf{A})\mathbf{x} - \mathbf{f}c) : 0 \leq \mathbf{z} \perp \mathbf{\Phi}(\mathbf{z}) \geq \mathbf{0}$. By nonnegativity of the components of $\mathbf{z}$ and $\mathbf{\Phi}(\mathbf{z})$, this economy-wide complementarity is equivalent to component-by-component complementarity. The parameters which are no variables define the *structure* of the economy, that is, $\mathbf{l}, \mathbf{A}, \mathbf{f}, N$. These are the input coefficients of production and consumption and the endowment of the economy. The generalized loss function $\mathbf{\Phi}$ is parametrized by the structure of the economy. An equilibrium is a solution to the complementarity problem $\mathbf{0} \leq \mathbf{z} \perp \mathbf{\Phi}(\mathbf{z}) \geq \mathbf{0}$ (Ferris and Pang, 1997). As different economies have different equilibria, an equilibrium is a function of the loss function: $\mathbf{z}^* = \mathbf{Z}(\Phi)$. If the economy is parametrized by its input–output structure, we may write $\mathbf{z}^* = \mathbf{Z}(\mathbf{l}, \mathbf{A}, f, N)$.

3. Stochastic Analysis

Stochastic analysis studies the transmission of uncertainty in the structure of the economy, $\mathbf{\Phi}$, possibly parametrized by input–output structure $(\mathbf{l}, \mathbf{A}, f, N)$ to the equilibrium. The uncertainty is given by a distribution of the structure, $\mathbf{\Phi} \sim F$. Then $\mathbf{z}^* \sim G = F(\mathbf{Z}^{-1})$. There is no need to invert reduced form $\mathbf{Z}$ of the solution, it suffices to take Monte Carlo drawings from F, to determine the respective equilibrium values, and to build their distribution, G. Although each Monte Carlo iteration involves solving a big model, this methodology is feasible because the nonlinear complementarity problem routine of GAMS takes extremely little time computing the equilibria of the draws.

If the structure of the economy is parametrized, distribution F has components, $F_{\mathbf{l}}, F_{\mathbf{A}}, F_{\mathbf{f}}, F_N$. Ideally, these components are derived from micro data (Mattey and ten Raa, 1997; ten Raa and Rueda-Cantuche, 2007), but the uncertainty may be a subjective summary of the uncertainty that surrounds a policy, as we illustrate now by extension to environmental economics.

Analogous to the factor input coefficients $\mathbf{l}$ and the endowment N, include emission coefficients $\mathbf{m}$ and a pollution cap M in the structure of the economy. Then, the variables and the model become

$\mathbf{0} \leq \mathbf{z} = (\mathbf{x}, c, w, t, \mathbf{p}) \perp \mathbf{\Phi}(\mathbf{z}) = (w\mathbf{l} + t\mathbf{m} + \mathbf{p}(\mathbf{I} - \mathbf{A}), \mathbf{pf}c - wN - t\mathbf{M}, N - \mathbf{lx}, \mathbf{M} - \mathbf{mx}, (\mathbf{I} - \mathbf{A})\mathbf{x} - \mathbf{f}c) \geq 0$. Similar inclusion of capital coefficients and endowment, aggregation of all but the last components of $\mathbf{z}$ and $\mathbf{\Phi}(\mathbf{z})$ by national economy i(= Spain, Denmark or Belgium), replacement of the last component of $\mathbf{\Phi}(\mathbf{z})$ by the same expression but summed over national economies, and a minor modification to accommodate trade imbalances yields the model of ten Raa and Shestalova (2014). The pollution caps M^i for each national economy were taken from the Kyoto agreement (reductions of base-year emissions). While in principle the allowed environmental damage levels are exogenously determined by international treaties, problems of implementation or uncertainty about the propagation of the environmental changes may lead us to treat them as random parameters. The environmental economics literature stresses the presence of uncertainty both about the measurement of emission as about their effects. For example, with respect to greenhouse gases, uncertainty is large for non-CO_2 greenhouse emission trends and abatement options (e.g. Gielen and Kram, 1998). In addition, there is also uncertainty regarding the effects of emissions on environment (Manne *et al.*, 2004). Therefore, the illustrative example provided below focuses on the environmental uncertainty, ignoring the uncertainty that surrounds the input and output data. We assume the distributions of the emission caps (one for each country) to be one-sided (implementation problems may yield under achievements) and uniform (there are few observations hence the least informative distribution is the natural prior): $F_M^i = M - M^i/(M^i\varepsilon^i)$ *on* $M^i \leq M \leq M^i(1+\varepsilon^i)$. We assume $\varepsilon^i = 0.5$ (50%), and compute statistics based on 100 runs of the model. The most interesting components of solution $\mathbf{z}$ are the expansion factors, $c^i \sim G_{c^i}$. They are dependent, but it is straightforward to compute their marginal distributions and, in particular, their means and 95% confidence intervals.

4. Illustration

To demonstrate the applicability of the approach, we extend the illustrative example from our earlier paper (ten Raa and Shestalova, 2014) to the case of uncertainty about environmental effects. The example features three developed economies, namely Belgium,

Denmark and Spain, as their data sets were completed and made available to us. For the sake of simplicity, we restrict attention to the main greenhouse gas, CO_2, which accounts for about 80% of greenhouse pollution of the EU-15 (Gielen and Kram, 1998). However, the extension to an interregional model of all EU member states and more pollutants is straightforward once the respective data become available.

We first describe the data and then compare the model outcomes in the deterministic case to those in the stochastic case. The data description section and the deterministic case are drawn from ten Raa and Shestalova (2014).

4.1. *Data*

The data, provided to us by the Institute for Prospective Technological Studies (IPTS), are based on the national and environmental accounts of each country, published by Eurostat for the year 2000. The use and supply tables, **U** and **V**, incorporate 59 products and industries. The tables are expressed in producer prices. The supply tables of the Eurostat are published in producer prices, while the use tables were estimated by the IPTS. For Denmark, the data have been converted into euros using the average exchange rate of 2000.[2] We treat the commodities with negligible values of the observed net export as non-tradable.[3] The trade with the rest of the world has been held fixed at the observed level.

Labour data (number of employed persons) originate from the EU KLEMS data (O'Mahony and Timmer, 2009). Labour unemployment rates in 2000 were as follows: Belgium 6.9%; Denmark 4.3%; Spain 11.1% (Eurostat, 2010). These percentages represent "unemployed persons as a percentage of the labor force, where the labor force is the total number of people employed and unemployed".

---

[2]Since we consider the aggregated production technology for each industry, the analysis does not account for within industry reallocations and environmental improvements.

[3]In this application, non-tradable commodities are as follows: secondary metals, water, sewage, transportation, real estate, education, health care, public services, services of membership organization and private households, and other services.

The total private capital stock in each country comes from the Kiel Institute of the World Economy's Database on Capital Stocks in OECD countries (Kamps, 2006). As usual, capital employment data are a bottleneck. Since no detailed capital employment data were available by industry (in our industry classification), capital employment has been allocated across industries proportionally to the industrial gross operating surpluses, assuming capacity utilization rates around 0.82, in accordance with the EU average utilization rates for that period (World Bank, 2010).

The environmental impact data come from the database of the IPTS, that builds upon the environmental accounts published by the Eurostat. We focus on CO_2-emissions and assume the policy parameters, emission limits μ^i, to reflect the respective Kyoto targets on the reduction of greenhouse gas emissions.[4] The original Kyoto targets (−7.5% for Belgium, and −21% for Denmark, and +15% for Spain) specify the percentage of the emission reduction compared with the level of 1990, while our data correspond to 2000. Therefore, we have transformed them by the following formula: $\mu_{2000} = \mu_{1990}/1 + \text{g})$, in which the subscripts refer to the two base years, and g denotes the change in the CO_2-emission level between these years. The data on g are derived from EEA (2002): 7.7% for Belgium, −0.4% for Denmark, and 34.9% for Spain. Plugging these values into the 1990–2000 transformation formula above yields the values of the Kyoto reduction factors: emission limits μ^i.

4.2. Results

In Table 1, the first line shows emission limits μ^i, the second line the unconstrained equilibrium consumption values — without the

[4]The Kyoto targets cover emissions of the six main greenhouse gases, namely carbon dioxide (CO_2), methane (CH_4), nitrous oxide (N_2O), hydrofluorocarbons (HFCs), perfluorocarbons (PFCs), and sulphur hexafluoride (SF_6). The total value of greenhouse gas emissions is constructed as a weighted average of each gas emissions with global warming potentials as weights. The targets specify the percentage of reductions of the total emission level to be achieved in the period 2008–2012 compared with the level of 1990. In addition to these national caps, there is the EU trading scheme currently covering only CO_2 emissions of major installations. Not all industries are covered by the EU emission trading scheme.

Table 1. Effect of environment policy targets on expansion factors under international trade in CO_2-emission permits and the effects of uncertainty.

Consumption levels	Spain	Denmark	Belgium
Emission limits	0.85	0.79	0.86
Unconstrained emissions	1.049	1.133	1.115
With caps and permits trade	0.903	1.015	1.094
One-sided uncertainty	1.031	1.134	1.105
95% confidence interval	(1.025, 1.038)	(1.127, 1.141)	(1.098, 1.112)

emission caps — and the third line the equilibrium consumption values with caps and international trade in CO_2-emission permits in the deterministic case. These lines are taken from ten Raa and Shestalova (2014). The fourth line shows the consumption levels under one-sided uncertainty, and the fifth line the 95% confidence interval.

As can be seen from Table 1, a 50%-uncertainty about the realization of μ's results in a relatively small variance of the resulting expansion factors.

5. Conclusion

The complementarity between the quantity and value systems of input–output analysis is shown to be the basis of the complementarity problem approach to computable general equilibrium. Environmental regulatory constraints are incorporated in the same vein as primary input constraints. The numerical illustration demonstrates the applicability of the model to stochastic analysis of input–output scenarios under uncertainty concerning the measurement of environmental changes and their effects.

Acknowledgments

The authors are grateful to Bart Los and two anonymous referees for their comments.

References

Brody, A. (2005). *Near Equilibrium*, Budapest: Aula Publishing House, vi + 137 pp.

EEA (European Environment Agency). (2002). *Annual European Community Greenhouse Gas Inventory* 1990–2000 *and Inventory Report* 2002, European Environmment Agency, Copenhagen.

Eurostat. (2010). *Unemployment Statistics.* http://epp.eurostat.ec.europa.eu/tgm/table.do?tab=table&init=1&language=en&pcode=tsiem110&plugin=1.

Ferris, M. C. and T. S. Munson. (2000). *GAMS/PATH User Guide.* http://www.gams.com/docs/pdf/path.pdf.

Ferris, M. C. and J. S. Pang. (1997). Engineering and economic applications of complementarity problems. *SIAM Review*, **39**, 669–713.

Gielen, D. and T. Kram. (1998). The role of non-CO2 greenhouse gases in meeting Kyoto targets, Ch. 12 Proceedings of the OECD Workshop "Economic Modelling of Climate Change", Paris.

Kamps, C. (2006). New estimates of government net capital stocks for 22 OECD countries, 1960–2001. *IMF Staff Papers*, **53**, 120–150.

Manne, A., R. Richels and T. Wigley. (2004). Moving beyond concentrations: Challenge for limiting temperature change. AEI-Brookings Joint Center Working Paper No. 04–11.

Mattey, J. and T. ten Raa. (1997). Primary versus secondary production techniques in U.S. manufacturing. *Review of Income and Wealth*, **43**, 449–464.

O'Mahony, M. and M. P. Timmer. (2009). Output, input and productivity measures at the industry level: The EU KLEMS database. *The Economic Journal*, **119**, F374–F403.

ten Raa, T. and H. Pan. (2005). Competitive pressures on China: Income inequality and migration. *Regional Science and Urban Economics*, **35**, 671–699.

ten Raa, T. and J. M. Rueda-Cantuche. (2007). Stochastic analysis of input-output multipliers on the basis of use and make matrices. *Review of Income and Wealth*, **53**, 318–334.

ten Raa, T. and V. Shestalova. (2014). Supply-use framework for international environmental policy analysis. *Economic Systems Research*, **27**, 1, 77–94 (2015).

World Bank. (2010). *Weekly Global Economic Brief of the Development Prospects Group*, Washington, DC: World Bank Group, 43, April 1.

Chapter 8

Efficiency Measures for Industrial Organization*

Thijs ten Raa
Department of Economics, Tilburg University, Tilburg, The Netherlands
tenraa@uvt.nl

Abstract. The aim of the paper is to measure the efficiency of an industry, and to decompose it in firm efficiencies — which indicate how close firms approximate best practices — and an organization efficiency — which indicates the degree of optimality of the number of firms and their distribution. The latter component provides an efficiency measure for the industrial organization. Economies or diseconomies of scale and of scope play a big role in the determination of the optimal industrial organization and the consequent measurement of the efficiency of an observed industry. Different approaches to the modeling of scale economies will be reviewed. The paper shows in detail how the efficiency of an industrial organization can be measured as a gap between mean firm efficiency and overall industry efficiency. The analysis is extended to dynamic models, to measure the role of entry and exit in the efficiency of the industrial organization.

1. Efficiency and Industrial Organization

If you want to rank firms in an industry, you better use a uniform set of weights for performance components across the firms

*Reprinted from *Benchmarking for Performance Evaluation: A Production Frontier Approach*, 221–250, 2015, with permission from Springer India.

one compares. This paper explains how potentially conflicting performance aspects can be balanced by assigning rational weights. Here we distinguish between internal and external (or competitive) benchmarking.

Internal benchmarking helps to spot exemplary business units within big companies, such as hotel chains. For every unit it spots the relevant benchmarks, suggests cost components that can be cut and potential revenue sources that would boost performance. *External benchmarking* includes the competition in the pool of examples and, therefore, is also called *competitive* benchmarking. It is a more demanding management tool, if only because data are hard to get from competitors, but potentially rewarding. By extending the pool to which you compare, the benchmark will be better and, therefore, the achievement level higher. External benchmarking is relevant to the analysis of industrial organization.

The performance of an industry is more than the sum of the parts. Not only do some firms under perform, but also the reallocation of resources between firms may be suboptimal. Obvious improvements could be achieved by reallocating resources from less to more efficient firms, but more subtle gains can be made by reallocating between efficient firms. Roughly speaking, a better industrial organization would alleviate shortages. In this paper we measure how much could be gained not only by eliminating firm inefficiencies, but also by a more efficient allocation of resources between the firms. The latter component measures the inefficiency of an industrial organization.

Benchmarking, particularly data envelopment analysis based, is yet to be integrated with other management tools. The airline industry is perhaps the one with the most widespread use of benchmarking. Here managers routinely measure the performance of their company in comparison to the competition and consumers visit websites to compare not only prices but also flight statistics, to assess costs and value aspects, such as the reliability of departure and arrival times. Nonetheless, Francis, Humphreys and Fry (2005) report that benchmarking is the most popular performance measurement tool in the industry, but that only one airline beefs it up with DEA. The perceived incapacity to value alternative performance components may be a hurdle and we will overcome it.

Most applications of benchmarking are basically alternative performance measurements and rankings, both financial and non-financial, and the bulk is based on *output* scores, such as revenues, net earnings, and customer satisfaction. I find it important though to bring in the inputs, if only to separate size effects from true performance scores. I will do so throughout the paper and we will encounter a number of interesting findings. For example, the use of output to input value *ratios* will emerge as natural performance measures, instead of difference based level concepts, such as profit (which is revenue minus cost). There is a close connection between the subtle distinction between ratios and difference on one hand and the distinction between the concepts of efficiency, productivity and profitability on the other. All this tends to be a smorgasbord and it is high time to disentangle the concepts and to clarify which is appropriate for performance measurement and ranking. This paper provides the analysis.

External or competitive benchmarking is applicable both to business units and to corporations. In the former case comparable intra-company information is required for different companies. In Table 1 this case is denoted by the box "Competitive benchmarking." In the latter case aggregate company data are compared, which is less demanding. This case is box "External benchmarking" in Table 1 and is relevant to industrial organization.

There is an interesting intermediate level of benchmarking, in between internal and external/competitive benchmarking. It is the benchmarking of an industrial organization by measuring it up against its constituent firms. The idea is borrowed from economic theory, which has developed a subtle technique to measure the efficiency of an economy *without* comparing it to other economies. Here inefficiency encompasses not only suboptimal production of outputs by firms (excessive use of inputs), but also the subtle of form of

Table 1. A taxonomy of benchmarking.

	Reference organization:	
Firm:	**Corporation**	**Industry**
Business Unit	Internal benchmarking	Competitive benchmarking
Corporation	Organization benchmarking	External benchmarking

inefficiency called *allocative* inefficiency. There may be scope for performance improvement by reallocating resources between firms. If so, the firms may be efficient, but the industry is not. This source of inefficiency can be exposed without benchmarking the industry against its foreign competitors, but by benchmarking the industry against its own firms. If we benchmark an industry internally, a subtle conceptual issue emerges, benchmarks are specific to the firm considered. While internal and competitive benchmarking are the same ballgame from the point of view of technical analysis, *industrial organization benchmarking* is distinct in that it requires some extra work to remove the dependence.

If we benchmark an industry against its own firms, then we analyze the performance of the industrial organization given the industry's *total* inputs and *total* outputs. We will do so by analyzing how much better the industry could perform if not only each firm operates efficiently, but also the industry's resources are allocated optimally. This problem will be solved by the operations research technique of linear programming, but this time the benchmark valuations or shadow prices pertain to the industry as a whole. In this way the results are no longer specific to firms and can be used to *rank* them objectively.

The remainder of this paper is organized as follows. Section 2 introduces efficiency measurement at the level of the firm. Section 3 discusses the subtle interrelations between efficiency, productivity and profitability. Section 4 discusses ranking and pricing issues. Section 5 discusses economies of scale and Section 6 presents the ramifications for efficiency measures, including for industries. Section 7 decomposes industrial efficiency into firm and organization components and accounts for changes through time, including entry and exit. Section 8 concludes.

2. Efficiency Measurement of Firms

An *industry* consists of I *firms*. Firm i(where $i = 1, \ldots, I$) is a black box that transforms *input* quantities $x_1^i, \ldots, x_k^i$ into *output* quantities $y_1^i, \ldots, y_l^i$. Here subscript k is the number of inputs and subscript l is the number of outputs. Superscript i indicates the firm of which we take the data. We wish to know at which level a firm operates compared to its full potential (i.e. full efficiency). In other words, we pose the question how much more *could* the firm deliver? To answer this question we conduct a thought experiment.

We allow the firm to redistribute its inputs over the activities represented by the inputs and outputs of all firms. Hence imagine firm i would employ its inputs to run the activities of firms $1, \ldots, I$ with *intensities* $\theta_1, \ldots, \theta_I$, where I is the total number of firms. The firm would need quantities $x_1^1\theta_1 + \cdots + x_1^I\theta_m$ of input $1, \ldots, x_k^1\theta_1 + \cdots + x_k^I\theta_I$ of input k, and produce quantities $y_1^1\theta_1 + \cdots + y_1^I\theta_I$ of output $1, \ldots, y_l^1\theta_1 + \cdots + y_l^I\theta_I$ of output l.

The envisaged operation is feasible if the required inputs do not exceed firm i's available inputs. The operation improves the output level if the hypothetical outputs exceed some multiple of the respective actual outputs of firm i. This output multiple is modeled by means of the so called *expansion* factor, e. The maximum expansion of output of firm i is determined by the following linear program:

$$\max_{\theta_1,\ldots,\theta_I,e\geq 0} e :$$

$$\begin{aligned} x_1^1\theta_1 + \cdots + x_1^I\theta_I \leq x_1^i, \quad \ldots, \quad x_k^1\theta_1 + \cdots + x_k^I\theta_I \leq x_k^i \\ y_1^1\theta_1 + \cdots + y_1^I\theta_I \geq y_1^i e, \quad \ldots, \quad y_l^1\theta_1 + \cdots + y_l^I\theta_I \geq y_l^i e \end{aligned} \quad (1)$$

In program (1) the expansion factor is maximized subject to the feasibility constraints on the inputs and proportionate expansion of the outputs. *All* that is needed to run benchmarking program (1) are the inputs and the outputs of all firms. Implicitly, program (1) assumes constant returns to scale. In Section 5 we will analyze more complicated models.

The assumption of constant returns to scale enables us to normalize the activities. For example, if there are two inputs and one output, it is natural to rescale such that the outputs of all activities are equal to one. After this rescaling, firms differ in their inputs only and we may plot a scatter diagram in input space, see Figure 1.

In Figure 1, firm 4 can reduce its distance to the origin from 100% to 75%. That way it is moved to the midpoint between firms 3 and 5. Indeed, if we run activities 3 and 5 at intensities 1/2 each, the required inputs are the average of the inputs of firms 3 and 5, which is represented by the midpoint, while the output would be $1/2+1/2 = 1$, hence unchanged. This way firm 4 can produce its output using only 75% of its inputs. The remainder, 25% of the inputs,

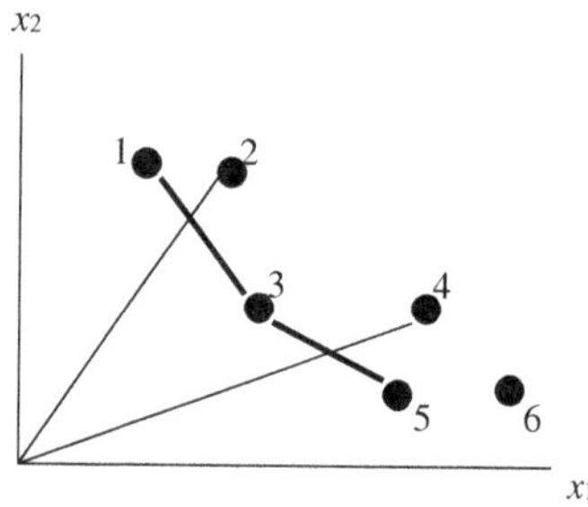

Fig. 1. An industry with two inputs and a single output.

Note: Firms 1, 3 and 5 use minimal input. Firms 2, 4 and 6 can contract their inputs.

can be considered wasted (and be reallocated without reducing output). Because of the constant returns-to-scale assumption, the capacity to produce output with 3/4ths of the inputs is equivalent to the capacity to produce 4/3rds of the output with the given input. Application of program (1) to unit 4 yields an expansion factor $e = 4/3$.

Firm 2, also in Figure 1, needs only some 80% of its inputs if it would employ the techniques of firms 1 and 3; 20% of its input can be considered waste for this firm. Application of program (1) to unit 2 yields an expansion factor $e = 5/4$. The lower envelop of the observations, the thick lines connecting firms 1, 3 and 5, represents the minimally required inputs for the production of one unit of output. These three units are the *benchmarks*. The distance between the envelope and a firm measures the unnecessary input, or inefficiency. This technique is called *Data Envelopment Analysis* or DEA for short.

In general it is impossible to identify an all-purpose best practice or practices. It depends on the unit you benchmark. For example, in Figure 1 there is *no* general purpose best practice. To firm 4 the benchmarks are firms 3 and 5, but to firm 2 the benchmarks are firms 1 and 3. Basically, the relevant best practices must be compatible with the mix of resources of the unit one investigates. In Figure 1 firm 4 is well endowed with the first input. The technique of firm 1, though efficient, requires a lot of the other input and, therefore, is not relevant to firm 4.[1]

[1]In Figure 1 firm 6 has only one benchmark, namely firm 5.

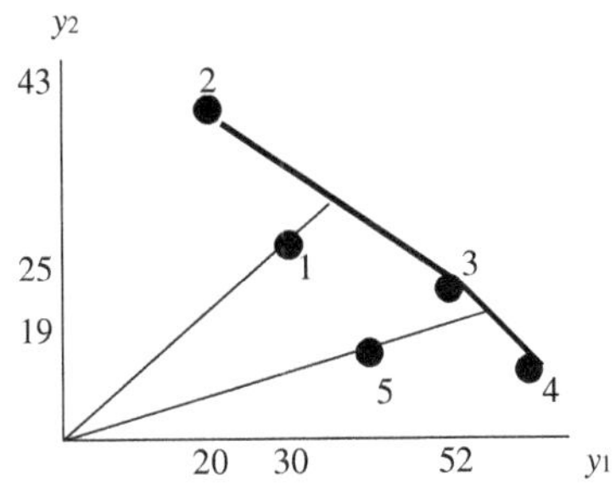

Fig. 2. An industry with a single input and two outputs.
Note: Firms 2, 3 and 4 produce maximal output. Firms 1 and 5 can expand their outputs.

Let me move from the example depicted in Figure 1 — where two inputs are combined to produce a single output — to the mirror image, where one input, say labor can be used to produce two outputs, such as serving meals and cleaning tables. In this case it is natural to exploit the assumption of constant returns to scale to the activities such that all inputs are equal to one. Upon this rescaling firms differ in their outputs only and we may plot a scatter diagram in *output* space, as depicted in Figure 2.

In output space the most efficient firms are on the North-Eastern frontier. We envelop the data again, but now from above. If firm 1 were to divide its input between the techniques employed by firms 2 and 3, it could produce their average output, which is represented by the midpoint. This way firm 2 can expand its output by some 20%. The precise output expansion figure is 22%. Figure 2 also shows that firm 5 can produce more by adopting the techniques of firms 3 and 4.

Having developed some intuition what is going on when we calculate wasted inputs, we now proceed with our formal analysis, to pave the way for the determination of the accounting prices, a key tool in the economic analysis. Accounting prices are associated with constraints. Now linear program (1) features $k + l$ ordinary constraints (k for the inputs and l for the outputs) plus I nonnegativity constraints (for the intensities with which the activities are run). Constraints are characterized by the coefficients of the variables. The variables in program (1) are the intensities $\theta_1, \ldots, \theta_I$ *and* expansion factor e. Mind that the input and output quantities are *no* variables, but given, fixed data. Formally, they are *coefficients* and, in case of the inputs $(x_1^i, \ldots, x_k^i)$, *bounds*.

Multiplying through the output constraints in (1) by -1, to write them in standard linear programming format (with an $\leq$-sign), the coefficients in the input constraints are $(x_1^1 \ldots x_1^I\ 0), \ldots, (x_k^1 \ldots x_k^I\ 0)$ and the coefficients in the output constraints are $(-y_1^1 \ldots -y_1^I\ y_1^1), \ldots, (-y_l^1 \ldots -y_l^I\ y_l^1)$, where the last components reflect the right hand sides of the second line of inequalities in program (12). These right hand side output terms are products of outputs (coefficients) and the expansion variable. They are *not* bounds! The output constraints have no bounds; formally they are zero. The objective functions coefficients of the variables ($\theta_1, \ldots, \theta_I$ and e) are $(0\ \ldots\ 0\ 1)$, since the intensities θ are tools and only the last variable feeds the objective function. This sums up the formal structure of benchmarking program (1) and we are ready to invoke the accounting prices.

It is customary to denote the accounting prices of the inputs by $w_1, \ldots, w_k$ and of the outputs by $p_1, \ldots, p_l$. Thus, the dual equation becomes:

$$\begin{aligned}
0 &\leq w_1x_1^1 + \cdots + w_kx_k^1 - p_1y_1^1 - \cdots - p_ly_l^1; \quad \ldots; \\
0 &\leq w_1x_1^I + \cdots + w_kx_k^I - p_1y_1^I - \cdots - p_ly_l^I; \\
1 &\leq p_1y_1^i + \cdots + p_ly_l^i; \quad w_1, \ldots, w_k \geq 0, p_1, \ldots, p_l \geq 0
\end{aligned} \tag{2}$$

One of the inequalities in (2) is in fact an equality, as I will argue now. The optimal value of expansion factor e is *at least one*, as is seen by the following choice of the intensity variables: $\theta_1 = 1$ and $\theta_2 = \ldots = \theta_I = 0$; this amounts to a simple reproduction of firm i itself. Hence the nonnegativity constraint for the last variable, e, is *non*binding. The phenomenon of complementary slackness yields that the slack in the dual constraint is zero. Since this is the last component in (2), we obtain the following condition:

$$p_1y_1^i + \cdots + p_ly_l^i = 1 \tag{3}$$

Equation (3) is the so called *price normalization* constraint. It resolves arbitrariness in the program that maximizes output, (1), as I will explain now. It has to do with the units of measurements. Imagine that all outputs are in kilograms but would be rescaled in metric pounds. Since there are two metric pounds to the kilogram, this would double all y's. The optimal x's would not be affected, nor the relative accounting prices of either the inputs or the outputs. By equation (3) all the output prices would be halved, precisely as one expects when the unit of measurement is halved. This concludes the explanation of equation (3).

The other components of dual equation (2) read as follows:

$$p_1 y_1^1 + \cdots + p_l y_l^1 \leq w_1 x_1^1 + \cdots + w_k x_k^1; \quad \ldots; \\ p_1 y_1^I + p_l y_l^I \leq w_1 x_1^I + \cdots + w_k x_k^I \tag{4}$$

Dual inequality (4) highlights an important fact: *Accounting prices render all activities unprofitable or zero.* The distinction between negative and zero accounting profits is crucial. It signals which activities are undertaken with positive intensity, in other words which are the benchmarks. It is easy to confirm. By the phenomenon of complementary slackness we know that if an activity is run with positive intensity, $\theta_i^* > 0$, then there is no slack in the dual constraint, $p_1 y_1^i + p_l y_l^i \leq w_1 x_1^i + \cdots + w_k x_k^i$, and, therefore, such activities must break even indeed.

Since accounting prices are shadow prices, we can invoke their marginal productivity interpretation. In the present context an input price measures by how much the output level could be raised if an additional unit of that input were available and an output price measures how much the overall output *level* could be raised if a unit of that output were gifted. The latter argument is subtle, because in benchmarking we fix the proportions of the outputs. Hence, if a unit of some output arrives as a gift, the resources must be slightly reallocated away from the production of this output, producing a little more of the other outputs, in order to preserve the proportions. If a price of an output component is higher, than of some other, it means that one unit releases more productive resources. *Output accounting prices measure their values in terms of* resource costs.

In general accounting prices make some firms *other* than themselves break even. It is extremely interesting to identify them, because they constitute the best available practices. So, focus on the firms for which the associated equations in (4) are binding. It constitutes the set of activities that would be run if the resources available to firm i are used optimally. The definition of efficiency is straightforward.

Compare a firm to its peers in the industry. More precisely, calculate how much more it could produce by solving program (1). Let the expansion factor be e. For example, if $e = 1.1$, it could produce 10% more and, therefore, it produces only $1/e = 0.91$ of its potential output. Hence *efficiency* is simply defined by the inverse value of the expansion factor of benchmarking program (1), $1/e$. Since the expansion factor is at least one, it follows by sheer arithmetic that *efficiency is a measure between zero and one*. Full efficiency ($1/e = 1$) represents the situation where a firm cannot improve its performance, is a leader.

We now use our apparatus to develop a nice alternative expression for efficiency, highlighting the performance of a firm we are interested in. The main tool is the main theorem of linear programming, which equates the value of the objective function with the value of the bounds. In benchmarking the objective function is the expansion factor, e, see program (1). As noted, the value of the bounds in this program is $w_1x_1^1 + \cdots + w_kx_k^1$. Invoking the price normalization constraint, equation (3), we conclude that the expansion factor is equal to the accounting cost/revenue ratio:

$$e = (w_1x_1^i + \cdots + w_kx_k^i)/(p_1y_1^i + \cdots + p_ly_l^i). \tag{5}$$

Formula (5) renders the expansion factor robust with respect to price level changes. For example, halving all prices (as in the transition from kilograms to metric pounds) does not affect expression (5), because halving the numerator *and* the denominator cancel. Formula (5) is important, because it weighs the importance of the inputs and the outputs for efficiency. Obviously, efficiency is increased by reducing inputs or increasing outputs. An input reduction by a unit is more effective if the shadow price is higher and the same holds for an output increase.

Since efficiency has been defined as the inverse of the expansion factor, equation (5) implies

$$\textit{Efficiency} = (p_1y_1^i + \cdots + p_ly_l^i)/(w_1x_1^i + \cdots + w_kx_k^i). \tag{6}$$

In words, the performance of a firm is measured by the *revenue/cost ratio* at accounting prices. Equation (6) admits a frequently used interpretation of efficiency measurement. Imagine the outputs are produced by a hypothetical, efficient firm. In fact the efficient inputs are given by the solution of program (1), $x_1^1\theta_1 + \cdots + x_1^I\theta_I, \ldots, x_k^1\theta_1 + \cdots + x_k^I\theta_I$, if the outputs are inflated by expansion factor e, hence a fraction $1/e$ of these inputs is enough to produce $y_1^1, \ldots, y_l^1$. The efficiency of the hypothetical firm is one. Applying formula (6) to the hypothetical unit, we see that it would break even: revenue equals cost. Here 'cost' is the value of the minimally required inputs to produce the outputs, $y_1^1, \ldots, y_l^1$. Substituting this back in the original formula (6), we conclude the following intuitive, yet powerful statement. *Efficiency is the Cost/Value ratio of inputs*, where 'cost' is the value of the *minimally* required inputs, 'value' refers to the *actual* inputs, and *both* types of inputs are valued at accounting prices.

3. Efficiency, Productivity, and Profitability

We discuss and distinguish some important business concepts which are often confused. An example from the literature is the following quote. Discussing farming enterprises in Finland, Anja Yli-Viikari *et al.* (2002, p. 20) write

> "To guarantee the continuation of the production the enterprises have to be profitable. The prerequisite of the profitability is efficiency."

Now particularly in agriculture there is *no* simple connection between profitability and efficiency. The breakdown of the relationship goes both ways. On one hand, many inefficient farms are quite profitable, because the prices are maintained at artificially high levels. On the other, efficient firms are not necessarily the most profitable ones. While it is true that a prerequisite for maximum profitability is efficiency, cost-cutting is but one way to boost profit. A notorious alternative procedure is the exercise of monopoly power; it deters more efficient firms and creates rents. As J.R. Hicks (1935, p. 8) quipped, "The best of all monopoly profits is a quiet life." In other words, profit need not signal efficiency!

Although there are interrelations between efficiency, productivity and profitability — and we will discuss them — the concepts are fundamentally *different*. I will explain the subtleties by means of a simple example. Consider a single input-single output industry with two firms, a duopoly. Denote the input quantities by x and the output quantities by y. Use w and p for the prices of the input (the labor wage) and the output (the product price), respectively, and use superscripts to indicate to which firm a symbol pertains: firm 1 or firm 2.

In our discussion we must distinguish market prices from accounting prices. Market prices are observed and may vary. Some firms negotiate tighter labor conditions than others; and some firms may have shrewder salesmen, extracting higher prices. A well-cited example is someone who "could sell sand to the Arabs." Indeed, in this situation *any* price above zero represents market power.

Denote market prices by an underscore and reserve the regular symbols for accounting prices. In short, the symbols for firm 1 are input and output *quantities* x^1 and y^1, input and output *market prices* $\underline{w}^1$ and $\underline{p}^1$, and input and output *accounting prices* w^1 and p^1. The symbols for firm 2 are similar, but with superscript1 replaced by superscript 2. The techniques implicit in the firm input-output observations (x^1, y^1) and (x^2, y^2) are given by the output/input ratios y^1/x^1 and y^2/x^2. These numbers give the amount of output one can produce with a unit of input, and, therefore, constitute the *productivities* of the respective firms. The concept of productivity gets a bit more involved in the presence of multiple inputs and outputs, but this issue can wait. In our simple duopoly, let the first firm be the more productive than the second: $y^1/x^1 > y^2/x^2$. (This is an innocent assumption, because we are free to relabel the firms.) Then firm 1 can produce no more than it produces, at least under the assumption that the data represent all conceivable practices of production. Firm 2, however, could perform better by adopting the technology of firm 1. That way it would produce y^1/x^1 units per unit of input and since it commands x^2 inputs, its potential output is $(y^1/x^1)x^2$. By the presumed productivity inequality this exceeds the actually produced quantity y^2.

The expansion factor, e, measures how much firm 2 could produce relative to what it produces; it equals $e = (y^1/x^1)x^2/y^2$. Now, as we have seen in Section 2, efficiency is the inverse expansion factor, measuring the actual output as a fraction of potential output: $1/e = y^2/(y^1/x^1)x^2 = (y^2/x^2)/(y^1/x^1)$. Since firm 1 can do no better than using its own technology, its expansion factor equals 1, and, therefore, its efficiency is also $1 = (y^1/x^1)/(y^1/x^1)$, to present it in the same format as for firm 2. For both firms we thus have the following result. *Efficiency* equals relative productivity. Here productivity is taken relative to the best practice; indeed, firm 1's productivity features in either denominator.

A further, interesting relationship between the concepts of productivity and efficiency is established in a dynamic setting, where we track the measures through time. If we proceed to the next year, all quantities will be different. Let me assume that the changes are slight, so that firm 1 remains the productivity leader. Imagine that firm 2 has become more efficient. What does it mean? That management does a better job, producing more output per input? Not necessarily. Positive efficiency change only means that relative productivity has increased. One way to boost efficiency is indeed to improve productivity, but another comes with stalling leadership. If the industry leader slips in terms of productivity, the followers get closer and formally this shows as positive efficiency change! Think of deteriorating industry conditions. Examples abound. In the mining industry the quality of the ore lessens as time progresses, simply because the easiest available ores are mined first. Conditions may also deteriorate due to demand, particularly when a product approaches the end of its life cycle, with new substitutes taking over. And conditions are influenced by world markets. For example, if a low wage country enters the industry and the incumbents are sluggish in making adjustments, such as reallocations to newly developing economies, costs may press harder on smaller numbers of output.

Conversely, without any change in the firm, its efficiency may change. In fact, in a world of technical progress the best practice productivity increases and since efficiency is productivity relative to the best practice it will go down by the denominator effect if there is *no* change in the inputs or outputs of the firm we analyze. The Dutch proverb *Standstill is decline* is particularly relevant to the concept of efficiency, because the latter is a *relative* concept. The underlying concept of productivity — output per input — is an absolute concept though. There are many physical examples. The fuel "efficiency" concept of miles per gallon is a productivity measure, indicating how much output one gets per unit of input. If, however, the input and output are of the same dimension, as in energy conversion, we are back in the situation where the "best" is a ratio of one (1 Watt of converted energy per Watt of basic energy). Here a ratio equal to one represents the case of no waste, hence full efficiency. Another physical example of a productivity measure is tons harvested (say of rice) per acre. To assess if it signals a good performance, we must know the size relative to the maximum observed magnitude, and *that* is efficiency.

Bring in profitability, a third related concept. In the single input-single output duopoly, with firm 1 more productive ($y^1/x^1 > y^2/x^2$), is firm 1 necessarily more *profitable*? Now we must disentangle a number of issues. First, there is the *size* issue. Firm 1 may enjoy a better margin between revenue and cost per unit of output (because it needs less input) and hence be the more profitable firm per unit of output, but firm 2 may have a bigger market share and hence generate a greater sum of profits. The size effect may outweigh the productivity effect. We correct for it by measuring profit per unit of sales. In other words, instead of profits $\underline{p}y - \underline{w}x$ we compare the profit *rates* $(\underline{p}y - \underline{w}x)/\underline{p}y$.

The second issue is the presence or absence of well functioning markets, both on the input and the output side. If the firms face *common market prices*, both on the input and the output sides, we may compare the profit rate of the more productive firm, which is $(\underline{p}y^1 - \underline{w}x^1)/\underline{p}y^1$, with that of the less productive firm, namely $(\underline{p}y^2 - \underline{w}x^2)/\underline{p}y^2$, and conclude that the former is bigger. The proof of this inequality is easy: The leading terms are equal (namely 1), while the second terms are inverse productivities (x/y) with a common coefficient ($-\underline{w}/\underline{p}$). Inverse productivity is obviously negatively related to productivity, but the minus sign makes the relationship between productivity and profitability per unit sales a positive one.

However — and this takes us to the third issue — the relationship between efficiency and profitability breaks down the moment we drop the single input-single output assumption. Figure 3 provides a simple example.

In Figure 3 three firms each produce one unit of output using two inputs, namely labor and capital. Firm 2 is inefficient, because it can contract its labor and capital inputs to the midpoint of techniques 1 and 3, as explained in Section 2. Then, by dividing its inputs between the techniques 1 and 3, it would produce $1/2+1/2 = 1$ unit of output. However, if capital is very incxpensive, relative to labor, firm 2 will be more profitable than firm 3, simply because it is more economical, using the inexpensive input, capital.

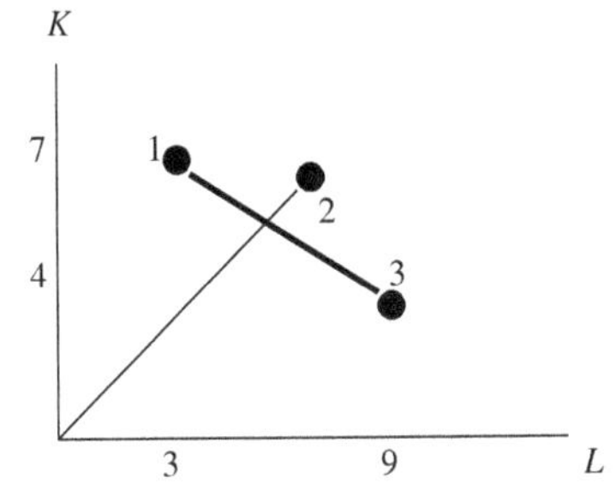

Fig. 3. An industry with two inputs and a single output.

Note: Firms 1 and 3 are efficient. Firm 2 is not. Yet, if labor is very expensive, input combination 3 is more costly than input combination 2.

It makes a difference — even for multi input-multi output industries — if profits are based on accounting prices. It is preferable, because it restores the relationship between efficiency and profit per unit of sales. The key to the analysis is equation (6), which equates efficiency to the revenue/cost ratio at accounting prices. Simple manipulation modifies that equation into the following:

$$\frac{(p_1 y_1^1 + \cdots + p_l y_l^1) - (w_1 x_1^1 + \cdots + w_k x_k^1)}{p_1 y_1^1 + \cdots + p_l y_l^1} = 1 - \mathit{Efficiency}^{-1}. \quad (7)$$

Because the right hand side of equation (7) is positively related to efficiency (as there are two minus signs) we once more have a positive relationship between efficiency and profitability. But be careful. Under accounting prices, fully efficient firms break even and inefficient units operate at a loss. Indeed, if efficiency is one in formula (7), as is the case fully efficient firms, then the right hand side is zero, hence profit must be zero. If the efficiency is less than full, for example 3/4, then the right hand side would be $-1/3$, creating a loss on the left hand side.

It is not difficult to evaluate the expressions numerically and I will illustrate this for the example of Figure 3. Accounting prices can be computed using the zero profit conditions for the efficient firms. In Figure 3 the accounting profit of firm 1 is $1-(3w+7r)$, where w is the wage rate and r the rental rate, while the accounting profit of firm 3 is $1 - (9w + 4r)$.[2] Setting these two profits equal to zero, we obtain two simple equations: $3w + 7r = 1$ and $9w + 4r = 1$. The solution is $w = 1/17$ and $r = 2/17$. These figures can be used to calculate the total cost of firm 2, hence its accounting profit (which will be negative) and efficiency, using formula (7). Let me carry out the calculation. Reading Figure 8, firm 2's inputs are 7 units of labor and 6 of capital, hence its profit is $1-(7/17+6\times 2/17) = 1-\mathit{Efficiency}^{-1}$, using formula (7). Solving, the efficiency of firm 2 amounts 17/19. In general, the numbers are given simply as output by the linear programming routine.

The crucial difference between market prices and accounting prices is that the former are observed and the latter are not. Market prices are exogenous, meaning that they are considered given, as *data*. Accounting prices are endogenous, meaning that they are derived from the data, not from price data, but from input and output data. It is instructive to see the difference in the simple single input-single output duopoly, where firm 1's data are input x^1, output y^1, prices $\underline{w}^1$ and $\underline{p}^1$, and firm 2's data are x^2, y^2, $\underline{w}^2$ and $\underline{p}^2$. Different price normalizations are allowed. If we stick to Section 2, equation (3), it is $py^1 = 1$ and the zero profit condition, $py^1 - wx^1 = 0$, yields $w = py^1/x^1 = 1/x^1$. Instead of the accounting prices $p = 1/y^1$, $w = 1/x^1$ we may use $p = 1$, $w = y^1/x^1$ as the relative prices are the same and that is all what matters. There are two ways to understand this. One is via result (6), equating efficiency with the revenue/cost *ratio*. This measure is clearly insensitive with respect to proportionate price changes. The other is to visualize a change in the scale of measurement. For example, if firm 1 produces 100 kilograms of rice, then the normalization condition $py^1 = 1$ reads $p = 1/100 = 1$ cent per kilogram. Now we *could* choose this as a new currency unit; i.e. the cent instead of the dollar. Then the value of output would not be 1 but 100 cents and the price would be 1 cent or 0.01 only.

The bottom line is that accounting prices must be *derived* from quantity data, in a way such that the most productive firms break even. Profitability implications of performance may be misleading when external, possibly distorted prices are used. For example, if the

[2]Revenue is 1 because of the single output variant of price normalization condition (3), Section 2.

less productive firm, firm 2, commands a lower input price, $\underline{w}^2 < \underline{w}^1$, it may be equally profitable or even more so than firm 1, if the input price discount is strong. The question arises what to do in such a situation. Is it advantageous to stimulate the *productive*, firm 1, or the *profitable*, firm 2? In other words, where should one allocate the industry's resources?

The answer may vary with the setting, but a general observation is in order. *Both* firms would benefit from adopting the most productive technique. In the simple example this would not change a thing to firm 1 (which already is the best practice firm), but it clearly would make firm 2 more profitable. Firm 2 earns a profit of $\underline{p}^2y^2 - \underline{w}^2x^2$, but replacement of output y^2 by potential output $(y^1/x^1)x^2$ would add to the revenue term, hence increase profit. Here we recognize y^1/x^1 as the best-practice productivity. Alternatively, should the market not bear the additional output, the profit could be increased by cutting back input x^2 to what is necessary given the best practice technique, namely $(x^1/y^1)y^2$.[3] Here we recognize x^1/y^1 as the minimal technical coefficient.

The productivity and the technical coefficient are each other's inverse, which is no surprise, because productivity is basically output per unit of input and a technical coefficient is input required per unit of output. The lesson of this example is that to improve performance, one must be on the look for the most *productive* practice, not the most profitable. This is the relevant rule of thumb even if the criterion is profit. In other words, the profit of a firm is enhanced by adopting best practice techniques, not by adopting the most profitable practices. In our duopoly example the adoption of the technique of the most profitable firm (firm 2) would even be detrimental to the profit of firm 1!

This paradoxical relationship between productivity and profitability rests on the following fact: *One may copy techniques, but not prices.* Emerging economies rightly adopt Western production practices in manufacturing and the service sectors, because like everyone they benefit from efficiency. Conversely, these Western plants do not copy their Eastern counterparts, even though they may be

[3]The latter is indeed less than x^2 by assumption that firm 1 is more productive, $y^1/x^1 > y^2/x^2$.

more profitable. The low wages prevailing in China and its Southern neighbors cannot be copied. They are reflections of conditions beyond business control, such as the endowments of nations. If a nation is well endowed with labor relative to other resources such as minerals, local wages will be low. This argument is valid even in the absence of exploitation.

4. Ranking

Ranking is a persuasive management tool that provides a sense of direction and infiltrates all corners of the information society. This section discusses the subtleties that surround this main application of benchmarking. The basic idea is to calculate the efficiencies of firms and to line them up between 0 to 100 percent, but there is a complication. Efficiency is measured by the revenue/cost ratio at accounting prices — see Section 2, equation (6) — but these prices vary across firms. The accounting price of an input measures how much more output could be produced if an extra unit of the input were available. Now if an input is scarce in a firm, it acts as a bottleneck and, therefore, carries a high accounting price. Since the mix of inputs may differ across firms, an input may be relatively scarce somewhere and abundant elsewhere. This is why accounting price vary across units. If the industry is well organized, such differences are leveled. This observation will be clue to the measurement of industrial organization efficiency. The rule of thumb is as follows.

Reallocate the excess resources of less efficient firms to an efficient firm where the accounting price is relatively high.

The rationale of this rule of thumb is that resources are best put to work where they are most productive and *accounting* prices are equal to marginal productivities. Market prices do not have the power to signal where resources are best put to work, simply because they are equal for different firms. On the product side the relationship is the opposite.

Idiosyncratic accounting prices are higher for outputs which are produced relatively abundantly.

This result is perhaps paradoxical, because we tend to associate abundance with low prices. However, large-scale production drains resources and, therefore, is costly indeed. The negative relationship between quantity and price is a property of demand functions, whereas here we analyze the supply side of a firm. Then the relationship is opposite indeed.

Recall that we have firms i with input vectors x^i and output vectors y^i. We calculate the maximally producible output ey^i, given the input x_i and the practices (x^i, y^i), see program (1), where symbol e stands for the expansion factor to be maximized. The dual equation (2) generates the accounting prices of the inputs, $w_1, \ldots, w_k$, and of the outputs, $p_1, \ldots, p_l$. (Here k and l are the numbers of the inputs and the outputs, respectively.) The problem is that these prices are specific to the object we benchmark: firm I, because inputs may be scarce at some firms and abundant at others and outputs may be produced in costly volumes.

In the inequalities of program (1) the intensities $\theta_1, \ldots, \theta_I$ are the variables and the right hand sides are firm specific and prompt the accounting prices to be idiosyncratic. Imagine that we have the power to improve the performance of firms not only by letting them adopt best practices, but also by reallocating their resources. The formal analysis involves the assessment of the overall efficiency of the industry by calculating how much more total output it could produce given its *total* input. Instead of benchmarking firms, we benchmark the entire industry. The benchmarking continues to be done on the same reference group of peers, i.e. on its own firms and *not* on others. This procedure amounts to replacement of the right hand sides of constraints (1) by the *total* industry resources or inputs $x_1, \ldots, x_k$ and (potential) outputs $ey_1, \ldots, ey_k$, where e is the expansion factor, as before. These total figures are defined by the following equations:

$$\begin{aligned} x_1 &= x_1^1 + \cdots + x_1^I, \quad \ldots, \quad x_k = x_k^1 + \cdots + x_k^I, \\ y_1 &= y_1^1 + \cdots + y_1^I, \quad \ldots, \quad y_l = y_l^1 + \cdots + y_l^I. \end{aligned} \tag{8}$$

The overall efficiency of the industry is the inverse of the expansion factor, e, where the latter is the solution to benchmarking program (1) with equation (8) used to modify the right hand sides:

$$\max_{\theta_1,\ldots,\theta_I,e\geq 0} \; e:$$

$$\begin{aligned} &x_1^1\theta_1 + \cdots + x_1^I\theta_I \leq x_1, \quad \ldots, \quad x_k^1\theta_1 + \cdots + x_k^I\theta_I \leq x_k \\ &y_1^1\theta_1 + \cdots + y_1^I\theta_I \geq y_1e, \quad \ldots, \quad y_l^1\theta_1 + \cdots + y_l^I\theta_I \geq y_le \end{aligned} \tag{9}$$

As we did in Section 2 for firm i, associate input and output accounting prices $w_1, \ldots, w_k$ and $p_1, \ldots, p_l$ with benchmarking program (9). The attractive property of these prices is that they measure the marginal productivity of inputs and outputs to the industry as a whole. The accounting prices thus constructed are independent of the firm under consideration.

The resolution of the weighting problem rests on the replacement of firms scarcities and abundances by their overall counterparts. For a single-output industry the accounting prices of a firm with a representative mix of inputs are the ones which reflect the values to the industry as a whole, in the sense of marginal productivities. An analogous observation can be made for a single input-multiple output industry. *The performance weights generated by the benchmarking program of a firm with a representative mix of scores agree with the optimal ones (relevant to the industry as a whole).* There is no need to identify the firm of which the accounting prices can be used to measure and compare the performance of all units. It suffices to solve the industry's benchmarking program, (9). The output contains the shadow prices.

Having settled the issue of weighting performance dimensions, let us now tackle the issue of ranking. We employ the input and output accounting prices $w_1, \ldots, w_k$ and $p_1, \ldots, p_l$ associated with benchmarking program (9). The efficiency of firm i is given by the revenue/cost ratio (6). The weights are independent of the firm! The firms are considered machines which transform inputs into outputs. The outputs are aggregated using the weights $p_1, \ldots, p_l$ and the inputs with the weights $w_1, \ldots, w_k$. Expression (6) measures efficiency as aggregated output per unit of aggregated input. The theory of Section 3 applies, in particular the observation that efficiency is a measure between zero and one. The reason is that the duality analysis — see equation (4) by which the value of the outputs is less than or equal to the value of the inputs — happens to be *independent* of the object that is benchmarked (i.e. firm i in Section 2 or the entire industry in the present Section).

5. Economies of Scale

There are four types of returns to scale, namely constant returns, decreasing returns, increasing returns, and variable returns to scale.

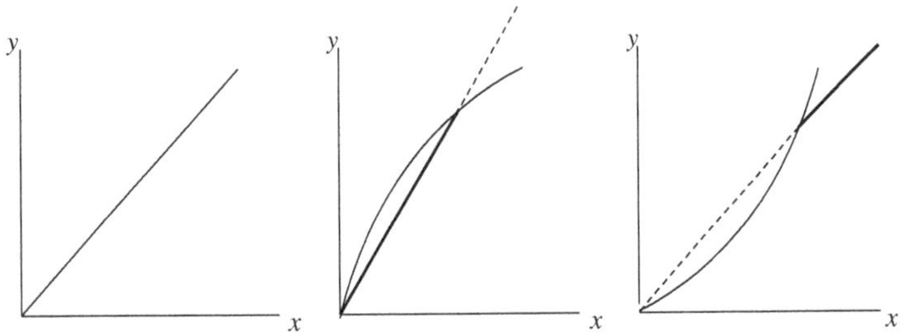

Fig. 4. Constant, decreasing, and increasing returns to scale defined.

Note: In each panel input is along the horizontal axis and output along the vertical. The unbroken lines are below the production function. The thin dashed lines are above the production function and, therefore, not feasible.

The principles are easiest understood for a single input-single output production unit, where the input and output are denoted by x and y, respectively.

In Figure 4 the first panel represents the case of *constant returns to scale.* An increase in the input quantity yields a proportionate increase in the output quantity. The second panel represents the case of *decreasing returns to scale.* Here the returns of additional input are less than proportionate, for example 1% of extra input yields only 0.9% of extra output. The third panel represents the case of *increasing returns to scale*, where the returns become more than proportionate.

If there are constant returns to scale — the left panel — any feasible activity, represented by an input-output combination (x, y) on the graph (or under it, but that would be wasteful) can be run with *any* nonnegative intensity, θ. If (x, y) is feasible, then so are $(\theta x, \theta y)$ with $\theta \geq 0$.[4] In other words, if a point is feasible, then so is *any* other point on the *half-line* through that point and the origin. However, if there are decreasing returns to scale — as in the central panel of Figure 4 — any feasible activity can be run with *lower* intensity only. In other words, if (x, y) is feasible, then so are $(\theta x, \theta y)$ with $0 \leq \theta \leq 1$. If a point is feasible, then so is any other point on the line unbroken *segment* connecting that point with the origin. Finally, if there are increasing returns to scale — as in the right panel

[4]$(\theta x, \theta y)$ can be denoted briefly by $\theta(x, y)$.

Table 2. Returns to scale and feasible intensities.

Returns to scale	Feasible intensities	Geometry	Panel in Figure 1
Constant	$\theta \geq 0$	Half-line	Left
Decreasing	$0 \leq \theta \leq 1$	Line segment	Central
Increasing	$\theta \geq 1$	Outer half-line	Right

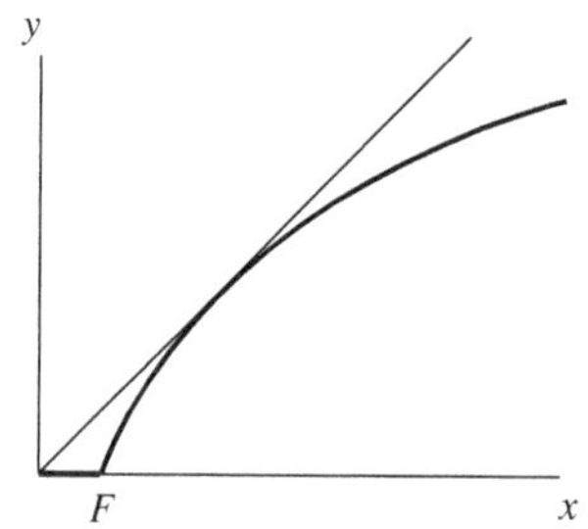

Fig. 5. An S-shaped production function.

Note: Input is along the horizontal axis and output along the vertical. There is a fixed cost (F).

any feasible activity can be run with *higher* intensity only. If (x, y) is feasible, then so are $(\theta x, \theta y)$ with $\theta \geq 1$. In other words, if a point is feasible, then so is any other point on the unbroken *outer half-line* through the point, away from the origin. These observations are summarized in Table 2.

Now let me turn to the case of variable returns. First I review some basic production theory. A flexible form for a production function, is the S-shaped function. It features first increasing and eventually decreasing returns to scale, see Figure 5.

In Figure 5 a minimum quantity of input, F, is required to produce any positive amount of output, however little. This is called the fixed cost or overhead. Now, if output is increased, the fixed cost can be spread among more units and this causes the returns to scale to be initially increasing. The effect peters out though. For big corporations overhead costs — however sizable in an absolute sense — become a small percentage of total cost, and another scale effect sets in, namely that of bottlenecks. Some inputs are just very hard to increase, think of land, and eventually limit output as the variable

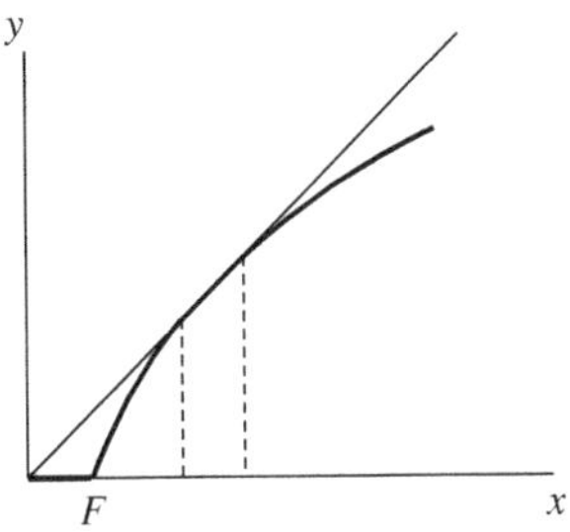

Fig. 6. Another S-shaped production function.

Note: Input is along the horizontal axis and output along the vertical. In the region between the dashed lines productivity is maximal.

inputs are increased. At some intermediate level the two scale effects balance and productivity (output-input ratio y/x) is maximal. This is where the line to the origin is steepest, see the straight line in Figure 5. To the left of this point of tangency the returns to scale are increasing and to the right decreasing. Productivity may be maximal in a *region*, see Figure 6.

With a little imagination one recognizes an S-shape in Figures 5 and 6. Better known is the so-called U-shaped average cost, the other side of the coin. The reason is simple: Average cost is determined by input per unit of output, which is x/y or inverse productivity. Since productivity is initially increasing and eventually decreasing, average cost is initially decreasing and eventually increasing, hence U-shaped. The U-shaped average cost associated with the production function of Figure 6 has a flat bottom.

The S-shaped production function is realistic, because it combines set-up costs with bottleneck effects. It is also flexible, because the point of maximal productivity may be reached when input is arbitrarily small — in which case the returns to scale are decreasing right away — or when input is arbitrarily large — in which case the returns to scale remain increasing for all relevant levels of activity. In other words, the S-shaped production function *encompasses* the cases of decreasing and increasing returns. In this sense it is quite general and it is desirable to have a counterpart in a multi input-multi output framework for efficiency measurement.

The counterpart exists and is called *variable returns to scale*. The model is due to Afriat (1972) and Førsund and Hjalmarsson (1974)

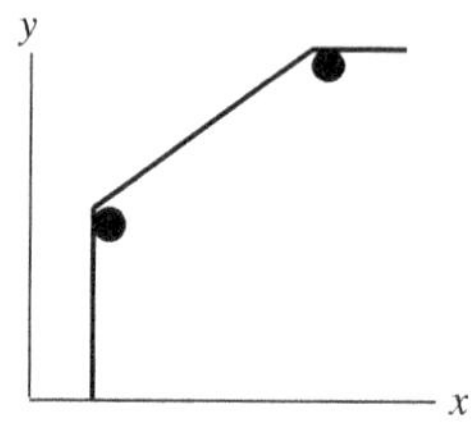

Fig. 7. S-shaped production observed.

Note: Input is along the horizontal axis and output along the vertical. The fixed cost cannot be escaped.

and has been launched in a DEA setting by Färe, Grosskopf and Logan (1983) and Banker, Charnes and Cooper (1984). The idea is that fixed costs cannot be dissolved by running firms, including their inputs, at small intensities. One may combine firms, but the level of operation must remain the same. Formally, *the sum of the intensities must be one*. A simple example illuminates, see Figure 7.

Figure 7 features a small firm (the lower dot) and a big one (the upper dot). It is drawn such that the small firm is more productive (more output per input, the line to the origin is steeper), but that does not matter and could have been the other way round. The tenet of DEA with variable returns is that any weighted average of the observed firms is feasible. These weighted averages are represented by the line segment connecting the two dots. It is assumed that it is impossible to run single activities at lower intensity. If allowed, variable returns to scale would degenerate into decreasing returns to scale. The variable returns to scale model also exclude the possibility to run activities at higher intensities. Doing so would take us back to the case of increasing returns to scale.

An implicit but important assumption of DEA with variable returns to scale is that the hypothetical firm representing inactivity — with zero input and zero output — is ruled out. The reason is simple. If it were allowed, any firm could dissolve its fixed cost by averaging out with the inactivity point (the origin in Figure 7) and this trick would take us back to the small-is-beautiful world of decreasing returns to scale, such as Figure 1, middle panel. The bottom line is that the smallest observed fixed cost is accepted as inescapable.

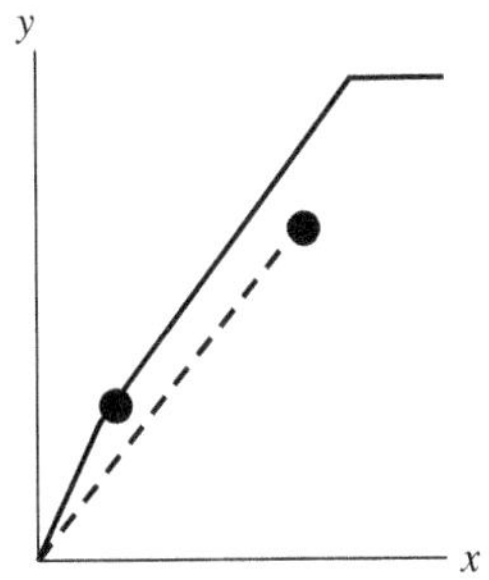

Fig. 8. Same data as Figure 7, but assuming decreasing returns.

Note: Input is along the horizontal axis and output along the vertical. The two points sum to the unidentified.

The relationship between the analysis of returns to scale and data envelopment involves a subtle distinction. The issue can be explained in the context of the simple Figure 7. Perhaps the most natural assumption in this example would be that of decreasing returns to scale, for the small unit has a greater output/input ratio than the big unit. The consequent production function is depicted in Figure 8.

Let me explain Figure 8. Under the assumption of decreasing returns to scale any activity can be run at a lower scale as well. This explains the line segment connecting the origin with the small unit and also the one connecting the origin with the big unit. At small levels of input the maximum level of output is determined by the output/input ratio of the small unit, as it is greater than the output/input ratio of the big unit. Now suppose we command a level of input slightly above the size of the small unit. What is the maximum amount of producible amount? Well, first employ the first unit up to capacity, as it is the more productive. The remaining available inputs are employed in the second unit and increase output beyond the first data point in Figure 8, at a rate determined by the productivity of the second data point, which is the slope of the dashed chord. We translate that chord from the origin to the first data point and thus continue the production.

Figure 7 shows the tricky difference between scale economies in economic theory and DEA. For example, imagine the total input is reduced to the input of the big unit: an accident kills the workers in the small business. Then it would be optimal to relocate workers from the big business to the small business, which is more productive in Figure 8. This would increase output. Hence the output of the big business is not the maximum producible output. In other words, the second data point resides *within* the production possibility frontier and the frontier is *not* the closest envelopment of the data.

Although it is not clear if it is desirable, the discrepancy between returns to scale assumptions and data envelopment can be resolved. If we reason like many free market economists do, we would argue that if the big business could produce more it would produce more and, therefore, it better resides on the production possibility frontier. This mildly dogmatic reasoning can be accommodated by the following modification, which is motivated by the analysis of variable returns to scale. Instead of assuming that *each* firm's intensity is less than unity (Table 1, decreasing returns), assume that the *total* intensity is less than unity: $\theta_1 + \theta_2 \leq 1$. (This is for two units, as in Figure 8. The extension to more units is straightforward.)

In DEA, enveloping the data, output expansion beyond the full utilization of the productive, small business is possible only by simultaneously shrinking the utilization of that same business. This process continues gradually until the next unit is fully utilized and the first, small unit no longer. Hence, the connection between the two data points in Figure 9. The consequent frontier is below the one of ordinary decreasing returns, depicted in Figure 8.

The concept of increasing returns to scale can be modified similarly. Instead of assuming that *each* firm's intensity is greater than unity (Table 2, increasing returns) we assume that the *total* intensity is greater than unity.

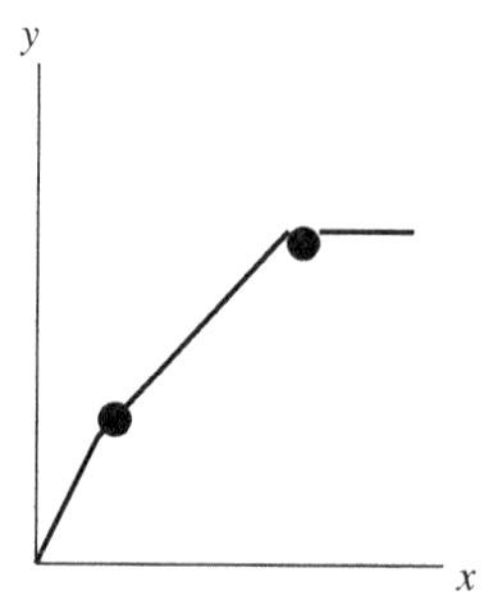

Fig. 9. Enveloping the data of Figure 7 or 8.

Note: Input is along the horizontal axis and output along the vertical.

Table 3. Returns to scale in economics and DEA.

	Feasible intensities		
Returns to scale	Economics	Relationship	DEA
Constant	$\theta_i \geq 0$	=	$\theta_i \geq 0$
Decreasing	$0 \leq \theta_i \leq 1$	<=	$\theta_i \geq 0$ and $\sum \theta_i \leq 1$
Increasing	$\theta_i = 0$ or ≥ 1	=>	$\theta_i \geq 0$ and $\sum \theta_i \geq 1$
Variable	Closed interval	<=	$\theta_i \geq 0$ and $\sum \theta_i = 1$

All the forms of returns to scale we have encountered are applicable to organizations with multiple inputs and outputs. It is a bit messy in the framework of production functions, see, e.g., Baumol (1977), but in the application to benchmarking the analysis becomes pleasantly crisp. The different returns to scale cases can be described by alternative restrictions on the intensities with which best practices are run to assess the potential output of a firm. Table 3 collects the encountered returns to scale cases.

Roughly speaking, Table 3 shows that constant/decreasing/increasing/variable returns to scale are a matter of feasible intensities to be any/below unity/above unity/unity. Here "intensities" are individual intensities in the economics literature and total intensities in the DEA literature. Under constant returns to scale there is full consistency between the two approaches.

Under decreasing returns to scale, there is a one-way consistency. Here DEA feasible intensities are also feasible in the sense of economics. This means that the feasible production possibility set in DEA is smaller than in economics. Hence the DEA frontier will be closer than the economics frontier. *Hence under decreasing returns DEA overestimates efficiency relative to the economic model.*

With increasing returns to scale, there is also consistency, but the other way. Now intensities feasible in the sense of economics are also feasible in the sense of DEA decreasing returns. This means that the feasible production possibility set in DEA is bigger than in economics. Hence the DEA frontier will be farther out than the economics frontier. *Hence under increasing returns DEA underestimates efficiency relative to the economic model.*

Variable returns to scale are locally increasing or decreasing, at least at frontier points. Intensities may increase or decrease, respectively. The feasible set is $[1, \theta_{\max}]$ or $[\theta_{\min}, 1]$, respectively. For non-frontier points it is $[\theta_{\min}, \theta_{\max}]$. It is not possible to specify these intervals without external information. Hence in this paper only the DEA variant of variable returns to scale will be considered. The DEA variant is restrictive. Observations are considered efficient, except when they are dominated by convex combinations of others. *Variable returns to scale in the sense of DEA are an instance of variable returns to scale in the economics sense.*

Following our discussion, summarized in Table 3, we can limit the intensities of activities. This amounts to the addition of alternative constraints to program (1). In the case of *decreasing* returns to scale the condition that an intensity of a benchmark (or the sum of these intensities if we take the DEA tack) must be between 0 and 1 automatically includes the possibility of ignoring bad examples (by setting their intensities equal to corner value zero). This straightforward extension preserves the linearity of program (1). *Increasing* returns to scale, however, includes the possibility $\theta = 0$ as a distinct event, creating a nonconvexity. Under *variable* returns to scale this complication is happily dissolved again. The set of admissible intensities is defined by the simple summing up condition given in Table 3, which admits smooth transitions between potential benchmarks. The variable returns to scale model also inherits the property of S-shaped production function that it encompasses the cases of decreasing and increasing returns. Related to this flexibility is the better fit to the data. As there is empirical support for S-shaped production functions (or U-shaped average costs), the variable returns to scale model of benchmarking outperforms its counterparts. The variable returns to scale model can be used to locate firms, placing them in the initial region of increasing returns, the intermediate efficient region of constant returns, or the eventual region of decreasing returns.

6. Alternative Efficiency Measures

In the *decreasing returns to scale* model we add the *capacity* constraints, $\theta_1, \ldots, \theta_I \leq 1$ (the economics approach) or $\theta_1 + \cdots + \theta_I \leq 1$ (DEA). Denoting the shadow prices of the separate capacity constraints by $\tau_1, \dots, \tau_I \geq 0$, the dual constraints associated with the intensity variables become:

$$py^1 \leq wx^1 + \tau_1, \quad \dots, \quad py^I \leq wx^I + \tau_I \tag{10}$$

The dual constraint associated with the final variable (e) is the price normalization constraint (3). If the constraints are pooled (the DEA approach) we have *commonality* of the shadow prices, $\tau_1 = \dots = \tau_I$. In either case the difference with the basic model is that decreasing returns to scale generate *profits*. The profits are determined by the shadow prices of the intensity constraints ($\theta_1, \dots, \theta_I \leq 1$).

By the phenomenon of complementary slackness positive profit implies that the unitary intensity constraint must be binding. This implies that its nonnegativity constraint is not binding. This implies — once more invoking complementary slackness — that there is no slack in the shadow prices of the nonnegativity constraints. By the theory of linear programming this means that the inequality for such a firm in equation (10) reduces to an equality. In short, profit $\tau_i > 0$ implies equality for unit i in (10). Conversely — the logical negation of the last sentence — inequality for a unit in (10) must yield no profit, $\tau_i = 0$. Incorporating these insights, equation (10) may be rewritten as follows:

$$py^j = wx^j + \tau_j \text{ or } py^j < wx^j \tag{11}$$

The left hand side of equation (11) are the benchmarks for the decision unit we assess. On the right hand side are units which have positive shadow prices of their nonnegativity constraints. By the phenomenon of complementary slackness these units have binding nonnegativity constraints, hence are inactive and, therefore, constitute no benchmark.[5]

Efficiency is the inverse of the expansion factor, e. By the main theorem of linear programming e is the value of the bounds in program (1) and the added constraint from Table 3. The former is x^i, applied to the inputs. The latter are 1, applied to the intensities (individual in the economic frame or total in DEA).

[5]It is possible that $\tau_j = 0$ in equation (11). This corresponds to a benchmark for which neither the nonnegativity constraint (as signaled by the equality) nor the capacity constraint (as signaled by the zero value of its shadow price, τ_j) is binding, i.e. the unit is hovering at partial capacity: $0 < \theta_j < 1$.

Hence $e = wx^i + \tau_1 + \cdots + \tau_I$, or, invoking price normalization constraint (3),

$$Efficiency = py^i/(wx^i + \tau_1 + \cdots + \tau_I) \qquad (12)$$

Remark on formula (12). In the DEA variant profit $\tau_1 + \cdots + \tau_I$ is replaced by just the single (common) profit. Since this profit depends on the unit we benchmark, i, I denote it by τ^i. This confirms Table 3 and the ensuing discussion by which the DEA efficiency level is greater. Also, if the unit is its own benchmark, the left hand side holds in equation (11), or $py^i = wx^i + \tau^i$, so that $Efficiency = py^i/(wx^i + \tau^i) = 1$, as should be.

In the *increasing returns to scale* model, the benchmarks can be determined in a similar way, albeit that we must now consider the many discrete possibilities mentioned before. Suppose we have done this and let $\underline{I}$ be the subset of *active* units j in program (1) (augmented with an increasing returns condition of Table 3), for which θ_j are positive. The other, *inactive*, units do not contribute to the determination of the maximal producible output and, therefore, maybe ignored. I relabel the units such that the active ones are listed up front, $i = 1, \ldots, \underline{I}$. The inactive units are $i = \underline{I} + 1, \ldots, I$. It follows that program (1) may be replaced by,

$$\max_{\theta_1,\ldots,\theta_{\underline{I}} \geq 1, e} e : x^1\theta_1 + \cdots + x^{\underline{I}}\theta_{\underline{I}} \leq x^i, y^1\theta_1 + \cdots + y^{\underline{I}}\theta_{\underline{I}} \geq y^i e \qquad (13)$$

Program (13) modifies program (1) in two ways: the value of the lower bounds, 0, becomes 1, and the replacement I becomes $\underline{I}$. Hence the dual equation is the same as in the basic case, (10) without τ's, and with $\underline{I}$ instead of I:

$$py^1 \leq wx^1, \quad \ldots, \quad py^{\underline{I}} \leq wx^{\underline{I}} \qquad (14)$$

If an inequality in (14) is strict (<), the slack is positive. Since the slack is the shadow price of the ≥ 1 constraint, the intensity equals 1 (by the phenomenon of complementary slackness). By the main theorem of linear programming e is the value of the bound in program (1), x^i, and the added constraint from Table 3, number(s) 1 (individual in the economic framework or total in DEA). The added constraint is flipped compared to the decreasing returns case. Hence the shadow prices are $\tau_1, \ldots, \tau_I \leq 0$: profits turn *losses*. With this modification, *efficiency formula* (12) *and the remark on the latter remain valid.*

Last but not least, let me address the case of *variable returns to scale.* The analysis follows the decreasing returns to scale case, with two tricks added. The first trick is that we now add a *single* capacity constraint to the basic model: $\theta_1 + \cdots + \theta_I = 1$. I denote the shadow price of this constraint by τ. Since the constraint is an equality, this shadow price is now *unsigned* and dual constraint (10) becomes as follows:

$$py^1 \leq wx^1 + \tau, \quad \ldots, \quad py^I \leq wx^I + \tau \tag{15}$$

The main difference of equation (15) compared to the basic model is that with variable returns to scale accounting prices admit profits *or* losses. Moreover, compared to the case of decreasing returns the accounting prices are now such that the profit is uniform across the benchmarks. Efficiency remains given by the DEA variant of equation (12), with $\tau_1 + \cdots + \tau_I$ replaced by τ^i (see the remark):

$$\textit{Efficiency} = py^i/(wx^i + \tau^i) \tag{16}$$

The variable returns to scale model seems the most popular benchmarking tool. It envelops the data closely, hence reduces the estimates of inefficiency, because the latter is measured by the gap between an observation and the frontier representing potential output. This reduction is considered not bad, because it offsets a shortcoming of DEA, namely its tendency to overestimate inefficiency.[6]

Scale returns may vary by nature (constant/decreasing/increasing/variable) and by frame of reference (economic/DEA). The alternatives are represented by alternative constraints on the feasible intensities (Table 3). These translate in alternative shadow prices. In view of the (non)convexity of the different cases it is perhaps surprising that a single efficiency formula, (12), applies to *all.* The profits are nonnegative (decreasing returns), nonpositive (increasing returns), or

[6]The problem is that DEA is sensitive with respect to errors of measurement, particularly of best practice observations. Overstatement of output or understatement of input may falsely identify decision making units as benchmarks and, as a consequence, throw back the other decision making units. The latter are thus suggested being relatively inefficient, but it is a fluke in the data.

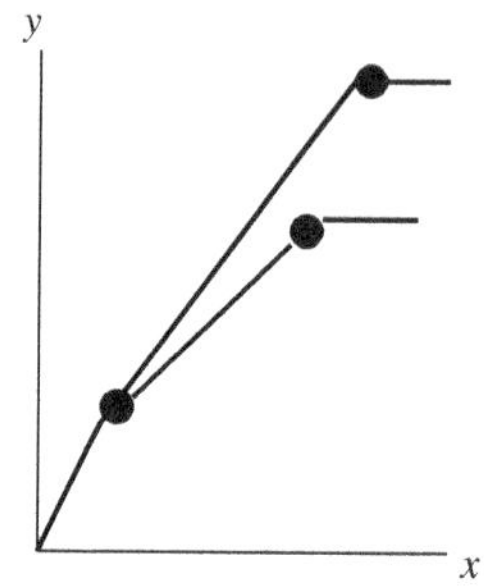

Fig. 10. Same data as Figure 8, total input/total output added.

Note: Input is along the horizontal axis and output along the vertical.

either (variable returns). Moreover, the profits are firm specific in the economics framework and uniform in DEA.

A central concept in industrial organization is the industry production function. The concept is best introduced for a single-input/single-output industry. Let the production function be F. Examples are depicted in Figure 1. With I firms the producible output is $y = F_I(x) = \max F(x^1) + \cdots + F(x^I)$ subject to $x^1 + \cdots + x^I = x$. With free entry (and exit) the industry production function is defined by $y = \max_I F_I(x)$.

With *constant* returns to scale the number of firms is irrelevant and the program that defines the potential output of the firm, (1), also specifies the industry output.

Ever since McKenzie (1959) it is known that if the production function features *decreasing* returns to scale, the free entry industry production function has constant returns to scale, with the optimal $I = \infty$. Because of this incompatibility it is common to preserve the number of firms, I. Let us return to the example of two firms (discussed in section 3). Combining Figures 8 and 9 and adding the total input/total output bundle, we get Figure 10.

What is the value of the industry production function at the level of total input? Well, it depends on the framework. The upper graph represents the economics production function and the lower graph the DEA production function or envelop. To determine the value of the industry production function, in either case we may reallocate the inputs of the two firms, given by x^1 and x^2, to $x^{1'}$ and $x^{2'}$, respectively, such that total input is preserved — $x^{1'} + x^{2'} = x^1 + x^2$ — and apply program (1) to each part, $x^{1'}$ and $x^{2'}$. The 'new' firm, now commanding $x^{1'}$, runs the activities (represented by the two firms) with intensities θ_1^1, θ_2^1. The new firm now commanding $x^{2'}$ runs the activities with intensities θ_1^2, θ_2^2. By linearity, this is equivalent to running the two activities with intensities $\theta_1^1 + \theta_1^2, \theta_2^1 + \theta_2^2$. Call these θ_1, θ_2. The question of feasibility (not using more than total input) can be addressed by transforming the intensity constraints defining alternative returns to scale (on the superscripted θ's) from the level of the firms to the level of the industry (the non-superscripted θ's).

In *DEA* the decreasing returns to scale constraints are $\theta_1^1 + \theta_2^1 \leq 1$ and $\theta_1^2 + \theta_2^2 \leq 1$. The *industry constraint* becomes $\theta_1 + \theta_2 \leq 2 = I$. Put numbers on Figure 10, say inputs 1 and 3 and outputs 2 and 4, respectively. Consider a departure from the observed intensities, $\theta_1 = \theta_2 = 1$, to say $\theta_1 = 1.1$, $\theta_2 = 0.9$. The inputs change by $0.1 - 0.1 \times 3$, which is feasible. The outputs change by $0.2 - 0.4$, which is suboptimal. We may also consider a contraction of θ_1, but the released input will be less productive in the other activity. Hence $\theta_1 = \theta_2 = 1$ determines the value of the 2 firms industry production function under decreasing returns to scale of the DEA variety.

In the *economics* approach the returns to scale constraints are θ_1^1, $\theta_2^1 \leq 1$ and θ_1^2, $\theta_2^2 \leq 1$. The *industry constraint* becomes θ_1, $\theta_2 \leq 2 = I$. In Figure 9 it is optimal to maximize the small, more productive process: $\theta_1 = 2$. The residual input (net of the endowments), $1 + 3 - 2 \times 1 = 2$, determines the activity level of the other process, hence $\theta_2 = 2/3$.

One rule holds for either decreasing returns to scale approach (see Table 3): *The transition to the industry production function is achieved by replacement of 1 by I as the intensity constraint.* This procedure reflects the pooling of the inputs — $x^{1'} + x^{2'} = x^1 + x^2$.

The case of *increasing* returns to scale is also defined by separate intensity constraints (economics) or a pooled one (DEA). The difference is that the inequalities are flipped from $\leq$ to ≥ 1. Hence *the same procedure holds for increasing returns to scale.*

As defended in section 3, of *variable* returns to scale only the DEA variant is considered. It is defined by the condition that for each firm activity intensities sum to unity. Repeating the reallocation argument introduced in our discussion of decreasing returns, this translates into the condition that intensities sum to the number of firms. Hence *the same procedure holds for variable returns to scale.*

The final step is to allow for free entry, varying the number of firms. This is problematic, particularly when there are variable returns to scale. The problem is well-known for single input-single output industries with an S-shaped production function, which translates into U-shaped average costs. Output is maximized when firms minimize unit costs. The optimal number of firms is output divided by the output produced at minimum unit cost, but this number need not be an integer. This integer problem diminishes as the optimal number becomes large, and even disappears completely at some point if average costs are flat-bottomed (minimized at an interval of outputs instead of a single one). There are bounds for the magnitude of this problem, and they may be reestablished in the present DEA context. If the problem is ignored, admitting real values of the number of firms, I, it can be shown that the industry intensity constraints reduce to nonnegativity constraints, even in all three cases of scale economies. If the problem is not ignored, the optimal integer number of firms must be determined, for every total input/total output combination, by solving the following variable returns to scale industry program for every integer number of firms, I'.

$$\begin{aligned} &\max_{\theta_1,\ldots,\theta_I \geq 0, \theta_1+\cdots+\theta_I = I', e} e : \\ &x^1\theta_1 + \cdots + x^I\theta_I \leq x^1 + \cdots + x^I, y^1\theta_1 + \cdots + y^I\theta_I \\ &\quad \geq (y^1 + \cdots + y^I)e \end{aligned} \tag{17}$$

The difference vis-à-vis the efficiency program for a firm is in the coefficient of the expansion factor, e, and in the input and intensity bounds. That coefficient change merely affects the dual price normalization constraint. The bounds changes merely affect the value of the primal or dual program. Dual constraint (15) is not changed. Efficiency equation (16) becomes equation (18).

$$\textit{Efficiency} = p(y^1 + \cdots + y^I)/[w(x^1 + \cdots + x^I) + \tau I] \tag{18}$$

If the integer problem is not important, $\tau = 0$ in equation (18).

7. Firms and Industrial Organization Efficiencies

We have seen how the measurement of efficiency can be transplanted from the firm to the industry, under alternative returns to scale assumptions. The industry efficiency, (18), is less than the market share weighted harmonic mean of the firm efficiencies, (16), and the ratio of the two is the efficiency of the industrial organization, as will be detailed in this section. Point of departure is industry program (9). Potential output is determined by not only letting firms adopt best practices, but also by relocating resources between them. In other words, potential industry output exceeds the sum of the potential firm outputs. Since the gap between observed output and potential output measures inefficiency, it follows that the efficiency of the industry is less than what one would expect on the basis of the firm efficiencies. More precisely, ten Raa (2010) has shown that $1/e \leq 1/(s^1e^1 + \cdots + s^Ie^I)$, where s^i are the market shares of the firms, $py^i/p(y^1 + \cdots + y^I)$, evaluated at the shadow prices of program (9) (the Lagrange multipliers of the output constraints). The right hand side of this inequality is the harmonic mean of the firm efficiencies, $1/e^1, \ldots, 1/e^I$. If, for example, the harmonic mean of the firm efficiencies is 80%, but the industry efficiency is 60%, the allocation of the resources between the firms is such that full firm efficiency attains only $60/80 = 75\%$ of full industry efficiency and we say that the efficiency of the industrial organization is 75%. Formally, *industrial organization efficiency* is defined by the ratio of industry efficiency to mean firm efficiency: $\varepsilon^{IO} = (s^1e^1 + \cdots + s^Ie^I)/e$.

Full efficiency of an industry requires that all firms are efficient and that the industrial organization is efficient. Ten Raa (2010) has shown that a necessary and sufficient condition is that the industrial organization is supportable (Sharkey and Telser, 1978), meaning invulnerable to entry. This one expects in a contestable market (Baumol, Panzar and Willig, 1982).

An immediate consequence of the definition of industrial organization efficiency is that industry efficiency is the product of mean firm efficiency and industrial organization efficiency.

We commingle efficiency change and technical change into productivity growth and bring in industrial organization change. For a solid conceptual foundation consider the structure of an efficiency program. Efficiency is the inverse expansion factor, $\varepsilon = 1/e$. It is a function of the parameters in the efficiency program, such as (1). The right hand sides of the constraints feature the inputs and outputs of the unit of which the efficiency is assessed, (x^i, y^i). The left hand sides feature the inputs and outputs of all firms, which we write formally by (X, Y), where X is the matrix of all inputs (across firms), and Y the matrix of all outputs.

The efficiency of firm i is a function of its (own) input/output vectors and of the family of all these vectors (representing the industry): $\varepsilon^i = 1/e^i = f((x^i, y^i), (X, Y))$, where function f summarizes the efficiency program, presenting the inverse of the expansion factor as a function of the program parameters. The data, $((x^i, y^i), (X, Y))$, are a function of time and, therefore, so is efficiency. *Efficiency change* is defined by the percentage expression $EC = (d\varepsilon^i/dt)/\varepsilon^i$. Total differentiation of efficiency function f yields the following equation:

$$EC = \left(\frac{\partial f}{\partial x^i}\frac{\partial x^i}{\partial t} + \frac{\partial f}{\partial y^i}\frac{\partial y^i}{\partial t}\right)/f + \left(\frac{\partial f}{\partial X}\frac{\partial X}{\partial t} + \frac{\partial f}{\partial Y}\frac{\partial Y}{\partial t}\right)/f \quad (19)$$

The first term on the right hand side of equation (19) measures the contribution of the firm, (x^i, y^i), by contracting its inputs or expanding its outputs, in short by improving its output/input ratio. Hence this term defines *productivity growth*, $PG = (\frac{\partial f}{\partial x^i}\frac{\partial x^i}{\partial t} + \frac{\partial f}{\partial y^i}\frac{\partial y^i}{\partial t})/f$. In the second term on the right hand side of equation (19) the firm data are fixed, but the environment changes. Now we must reason carefully. If there is technical progress, the efficiency of the firm will be *lower* in the next point of time, as its potential output will be greater under the new technology. Hence the effect of the second argument measures *technical change*, but with a minus sign: $T = -(\frac{\partial f}{\partial X}\frac{\partial X}{\partial t} + \frac{\partial f}{\partial Y}\frac{\partial Y}{\partial t})/f$. If we rearrange the terms in equation (19), we conclude that $PG = EC + TC$: *productivity growth is the sum of efficiency change and technical change.*

All these concepts have discrete time variants, of which Malmquist indices have attractive theoretical properties. For productivity growth the derivation is as follows. Since the derivative of $\ln f$ is $1/f$, $PG = \frac{\partial \ln f}{\partial x^i}\frac{\partial x^i}{\partial t} + \frac{\partial \ln f}{\partial y^i}\frac{\partial y^i}{\partial t}$, which in turn may be approximated by $\ln f(x^i_{t+1}, y^i_{t+1}, \cdot, \cdot) - \ln f(x^i_t, y^i_t, \cdot, \cdot) = \ln \frac{f(x^i_{t+1}, y^i_{t+1}, \cdot, \cdot)}{f(x^i_t, y^i_t, \cdot, \cdot)}$.

(Subscripts t and $t+1$ represents points in time, not components.) The dots represent the environment, (X,Y); evaluating it in times t and $t+1$ and taking the average, $PG = \ln\sqrt{\frac{f(x^i_{t+1},y^i_{t+1},X_t,Y_t)}{f(x^i_t,y^i_t,X_t,Y_t)}\frac{f(x^i_{t+1},y^i_{t+1},X_{t+1},Y_{t+1})}{f(x^i_t,y^i_t,X_{t+1},Y_{t+1})}}$, which can be approximated by $\sqrt{\frac{f(x^i_{t+1},y^i_{t+1},X_t,Y_t)}{f(x^i_t,y^i_t,X_t,Y_t)}\frac{f(x^i_{t+1},y^i_{t+1},X_{t+1},Y_{t+1})}{f(x^i_t,y^i_t,X_{t+1},Y_{t+1})}} - 1$. It is tradition not to subtract the one, so a *Malmquist productivity index* is simply defined by the geometric mean of productivity growth rates measured against the backdrops of times t and $t+1$, $M_t = \sqrt{\frac{f(x^i_{t+1},y^i_{t+1},X_t,Y_t)}{f(x^i_t,y^i_t,X_t,Y_t)}\frac{f(x^i_{t+1},y^i_{t+1},X_{t+1},Y_{t+1})}{f(x^i_t,y^i_t,X_{t+1},Y_{t+1})}}$, and a Malmquist index of say 1.02 thus represents 2% growth. To evaluate a Malmquist productivity index one must determine four values of function f, hence solve four linear programs.

If we apply this analysis to an industry instead of a firm i, we trace the effects in $\varepsilon = f((x,y),(X,Y))$ and get the same decomposition, but since industry efficiency change is the product of mean firm efficiency and industrial organization efficiency, we obtain that *industry productivity growth equals industrial organization efficiency change plus mean firm efficiency change plus technical change.* Ten Raa (2010) details the straightforward but tedious decomposition, with the result $M_t = \frac{\varepsilon^{IO}_{t+1}}{\varepsilon^{IO}_t} \cdot \frac{\sum s^i_t/f((x^i_t,y^i_t),(X_t,Y_t))}{\sum s^i_{t+1}/f((x^i_{t+1},y^i_{t+1}),(X_{t+1},Y_{t+1}))} \cdot \sqrt{\frac{f((x_t,y_t),(X_t,Y_t))}{f((x_t,y_t),(X_{t+1},Y_{t+1}))} \cdot \frac{f((x_{t+1},y_{t+1}),(X_t,Y_t))}{f((x_{t+1},y_{t+1}),(X_{t+1},Y_{t+1}))}}$. Symbols without superscripts represent industry totals, summed inputs or outputs, with all summations over firms $i = 1,\ldots,I$. The first quotient is the index for industrial organization efficiency change, the second for mean firm efficiency change, and the third for technical change.

So far we have remained silent about entry and exit; the number of firms, I, has been constant. The idea that industry efficiency is a combination of firm efficiencies and organization efficiency is an aggregation result for firms that can be extended to groups of firms. Entry can be modeled as an extension of the number of firms and exit as the transition to dormant, $x^i = 0$, $y^i = 0$. The number of firms becomes $I + E$, where the first term represents the incumbents and the second the entrants. We now have that industry efficiency is less than the harmonic means of the incumbent and entrant efficiencies, $\varepsilon = 1/e = f((x^I + x^E, y^I + y^E),(x,y)) \leq 1/[s^I/f((x^I,y^I),(X,Y)) + s^E/f((x^E,y^E),(X,Y))] = 1/(s^I/\varepsilon^I + s^E/\varepsilon^E)$, where s are the market shares of total incumbent output y^I and total entrant output y^E (both evaluated at the shadow of the industry efficiency program) and x^I and x^E represent total incumbent input and total entrant input. The relative gap, $\varepsilon^E = f((x^I + x^E, y^I + y^E),(X,Y))[s^I/f((x^I,y^I),(X,Y)) + s^E/f((x^E,y^E),(X,Y))]$, measures *entry efficiency*. We now have that *industry productivity growth equals entry efficiency plus mean incumbent and entrant efficiency change plus technical change*: $M_t = \varepsilon^E_{t+1} \cdot \frac{\sum s^i_t/f((x^i_t,y^i_t),(X_t,Y_t))}{\sum s^i_{t+1}/f((x^i_{t+1},y^i_{t+1}),(X_{t+1},Y_{t+1}))} \cdot \sqrt{\frac{f((x_t,y_t),(X_t,Y_t))}{f((x_t,y_t),(X_{t+1},Y_{t+1}))} \cdot \frac{f((x_{t+1},y_{t+1}),(X_t,Y_t))}{f((x_{t+1},y_{t+1}),(X_{t+1},Y_{t+1}))}}$. It is possible to further disentangle the middle factor, representing mean incumbent and entrant efficiency change, in individual firm effects and intra-organization effects (of the incumbents and of the entrants), but I leave that for future work.

8. Conclusion

In this paper we have shown that a simple linear program that can be used to measure the efficiency of a firm relative to the industry it belongs to can be applied to the industry as a whole and that the solution decomposes the efficiency of the industry in firm effects and an industrial organization effect. The simple linear programming technique can even be extended to dynamic analysis and then encompasses the measurement of productivity growth and the contributions of a better industrial organization and entry and exit.

Acknowledgments

I am grateful to editor Subhash Ray for numerous comments and suggesting to let the static efficiency model encompass productivity growth analysis.

References

Afriat, S. N. (1972). Efficiency estimation of production functions. *International Economic Review*, **13**, 568–598.

Banker, R. D., A. Charnes, and W. W. Cooper. (1984). Some models for estimating technical and scale inefficiencies in data envelopment analysis. *Management Science*, **30**, 1078–1092.

Baumol, W. J. (1977). On the proper cost tests for natural monopoly in a multiproduct industry. *The American Economic Review*, **67**, 809–822.

Baumol, W. J., J. C. Panzar and R. D. Willig. (1982). *Contestable Markets and the Theory of Industry Structure*, New York: Harcourt Brace Jovanovich.

Färe, R., S. Grosskopf and J. Logan. (1983). The relative efficiency of illinois electric utilities. *Resources and Energy*, **5**, 349–367.

Førsund, F. R. and L. Hjalmarsson. (1974). On the measurement of productive efficiency. *The Swedish Journal of Economics*, **76**, 141–154.

Francis, G., I. Humphreys and J. Fry. (2005). The nature and prevalence of the use of performance measurement techniques by airlines. *Journal of Air Transport Management*, **11**, 207–217.

Hicks, J. R. (1935). Annual survey of economic theory: The theory of monopoly. *Econometrica*, **3**, 1–20.

McKenzie, L. W. (1959). On the existence of general equilibrium for a competitive market. *Econometrica*, **27**, 54–71.

ten Raa, Th. (2010). Benchmarking and industry performance, *Journal of Productivity Analysis* **36**, 3, 285–292 (2011).

Sharkey, W. W. and L. G. Telser. (1978). Supportable cost functions for the multiproduct firm. *Journal of Economic Theory*, **18**, 23–27.

Yli-Viikari, A., H. Risku-Norja, V. Nuutinen, E. Heinonen, R. Hietala-Koivu, E. Huusela-Veistola, T. Hyvönen, J. Kantanen, S. Raussi, P. Rikkonen, A. Seppälä and E. Vehmasto. (2002). Agri-environmental and rural development indicators: A proposal. Agrifood Research Reports 5, MAA Agrifood Research Finland.

Chapter 9

Monopoly, Pareto and Ramsey Mark-ups*

Thijs ten Raa

Department of Economics, Tilburg University, Tilburg, The Netherlands

tenraa@uvt.nl

Abstract. Monopoly prices are too high. It is a price level problem, in the sense that the relative mark-ups have Ramsey optimal proportions, at least for independent constant elasticity demands. I show that this feature of monopoly prices breaks down the moment one demand is replaced by the textbook linear demand or, even within the constant elasticity framework, dependence is introduced. The analysis provides a single Generalized Inverse Elasticity Rule for the problems of monopoly, Pareto and Ramsey.

Keywords: Monopoly Prices, Ramsey Prices, Inverse Elasticity Rules

JEL-codes: D40, D60, L50

1. Introduction

Monopoly prices are too high. It is a price level problem, in the sense that the relative markups have Ramsey optimal proportions, at least for independent constant elasticity demands. By the same

*Reprinted from *Journal of Industry, Competition and Trade*, **9**, 57–63, 2009, with permission from Springer Nature.

token, Ramsey pricing is considered business oriented (Laffont and Tirole, 2000, p. 63). This attractive feature of monopoly prices breaks down for variable elasticity's. The reason is that both monopoly prices and Ramsey prices are governed by local inverse elasticity rules, but if the elasticity's differ at the (low) monopoly output and the (high) Ramsey output, the mark-ups will differ as well. Hoeffler (2006) illustrates this phenomenon using a kinked demand curve. The break-down of the optimality of relative monopoly mark-ups already occurs once a constant-elasticity demand is replaced by the textbook linear demand. And worse — remaining within the framework of constant elasticity's — the break-down also occurs the moment dependence is introduced. Our counterexamples are strong: even the *orders* of monopoly and Ramsey price components differ! These negative results follow a novel, unifying framework, featuring a Generalized Inverse Elasticity Rule for alternative pricing rules. Hitherto Ramsey rules have been less transparent for interdependent demands (Mohring, 1970).

2. Monopoly, Pareto and Ramsey Pricing: One Rule

I will analyze the alternative pricing rules using a single framework. It is general yet simple and parameterizes the problems of monopoly, Pareto and Ramsey (through variable μ defined below).

Consider an industry with n products. List the prices in the n-dimensional row vector p. Demand is given by the n-dimensional column vector $D(p)$ and revenue is $pD(p)$. Subtraction of costs $C(D(p))$ defines profit. Welfare is the sum of profit and consumers' surplus, the area under the demand curve (or surface): $\int_p^\infty D(\tilde{p}) \bullet d\tilde{p}$, where the dot denotes the inner product. Because demand is assumed to be independent of income, this line integral is path-independent. It has the property that its derivative with respect to p_i equals $-D_i(p)$. Ramsey prices maximize welfare subject to the constraint that profit is nonnegative. The Lagrangian function is:

$$\int_p^\infty D(\tilde{p}) \bullet d\tilde{p} + (1+\lambda)[pD(p) - C(D(p))], \lambda \geq 0 \qquad (1)$$

Profit enters both the objective function (the term with coefficient 1) and the constraint part (the term with coefficient λ) of the

Lagrangian function. Equation 1 is not a Lagrangian function in the narrow sense, because I want to be able to consider cases in which λ is set exogenously. Ignoring the profit constraint defines Pareto optimality. This is encompassed by $\lambda = 0$. Conversely, if all weight in the Lagrangian function is on the constraint function, profit, we have the problem of the monopolist. This is encompassed by $\lambda \to \infty$. The profit constraint is binding in the Ramsey problem. This is the intermediate case, $0 < \lambda < \infty$.

It is convenient to change variable $0 \leq \lambda \leq \infty$ into $\mu = \lambda/(1+\lambda), 0 \leq \mu \leq 1$. The cases of Pareto, monopoly and Ramsey pricing are then encompassed by $\mu = 0$, 1, and $0 < \mu < 1$, respectively. Now in each case, the first-order conditions are obtained by setting the price derivatives of expression (1) zero. For this purpose it is convenient to use the row vector of relative mark-ups or *Lerner indices*, $L(p) = [p - C'(D(p))]\hat{p}^{-1}$ where C' is the row vector of marginal costs and the hat is transforms a vector to a diagonal matrix. And instead of the matrix of demand derivatives, $D' = (\partial D_i/\partial p_j)_{i,j=1,\ldots,n'}$ it is customary to use that of elasticities: $\varepsilon = (\varepsilon_{ij})_{i,j=1,\ldots,n} = [(p_j/D_i)\partial D_i/\partial p_j]_{i,j=1,\ldots,n} = \hat{D}^{-1}D'\hat{p}$ The following formula generalizes the Inverse Elasticity Rule (Baumol and Bradford 1970) with respect to demand, costs, and problem setting. It follows Cuthbertson and Dobbs (1996) and solves for the Lerner indices:

Proposition 1 (Generalized Inverse Elasticity Rule). *The first order conditions read* $L_i(p^\mu) = -\mu \sum_{j=1}^{n} p_j D_j(p)(\varepsilon^{-1})_{ji}/[p_i D_i(p)]$. *Here problem identifier* μ *is* 0 *(Pareto prices),* 1 *(monopoly prices) or intermediate (Ramsey prices).*

Proof: The partial derivatives of consumers' surplus with respect to price, organized in a row vector, are given by $D^\top(p)$, where $\top$ is the transposition sign. Setting the price derivative of expression (1) equal to zero: $-D^\top(p) + (1+\lambda)[D^\top(p) + pD'(p) - C'(D(p))D'(p)] = 0$ or $L(p)\hat{p}D'(p) = -\mu D^\top(p)$. Solving for the Lerner indices, $L(p) = -\mu D^\top(p)D'^{-1}(p)\hat{p}^{-1} = -\mu D^\top(p)\hat{p}\varepsilon^{-1}\hat{D}^{-1}\hat{p}^{-1}$. Taking the i-th component completes the proof. □

The i-th (Pareto, monopoly or Ramsey) optimal Lerner index is a weighted average of elements of the inverse elasticity matrix $\varepsilon - 1$; the weights are the budget ratios $p_j D_j(p)/[p_i D_i(p)]$. Proposition 1 has two corollaries, both well-known results. Before I present them, I define two concepts. First, demand is *independent* if $\partial D_i/\partial p_j = 0$ for all $i \neq j$. Second, two price vectors have the same *structure*, if the vectors of Lerner indices are proportionate (collinear).

Corollary 1. *Pareto prices equal marginal costs.*

Proof: Pareto prices are encompassed by $\mu = 0$. By Proposition 1, the Lerner indices are zero. By definition of the latter, $p = C'$. □

Corollary 2. *Monopoly prices and Ramsey prices have the same structure, if elasticity's are constant and demand is independent.*

Proof: Independent demand means that D' is a diagonal matrix. Hence ε is a diagonal matrix. Hence ε^{-1} is the diagonal matrix with elements ε_{ii}^{-1}. Recall that elasticities are functions of prices. By independence, they depended only on own prices. By Proposition 1, $L_i(p_i^{\mu}) = -\mu\varepsilon_{ii}^{-1}$ because the elasticity's are assumed constant, we conclude $L_i(p_i^{\mu}) = -\mu L_i(p_i^1)$. □

The upshot of Corollary 2 is that monopoly prices may be too high, but their structure (the proportions of the mark-ups) is right. This has the policy implication that regulation can be limited to the price level, leaving the fine-tuning of the mark-ups to the monopolist. Vogelsang and Finsinger (1979) detail the regulatory process which, perhaps surprisingly, holds for interdependent demands. Anyway, a monopolist can and will charge high prices for products with inelastic demand — without eroding the market too much — while a social planner charges high prices for products with inelastic demand, because the allocation is little distorted.

Corollary 2 provides sufficient conditions for the similarity of monopoly and Ramsey prices, but they are not necessary. Non-constant elasticity's and demand dependencies are sources which drive a wedge between the structures of monopoly and Ramsey prices, but, at least in principle, these sources may neutralize each other. In other words, monopoly prices and Ramsey prices *may* be similar in industries with complicated demands.

3. Two Counterexamples

I will now demonstrate that both the constant elasticity's and the independence of demand are critical to the result that monopoly prices have a Ramsey structure. Counterexample 1 presents a violation of constant elasticity's (while demand is independent) and Counterexample 2 presents a violation of independence (while all elasticity's are constant).

Counterexample 1. Consider two, independent demands. The first has constant elasticity: $D_1(p_1) = p_1^{-2}$. The second demand is from the textbooks, the simple linear $D_2(p_2) = 1 - p_2$. There is a small fixed cost, f, and the variable production costs are constant, $\frac{1}{2}$ per unit of (either) output. In market 2, the elasticity is $-\frac{p_2}{1-p_2}$. By Proposition 1, the Generalized Inverse Elasticity Rule reads $\frac{p_1-\frac{1}{2}}{p_1} = \frac{\mu}{2}\frac{p_1-\frac{1}{2}}{p_2} = \mu\frac{1-p_2}{p_2}$ The solution is $p_1^\mu = \frac{1}{2-\mu}, p_2^\mu = \frac{\frac{1}{2}+\mu}{1+\mu}$.

First consider the monopoly case, $\mu = 1$. Then $p1 = 1$, $p_2 = \frac{3}{4}$ and the Lerner indices are 1/2 and 1/3, respectively. Thus, a monopolist charges a high price (and Lerner index) in the *first* market.

Next consider the Ramsey case, where μ is determined by the profit constraint, $(p_1 - \frac{1}{2})p_1^{-2} + (p_2 - \frac{1}{2})(1 - p_2) = f$. Substitution of the prices yields $\frac{\mu}{2}(2-\mu) + \left(\frac{\frac{1}{2}+\mu}{1+\mu} - \frac{1}{2}\right)\left(1 - \frac{\frac{1}{2}+\mu}{1+\mu}\right) = f$. This equation determines μ as an increasing function of f, starting in $\mu = 0$ for $f = 0$ (the Pareto case). For example, $\mu = 1/3 \approx 0.33$ corresponds with $f = 187/576 \approx 0.32$. In this case, $p_1 = \frac{1}{2-\mu} = 0.6, p2 = \frac{\frac{1}{2}+\mu}{1+\mu} = 0.625$ and the Lerner indices are $1/6 \approx 0.17$ and $1/5 = 0.20$, respectively. The prices and Lerner indices are collected in Table 1.

Contrary to a monopolist, a regulator would charge the higher price (and Lerner index) in the *second* market. Not only the proportions of monopoly prices are off, but even the order of price components is reversed.

Counterexample 2. Consider $D_1(p_1) = p_1^{-1}$ and $D_2(p_{1,}, p_2) = p_1^{-1}p_2^{-2}$. (The products are complements.) There is a small fixed cost, f, and the variable production costs are constant, $2/3 \approx 0.67$ per unit of output 1 and $\frac{1}{2} = 0.50$ per unit of output 2. $\varepsilon = \begin{pmatrix} -1 & 0 \\ -1 & -2 \end{pmatrix}$ and, therefore, $\varepsilon^{-1} = \begin{pmatrix} -1 & 0 \\ \frac{1}{2} & -\frac{1}{2} \end{pmatrix}$. By Proposition 1, the Generalized Inverse Elasticity Rule reads $L_1 = \frac{p_1-2/3}{p_1} = \mu - \mu p_1^{-1}p_2^{-1}\frac{1}{2}, L_2 = \frac{p_2-\frac{1}{2}}{p_2} = \mu/2$. The solution is $p_1^\mu = \frac{1}{6(1-\mu)} + \frac{1-\mu}{2}, p_2^\mu = \frac{1}{2-\mu}$. The first price is minimal, in fact $p_1^\mu = 1/\sqrt{3} \approx 0.58$, at $\mu = 1 - 1/\sqrt{3} \approx 0.42$, whilst

Table 1. Pareto, Ramsey and monopoly prices and Lerner indices in Counterexample 1.

Problem	μ	p_1	p_2	L_1	L_2
Pareto	0	0.50	0.50	0	0
Ramsey	0.33	0.60	0.625	0.17	0.20
Monopoly	1	1	0.75	0.50	0.33

Table 2. Pareto, Ramsey and monopoly prices and Lerner indices in Counterexample 2.

Problem	μ	p_1	p_2	L_1	L_2
Pareto	0	0.67	0.50	0	0
Ramsey	0.42	0.58	0.63	−0.15	0.21
Monopoly	1	∞	1	1	0.50

there $p_2^\mu = \frac{1}{1+1/\sqrt{3}} = 0.63$. The Lerner indices are $L_1 = 1 - \frac{2/3}{p_1^\mu} = 1 - \frac{2}{3}[\frac{1}{6(1-\mu)} + \frac{1-\mu}{2}]^{-1} = 1 - \frac{4(1-\mu)}{1+3(1-\mu)^2}$, $L_2 = \mu/2$. In the Ramsey case, μ is determined by the profit constraint. One can show that the profit constraint reads $f = \mu$. (The demonstration involves the tedious but straightforward calculation by which variable profit, $(p_1 - 2/3)D_1(p_1) + (p_2 - \frac{1}{2})D2(p1, p2)$, reduces to a simple μ.) For the case of $\mu = f = 1 - 1/\sqrt{3} \approx 0.42$ the Lerner indices reduce to $L_1 = 1 - 2/\sqrt{3} \approx -0.15$ and $L_2 = \frac{1}{2} - \frac{1}{2}/\sqrt{3} \approx 0.21$. For this case, prices and Lerner indices are collected in Table 2.

As is well known, a monopolist ($\mu = 1$) increases the price of the good with unitary demand elasticity (product 1) without limit; the Lerner index for good 1 is a full 1. The monopolist charges a limited price for the good with elastic demand; that Lerner index is only 0.50. A regulator, however, charges a *low* price for the good with relatively inelastic demand (product 1), namely 0.58, which is even below cost. The price cut boosts the demand for the complement, which generates the funds required to defray the fixed cost. As in Counterexample 1, not only the proportions of monopoly prices are off, but even the order of price components is reversed.

Ever since Baumol *et al.* (1979) it is indeed known that Ramsey prices may involve a cross-subsidy. In Counterexample 2 the second market cross-subsidizes the first. This flow of funds renders the second market vulnerable to entry. In other words, the Ramsey optimum is not sustainable. Indeed, a condition of the Weak Invisible Hand Theorem (by which the Ramsey optimum is sustainable, see Baumol *et al.* 1977) is not fulfilled (namely weak gross substitutability).

4. Discussion

The examples show that monopoly prices and Ramsey prices can have very different structures, even to the extent that the order of price components is reversed. It shows that the problem of monopoly pricing by a multi-product monopolist is not solved by just reducing all prices by some proportion. An RPI-X price cap for each product need not yield the desired result of approaching Ramsey efficient prices. In the RPI-X price cap system the price cap is allowed to increase at the rate of inflation, measured by the retail price index, less some "X factor" to account for productivity gains or to reduce the regulated firm's rents, but otherwise the regulated firm is allowed to adjust its own prices, unlike rate of return based regulation. When should the regulator be alerted to the fact that only the level but also the structure of the prices better be adjusted?

The first situation that springs to mind is the case of non-constant elasticity's. In this case it is quite intuitive that monopoly and Ramsey prices have different structures, because the pricing rules are local and, therefore, may produce different results. From an applied point of view, however, such variations are hard to estimate and the other cause of trouble, the violation of the independence assumption is more serious. To develop some intuition, recalls the Generalized Inverse Elasticity Rule (Proposition 1): $L_i(p^\mu) = -\mu \sum_{j=1}^n p_j D_j(p)(\varepsilon^{-1})_{ji}/[p_i D_i(p)]$. By definition, the monopoly price vector p^1 has the same structure as the Ramsey price vector p^μ if $L_i(p^1)$ and $L_i(p^\mu)$ are collinear, i.e. if $\sum_{j=1}^n p_j D_j\ (p)(\varepsilon^{-1})_{ji}/[p_i D_i(p)]$ is constant. Clearly, it is not enough if the demand elasticities (ε) are constant, but also the budget shares must be constant. In other words, *income effects between the products* break down the similarity between monopoly and Ramsey prices.

The upshot for regulators is that doubt is shed on standard tools such as RPI-X price caps when a monopolist produces final consumption goods with mutual income effects. The most prominent example is a firm that offers a quality ladder of products. Think of a window producer. Its monopoly prices are not only high — the standard tool to restrain the market and exercise market power — but also take output in a region where the market share of double glazed windows is smaller (because of the negative income effect).

It is possible to analyze this one step further by a first order approximation of the inverse elasticity rule about the benchmark of independent demands, which is not plagued by the dissimilarity problem (Corollary 2). Thus, rewriting the elasticity's matrix ε as the sum of diagonal matrix $\hat{\varepsilon}$ — representing the own elasticity's — and off-diagonal matrix $\tilde{\varepsilon}$ — representing the cross elasticity's, let the latter be small compared to the former. Then $\varepsilon^{-1} = (\hat{\varepsilon} + \tilde{\varepsilon})^{-1} = [\hat{\varepsilon}(I + \hat{\varepsilon}^{-1}\tilde{\varepsilon})]^{-1} = (I + \hat{\varepsilon}^{-1}\tilde{\varepsilon})^{-1}\hat{\varepsilon}^{-1} \approx (I - \hat{\varepsilon}^{-1}\tilde{\varepsilon})\hat{\varepsilon}^{-1}$ and, therefore, the Generalized Inverse Elasticity Rule becomes $L_i(p^\mu) \approx \mu \sum_{j=1}^{n} p_j D_j(p)(I - \hat{\varepsilon}^{-1}\tilde{\varepsilon})_{ji}/[p_i D_i(p)(-\varepsilon_{ii})] = \mu/(-\varepsilon_{ii}) + \mu \sum_{j \neq 1} p_j D_j(p)(-\varepsilon_{jj}^{-1}\varepsilon_{ji})/[p_i D_i(p)(-\varepsilon_{ii})]$. For quality ladders, the commodities are substitutes, hence $\varepsilon_{ji}(j \neq i)$ are positive. If commodity i is a top-of-the-line product, such as a double glazed windows, the exercise of monopoly power (with its negative income effect) reduces $p_i D_i(p)/p_j D_j(p)(j \neq i)$, hence increases the Lerner index disproportionally much. Quality is overprized and a regulator might consider imposing a stiffer cap on high-quality products.

In this case, however, the critical condition of the Weak Invisible Hand Theorem, namely weak gross substitutability, is fulfilled, and a more practical regulation would be to reduce barriers to entry, to introduce the disciplinary sway of potential competition.

5. Conclusion

The Generalized Inverse Elasticity Rule presented in this note encompasses the problems of monopoly, Pareto and Ramsey. The result that monopoly prices are merely too high, while their structure is right in the sense that relative mark-ups have the same proportions as of Ramsey prices, is confined to industries with demands that feature constant elasticity's and are independent. Otherwise even the rankings of monopoly and Ramsey price components can be different. If there are income effects, a regulator may consider to cap some prices more strictly than others.

Acknowledgments

I am grateful to Felix Hoeffler for stimulating suggestions and feedback. An anonymous referee induced me to discuss the break-down of the similarity result (Corollary 2) and the implications for regulators, for which I am extremely grateful.

Open Access

References

Baumol, W. J., E. E. Bailey and R. D. Willig. (1977). Weak invisible hand theorems on the sustainability of multiproduct natural monopoly. *American Economic Review*, **67**(3), 350–365.

Baumol, W. J. and D. F. Bradford. (1970). Optimal departures from marginal cost pricing. *American Economic Review*, **60**(3), 265–283.

Baumol, W. J., D. Fischer and Th. ten Raa. (1979). The Price-Iso return locus and rational rate regulation. *Bell Journal of Economics*, **10**(2), 648–658.

Cuthbertson, K. and I. M. Dobbs. (1996). A robust methodology for Ramsey pricing with an application to UK postal services. *Journal of Industrial Economics*, **44**(3), 229–247.

Hoeffler, F. (2006). Monopoly prices versus Ramsey Boiteux prices: Are they "similar" and: Does it matter? *Journal of Industry, Competition and Trade*, **6**(1), 27–43.

Laffont, J.-J. and J. Tirole. (2000). *Competition in Telecommunications*, Cambridge: MIT Press.

Mohring, H. (1970). The peak load problem with increasing returns and pricing constraints. *American Economic Review*, **60**(4), 693–705.

Vogelsang, I. and J. Finsinger. (1979). A regulatory adjustment process for optimal pricing by multiproduct monopoly firms. *Bell Journal of Economics*, **10**(1), 157–171.

Chapter 10

Consumer Surplus and CES Demand*

Thijs ten Raa

Department of Economics, Tilburg University,
Tilburg, The Netherlands
tenraa@uvt.nl

Abstract. This article presents the consumer surplus formula for constant elasticity of substitution (CES) demands. The formula is used to compare the monopoly and optimum provisions of product variety. It is shown that a monopolist under-provides variety. This result is contrasted with Lambertini's analysis of the monopolist's optimal R&D portfolio. I also contrast my approach with the indirect utility technique of Anderson, de Palma, and Thisse's discrete choice theory of product differentiation.

Keywords: Consumer Surplus, CES, Monopoly Variety

JEL-codes: D61, L12

1. Introduction

Alternative measures of consumer's welfare coexist. There are utility measures and surplus measures. Utility measures are direct (defined on the commodity quantities consumed) or indirect (defined on the commodity prices and the available budget). Surplus measures the difference between the willingness to pay, i.e. inverse demand, and

*Reprinted from *Oxford Economic Papers*, **67**, 1165–1173, 2008, with permission from Oxford University Press.

price. (This difference is zero at the margin of the last unit purchased of any of the commodities, but positive for the other units purchased.) Marshall (1920) measured surplus using the ordinary demand function, while Hicks (1942) did so using the compensated demand functions. The term consumer surplus refers to Marshallian surplus, while the Hicksian measures are called equivalent and compensating variations.

Chipman and Moore (1980) provide an elegant consolidation. They consider line integrals of vector-valued functions of the prices and the budget. If a vector-valued function yields a path-independent line integral and is nonnegative if and only if indirect utility in the terminal point is at least as great as in the initial point, then the function is said to furnish an acceptable integral measure of welfare change. If the function is the gradient of indirect utility (where the derivatives with respect to price can be expressed as the product of demand and the marginal utility of income, by Roy's lemma), we get indirect utility. If the function is demand, we get consumer surplus. If the function is the gradient of an expenditure function, we get a Hicksian variation. Chipman and Moore (1980) investigate if these functions furnish acceptable measures of welfare change. This is trivially true for the first case, indirect utility. It is also true for the Hicksian compensating variation, but not for the Hicksian equivalent variation. The case of consumer surplus has two interesting results. If the budget is constant, then consumer surplus furnishes an acceptable measure of welfare change if and only if utility is homothetic. If one price is constant, then consumer surplus furnishes an acceptable measure of welfare change if and only if utility is quasi-linear, with the linear term representing the commodity of which the price is constant. I consider constant elasticity of substitution (CES) demands with and without a residual commodity, and these two cases will fulfil the respective Chipman and Moore (1980) conditions of homotheticity and quasi-linearity.

Consumer surplus has gone through a roller coaster. It started as a popular welfare measure to evaluate price changes; all you need are ordinary demand functions. However, theorists argued that it is "inexact" and should be replaced by the Hicksian variations. Willig (1976) restored consumer surplus by showing it is a good approximation. Hausman (1981) showed that there is no need for approximation, as the "exact" concepts can be derived from ordinary demand functions. Takayama (1982) shows that the "exact" concepts do *not* measure the welfare impact of a price change correctly, while consumer surplus *does*, at least for homothetic demands. Takayama's result justifies the use of consumer surplus in applied theory.

The main applications of consumer surplus involve linear and log-linear demands, not CES demands. This is surprising, because CES demands are the workhorse of empirical models. CES functions admit the selection of commodities, without reducing utility to zero as for the Cobb-Douglas and Leontief specifications. Moreover, CES functions facilitate tractable analysis, not only of equilibrium prices and quantities under alternative behavior assumptions, such as Bertrand versus Cournot competition, but also of competitive versus non-competitive imports, via the Armington (1969) specification. However, CES functions are deemed too complicated for surplus measurement. No analytical benefit formula exists according to De Borger (1989, p. 216). Lambertini (2003, p. 563) addresses the monopoly provision of differentiated products by computing producer plus consumer surplus. He stresses that his linear demand parameter is an imperfect indicator of complementarity and suggests that one should use a CES utility function, 'which however would complicate calculations'. Tohamy and Mixon (2004, p. 255) were unable to integrate the CES demand curve and instead used a numerical routine.

This article presents the missing formula and uses it to implement Lambertini's (2003) suggestion to extend his monopoly sub-optimality result to CES demand. This extension result could also be obtained by using the indirect utility technique of Anderson *et al.* (1992). An advantage of consumer surplus over the indirect utility technique is its wider applicability. The moment we depart from the representative consumer implicit in Anderson *et al.* (1992), indirect utility is no longer available, but consumer surplus still is.

Section 2 presents the consumer surplus formula for CES demand. Section 3 shows how a residual commodity, representing the rest of the economy (outside the industry considered) can be accommodated. Section 4 determines the monopoly and optimum provisions of variety. Section 5 contrasts the result with that of Lambertini (2003) and discusses the contribution of the formula vis-à-vis the CES model of Anderson *et al.* (1992).

2. CES Consumer Surplus

For n commodities the CES utility function is $U(x_1,\ldots,x_n) = (\alpha_1 x_1^\rho + \cdots + \alpha_n x_n^\rho)^{1/\rho}$, where $x_1,\ldots,x_n$ are the commodity quantities, and generates ordinary demands $D_i(p_1,\ldots,p_n;I) = \frac{(\alpha_i/p_i)^\sigma I}{\alpha_1^\sigma p_1^{1-\sigma}+\cdots+\alpha_n^\sigma p_n^{1-\sigma}}$, where $p_1,\ldots,p_n$ are the commodity prices, I is the available budget, and commodity index $i = 1,\ldots,n$. α_i are share parameters. Parameter ρ ranges from minus infinity (Leontief utility) via zero (Cobb-Douglas utility) to one (linear utility). A monotonic transformation is $\sigma = 1/(1-\rho)$, ranging from zero via one to infinity, respectively; σ is the elasticity of substitution. In a monopolistic competition setting σ is also the elasticity of demand. As is customary for consumer surplus calculations, I analyze the effect of a price change of a single commodity, i, from p_i to p_i'. The *variation of consumer surplus* is defined by $-\int_{p_i}^{p_i'} D_i(p_1,\ldots,p_{i-1},p_i'',p_{i+1},\ldots,p_n;I)dp_i''$. The extension to price vector change is much debated, but straightforward for homothetic demand, as argued by Takayama (1982, p. 40), and trivial for the symmetric demand used in the product variety literature, as shown after the proof of the Proposition. The homotheticity ensures that the variation of consumer surplus furnishes an acceptable measure of welfare change in the sense of Chipman and Moore (1980).

Proposition 1. *The CES variation of consumer surplus equals* $\frac{-I}{1-\sigma}\ln\left\{1+\left[\left(\frac{p_i'}{p_i}\right)^{1-\sigma}-1\right]\frac{p_i x_i}{I}\right\}$.

Let us first check the sign for a price increase, $p_i' > p_i$. If $\sigma < 1 (> 1)$, the square bracketed expression hence the accolade bracketed expression is positive (negative) and the coefficient is negative (positive), making the product expression negative indeed for both $\sigma < 1$ and $\sigma > 1$.

For $\sigma \to 1$ the logarithm and the denominator both go to zero, but l'Hôpital's rule confirms the Cobb-Douglas variation of consumer surplus, as I will show now. By this rule we may take the ratio of the derivatives of the numerator and the denominator (with respect to σ), which yields $\frac{-I}{-1}\left\{1+\left[\left(\frac{p_i'}{p_i}\right)^{1-\sigma}-1\right]\frac{p_i x_i}{I}\right\}^{-1}\frac{p_i x_i}{I}\left(\frac{p_i'}{p_i}\right)^{1-\sigma}(-1)\ln\left(\frac{p_i'}{p_i}\right)$. For $\sigma \to 1$ this expression reduces to $p_i x_i \ln\left(\frac{p_i}{p_i'}\right)$. Indeed, for

Cobb-Douglas demand we have $p_i x_i = \alpha_i I$ or $x_i = \frac{\alpha_i I}{p_i}$ with variation of consumer surplus $-\int_{p_i}^{p_i'} D_i(p_i'', I)dp_i'' = -\int_{p_i}^{p_i'} \frac{\alpha_i I}{p_i''} dp_i'' = \alpha_i I \ln\left(\frac{p_i}{p_i'}\right)$, which is perfectly consistent.

Proof of Proposition 1. By definition the variation of consumer surplus is $-\int_{p_i}^{p_i'} D_i(p_1, \ldots, p_{i-1}, p_i'', p_{i+1}, \ldots, p_n; I)dp_i'' = -I \int_{p_i}^{p_i'} \frac{(\alpha_i/p_i'')^\sigma}{\alpha_1^\sigma p_1^{1-\sigma} + \cdots + \alpha_i^\sigma p_i''^{1-\sigma} + \cdots + \alpha_n^\sigma p_n^{1-\sigma}} dp_i''$. The primitive function with respect to p_i'' is $\frac{1}{1-\sigma} \ln(\alpha_1^\sigma p_1^{1-\sigma} + \cdots + \alpha_i^\sigma p_i''^{1-\sigma} + \cdots + \alpha_n^\sigma p_n^{1-\sigma})$ plus an arbitrary constant, for which I pick $\frac{1}{1-\sigma} \ln(p_i^\sigma x_i/\alpha_i^\sigma)$. The addition of this term is equivalent to replacement of the n terms under the ln in the primitive function by $(\alpha_1/\alpha_i)^\sigma (p_1/p_i)^{-\sigma} p_1 x_i, \ldots, (p_i''/p_i)^{-\sigma} p_i'' x_i, \ldots, (\alpha_n/\alpha_i)^\sigma (p_n/p_i)^{-\sigma} p_n x_i$. However, since the demand function is generated by budget constrained utility maximization, the ratio of the marginal utilities equals the price ratio, $(\alpha_1/\alpha_i)(x_1/x_i)^{\rho-1} = p_1/p_i$ or $(\alpha_1/\alpha_i)^\sigma (p_1/p_i)^{-\sigma} = x_1/x_i$, and the first of the latter n terms reduces to $p_1 x_1$ and similar for the other terms; only the ith term stays $(p_i''/p_i)^{-\sigma} p_i'' x_i = p_i''^{1-\sigma} p_i^\sigma x_i$, where $p_i'' = p_i'$ or p_i (the upper and lower bounds of the integral). Summing these terms the expression under the ln function reads $I + (p_i''^{1-\sigma} p_i^\sigma - p_i)x_i$ and, therefore, the variation of consumer surplus becomes $\frac{-I}{1-\sigma} \ln \frac{I + (p_i'^{1-\sigma} p_i^\sigma - p_i)x_i}{I} = \frac{-I}{1-\sigma} \ln \left\{1 + \left[\left(\frac{p_i'}{p_i}\right)^{1-\sigma} - 1\right] \frac{p_i x_i}{I}\right\}$. This completes the proof.

Corollary 1. *In the symmetric case, with equal coefficients, the CES demand functions reduce to* $D_i(p_1, \ldots, p_n; I) = \frac{I/p_i^\sigma}{p_1^{1-\sigma} + \cdots + p_n^{1-\sigma}}$. *For a symmetric price vector change, from* $(p, \ldots, p)$ *to* $(p', \ldots, p')$, *the variation in consumer surplus is* $-I \ln \frac{p'}{p}$, *as shown in Appendix* 1.

Remark. The budget share in the formula is $\frac{p_i x_i}{I} = \frac{(\alpha_i/p_i)^\sigma}{\alpha_1^\sigma p_1^{1-\sigma} + \cdots + \alpha_n^\sigma p_n^{1-\sigma}}$. The price elasticity is unitary, which explains that the variation of consumer surplus is logarithmic and not summable. Hence consumer surplus at p_i (with reference price p_i' infinity) is not defined. This problem does not occur when there is residual income.

3. CES Consumer Surplus with Residual Demand

For n commodities with residual demand the CES utility function is $U(x_0, x_1, \ldots, x_n) = x_0 + (\alpha_1 x_1^\rho + \cdots + \alpha_n x_n^\rho)^{m/\rho}$. The quasi-linearity ensures that consumer surplus will furnish an acceptable measure of welfare change in the sense of Chipman and Moore (1980).

If $m = 1$, utility is homothetic and demand will be concentrated in either the differentiated commodities or the residual commodity, bringing us back to the previous section. From this section onwards I assume that $0 < m < 1$. Then demands for both commodity types are positive. The available budget, say $\underline{I}$, is now divided between expenditure I on the differentiated commodities and residual demand x_0, where numeraire residual demand has been scaled such that its price is one. The demand for the differentiated commodities are $D_i(p_1, \ldots, p_n; I) = \frac{(\alpha_i/p_i)^\sigma I}{\alpha_1^\sigma p_1^{1-\sigma} + \cdots + \alpha_n^\sigma p_n^{1-\sigma}}$. The expenditure on the differentiated commodities or, equivalently, the residual demand, is determined by the condition that the marginal utility of the bundle of differentiated commodities with respect to expenditure equals one. The differentiated commodities contribute utility $(\alpha_1^\sigma p_1^{1-\sigma} + \cdots + \alpha_n^\sigma p_n^{1-\sigma})^{\frac{m}{\sigma-1}} I^m$. Differentiating with respect to I the optimality condition reads $m(\alpha_1^\sigma p_1^{1-\sigma} + \cdots + \alpha_n^\sigma p_n^{1-\sigma})^{\frac{m}{\sigma-1}} I^{m-1} = 1$. Solving, the expenditure on the differentiated commodities is $I(p_1, \ldots, p_n) = m^{1/(1-m)}(\alpha_1^\sigma p_1^{1-\sigma} + \cdots + \alpha_n^\sigma p_n^{1-\sigma})^{\frac{1}{(1/m-1)(\sigma-1)}}$. Substituting back, demand becomes $D_i = m^{1/(1-m)}(\alpha_i/p_i)^\sigma(\alpha_1^\sigma p_1^{1-\sigma} + \cdots + \alpha_n^\sigma p_n^{1-\sigma})^{\frac{1/(1-m)-\sigma}{\sigma-1}}$.

Proposition 2. *With residual demand CES consumer surplus equals* $(1/m - 1)m^{1/(1-m)}(\alpha_1^\sigma p_1^{1-\sigma} + \cdots + \alpha_n^\sigma p_n^{1-\sigma})^{\frac{1}{(1/m-1)(\sigma-1)}}$.

Proof of proposition 2. Consumer surplus is $m^{1/(1-m)} \int_{p_i}^\infty (\alpha_1^\sigma p_1^{1-\sigma} + \cdots + \alpha_i^\sigma p_i'^{1-\sigma} + \cdots + \alpha_n^\sigma p_n^{1-\sigma})^{\frac{1/(1-m)-\sigma}{\sigma-1}} (\alpha_i/p_i')^\sigma dp_i'$. The primitive function with respect to p_i' is $\frac{1}{1-\sigma}\frac{1/m-1}{1/\rho-1}(\alpha_1^\sigma p_1^{1-\sigma} + \cdots + \alpha_i^\sigma p_i'^{1-\sigma} + \cdots + \alpha_n^\sigma p_n^{1-\sigma})^{\frac{1}{(1/m-1)(\sigma-1)}} = (1 - 1/m)(\alpha_1^\sigma p_1^{1-\sigma} + \cdots + \alpha_i^\sigma p_i'^{1-\sigma} + \cdots + \alpha_n^\sigma p_n^{1-\sigma})^{\frac{1}{(1/m-1)(\sigma-1)}}$. This behaves like $p_i'^{(1-\sigma)\frac{1/\rho-1}{1/m-1}} = p_i'^{\frac{1}{1-1/m}}$, which tends to 0 since $m < 1$. Hence consumer surplus is $m^{1/(1-m)}(1/m-1)(\alpha_1^\sigma p_1^{1-\sigma} + \cdots + \alpha_i^\sigma p_i^{1-\sigma} + \cdots + \alpha_n^\sigma p_n^{1-\sigma})^{\frac{1}{(1/m-1)(\sigma-1)}}$.

Corollary 2. In the symmetric case, $\alpha_i = \alpha$ and $p_i = p$, demand is $D_i = m^{1/(1-m)}(\alpha/p)^{\sigma}(n\alpha^{\sigma}p^{1-\sigma})^{\frac{1/(1-m)-\sigma}{\sigma-1}}$. The price elasticity is $-1/(1-m)$, which is independent of the elasticity of substitution. The elasticity of substitution does impact the level of demand (through the power of α, namely $\sigma(1+\frac{1/(1-m)-\sigma}{\sigma-1}) = \frac{\sigma}{\sigma-1}(-1+\frac{1}{1-m}) = \frac{1/\rho}{1/m-1}$). Complementarity (as measured by a lower value of ρ or, equivalently, σ) boosts demand and hence consumer surplus (for $\alpha > 1$, as will be the case). Consumer surplus reduces to $(1/m-1)m^{1/(1-m)}n^{\frac{1}{(1/m-1)(\sigma-1)}}\alpha^{\frac{\sigma}{(1/m-1)(\sigma-1)}}/p^{\frac{1}{1/m-1}}$.

4. Monopoly and Optimum Provision of Variety

Dixit and Stiglitz (1977, p. 301) "have a rather surprising case where the monopolistic competition equilibrium is identical with the optimum constrained by the lack of lump sum subsidies." In their case utility is a function of the numeraire and the symmetric CES aggregate $(x_1^{\rho}+\cdots+x_n^{\rho})^{1/\rho}$. The number of varieties, n, is determined by market forces or a nonnegative profit constrained welfare optimization. Consumers have taste for variety. The utility gain derived from spreading a unit of production between n differentiated products is $[(1/n)^{\rho}+\cdots+(1/n)^{\rho}]^{1/\rho}/1 = [n(1/n)^{\rho}]^{1/\rho} = n^{(1-\rho)/\rho}$. Benassy (1996) defines the elasticity of the taste variety in the obvious way and thus shows it equals to $1/\rho - 1$ in the Dixit-Stiglitz framework. The elasticity of demand is $\sigma = 1/(1-\rho)$ and monopolistic profit maximization yields that the markup relative to price is the inverse elasticity $\frac{p-c}{p} = \sigma^{-1}$ or that the markup relative to cost c is $\frac{p-c}{c} = \frac{p}{c} - 1 = (1-\sigma^{-1})^{-1} - 1 = [1-(1-\rho)]^{-1} - 1 = 1/\rho - 1$. Benassy (1996) shows that this coincidence between taste for variety and markup explains the Dixit-Stiglitz result and introduces a multiplicative power function of n in the CES aggregate to control for the variety elasticity independent of the demand elasticity or markup.

In the symmetric Dixit-Stiglitz model consumers maximize $U(\underline{I} - npx, (x^{\rho}+\cdots+x^{\rho})^{1/\rho}) = U(\underline{I}-npx, n^{1/\rho}x)$. Denoting partial derivatives by subscripts 0 for numeraire and 1 for the differentiated commodities, the first order condition is that the marginal rate of substitution is $U_1/U_0 = n^{1-1/\rho}p$. If U is Cobb-Douglas with coefficients α for the differentiated commodity aggregate and $1-\alpha$ for the numeraire, as in Anderson, de Palma and Thisse (1992), we have $npx = \alpha \underline{I}$. The elasticity of demand is one, and the monopoly price becomes infinite. If U is linear (as in partial equilibrium analysis), the marginal rate of substitution is constant and can be set equal to one by choice of differentiated commodities unit, so that utility is $I - npx + n^{1/\rho}x$. The consumer maximizes $(n^{1/\rho} - np)x$; if p is greater than $n^{1/\rho - 1}$ demand is zero and otherwise the budget will be exhausted: $npx = \underline{I}$. Since revenue is constant the monopolist minimizes cost by offering no variety, $n = 1$. To avoid the just discussed bang-bang behavior featuring uninteresting monopoly solutions, I raise the CES aggregate to a power m, a constant between 0 and 1, so that for any given number of varieties there is diminishing marginal utility. I also include a power of n, to control for the taste of variety.

The *utility function* I use is $U(x_0, x_1, \ldots, x_n) = x_0 + n^{\nu+m-m/\rho}(x_1^\rho + \cdots + x_n^\rho)^{m/\rho}$. Here the multiplicative coefficient has been chosen following Benassy (1996): If the prices are equal and the expenditure is split accordingly, then the contribution to utility is $n^{\nu+m-m/\rho}[(\frac{I}{np})^\rho + \cdots + (\frac{I}{np})^\rho]^{m/\rho} = n^{\nu+m-m/\rho}[n(\frac{I}{np})^\rho]^{m/\rho} = n^\nu (I/p)^m$, which has variety elasticity ν.

4.1. *Monopoly Variety*

The budget constraint of the consumer is binding and can be used to eliminate residual income x_0. The constant income term may be deleted and utility reduces to $n^{\nu+m-m/\rho}(nx^\rho)^{m/\rho} - npx = n^{\nu+m}x^m - npx$. The first order demand condition (with respect to x) can be rewritten as $npx = n^{\nu+m}mx^m$. This is *revenue*. The implicit assumption is that income is greater than this expression, ruling out the corner solution where all income is spent on the differentiated commodities offered by the monopolist. (Because we will solve for quantities and variety, the lower bound of income is a function of the parameters.) Dividing revenue by np and rewriting we see that *demand* is $x = (n^{\nu+m-1}m/p)^{1/(1-m)}$. For each variety let the set-up cost be F and the marginal cost be c. Then *profit* is $n^{\nu+m}mx^m - cnx - nF$. The first order condition with respect to x yields $x = (n^{\nu+m-1}m^2/c)^{1/(1-m)}$. The first order condition with respect to n is $(\nu+m)n^{\nu+m-1}mx^m - cx - F = 0$, ignoring the integer problem (following Dixit and Stiglitz, 1977, Anderson, de Palma and Thisse, 1992, and Benassy, 1996). I assume that there is taste for variety, but with diminishing returns: the elasticity fulfills the following maintained.

Assumption. The variety elasticity, ν, is less than $1-m$, where m is the utility elasticity of the differentiated products.

This ensures the first-order conditions solve, barring bang-bang behavior. In fact, the monopoly variety is $n = \left(\frac{\nu m^{(1+m)/(1-m)}}{Fc^{m/(1-m)}}\right)^{\frac{1-m}{1-m-\nu}}$. The derivation is in Appendix 2.

4.2. *Second Best Variety*

As I confirm later, in the first best solution price equals marginal cost, hence profit is negative. In the second best solution producer surplus must be at least zero (and this constraint is binding). From subsection 4.1 we see that the zero-profit condition reads $n^{\nu+m}mx^m - cnx - nF = 0$. It implies a marginal rate of substitution (between variety n and quantity x) of $\frac{(\nu+m)n^{\nu+m-1}mx^m - cx - F}{n^{\nu+m}m^2x^{m-1} - cn} = \frac{(\nu+m-1)n^{\nu+m-1}mx^m}{n^{\nu+m}m^2x^{m-1} - cn}$, where we substituted the zero-profit condition. By Corollary 2, with $\alpha^{m/\rho} = n^{\nu+m-m/\rho}$, or $\alpha^{\sigma} = n^{(\nu+m-m/\rho)\rho\sigma/m} = n^{[(\nu+m)(\sigma-1)-m\sigma]/m} = n^{\nu(\sigma-1)/m-1}$, consumer surplus reduces to $(1/m-1)m^{1/(1-m)}n^{\frac{\nu}{1-m}}/p^{\frac{1}{1/m-1}}$. Substituting inverse demand, which is readily available from revenue expression $npx = n^{\nu+m}mx^m$, and simplifying, consumer surplus can be rewritten as $(1/m-1)m^{1/(1-m)}n^{\frac{\nu}{1-m}}/(n^{\nu+m-1}mx^{m-1})^{\frac{1}{1/m-1}} = (1-m)n^{\nu+m}x^m$. It implies a marginal rate of substitution (between n and x) of $\frac{(\nu+m)/n}{m/x} = (1+\nu/m)x/n$.

The first-order condition of the maximization of consumer surplus subject to the producer surplus constraint is that the marginal rates of substitution of producer and consumer surplus are equal. Solving, $x^{1-m} = \frac{n^{\nu+m-1}m}{(1+\nu/m)c}$. Comparison with the demand relationship, $npx = n^{\nu+m}mx^m$, yields $p = (1+\nu/m)c$. By the zero-profit condition the markup offsets the fixed cost: $(\nu/m)cx = F$. Hence $x = mF/\nu c$, which is independent of n. Combining the last two expressions for x, $(mF/\nu c)^{1-m} = \frac{n^{\nu+m-1}m}{(1+\nu/m)c}$. Hence the second best variety is $n = \left(\frac{m^m\nu^{1-m}}{F^{1-m}c^m(1+\nu/m)}\right)^{\frac{1}{1-m-\nu}}$.

4.3. *First Best Variety*

The derivative of consumer surplus with respect to p_i, is minus the demand for that commodity, $-D_i$. The derivative of producer surplus $(p_1-c)D_1 + \cdots + (p_n-c)D_n-nF$ with respect to p_i is $D_i + (p_1-c)\partial D_1/\partial p_i + \cdots + (p_n-c)D_n/\partial p_i$. Setting the sum of the derivatives equal to zero, the first-order condition of total surplus maximization with respect to price reads $(p_1-c)\partial D_1/\partial p_i + \cdots + (p_n-c)D_n/\partial p_i = 0$, $i = 1,\ldots,n$. By symmetry and (differentiated commodities) demand homogeneity (of degree $1/(m-1) < 0$), we conclude the familiar first best condition $p_i = c$. By subsection 4.2 consumer surplus is equal to $(1/m - 1)m^{1/(1-m)}n^{\frac{\nu}{1-m}}/c^{\frac{1}{1/m-1}}$ and producer surplus is $-nF$. The first order condition for total surplus maximization is $(1/m-1)m^{1/(1-m)}\frac{\nu}{1-m}n^{\frac{\nu}{1-m}-1}c^{\frac{-1}{1/m-1}} = F$. Solving, $n = \left(\frac{\nu^{1-m}m^m}{F^{1-m}c^m}\right)^{\frac{1}{1-m-\nu}}$.

The explicit variety solutions for the monopoly, second-best, and first-best cases admit direct comparisons.

Proposition 3. If the variety elasticity, ν, is less than $1-m$, where m is the utility elasticity of the differentiated products, then a monopolist under-provides variety relative to the second-best variety, which in turn is smaller than the first-best variety.

Proof of Proposition 3. From the results of Sections 4.1 and 4.2 we see that the ratio of the monopoly variety to the second best variety is $\left(\frac{\nu m^{(1+m)/(1-m)}}{Fc^{m/(1-m)}}\right)^{\frac{1-m}{1-m-\nu}} / \left(\frac{m^m\nu^{1-m}}{F^{1-m}c^m(1+\nu/m)}\right)^{\frac{1}{1-m-\nu}} = (m+\nu)^{\frac{1}{1-m-\nu}} < 1$, because $m+\nu < 1$ (and therefore the exponent is positive), by assumption. From the results of Sections 4.2 and 4.3 we see that the ratio of the second-best to the first-best variety is $\left(\frac{m^m\nu^{1-m}}{F^{1-m}c^m(1+\nu/m)}\right)^{\frac{1}{1-m-\nu}} / \left(\frac{\nu^{1-m}m^m}{F^{1-m}c^m}\right)^{\frac{1}{1-m-\nu}} = 1/(1+\nu/m)^{\frac{1}{1-m-\nu}} < 1$ (because the exponent is positive). This completes the proof.

5. Discussion

Proposition 3 is closely related to Lambertini's (2003) analysis of the monopoly provision of variety when demand is linear. When the commodities are substitutes we are in perfect agreement: a monopolist under-provides variety. When the commodities are complements I again obtain under-provision, but Lambertini (2003) finds that the provision is just right. One may question the robustness of this result, as Benassy (1996) questioned the robustness of the Dixit and Stiglitz (1977) result that the monopolistic competition equilibrium is identical with the second-best optimum. To be fair, Lambertini (2003) himself acknowledged that his linear demand is an imperfect model of complementarity. In fact, LaFrance (1985) has shown that the underlying utility function must be quasi-linear, with a quadratic nonlinear term and with the linear term representing the residual numeraire commodity. Lambertini's (2003) utility function captures the quadratic term, but misses the residual income term.

Anderson *et al.* (1992) use a CES utility function to compare optimum and monopolistic equilibrium product diversity of substitutes. They do capture the numeraire commodity, albeit in Cobb-Douglas, not quasi-linear fashion. Consumer surplus would not furnish an acceptable measure of welfare change in the sense of Chipman and Moore (1980). Instead, Anderson *et al.* (1992) derive and use the indirect utility function. Their (Cobb-Douglas) specification is not applicable to the monopoly problem addressed in this article — the monopoly price level would become infinite — but in principle I could have used their technique. This procedure would amount to an alternative proof of Proposition 3. The reason of this consistency is that the Chipman and Moore (1980) result renders the indirect utility and consumer surplus approaches equivalent for our quasi-linear CES function. However, an advantage of consumer surplus over the indirect utility technique is its wider applicability. The moment we depart from the representative consumer implicit in Anderson *et al.* (1992), indirect utility is no longer available, but consumer surplus still is. If the number of household types becomes as large as the number of varieties, all we can say is that demand fulfills Walras's law (Debreu, 1974). For example, in applied general equilibrium analysis the different household types are modelled by different CES demands. Consumer surplus can be evaluated, but not so indirect utility.

Acknowledgment

I am grateful to two anonymous referees and Associate Editor Sujoy Mukerji for insightful suggestions and stimulating me to expand the paper.

References

Anderson, S. P., A. de Palma and J.-F. Thisse. (1992). *Discrete Choice Theory of Product Differentiation*, Cambridge, MA: MIT Press.

Armington, P. S. (1969). A theory of demand for products distinguished by place of production. *International Monetary Fund Staff Papers*, **16**, 159–178.

Benassy, J.-P. (1996). Taste for variety and optimum production patterns in monopolistic competition. *Economics Letters*, **52**(1), 41–47.

Chipman, J. S. and J. C. Moore. (1980). Compensating variation, consumer's surplus, and welfare. *American Economic Review*, **70**(5), 933–949.

De Borger, B. (1989). Estimating the welfare implications of in-kind government programs. *Journal of Public Economics*, **38**(2), 215–226.

Dixit, A. K. and Stiglitz, J. E. (1977) Monopolistic competition and optimum product diversity. *American Economic Review*, **67**, 297–308.

Hausman, J. A. (1981). Exact consumer's and deadweight loss. *American Economic Review*, **71**(4), 662–676.

Hicks, J. R. (1942). Consumers' surplus and index-numbers. *Review of Economic Studies*, **9**(2), 126–137.

LaFrance, J. T. (1985). Linear demand functions in theory and practice. *Journal of Economic Theory*, **37**(1), 147–166.

Lambertini, L. (2003). The monopolist's optimal R&D portfolio. *Oxford Economic Papers*, **55**(4), 561–578.

Marshall, A. (1920). *Principles of Economics*, London: Macmillan.

Takayama, A. (1982). On consumer's surplus. *Economics Letters*, **10**(1–2), 35–42.

Tohamy, S. M. and J. Wilson Mixon Jr. (2004). Illustrating consumer theory with the CES utility function. *Journal of Economic Education*, **35**(3), 251–258.

Willig, R. D. (1976). Consumer's surplus without apology. *American Economic Review*, **66**(4), 589–597.

Appendix 1. Proof of Corollary 1.

The variation of consumer surplus can be evaluated by changing one price at the time. For a symmetric price vector change, from $(p, \ldots, p)$ to $(p', \ldots, p')$, the contribution to the variation of consumer surplus due to the first price component change is $-\int_p^{p'} D_1(p'', p, \ldots, p; I)dp'' = \frac{-I}{1-\sigma} \ln\left\{1 + \left[\left(\frac{p'}{p}\right)^{1-\sigma} - 1\right] \frac{pD_1(p,p,\ldots,p;I)}{I}\right\}$, with the argument of the ln equal to $1 + \left[\left(\frac{p'}{p}\right)^{1-\sigma} - 1\right] \frac{p^{1-\sigma}}{p^{1-\sigma}+\cdots+p^{1-\sigma}} = 1 + \frac{p'^{1-\sigma}-p^{1-\sigma}}{p^{1-\sigma}+\cdots+p^{1-\sigma}} = \frac{p'^{1-\sigma}+p^{1-\sigma}\cdots+p^{1-\sigma}}{p^{1-\sigma}+\cdots+p^{1-\sigma}}$.

The contribution due to the second price change is $-\int_p^{p'} D_2(p', p'', p, \ldots, p; I)dp'' = \frac{-I}{1-\sigma} \ln\left\{1 + \left[\left(\frac{p'}{p}\right)^{1-\sigma} - 1\right] \frac{pD_2(p',p,\ldots,p;I)}{I}\right\}$, with the argument of the ln equal to $1 + \left[\left(\frac{p'}{p}\right)^{1-\sigma} - 1\right] \frac{p^{1-\sigma}}{p'^{1-\sigma}+p^{1-\sigma}+\cdots+p^{1-\sigma}} = 1 + \frac{p'^{1-\sigma}-p^{1-\sigma}}{p'^{1-\sigma}+p^{1-\sigma}+\cdots+p^{1-\sigma}} = \frac{p'^{1-\sigma}+p'^{1-\sigma}+p^{1-\sigma}\cdots+p^{1-\sigma}}{p'^{1-\sigma}+p^{1-\sigma}+\cdots+p^{1-\sigma}}$.

And so on. The contribution due to the n-th price change is $-\int_p^{p'} D_n(p', \ldots, p', p''; I)dp'' = \frac{-I}{1-\sigma} \ln\{1 + [(\frac{p'}{p})^{1-\sigma} - 1] \frac{pD_n(p',\ldots,p',p;I)}{I}\}$, with the argument of the ln equal to $1 + [(\frac{p'}{p})^{1-\sigma} - 1] \frac{p^{1-\sigma}}{p'^{1-\sigma}+\cdots+p'^{1-\sigma}+p^{1-\sigma}} = 1 + \frac{p'^{1-\sigma}-p^{1-\sigma}}{p'^{1-\sigma}+\cdots+p'^{1-\sigma}+p^{1-\sigma}} = \frac{p'^{1-\sigma}+\cdots+p'^{1-\sigma}+p'^{1-\sigma}}{p'^{1-\sigma}+\cdots+p'^{1-\sigma}+p^{1-\sigma}}$. Summing the n contributions to the variation of consumer surplus we obtain $\frac{-I}{1-\sigma}$ times the sum of the n natural logarithms. That sum is the ln of the product of the n arguments. Because the denominator of an argument cancels against the numerator of the preceding argument, only the first denominator and last numerator remain. Hence the variation in consumer surplus is $\frac{-I}{1-\sigma} \ln \frac{p'^{1-\sigma}+\cdots+p'^{1-\sigma}}{p^{1-\sigma}+\cdots+p^{1-\sigma}} = -I \ln \frac{p'}{p}$.

Appendix 2. Derivation of the monopoly number of varieties.

The first order conditions of the interior solution are $x = (n^{\nu+m-1}m^2/c)^{1/(1-m)}$ and $(\nu+m)n^{\nu+m-1}mx^m - cx - F = 0$. Substituting the former into the latter, we obtain $(\nu+m)n^{\nu+m-1}m(n^{\nu+m-1}m^2/c)^{m/(1-m)} - c(n^{\nu+m-1}m^2/c)^{1/(1-m)} - F = 0$. Collecting powers, $c(1/c)^{1/(1-m)} = (1/c)^{1/(1-m)-1} = (1/c)^{m/(1-m)}$ and $n^{\nu+m-1}(n^{\nu+m-1})^{m/(1-m)} = (n^{\nu+m-1})^{1/(1-m)} = n^{(\nu+m-1)/(1-m)}$, we obtain $[(\nu+m)m(m^2)^{m/(1-m)} - (m^2)^{1/(1-m)}]$ $(1/c)^{m/(1-m)}n^{(\nu+m-1)/(1-m)} - F = 0$. Since the bracketed expression is simply $\nu m^{(1+m)/(1-m)} + m^{2/(1-m)} - m^{2/(1-m)} = \nu m^{(1+m)/(1-m)}$, we conclude $\nu m^{(1+m)/(1-m)}(1/c)^{m/(1-m)}n^{(\nu+m-1)/(1-m)} - F = 0$ or $n = \left(\frac{Fc^{m/(1-m)}}{\nu m^{(1+m)/(1-m)}}\right)^{\frac{1-m}{\nu-(1-m)}} = \left(\frac{\nu^{1-m}m^{1+m}}{F^{1-m}c^m}\right)^{\frac{1}{1-m-\nu}}$.

Chapter 11

Homothetic Utility, Roy's Lemma and Consumer's Surplus*

Thijs ten Raa

Department of Economics, Tilburg University, Tilburg, The Netherlands

tenraa@uvt.nl

Abstract. I provide a short proof that consumer's surplus normalized by income is the correct welfare measure when utility is homothetic.

Keywords: Consumer's Surplus, Compensating Variation, Equivalent Variation

JEL-codes: D60, I31

1. Introduction

Price effects on consumer's welfare are measured by Hicksian variations or by Marshallian consumer's surplus. Hicksian variations are compensating or equivalent. A compensating variation is an income subsidy that compensates a price increase and an equivalent variation is an income tax which yields an equivalent reduction of well-being. For normal goods an equivalent variation is smaller than the compensating variation, because money is more valuable before the price increase. Because the Hicksian variations have these crisp monetary

*Reprinted from *Economics Letters*, **161**, 133–134, 2017, with permission from Elsevier Science Publishers B.V.

interpretations, they are called "exact". Marshallian consumer's surplus is the area between the old and new price lines and the ordinary demand curve. It is easy to measure, falls between equivalent and compensating variations, and considered a good "approximation" (Willig, 1976). In a neglected paper Takayama (1982) has shown that not Hicksian variations are the correct theoretical measures, but a variant of consumer's surplus, at least for homothetic demands. This note presents a short alternative proof.

2. Analysis

A function U is *homothetic* if $U(x) = f(h(x))$, where x is an n-dimensional vector, h a homogeneous function of degree $d > 0$ and f an increasing function. If U is a utility function, we may just as well use any increasing transformation of U. Consequently we may set the degree of the homogeneous function equal to 1 and choose the logarithm for the increasing function. Hence a homothetic utility function U can be written

$$U(x) = \ln(u(x)) : u(sx) = su(x)(s > 0). \tag{1}$$

The essence of a homothetic utility function is that the solution of max $U(x)$:$px \leq I$ (p a price vector and I income, both positive) is $x = D(p)I$: Demand is multiplicatively separable in price and income. By equation (1) indirect utility, which is defined by $V(p, I) = U(x) = U(D(p)I)$, is additively separable:

$$V(p, I) = \ln(u(D(p)I)) = \ln(Iu(D(p))) = V(p, 1) + \ln I. \tag{2}$$

According to *Roy's Lemma* the local price effect on indirect utility equals minus the quantity purchased of that commodity, times the marginal indirect utility of money, which is given by equation (2):

$$\frac{\partial V(p, I)}{\partial p} = -x^* \frac{\partial V(p, I)}{\partial I} = -D(p)I/I. \tag{3}$$

Here $\frac{\partial V(p,I)}{\partial p}$ is the vector of partial derivatives with respect to the price components and $\frac{\partial V(p,I)}{\partial I}$ the marginal indirect utility of income.

In view of equations (2) and (3) the effect of a price change from p^0 to p^1 on indirect utility is given by the line integral

$$V(p^1, 1) - V(p^0, 1) = \int_{p^0}^{p^1} \frac{\partial V(p, 1)}{\partial p} dp = -\int_{p^0}^{p^1} D(p) I dp / I. \qquad (4)$$

Measure (4) is the integral of demand $D(p)I$, i.e. *consumer's surplus*, normalized by income (Takayama, 1982). *This* measure is exact, not the Hicksian variations. And since the latter variations are not exact for homothetic utility functions, there is no hope they are exact in general.

A referee insightfully suggested the analysis remains valid when income changes too, from I^0 to I^1. Indeed, in this case equations (2) and (4) yield that indirect utility effect (4) becomes

$$\begin{aligned} V(p^1, I^1) - V(p^0, I^0) &= V(p^1, 1) + \ln I^1 - [V(p^0, 1) + \ln I^0] \\ &= \int_{p^0}^{p^1} \frac{\partial V(p, 1)}{\partial p} dp + \ln(I^1/I^0). \end{aligned} \qquad (5)$$

The first term on the right hand side of equation (5) is, again, consumer's surplus normalized by income, equation (4). It is augmented by the logarithmic growth factor of income.

References

Takayama, A. (1982). On consumer's surplus. *Economics Letters*, **10**, 35–42.

Willig, R. D. (1976). Consumer's surplus without apology. *American Economic Review*, **66**(4), 589–597.

Chapter 12

The Consumer's Index*

Thijs ten Raa

Department of Economics, Tilburg University, Tilburg, The Netherlands

tenraa@uvt.nl

Abstract. Consumer's surplus measures the area under the demand curve between two prices, but is path dependent. There exists a path such that consumer's surplus tracks utility and an explicit formula is known for CES utilities. This paper shows that the CES based formula holds for any homothetic utility and I call it the consumer's index. The index modifies consumer's surplus in two ways: the change in income is measured by its growth factor and the area under the demand curve is normalized by income.

Keywords: Consumer's Surplus, Price-income Indices, Purchasing Power

JEL-codes: C43, D60

1. Introduction

A key issue is the measurement of purchasing power. Purchasing power is an index of price p, an n-dimensional nonnegative row vector, and income m, a positive scalar. An index is economic if it is based on the utility level of consumers. A consumer is supposed to

*Reprinted from *International Journal of Economic Theory*, 119–122, 2019, with permission from John Wiley & Sons.

$$\max U(x) : px \leq m, \tag{1}$$

where x is the consumption vector and U the utility function. The solution to the consumer's problem, (1), is demand $x = D(p, m)$, with value $V(p, m) = U(D(p, m))$. V is called the indirect utility function. An index, $I(p, m)$, *tracks utility* if it preserves the order of $V(p,m)$:$I(p^1, m^1) \geq I(p^0, m^0)$ if and only if $V(p^1, m^1) \geq V(p^0, m^0)$. An index cannot be (indirect) utility itself, because that is not observed. Indices are based on demand, which is observable.

The three main indices for price changes are equivalent variation EV, compensating variation CV, and consumer's surplus CS. The equivalent variation of just a price change, from p^0 to p^1, (while $m^0 = m^1 = m$) is the equivalent reduction of the budget, yielding the new utility level under the old price: $V(p^0, m - EV) = V(p^1, m)$. The compensating variation of the price change is the increase of the budget, yielding the old utility level under the new price: $V(p^1, m + CV) = V(p^1, m)$. The equivalent and the compensating variations are indirectly observable, by letting the consumer choose between the old and the new price regime and adjusting the budget in one of the two regimes up to the point where the consumer switches. More directly observable is consumer's surplus, $\int_{p^0}^{p^1} D(p, m)dp$. The three indices are increasing in the price change. They are transformed to purchasing power indices by inclusion of a minus sign and addition of the income change, $m^1 - m^0$. Thus, the consumer's surplus index is defined by

$$CS = m^1 - m^0 - \int_{(p^0, m^0)}^{(p^1, m^1)} D(p, m)dp. \tag{2}$$

Willig (1976) calls consumer's surplus an "approximation" to the "exact" measures of equivalent and compensating variation, but Takayama (1982) argues that consumer's surplus is the better foundation for an index. I side with Takayama, though consumer's surplus is problematic, but two modifications can straighten this out, at least when utility is homothetic. The essence of homotheticity is that demand is linear in income: $D(p, m) = mD(p,1)$. In the remainder of this paper I defend my siding with Takayama and discuss the issue of consumer's surplus. This will lead me to define a close cousin of consumer's surplus: the consumer's index.

2. Homothetic Utility

Utility is *homothetic* when it is an increasing transformation of a homogeneous function of positive degree. Without loss of generality, by taking an increasing transformation of the utility function, ten Raa (2017) shows that the indirect utility that comes with homothetic utility fulfills

$$V(p, m) = V(p, 1) + \ln m \tag{3}$$

and that, by Roy's Lemma, $\frac{\partial V(p,m)}{\partial p} = -D(p, m)\frac{\partial V(p,m)}{\partial m} = -D(p, m)/m$, we have

$$V(p^1, m^1) - V(p^0, m^0) = \ln m^1 - \ln m^0 - \int_{(p^0,m^0)}^{(p^1,m^1)} [D(p, m)/m]dp. \tag{4}$$

In equation (4) the leading terms stem from the last term of equation (3), while the last term stems from the first term of equation (3), $V(p,1)$, which is independent of m. Indeed, $D(p,m)/m$ is also independent of m for homothetic utility.

3. The Consumer's Index

I define the consumer's index by

$$CI = \ln m^1 - \ln m^0 - \int_{(p^0,m^0)}^{(p^1,m^1)} [D(p, m)/m]dp. \tag{5}$$

Obviously, definition (5) is motivated by equation (4), but, at least in principle, it is also applicable to non-homothetic utilities. For homothetic utility equation (4) shows that the consumer's index tracks utility.

The consumer's index, (5), is reminiscent of consumer's surplus, (2), but there are two modifications. The consumer's index measures the change in income by the logarithmic growth factor and it normalizes the area under the demand curve (or surface) by income. The latter modification resolves a well known flaw of consumer's surplus, at least for homothetic utility, namely the path dependence of the line integral in equation (2). This path dependence even plagues the consumer's surplus associated with homothetic utility. Indeed, in that case (2) reduces to

$$CS = m^1 - m^0 - \int_{(p^0,m^0)}^{(p^1,m^1)} D(p,1)mdp \tag{6}$$

and to illustrate the path dependence, take a path $(p^0, m^0) \rightarrow (p^0, m) \rightarrow (p^1, m) \rightarrow (p^1, m^1)$. I call such a path rectangular. The rectangularity merely concerns the division between price and income; the price path, $p^0 \rightarrow p^1$, need not be rectangular with respect to price components. For a rectangular path (6) reduces to

$$CS = m^1 - m^0 - m\int_{p^0}^{p^1} D(p,1)dp. \tag{7}$$

Equation (7) illustrates the path dependency of consumer's surplus, simply because path parameter m may vary. To the contrary, the consumer's index is not path dependent for homothetic utility. Equation (4) shows that the line integral of income normalized demand is $\ln m^1 - \ln m^0 - V(p^1, m^1) + V(p^0, m^0)$, irrespective the path of integration.

4. The Connection between the Consumer's Index and Consumer's Surplus

For a given pair (p^0,m^0) and (p^1,m^1) Stahl (1983) constructs a utility tracking path of consumer's surplus by tracing the old and new indifference surfaces in price space and joining them by an income jump at an arbitrary price vector. Income also varies along the two indifference surfaces (according to the expenditure function).

For CES utilities, ten Raa (2013, equations 5.12 and 5.13) offers an explicit result by showing that the rectangular path with

$$m = \frac{m^1 - m^0}{\ln m^1 - \ln m^0} \tag{8}$$

makes consumer's surplus (7) track utility (4). He also shows that (8) is an intermediate value of m^0 and m^1. The main contribution of this paper is that this result holds for any homothetic utility:

Proposition. *The intermediate income value* (8) *makes consumer's surplus* (7) *track utility* (4) *for any homothetic utility.*

Proof: For homothetic utility equation (5) reduces to $CI = \ln m^1 - \ln m^0 - \int_{p^0}^{p^1} D(p,1)dp$. Substitution in equation (7) yields

$$CS = m^1 - m^0 + m(CI - \ln m^1 + \ln m^0). \tag{9}$$

Since *CI* tracks utility, *CS* tracks utility if and only if *CS* has the same sign as *CI*. Substitute ten Raa's CES value (8) for m in *CS* expression (9). Then expression (9) reduces to $CS = m^1 - m^0 + \frac{m^1-m^0}{\ln m^1-\ln m^0}(CI - \ln m^1 + \ln m^0) = \frac{m^1-m^0}{\ln m^1-\ln m^0}CI = mCI$.

Because ten Raa (2013, equation 5.13) has shown that m is an intermediate value of m^0 and m^1, and both are assumed positive, we have $m > 0$. Hence *CS* with m given by (8) has the same sign as *CI* and, therefore, tracks utility. □

5. Conclusion

Consumer's surplus is plagued by the problem of path dependence, even when utility is homothetic. The consumer's index is a dimension-free modification of consumer's surplus. It tracks homothetic utility. Then it singles out the path on which consumer's surplus tracks utility. The use of the consumer's index for non-homothetic utility remains an open question.

References

Stahl, D. (1983). A note on the consumer surplus path-of-integration problem. *Economica New Series*, **50**(197), 95–98.

ten Raa, Th. (2013). *Microeconomics: Equilibrium & Efficiency*, Palgrave Macmillan, Basingstoke.

ten Raa. (2017). Homothetic utility, Roy's Lemma and consumer's surplus. *Economics Letters*, **161**, 133–134.

Takayama, A. (1982). On consumer's surplus. *Economics Letters*, **10**, 35–42.

Willig, R. D. (1976). Consumer's surplus without apology. *American Economic Review*, **66**(4), 589–597.

Chapter 13

Performance: The Output/Input Ratio*

Thijs ten Raa
Department of Economics, Tilburg University, Tilburg, The Netherlands
tenraa@uvt.nl

1. Introduction

A production unit, organization, firm, industry or economy performs well if it produces much output per unit of input, in other words, when the output/input ratio is high. The main performance measure is productivity. There are subtle connections between performance, productivity, efficiency, and profitability. Analysis of their interrelations will take us through many issues and concepts of measurement and will connect different bodies of literature, namely in economics and operations research.

The measurement of performance using an output/input ratio presumes that output components and input components can each be aggregated. This is particularly true for inputs. Production requires multiple inputs, typically labor and capital services. On the output side the aggregation issue is often circumvented. One way is to break down production in micro activities, one for each type of output. This approach moves the aggregation issue away from

*Reprinted from *The Palgrave Handbook of Economic Performance Analysis*, 77–95, 2019, with permission from Springer Nature.

commodities towards the micro performance measures (Blackorby and Russell, 1999). An obvious alternative way to circumvent output aggregation is to assume that there is a single performance criterion, such as profit, but this approach raises the question if profit is a better measure of performance than, say, real profit (profit divided by a price index). A windfall profit due to a price shock, without any change in the input-output structure of production, does not reflect an improvement in management performance. In other words, we better disentangle profit in a real performance component and a nominal price effect. This issue is related to the design of bonus schedules for managers, where profit is shown to be a good proxy for effort only if the distribution of the windfall component fulfills a certain property (the likelihood ratio monotonicity of Milgrom, 1981).

Throughout this chapter I assume constant returns to scale, unless explicitly stated otherwise. With increasing complexity I will discuss, first, single input-single output production; second, multiple input-single output production; third, single input-multiple output production; and, fourth, multiple input-multiple output production. The simplest of these cases, single input-single output production, suffices to discuss the relationship between performance, productivity, efficiency, and profitability.

Consider a single input-single output industry with two firms, a duopoly. Denote the input quantities by x and the output quantities by y. Use superscripts to indicate to which firm a symbol pertains: firm 1 or firm 2. Let the first firm be the more productive than the second: $y^1/x^1 > y^2/x^2$. (This is an innocent assumption, because we are free to relabel the firms.) Then firm 1 can produce no more than it produces, at least under the assumptions that the data represent all conceivable practices of production and that the firm's input is fixed. Firm 2, however, could perform better by adopting the production technique of firm 1. That way it would produce y^1/x^1 units per unit of input and since it commands x^2 inputs, its potential output is $(y^1/x^1)x^2$. By the presumed productivity inequality this exceeds the actually produced quantity, y^2.

In our discussion we must distinguish observed market prices and competitive shadow prices . Market prices are observed and may vary. Some firms negotiate tighter labor conditions than others; and some firms may have shrewder salesmen, extracting higher prices. Someone who "could sell sand to the Arabs" exercises market power but is not productive; the market price exceeds the production price.

Production prices are shadow prices which in turn are associated with the constraints of a program that determines the optimum allocation of resources. Later on optimality will be linked to the consumer's preferences, but in the introductory Mickey Mouse duopoly it reduces to the maximization of output subject to an input constraint. The maximization program can be applied to a firm (1 or 2) and to the industry (the duopoly), to determine firm and industry efficiencies. The simplest program features constant returns to scale and is applied to a firm, say firm 1:

$$\max_{\theta_1,\theta_2,c\geq 0} y^1 e : x^1\theta_1 + x^2\theta_2 \leq x^1, y^1\theta_1 + y^2\theta_2 \geq y^1 c. \tag{1}$$

In program (1) firm 1 runs activities 1 (input x^1, output y^1) and 2 (input x^2, output y^2) with intensities θ_1 and θ_2, respectively, and c is the expansion factor for output. The first constraint binds the required input by the available input. Denote the Lagrange multiplier or shadow price of this constraint by w (the labor wage). The second constraint binds the expanded output by the sum of the activity outputs. Denote the Lagrange multiplier or shadow price of this constraint by p (the product price). The shadow prices are relevant for performance measurement and are the variables of the dual program associated with the primal program, (1) in this case.

The dual program minimizes the value of the bounds subject to the dual constraint. The bounds are x^1 and 0, so the objective of the dual program is wx^1, or, equivalently, w. The dual constraint is $\begin{pmatrix} w & p \end{pmatrix} \begin{pmatrix} x^1 & x^2 & 0 \\ -y^1 & -y^2 & y^1 \end{pmatrix} \geq \begin{pmatrix} 0 & 0 & y^1 \end{pmatrix}$, featuring the row vector of shadow prices, the matrix of coefficient rows, and the objective coefficients. The first two components of the dual constraint, $wx^1 \geq py^1$ and $wx^2 \geq py^2$, state that the prices render the two activities unprofitable. Rewriting, $w/p \geq y^1/x^1$ and $w/p \geq y^2/x^2$. By assumption that the first firm is more productive and because w is minimized, the first dual constraint is binding, $w/p = y^1/x^1$. In other words, *the real wage rate equals the highest productivity* and, therefore, this activity would break even.

There is an interesting connection between shadow prices and competitive markets. Without loss of generality program (1) has been set up (by inclusion of coefficient y^1 in the objective function) such that the third component of the dual constraint, $py^1 = y^1$, normalizes the price system $(w \quad p)$ such that $p = 1$. Hence $w = y^1/x^1$. The second, less productive, activity would be unprofitable under these prices. In other words, if shadow prices prevail and entrepreneurs are profit maximizers, they would select the optimal activity to produce output. The solutions to the profit maximization problems are not unique, but there exists a combination of solutions which is consistent with equilibrium; see ten Raa and Mohnen (2002).

In the primal program, (1), the less productive activity is suppressed by setting $\theta_2 = 0$ and, therefore, $\theta_1 \leq 1$ and the maximum value is $c = 1$. Firm 1 cannot expand its output. Next consider firm 2. In program (1) in the right sides of the constraints superscripts 1 are replaced by 2. The first two dual constraints, $wx^1 \geq py^1$ and $wx^2 \geq py^2$, remain the same, as does the conclusion that the first activity would be adopted to produce output. The maximum expansion factor equals the ratio of the highest productivity to the actual productivity, $c = (y^1/x^1)/(y^2/x^2)$. For example, if this number is 1.25, potential output of firm 2 exceeds actual output by 25%. Conversely, actual output is only 80% of potential output. Firm 1, however, produces 100% of its potential output. The efficiency of firm 1 is 100% and the efficiency of firm 2 is 80%. Here efficiency is defined as the inverse expansion factor, $(y^2/x^2)/(y^1/x^1)$ firm 2 and $(y^1/x^1)/(y^1/x^1) = 1$ for firm 1. Efficiency is the performance measure. *Efficiency is equal to the ratio of actual to optimal productivity.* In the single input-single output case with constant returns to scale, introduced in this section, efficiency must be technical efficiency. However, in more general settings, the inverse expansion factor of efficiency will also encompass allocative efficiency, as we will see in sections 2 and 4.

2. Multiple Input-Single Output Production

In the bulk of the economic literature, including macro-economics, there are multiple inputs, such as labor and capital, but a single output. The inputs, x^1 for firm 1 and x^2 for firm 2, turn vectors and the input price will be represented by row vector w. The previous set-up is maintained and the extension to more than two firms is straightforward. However, because of the multiplicity of inputs several activities may now be activated when a firm maximizes output given its input vector, x. The potential output given an input vector is a scalar, the value of a function, $y = F(x)$. This is the reduced form of program (1) with y equal to scalar $y^1 e$ and x equal to vector x^1. Mind that potential output y is the product of actual output and the expansion factor. F is called the *production function*. To define productivity as an output/input ratio, we must aggregate the input components, if only because division by a vector is impossible. The way to do this is intuitive, making use of a well known property of Lagrange multipliers, namely that they measure the gain in output per unit of input. The rate of potential output with respect to input k is given by w_k, the shadow price of the constraint $\sum_i x^i \theta_i \leq x$. The productivity of input k is shadow price w_k. This is output per unit of input. Now the problem is that a unit of input is arbitrary. For example, sugar can be measured in kilograms or in metric pounds. Using the latter a unit has half the size of the former, the number of units is doubled, the shadow price is halved. We must aggregate across inputs in a way that is not sensitive with respect to the units of measurement. The way to do this is to first aggregate productivity over the units of the same input, k. The contribution to output of input i is $w_i x_i$ and in this product the two effects of taking metric pounds instead of kilograms cancel. Summing over inputs k, the value of the dual program is obtained. However, by the main theorem of linear programming the value of the dual program is equal to the value of the primal program, potential output y. The aggregate output/input ratio, $y/\sum_i w_i x^i$, is thus unity. The reason of this peculiar limitation is that output and input are different commodities; there is no common denominator. This is the economic problem of value and the classical solution is to express output in terms of resource contents, like labor values. Then, indeed, the output/input ratio is bound to be one.

Yet this framework is useful, because productivity levels are determined relative to a base economy, a base year. We do observe changes in the output/input ratio over time. For example, if the productive firm in section 1, firm 1, increases output in the next period, then $w = y^1/x^1$ remains valid, hence productivity w increases. This argument is extendable to the multi-input case. Dropping firm indices, productivity growth of input k is $\overset{\bullet}{w}_k$, where the dot stands for the derivative with respect to time. This, again, is sensitive with respect to the unit of measurement. However, aggregating across inputs, weighing by the units of inputs, $\sum_k \overset{\bullet}{w}_k x_k$, the sensitivity gets lost, because $\overset{\bullet}{w}_k x_k = \frac{\overset{\bullet}{w}_k}{w_k} w_k x_k$, in which the ratio is a growth rate while the subsequent product was already seen to be insensitive with respect to the unit of measurement. It is also customary to express the change in the output/input ratio as a growth rate, by dividing by the level, $\sum_k w_k x_k$. In short, the output/input ratio grows at the rate

$$TFP = \sum_k \overset{\bullet}{w}_k x_k / \sum_k w_k x_k. \tag{2}$$

Expression (2) is called *total factor productivity growth*. *TFP* is the most prominent performance measure. The expression can be rewritten as a weighted average of the factor productivity growth rates, $\overset{\bullet}{w}_k / w_k$, with weights $w_k x_k / \sum w_k x_k$. These weights sum to one.

This direct approach from Lagrange multiplier based input productivities to total factor productivity growth can be related to the Solow residual approach. Recall that the values of the primal and dual programs match, $py = wx$, where the right hand side is the product of row vector w and column vector x, and that we normalized $p = 1$. Differentiating totally, $\overset{\bullet}{w} x = \overset{\bullet}{y} - w \overset{\bullet}{x}$ and, therefore, expression (2) equals

$$TFP = (p\overset{\bullet}{y} - w\overset{\bullet}{x})/py. \tag{3}$$

Expression (3) is called the Solow residual; see ten Raa (2008), section 7, and the references given there. Solow (1957) modeled technical change by letting the production function depend on time,

$$y = F(x, t). \tag{4}$$

Differentiating production function (4) with respect to time, indicating partial derivatives by subscripts, $\overset{\bullet}{y} = F'_x \overset{\bullet}{x} + F'_t$ or

$$(\overset{\bullet}{y} - F'_x \overset{\bullet}{x})/y = F'_t/F, \tag{5}$$

Now if inputs are rewarded according to their marginal products, $w = pF'_x$, then the left hand sides of equations (3) and (5) match, and, therefore, the Solow residual (3) reduces to F'_t/F, i.e. *technical change*. This condition is fulfilled if the input prices are the shadow prices of the program that maximizes output subject to technical feasibility. The production possibility set, $\{(x, y){:}y \leq F(x, t)\}$, is the set which is either spanned by the observed input-output pairs or postulated by some functional form of function F. This distinction corresponds with nonparametric and parametric performance measurement. The first underpinning, by observed input-output pairs, is more fundamental, as the second underpinning, by a production function, can be shown to be generated by a distribution of input-output pairs, where the distribution represents the capacities of the activities. Houthakker (1955) demonstrated this for the Cobb-Douglas function, $Y = AK^{\alpha}L^{\beta}$, where K and L are inputs, Y is output, and A, α and β are parameters with $\alpha + \beta < 1$, meaning there are decreasing returns to scale. The returns to scale decrease because of constraining third input, as will be explained next. Output notation Y is customary in the Cobb-Douglas literature. Moreover, we may now reserve y for full capacity output.

An *activity* is a pair of proportionate inputs and an output. The assumption of input proportionality facilitates normalization of the activity by the output to $(k, l; 1)$, with $k = K/Y$ and $l = L/Y$ fulfilling $Ak^{\alpha}l^{\beta} = 1$. The activities can be parameterized by one input, e.g. k. Then $l = (Ak^{\alpha})^{-1/\beta}$ and, therefore, the technology set of activities is $\{(k, (Ak^{\alpha})^{-1/\beta}; 1) : k > 0\}$. Each activity can be run with intensity s_k. Total output will be $\int s_k dk$, where the integral is taken over the positive numbers. The constraints are $\int s_k k dk \leq K$ and $\int s_k l dl \leq L$, where K and L are the factor endowments. However, Houthakker (1955) assumes there is a capacity constraint for each activity. A fixed input causes the capacity constraint. The fixed input is different than the variable inputs, capital and labor. Houthakker (1955) suggests entrepreneurial resources. The distribution of the capacity constraint (of entrepreneurial resources) over activities $(k,\ l;\ 1)$, is considered to be given, $y(k, l)$. This distribution need not be concentrated on a frontier like $\{(k, l) : Ak^{\alpha}l^{\beta} = 1\}$. Some activities may dominate others, with both components of (k, l) smaller. Yet a dominated activity may be run, because the superior activity, like all activities, has a capacity constraint. Activities can be run with intensities $0 \leq s(k, l) \leq y(k, l)$. Subject to the factor constraints $\iint s(k, l)kdkdl \leq K$ and $\iint s(k, l)ldkdl \leq K$ we maximize output $\iint s(k, l)dkdl$. This is an infinite dimensional linear program, with a continuum of variables $s(k, l)$. Denote the shadow prices of the two factor constraints by r and w, respectively. By the phenomenon of complementary slackness unprofitable activities, with unit cost

$rk + wl > 1$, are not run, $s(k,l) = 0$. By the same argument, profitable activities, with unit cost $rk + wl < 1$, are run at full capacity, $s(k,l) <= y(k,l)$. Activities which break even, $rk + wl = 1$, have activity $0 \leq s(k,l) \leq y(k,l)$, but since the set of such activities has measure zero we may set $s(k,l) = y(k,l)$. It follows that inputs and output are $K = \iint_{rk+w|\leq 1} y(k,l)kdkdl$, $L = \iint_{rk+wl\leq 1} y(k,l)ldkdl$, and $Y = \iint_{rk+wl\leq 1} y(k,l)kdkdl$, respectively. The implicit assumption is that all factor input can be fully employed. There must be activities with factor intensity k/l below endowment ratio K/L and activities with factor intensity above the endowment ratio.

The three expressions, for inputs K and L and output Y, are interrelated by the two shadow prices r and w. The idea of Houthakker (1955) is to use the first to expressions to solve for r and w in terms of K and L. Substitution of the results in the third expression yields output as function of the inputs. Houthakker (1955) carries out this calculation for the capacity distribution with Pareto density function, $y(k,l) = \mu k^{\kappa-1} l^{\lambda-1}$, where μ, κ and λ are positive constants. The result is $Y = AK^{\alpha}L^{\beta}$ with $\alpha = \kappa(\kappa + \lambda + 1)$, $\beta = \lambda(\kappa + \lambda + 1)$ and A a positive constant depending on μ, κ and λ. In other words, a Pareto capacity distribution yields a Cobb-Douglas production function. This is Houthakker's Theorem. At the micro level activities have fixed input-output ratios — it takes given amounts of labor to operate given machinery and equipment — but a change in resources, such as the inclusion of the East German labor force in the year 1989, is accommodated by the activation of new activities and the deactivation of some incumbent activities. Reallocations of resources across activities manifest as substitutions.

The capacity distribution is not concentrated on a single isoquant in input space. Both k and l can be bigger, less efficient. In solving the output maximization, smaller input combinations are activated, but only to full capacity. Residual inputs are employed by more input intensive activities. The capacity constraints thus yield decreasing returns to scale. Indeed, the Cobb-Douglas function has exponents summing to a number less than one. Houthakker's activity foundation of neoclassical production functions works only if returns to scale are decreasing.

Clearly, different capacity distributions for the activity levels will generate different production functions. Houthakker (1955) has generated a stream of theoretical and applied research. The bulk of this literature features a lower dimension, with only one variable input, namely labor, and again one fixed output, which is now capital. In this one fixed-one variable input framework Levhari (1968) found the capital distribution for which total output is a CES function of the total fixed input (capital) and the total variable input (labor) and showed it encompasses the Cobb-Douglas function. Muysken (1983) has consolidated the Cobb-Douglas, CES and VES functions by showing they are all generated by beta distributions, with alternative parametrizations. Two books on the distribution approach to production are Johansen (1972) and Sato (1975). In this literature activities have fixed input-output proportions and capacity constraints explain the existence of inefficient activities. Increases in levels of inputs prompt the activation of less efficient activities, in Ricardian style. The law of one price yields rents to the more efficient activities. The activation of different activities prompts different proportions between the input totals and the output. Substitution is considered a symptom of the change in the range of active activities (run with positive intensity).

3. Single Input-Multiple Output Production

In classical economics labor is the only factor input. All other inputs are produced commodities, also called intermediate inputs. Production output is used to fulfill intermediate demand and final demand, where the latter is defined residually, as the difference between output and intermediate input. Production output is also called gross output; similarly, final demand is also called net output. In standard input-output analysis each output has a single technique to produce it. Assuming constant returns to scale, the input of commodity j, $j = 1, \ldots, n$, per unit of output, is denoted by the input vector $(a_{1_j}, \ldots, a_{nj}, l_j)$, of which the components represent the n intermediate inputs and the factor input (labor), respectively. If these unit input requirements are constant and fixed, they cannot be reduced and, therefore, are necessarily efficient (actual and optimal production coincide). If, however, there is a set of input vectors for each product j, there is room to reallocate labor between alternative techniques, which may save labor or, alternatively, increase output. This would increase the output/input ratio from actual productivity to optimal productivity. The ratio of the two would be efficiency. A deep result states that the optimal input vectors, one for each product, are independent of the composition of final demand. This is the substitution theorem, but for obvious reason also called non-substitution theorem, which goes back to Samuelson (1951). The proof of the theorem has a long history, in which details have been worked out and minor flaws eliminated. This culminated in a proof based on the efficiency program of maximizing the expansion factor of a some net output vector, determining the optimal input vectors, one for each product, and showing that this combination of input vectors remains optimal when the net output vector is replaced by another one (ten Raa, 1995).

The substitution theorem yields an all purpose optimal technology, featuring one technique for each product. Given any net output vector one can compare the optimal labor input to the actual labor input. The ratio is the efficiency of the economy.

4. Multiple Input-Multiple Output Production

The determination of efficiency is simple in the single output case: one maximizes output given the inputs and in the single input case one can minimize the input given the output. A mechanical extension to the multiple input-multiple output world would be to expand the output vector while preserving its component proportions. This procedure, however, presumes that the mix of outputs should not be changed, is optimal. Yet it is a useful procedure and I will detail it and discuss its merits. The fundamental paper of this approach is Debreu's (1951) now classic "The Coefficient of Resource Utilization," which will be discussed first.

The economy comprises m consumers with preference relationships $\succsim_i$ and observed l-dimensional consumption vectors $y^i(i = 1, \ldots, m)$, where l is the number of commodities.[1] Z is the set of possible l-dimensional input vectors (*net* quantities of commodities consumed by the whole production sector during the period

[1]I stick to the performance literature notation of (factor) inputs x, (consumed) outputs y, and intermediate inputs z. In the general equilibrium literature, including Debreu (1951), the notation is (factor) inputs z, (consumed) outputs x, and intermediate inputs y.

considered), including the observed one, z. A combination of consumption vectors and an input vector is *feasible* if the total sum — the economy-wide *net* consumption — does not exceed the vector of *utilizable physical resources*, l-dimensional vector x.[2] Vector x is assumed to be at least equal to the sum of the observed consumption and input vectors, ensuring the feasibility of the latter.

The set of net consumption vectors that are at least as good as the observed ones is

$$B = \left\{\sum y^{i'} : y^{i'} \succsim_i y^i, i = 1, \ldots, m\right\} + Z. \tag{6}$$

The symbol B stands for 'better' set. The minimal resources required to attain the same levels of satisfaction that come with x^i belong to $B^{\min}$, the South-western edge or subset of elements z' that are minimal with respect to $\geq$.[3] Assume that preferences $\succsim_i$ are convex and continuous, and that production possibilities form a convex and closed set, then the separating hyperplane theorem yields a supporting price row vector $p(x') > 0$ (all components positive) such that $x'' \in B$ implies $p(x')x'' \geq p(x')x'$. The *Debreu coefficient of resource utilization* is defined by

$$\rho = \max_{x'}\{p(x')x'/p(x')x : x' \in B^{\min}\}. \tag{7}$$

Coefficient ρ measures the distance from the set of minimally required physical resources, $x' \in B^{\min}$, to the utilizable physical resources, x, in the metric of the supporting prices (which indicate welfare indeed). Debreu (1951, p. 284) shows that the distance or the max in (7) is attained by

$$x' = \rho x \in B^{\min}. \tag{8}$$

In other words, the Debreu coefficient of resource utilization is the smallest fraction of the actually available resources that would permit the achievement of the levels of satisfaction that come with x^i. Coefficient ρ is a number between zero and one, the latter indicating full efficiency. In modern terminology, this result means that ρ is the *input-distance function*, determined by the program

$$\rho = \min_r\{r : \Sigma y^{i'} + z' \leq rx, y^{i'} \succsim_i y^i, z' \in Z\}. \tag{9}$$

---

[2]For example, if the last commodity, l, represents labor, and this is the only nonproduced commodity, then $x = Ne_l$, where N is the labor force and e_l the l-th unit vector.

[3]By convention, this vector inequality holds if it holds for all components.

5. The Farrell Efficiency Measure

Another classic paper is Farrell (1957), which decomposes efficiency in technical efficiency and price efficiency. Here technical efficiency is measured by the reduced level of proportionate inputs (as a percentage between 0 and 100) such that output is still producible. Price efficiency is the fraction of the value of an input vector with possibly different proportions (but the same output) to the value of the efficient input vector with the given proportions. Farrell (1957) notes the similarity between his technical efficiency and the Debreu coefficient of resource utilization: Both the Farrell technical efficiency measure and the Debreu coefficient of resource utilization are defined through proportionate input contractions, but the analogy is sheer formality and even confusing at a conceptual level. The analogy suggests that Farrell takes the Debreu coefficient to measure technical efficiency and augments it with a reallocative efficiency term, thus constructing a more encompassing overall measure. However, it is the other way round; the sway of the Debreu coefficient is far greater than that of Farrell's efficiency measure. Farrell's price efficiency measure is a partial (dis)equilibrium concept, conditioned on prices. It takes into account the cost reduction attainable by changing the mix of the inputs, given the prices of the latter.

The Debreu coefficient, however, is a general (dis)equilibrium concept. It measures the technical and allocative inefficiency in the economy given only its fundamentals: resources, technology, and preferences. Prices are derived and enter the definition of the Debreu coefficient, see (2). Debreu (1951) then *proves* that the coefficient can be freed from these prices, by equation (8) or non-linear program (9). The prices are implicit, supporting the better set in the point of minimally required physical resources. The Debreu coefficient measures technical *and* allocative inefficiency, both in production and consumption, solving the formidable difficulty involved in assessing prices, referred to by Charnes, Cooper, and Rhodes (1978, p. 438). Farrell refrains from this, restricting himself to technical efficiency and price-conditioned allocative efficiency, which he calls price efficiency.

The formal analogy between the Debreu coefficient and the Farrell measure of technical efficiency prompted Zieschang (1984) to coin the phrase "Debreu-Farrell measure of efficiency," a term picked up by Chakravarty (1992) and Grifell-Tatjé, Lovell and Pastor (1998), but this practice is confusing. Debreu's coefficient of resource allocation encompasses both Farrell's technical efficiency and his price efficiency measures, and frees the latter from prices. On top of this, Debreu's coefficient captures consumers' inefficiencies. The confusion persists. Färe, Grosskopf and Zelenyuk (2002) speak of the "Debreu-Farrell measure of technical efficiency." A recent review of Farrell's contribution states

> "(Debreu) worked only from the resource cost side, defining his coefficient as the ratio between minimised resource costs of obtaining a given consumption bundle and actual costs, for given prices and a proportional contraction of resources."
> Førsund and Sarafoglou (2002), footnote 4.

However, Debreu (1951) calculates the resource costs *not* of a given consumption bundle, but of an (intelligently chosen) Pareto equivalent allocation. (And the prices are not given, but support the allocation.) It is true, however, that the Debreu measure would become applicable if the aggregated consumption bundle can be considered given. Ten Raa (2008) demonstrates that this approach is doable and that it is exact if the preferences are Leontief.

6. The Debreu-Diewert Coefficient of Resource Utilization

Diewert (1983) had the idea that Leontief preferences remove misallocations between consumers as a source of inefficiency. The consequent coefficient of resource utilization yields a more conservative estimate of inefficiency than Debreu's coefficient resource of utilization. Ten Raa (2008) shows that Leontief preferences not only separate production efficiency from consumption efficiency, but also solve an aggregation problem: The Leontief preferences may vary between consumers, with different preferred consumption bundle proportions, but information of this preference variation need not be given. This useful fact is explained now.

Leontief preferences $\succsim_i$ with nonnegative bliss point y^i are defined for nonnegative consumption vectors by $y'' \succsim_i y'$ if $\min y''_k/y_k \geq \min y'_k/y_k$ where the minimum is taken over commodities $k = 1, \ldots, l$.

If so, the consumption term in better set (6) fulfills (ten Raa, 2008)

$$\left\{\sum y^{i'} : y^{i'} \succsim_i y^i, i = 1, \ldots, m\right\} = \left\{y' : y' \geq \sum y^i\right\}. \tag{10}$$

Equation (10) shows that "more is better" at the micro level if and only if "more is better" at the macro level. Equation (10) is a perfect aggregation result. One might say that if preferences are Leontief with varying bliss points (according to the observed consumption baskets), there is a social welfare function. The better set is freed from not only preferences, $\succsim_{i_i}$, but also from individual consumption baskets, y^i. Only *aggregate* consumption is required information.

This result creates the option to determine the degree of efficiency in terms of output. If the production set X features the impossibility to produce something from nothing and constant returns to scale, then $\gamma = 1/\rho$ transforms the input-distance function program (9) into the *output-distance function* program

$$1/\rho = \max\{c : c\sum y^i + z' \leq x, z' \in Z\}. \tag{11}$$

Output-distance program (11) determines the expansion factor and potential consumption i.e. net output. The ratio of actual output to potential output is equal to efficiency, the Debreu-Diewert coefficient of resource utilization, ρ. This has been applied and analyzed, including decompositions in different inefficiency components, for various economies.

Ten Raa and Mohnen (2001) evaluate the gains from free trade between the European and Canadian economies. The results show that bilateral trade liberalization would multiply the trade volume and let Canada, which is a small economy, to specialize in a few sectors. Perfect competition and free trade together will result in the expansion factors of 1.075 for Europe and 1.4 for Canada, while without free trade the economies expand to 1.073 and 1.18 respectively. The gains of free trade are evaluated at 0.2% for Europe and 22% for Canada. Sikdar *et al.* (2005) applies a similar model for measuring the effects of freeing bilateral trade between India and Bangladesh. The study was conducted against the background that Bangladesh was about to join the South Asian Association for Regional Cooperation (SAARC, established in 1985), in which India participated from the very beginning. Using the linear program version of the model, the authors locate comparative advantages in both economies, and contrast them with the observed trade pattern. While the patterns are generally comparable, there are notable differences for some products. For example, it turns out that although India is an exporter of 'Lifestock, fishing, forestry' and 'Other food products', the free trade model suggests that these should be import products for India. While on its own, each economy's expansion factor equals 1.37, the introduction of free trade would increase it to 1.43 for India and 1.97 for Bangladesh. This means that the potential gains of free trade for these two countries are 6% and 60%. Similarly to the previous paper, a small economy — Bangladesh — has much more to gain by joining the free trade agreement with a large economy. Ten Raa (2005) evaluates the contribution of international trade, disentangling trade efficiency from domestic efficiency, and splits the domestic efficiency of the economy into X-efficiency and allocative efficiency.

Another interesting decomposition of efficiency is provided by Cella and Pica (2001), who use a convex piecewise linear envelopment of the observed data (DEA) to disentangle sectoral inefficiencies in five OECD countries, Canada, France, Denmark, Germany and the United Kingdom, into internal sectoral inefficiencies and inefficiencies imported from other sectors through the price distortion of intermediate product prices. These imported inefficiencies are also called "spillovers" from other sectors. The study shows that inefficiency spillovers are empirically relevant in all sectors of the five considered countries.

Amores and ten Raa (2014) distinguish three levels of production efficiency of the Andalusian economy: a firm level, an industry level, and the economy level. *Firm level* efficiency measures the potential productivity gains (i.e., output/input ratios) that arise if the firm could choose to use production techniques of other firms from the same industry. (However, intellectual property rights may prevent this.) *Industry efficiency* measures the gains that can be achieved by pooling all the vectors of inputs and outputs of the firms that belong to this industry and reallocating production within the industry to maximize the total output value of the industry. Finally, the total *efficiency of the economy* measures the gains that can be achieved by the economy if there were no barriers to reallocation of inputs and outputs across firms and industries. Based on the results from these three problems, one can distinguish *industrial organization efficiency* and *industrial specialization efficiency.* The former captures the efficiency gains achieved by reorganization within industries, if each industry starts to produce a more valuable (i.e. efficient) output mix. The latter captures the additional efficiency that can be achieved by re-specialization of the output mix of the economy.

7. Interrelation between the Productivity and Efficiency Measures

Productivity growth, measured by the Solow residual (3), and efficiency, measured by the Debreu-Diewert coefficient of resource utilization (11), can be interrelated.

Productivity is output per input. For an economy input are the resources and output is the final consumption. Input x and output y are multi-dimensional. Denote the production possibility set at time t, the set of all pairs (x, y) such that x can produce y at time t, by P^t, the so-called *production possibility set.* Following equation (9) the input-distance function is

$$D(x, y, t) = \min\{r : (rx, y) \in P^t\}. \tag{12}$$

Input distance r is a number between zero and one. If $r = 1$, input cannot be contracted, is on the frontier of the production possibility set, is efficient. If $r < 1$, input can be contracted, is not on the frontier, is inefficient. An increase in the input distance signals an increase in efficiency. *Efficiency change* is the relative change in input-distance function (12) with a dot representing time derivative:

$$EC = \dot{D}/D. \tag{13}$$

The distance to the frontier may grow without any change in input x or output y, simply because the frontier shifts out. This shows as a decrease in the input distance. *Technical change* is minus the relative partial derivative of the input-distance function with respect to time, i.e. keeping input x and output y fixed:

$$TC = -D_t'/D. \tag{14}$$

To relate these efficiency change and technical change to the single output Solow residual analysis, we must replace Solow's implicit assumption that output is related to input by the production function, (4), by the more general relationship

$$y = D(x, y, t)F(x, t), \tag{15}$$

where potential output is reduced to actual output. Differentiating equation (15) with respect to time, $\overset{\bullet}{y} = \overset{\bullet}{D} F + D(F'_x \overset{\bullet}{x} + F'_t)$ or, dividing by expression (15),

$$(\overset{\bullet}{y}/y - F'_x \overset{\bullet}{x}/F) = \overset{\bullet}{D}/D + F'_t/F, \tag{16}$$

The left hand side of formula (16) features total factor productivity, see equation (3) with y 1-dimensional and p canceling out, and the right hand side features efficiency change (13) plus technical change. The last term is indeed consistent with equation (14), as output $y = D(x, y, t)F(x, t)$ and partial differentiation with respect to time yields $D'_t F + DF'_t = 0$. Summarizing,

$$TFP = EC + TC = \overset{\bullet}{D}/D - D'_t/D, \tag{17}$$

where the second equality holds term by term. Expression (17) holds for multi-output production with, however, constant returns to scale. Ten Raa (2008) proves that the efficiency change term is measured by the growth rate of the Debreu-Diewert coefficient of resource utilization and the technical change term by a generalized Solow residual of net frontier output growth evaluated at the supporting price vector.

In applied work time is in discrete periods and the main performance measure that accommodates this is the Malmquist productivity index (Caves, Christensen, and Diewert, 1982). Its derivation is as follows. The first term on the right hand side of equation (17) is the total derivative of input-distance $D(x, y, t)$ and the last term subtracts the third partial derivative. What remains are the first two partial derivatives,

$$TFP = \frac{\partial \ln D(x,y,t)}{\partial x}\frac{dx}{dt} + \frac{\partial \ln D(x,y,t)}{\partial y}\frac{dy}{dt}. \tag{18}$$

In discrete time expression (18) is a local approximation to

$$\ln D(x^{t+1}, y^{t+1}, \cdot) - \ln D(x^t, y^t, \cdot) = \ln \frac{D(x^{t+1}, y^{t+1}, \cdot)}{D(x^t, y^t, \cdot)}. \tag{19}$$

Evaluating this expression at t and $t+1$, taking the average of the two logarithms and exponentiating, one obtains the standard expression of the Malmquist productivity index:

$$TFP = \left[\frac{D(x^{t+1}, y^{t+1}, t)}{D(x^t, y^t, t)} \frac{D(x^{t+1}, y^{t+1}, t+1)}{D(x^t, y^t, t+1)} \right]^{1/2}. \tag{20}$$

The explicit price information in the Solow residual (3) has been replaced by implicit shadow price information, derived from the shape of the frontier; see Coelli and Rao (2001). The Malmquist productivity index assumes constant returns to scale. The decomposition of the Malmquist index into technical change and efficiency change, see equation (17), is straightforward; see Färe *et al.* (1989, 1996).

The Malmquist productivity index is popular because of its simplicity. Moreover, it can be bridged with other important TFP growth indices. The Törnqvist productivity index is defined by the discrete time approximation of (3) with value weights $w_k x_k / wx$ and $p_k y_k / py$ approximated by their arithmetic averages between periods t and $t+1$ and growth rates $\dot{x}_k / x_k$ and $\dot{y}_k / y_k$ approximated by the changes in the logs of x and y between periods t and $t+1$. Caves, Christensen and Diewert (1982) have shown that the Malmquist productivity index becomes a Törnqvist productivity index provided that the distance functions are of translog form with identical second order coefficients and that the prices support cost minimization and profit maximization. The Fisher productivity index is also defined by a discrete time approximation of (3), with the changes in the logs of x and y now evaluated at the prices in periods t and $t+1$ separately and then averaged arithmetically. Färe and Grosskopf (1992) have proved that the Malmquist productivity index approximates the Fisher productivity index under the assumption of profit maximizing behavior. Balk (2008) reviews comprehensively, including non-constant returns to scale.

A defect of the Malmquist, Törnqvist and Fisher indices is that they are not transitive. The changes from periods t to $t+1$ and from periods $t+1$ to $t+2$ do not add to the change from periods t to $t+2$. A necessary and sufficient condition for transitivity is that the index between periods can be written as a ratio of values of a function evaluated in the two periods. This property is fulfilled for the efficiency change component of productivity growth, but not for the technical change component, unless technical change is Hicks neutral. However, Balk and Althin (2008) shows that a modification of the Malmquist index, averaging out between firm observations, is transitive.

8. Conclusion

The key concept in performance analysis is productivity, which is the output/input ratio. Both output and input are aggregates. The appropriate weights are shadow prices of the program that determines potential output. The latter is based on observed input-output pairs or a production function, corresponding with nonparametric and parametric performance analysis, respectively. Parametric performance analysis can be conceived as nonparametric performance analysis with an appropriate distribution of observations. Hence nonparametric analysis is more fundamental. Replacing output by potential output, productivity becomes optimal productivity. The ratio of actual productivity to optimal productivity is equal to efficiency. Performance may increase because of efficiency change, technical change, scale economies or changes in the production environment. Technical change is a change in optimal productivity. All this can be grounded in economic theory, where optimality is defined in terms of consumer preferences. If consumers have Leontief preferences, with consumptions bundles preferred to be in fixed proportions, which may vary between consumers, then performance analysis is freed from micro consumer data requirements and shadow prices can be determined on the basis of production data and the proportions of final demand. Moreover, then the efficiency is measured by Debreu's coefficient of resource utilization and technical change by the Solow residual of net frontier output growth.

9. Acknowledgment

I am grateful to a referee for detailed criticism that prompted numerous improvements.

References

Amores, A. F. and T. ten Raa. (2014). Firm efficiency, industry performance and the economy: Three-way decomposition with an application to Andalusia. *Journal of Productivity Analysis*, **42**(1), 25–34.

Balk, B. (2008). *Price and Quantity Index Numbers*, Cambridge University Press, Cambridge.

Balk, B. M. and R. Althin. (1996). A new, transitive productivity index. *Journal of Productivity Analysis*, **7**(1), 19–27.

Blackorby, C. and R. R. Russell. (1999). Aggregation of efficiency indices. *Journal of Productivity Analysis*, **12**(1), 5–20.

Caves, D. W., L. R. Christensen and W. E. Diewert. (1982). The economic theory of index numbers and the measurement of input, output and productivity. *Econometrica*, **50**(6), 1393–1414.

Cella, G. and G. Pica. (2001). Inefficiency spillovers in five OECD countries: An interindustry analysis. *Economic Systems Research*, **13**(4), 405–416.

Chakravarty, S. R. (1992). Efficiency and concentration. *Journal of Productivity Analysis*, **3**, 249–255.

Charnes, A., W. W. Cooper and E. Rhodes. (1978). Measuring the efficiency of decision making units. *European Journal of Operational Research*, **2**, 419–444.

Coelli, T., and D. S. P. Rao (2001). Implicit value shares in Malmquist TFP index numbers. CEPA Working Paper No. 4/2001, University of New England, Armidale, Australia.

Debreu, G. (1951). The coefficient of resource utilization. *Econometrica*, **19**(3), 273–292.

Diewert, W. E. (1983). The measurement of waste within the production sector of an open economy. *Scandinavian Journal of Economics*, **85**(2), 159–179.

Färe, R. and S. Grosskopf. (1996). *Intertemporal Production Frontiers: With Dynamic DEA*, Boston: Kluwer Academic Publishers.

Färe, R., S. Grosskopf, B. Lindgren and P. Roos. (1989). Productivity development in Swedish hospitals: A malmquist output index approach. Discussion paper No. 89-3, Southern Illinois University, Illinois.

Färe, R., S. Grosskopf and V. Zelenyuk. (2002). Finding common ground: Efficiency indices. UPEG Working Paper 0305, presented at the North American Productivity Workshop at Union College, Schenectady, NY.

Farrell, M. J. (1957). The measurement of productive efficiency. *Journal of Royal statistical society*, **120**(3), 253–290.

Førsund, F. R. and N. Sarafoglou. (2002). On the origins of data envelopment analysis. *Journal of Productivity Analysis*, **17**, 23–40.

Grifell-Tatjé, E., C. A. K. Lovell and J. T. Pastor. (1998). A Quasi-Malmquist productivity index. *Journal of Productivity Analysis*, **10**(1), 7–20.

Houthakker, H. S. (1955). The Pareto distribution and the Cobb-Douglas production function in activity analysis. *Review of Economic Studies*, **23**(1), 27–31.

Johansen, L. (1972). *Production Functions: An Integration of Micro and Macro, Short Run and Long Run Aspects*, Amsterdam, the Netherlands: North-Holland.

Levhari, D. (1968). A note on Houthakker's aggregate production function in a multifirm industry. *Econometrica*, **36**(1), 151–154.

Milgrom, P. R. (1981). Rational expectations, information acquisition, and competitive bidding. *Econometrica*, **49**(4), 921–943.

Muysken, J. (1983). Transformed beta-capacity distributions of production units. *Economics Letters*, **11**(3), 217–221.

Samuelson, P. A. (1951). Abstract of a theorem concerning substitutability in open Leontief models. *Activity Analysis of Production and Allocation*, **13**, 142–146.

Sato, K. (1975). *Production Functions and Aggregation*, Amsterdam, the Netherlands: North-Holland.

Sikdar, C., D. Chakraborty and T. ten Raa. (2005). A new way to locate comparative advantages of India and Bangladesh on the basis of fundamentals only. In *Essays on International Trade, Theory and Policy for the Developing Countries*, Ed. Acharyya, R., Kolkata: Allied Publishers, pp. 169–197.

Solow, R. M. (1957). Technical change and the aggregate production function. *The Review of Economics and Statistics*, **39**(3), 312–320.

ten Raa, T. (1995). The substitution theorem. *Journal of Economic Theory*, **66**(2), 632–636.

ten Raa, T. (2005). *The Economics of Input-Output Analysis*, Cambridge: Cambridge University Press.

ten Raa, T. (2008). Debreu's coefficient of resource utilization, the Solow residual, and TFP: The connection by Leontief preferences. *Journal of Productivity Analysis*, **30**(3), 191–199.

ten Raa, T. and P. Mohnen. (2001). The location of comparative advantages on the basis of fundamentals only. *Economic Systems Research*, **13**(1), 93–108.

ten Raa, T. and P. Mohnen. (2002). Neoclassical growth accounting and frontier analysis: A synthesis. *Journal of Productivity Analysis*, **18**(2), 111–128.

Zieschang, K. D. (1984). An extended farrell technical efficiency measure. *Journal of Economic Theory*, **33**(2), 387–396.

Chapter 14

The Relative Performance of Formal and Informal Sectors in India*

Amarendra Sahoo[†] and Thijs ten Raa[‡]

[†] *Urban Institute, School of Planning and Environment Policy, University College Dublin (Richview), Ireland*
amarendra.sahoo@ucd.ie

[‡] *Department of Economics, Tilburg University, Tilburg, The Netherlands*
tenraa@uvt.nl

Abstract. We evaluate the relative performance of formal and informal sectors in India by looking into their productivity difference. Recognizing the intersectoral linkages in the economy, the competitive general equilibrium prices are computed; these signal the productivities. Our model synthesizes frontier analysis with the general equilibrium approach to generate shadow prices. The formal activities are found to be more productive than the informal. However, the informal services sector is as efficient as the formal one. There would be an overall productivity gain of 22% to the economy if factors were allocated to productive activities. The shadow prices from the model indicate that the formal capital and informal capital are scarce factors, while it has been the opposite for formal (regular) and informal (casual) labor. Formal labor is more productive than its informal counterpart; formal capital and informal capital are equally productive.

Keywords: Productivity, Formal and Informal Sectors, Competitive Prices, General Equilibrium

---

*Reprinted from *Economic Systems Research*, **21**, 151–162, 2009, with permission from Taylor & Francis.

1. Introduction

The existence of formal and informal sectors, particularly in developing countries, has led to much research on defining their differences.[1] Studies have shown that the formal sector is more productive than the informal sector because of size, the capital-intensive nature of production, self-selection by more productive employers for formal activities, taxation and productive public distribution to the formal sector (Esfahani and Salehi-Isfahani, 1989; Loayza, 1996; Webser and Fidler, 1996; Schaefer, 2002; Rogers and Swinnerton, 2004; Kenyon and Kapaz, 2005). Our study attempts to look into the relative performance of formal and informal activities producing similar commodities with different technologies in India, by way of evaluating their productivity levels.[2] We measure total productivity and account for intermediate inputs. As ten Raa and Shestalova (2006) contend that the main conceptual difference among alternative measures of total factor productivity turns out to be prices, we measure it with competitive prices instead of observed prices. Observed prices are generally not efficient as they are marked by distortions of several kinds. Competitive prices are the result of the removal of distortions with efficient utilization and allocation of resources when the economy is pushed to its production frontier. The observed prices in the productivity accounting framework are replaced by the shadow prices derived from a general equilibrium approach that incorporates intersectoral linkages. These shadow prices reflect the potential factor productivities under perfect competition. We focus on the productivity of existing technologies and do not address technological change induced by free trade. Besides finding the productivity differential between the formal and informal activities, this approach yields the potential productivity gain to the aggregate economy, if the resources were reallocated to the most productive activities.

The formal–informal division in developing countries is an important manifestation of the coexistence of traditional technologies and

[1]Morrisson (1995), and Fortin *et al.* (1997) described the differences in terms of scale, legal obligations and wage dualism.

[2]Instead of considering total factor productivity growth, which is useful for intertemporal comparisons, we use relative productivity levels more suitable for the comparison of formal and informal industries.

family enterprises on the one hand, and modern technology on the other (Stifel and Thorbecke, 2003). Like most of the sub-Saharan Africa and Latin American countries, the informal sectors in India contribute more than 60% of GDP and employ 87% of the labor force (Sinha *et al.*, 2003; Gibson *et al.*, 1986; Meagher, 1995; Schneider and Enste, 2000). Does this mammoth share of the informal sector contribute significantly to the health of the economy? The formal sector is generally thought to be more productive due to a better market, services accessibility and capital-intensive production (Webster and Fidler, 1996). It is often argued that the existence of the informal sector hinders the potential growth in productivity of the formal sector. In India, like some other developing countries, this debate has gathered currency at the outset of the new economic liberalization policy since the beginning of the 90s. Farrell (2004) contended that informal software companies in India reduce the overall industry's productivity and profitability by 90% and that Indian informal apparel maker's gain a 25% cost advantage over their law-abiding formal counterpart.

The informal sector is defined as the unregistered sector with self-employed microenterprises and family-owned activities. The informal sector is marked by less or no tax payment, less capital endowment, lower technology, less capital, lower wages and producing wage-goods compared to that of the formal sector (Gerxhani, 2004). The formal sector could feature mark-up pricing due to the existence of unionization, concentration in industries, and underutilization of capital (Gibson and van Seventer, 1995; Schaefer, 2002). Current measurement of the productivity differential between the formal and the informal activities requires removal of these mark-ups. The goods produced by formal and informal sectors can significantly compete with each other, as in Latin America, or they can be completely complimentary to each other, as in Africa (Kelley, 1994; Schaefer, 2002). We assume perfectly substitutable formal and informal commodities produced with different technologies. An efficient allocation of resources in a competitive environment would lead either to complete submission of production of some goods and services to one activity (formal or informal), or to sharing by equally productive activities. We evaluate the observed formal and informal activities at their potential competitive prices.

We draw our basic model from ten Raa and Mohnen (2001, 2002), which synthesizes Solow's growth accounting and the frontier data envelopment analysis (DEA) in an augmented input–output optimization model to measure aggregate productivity of the economy at shadow prices.[3] We maximize aggregate real consumption demand of the households with given commodity and factor constraints for both the formal and the informal activities. With the assumption of no technical change, the productivity level is solely due to utilization of inputs. Our index of productivity level is defined as the ratio of value-added to total factor input cost all evaluated at shadow prices. Value added is the sales value of produced output net of purchased materials, i.e. intermediate use. The value added concept is closely comparable to the amount of factors of production required, i.e. gross factor cost. Gross value added can be rationalized as a measure of output by imposing certain conditions on the production function. Bruno (1978) and Diewert (1978) had shown that if producers behave in a profit-maximizing manner, then the replacement of gross output by deflated value-added can be justified under conditions that inputs are used in fixed proportions to gross output, or the original gross-output production is functionally separable into the intermediate and all primary inputs, or if the prices of outputs and intermediate inputs vary in strict proportion. Given the Leontief type of production function in our analysis with respect to intermediate and factor inputs, the pattern of our productivity indices across the activities and between the sectors based on either gross value-added or gross output would be unbiased (see Theorem 2 from Diewert, 1978). The productivity index requires aggregation among inputs and within outputs with their relative importance or weights. Shadow prices generated by the competitive equilibrium explain the relative contribution of each factor input to the unit production at the frontier. Value added of an efficient-productive sector should account for its entire factor cost. The productivity index takes a value between zero and one. The inefficient industries, which do not match their productivity their high factor cost over the output prices, will have a productivity index less than one.

The rest of the paper is organized as follows. The next section gives an overview of the Indian formal and informal industries.

---

[3]DEA measures sectoral efficiency by using distance functions with respect to the production possibility frontier (Fare *et al.*, 1985, 1994).

Data and the structure of the Indian economy with respect to formal informal sectors are discussed in Section 3. Section 4 sets up the basic model, while the fifth section presents the empirical results. Section 6 concludes the paper.

2. The Formal and Informal Sectors in India

Before presenting a quantitative analysis of productivity differences between formal and informal sectors, we take a cursory look at the performance and prospects of Indian formal and informal industries in recent years. In our study, there are nine commodities and services in the economy. 'Agro processing', 'readymade garments', 'rice milling', 'other manufacturing' and 'other services' are produced by both the formal and the informal sectors. Besides these, 'agriculture' and 'construction' are all informal, and 'capital goods' and 'government administration' are all formal. The informal 'rice milling' industry, a separate unit from 'agro processing' is part of the rural economy. Once domestic and international competition was allowed for agriculture products (including rice) this industry started to grow in size with total investment of US$1.5 billion by the end of 2002, of which US$253.5 million was foreign investment. This induced the growth of the formal sector in the milling industry. 'Agro processing', which has been in the nascent stage in the 1990s, has been a key focus area for its value addition to agricultural produce. This industry consists of many fragmented units, namely diary sector, food, fish and meat processing sectors, etc., for which the share of the formal and informal sectors vary. The industry structure and ongoing transformation offer opportunities for organized players of the 'agro processing' (including 'rice milling') to grow (IBEF, 2006). Readymade garments constitute around 40% of the Indian textile industry, consisting of both large and small production retailing units. A study by Hashim (2005) shows that the textile industry is marred by inefficiency, contributing to the unit cost growth, and large-scale production (particularly in the ready-made garment sector) should be encouraged to make it more cost effective.

Subscribing to the terminology used by Gereffi (1994), the above-mentioned three activities ('rice milling', 'agro-processing' and 'readymade garments') could be treated as part of buyer-driven chains, where retailers govern the production. Traditionally, an overwhelming proportion of the retail market is occupied by the unorganized sector. But in order to cope with the intensifying competition and growing demand, the organized retail market is estimated to grow by 20% a year from the year 2000 (A.T. Kearney, 2006). Generally, 'other services' could comprise of small informal transport sectors, informal trade, and restaurants, self-employed software units, and other miscellaneous services. At the same time, the big enterprises, such as large transport and trading companies, hotels, banking and big software industries are also part of the 'other services'. This sector has marked a significant growth in the 1990s. Business services, communication, community services (education and health), hotels and restaurants have been fast rising growth sub-sectors (Gordon and Gupta, 2003).[4] These authors argued that this significant productivity gain in the service sector has been due to high-income elasticity of demand, increased use of input of services by other industries and economic reforms.

3. Database and Structure of the Economy

The basic data are drawn from the formal-informal social accounting matrix for 1999–2000 (Sinha *et al.*, 2004), with some modifications. There are five commodities and services produced by both the formal and the informal sectors. Besides these, 'agriculture' and 'construction' are all informal, and 'capital goods' and 'government administration' are all formal. The informal sector activities use 'casual labor' and 'informal capital' (owned by self-employed), while the formal activities use both casual and regular labor, 'informal capital' and 'formal capital', owned by entrepreneurs.[5] Casual labor (as opposed to regular labor) works on a short-term basis and can

[4]The average growth rate of service sector value added has been 7.5% per annum while the average aggregate GDP growth has been 5.8%.

[5]Capital is defined on the basis of its ownership, namely self-employed or employer (entrepreneur). 'Formal capital' is solely used by formal sector. Only the informal 'construction' activity requires 'formal capital' for its production. 'Informal capital' in the formal sector is owned by the self-employed, which is also an employer hiring less than six workers.

Table 1. Factor distribution across household groups.

Household groups	Casual labor	Regular labor	Informal capital	Formal capital	Profit
Rural – Casual Labor	0.63				
Rural – Regular Wage Earner		0.50			
Rural – Self-employed			0.26		
Rural – Entrepreneur				0.03	0.03
Urban – Casual Labor	0.37				
Urban – Regular Wage Earner		0.50			
Urban – Self-employed			0.74		0.24
Urban – Entrepreneur				0.97	0.73
Total	1.00	1.00	1.00	1.00	1.00

Source: Authors' calculation based on Sinha *et al.* (2004).

be easily displaced. Regular labor could be either relatively more efficient or at a more advantageous step of the job ladder. Part of the commodities is used as intermediate demand by both the formal and the informal sectors and the rest is absorbed by final demand. We assume intermediate consumption has the same pattern in the informal and formal sectors. There are eight categories of household groups, namely casual labor, regular labor, self-employed and entrepreneurs, all rural or urban; these coefficients are defined on the basis of ownership of factor endowments. Profit generated from each activity is distributed among the 'self-employed' and 'entrepreneur' households. Profit comes more from the formal activities than the informal.

The distribution of households' factor endowments is obtained from the SAM. Table 1 shows that casual labor is concentrated in the rural area, while regular labor is equally shared by the rural and the urban households. Most of the capital, both formal and informal, is held by urban households.

Table 2 shows that casual labor is mostly used by the informal sector ('agriculture', 44%; 'construction', 15%; 'other services', 17%), while regular labor is largely used by the formal sector 'other services' and 'government services'. Although there is not a big gap between the share of informal capital in the formal and informal activities, this factor is concentrated in a few sub-sectors, namely 'agriculture' (26%), informal 'other services' (21%), formal 'other services' (30%).

Table 2. Distribution of factors and output across formal and informal activities.

Sectors	Casual labor	Regular labor	Informal capital	Formal capital	Profit	Output
Informal						
Agriculture	44.04		26.14		2.00	15.73
Agro Processing	0.86		1.11		0.36	1.79
Rice Milling	0.33		0.42			0.19
Readymade Garments	0.08		0.10		0.09	0.14
Other manufacturing Goods	4.11		5.26		23.92	7.54
Capital Goods	0.00		0.00			0.00
Construction	14.74		2.49	6.00		6.40
Other Services	16.88		21.00			13.74
Government Services	0.00		0.00			0.00
Subtotal	81.04		56.52	6.00	26.37	45.52
Formal						
Agriculture	0.00	0.00				0.00
Agro Processing	0.46	0.97	1.27	2.80	0.69	2.35
Rice Milling	0.26	0.00	0.29	0.60		0.14
Readymade Garments	0.08	0.23	0.26	0.70	0.27	0.43
Other manufacturing Goods	3.90	6.90	9.72	22.28	50.83	16.04
Capital Goods	0.21	2.34	2.02	5.34	21.83	4.09
Construction						0.00
Other Services	4.03	33.26	29.91	62.27		21.43
Government Services	10.01	56.31	0.00	0.00		10.00
Subtotal	18.96	100.00	43.48	94.00	73.62	54.48
Total	100.00	100.00	100.00	100.00	100.00	100.00

Source: Authors' calculation based on Sinha *et al.* (2004)

The 'other services' in the formal sector takes the major chunk of formal capital (62%), followed by the formal 'other manufacturing', (22%). The formal sector generates more profit for the entrepreneurs. Production of 'other manufacturing goods' is the most profitable activities in both formal and informal sectors, followed by the 'capital goods' in the formal sector. Finally, for our experiment, we assume a 7% unemployment rate (Government of India, 2000) and a 70% capital utilization rate for the Indian economy.

4. Assumptions and the Model

Since we assume the same intermediate technology for both formal and informal sectors, the technological heterogeneity comes from differences in the intensities of primary factors of production. We model informal labor (casual) and informal capital qualitatively differently than their formal counterparts. While casual labor can freely move between the formal and informal sectors, regular workers are mobile only within the formal sector; the two types of labor are complements and regular workers have the capacity to perform tasks of casual labor (if they are left unemployed in the regular formal work), but not vice-versa.[6] This asymmetry generates a non-negative competitive premium for regular labor in the formal sector over the wage of casual labor. 'Formal capital' and 'informal capital' are mobile across the activities and both types of capital are complements. However, if formal capital is found to be in excess supply, it can perform the tasks of 'informal capital', not the other way around, resulting in a premium for 'formal capital'.

Productivity measurement requires competitive valuations of commodity and factors, which we derive from the following general equilibrium model. Assuming Leontief preferences and noting that the conditions of the second welfare theorem hold, the competitive allocation can be determined by the maximal expansion of total final household consumption subject to the commodity and factor constraints, while preserving the composition of the vectors of private consumption of the household groups.

$$\text{Max } D\mathbf{e}\sum_{h}^{8}\mathbf{f}d_h$$

$$D, \mathbf{x}^f, \mathbf{x}^i \geq 0$$

[6]Stark (1982) assumed the existence of a 'downward linkage' between the formal sector and the informal sector in order to capture the impact of formal sector job creation on the informal sector.

$$\mathbf{x}^f + \mathbf{x}^i \geq \mathbf{A}^f\mathbf{x}^f + \mathbf{A}^i\mathbf{x}^i + \sum_h^8 \mathbf{f}d_h D + \mathbf{g} \qquad (\mathbf{p})$$

$$\mathbf{l}^f\mathbf{x}^f \leq N^f \qquad (\omega)$$

$$\boldsymbol{\lambda}^f\mathbf{x}^f + \boldsymbol{\lambda}^i\mathbf{x}^i \leq N^i + (N^f - \mathbf{l}^f\mathbf{x}^f) \qquad (w)$$

$$\mathbf{k}^f\mathbf{x}^f + \mathbf{k}^i\mathbf{x}^i \leq K^f \qquad (\rho)$$

$$\boldsymbol{\kappa}^f\mathbf{x}^f + \boldsymbol{\kappa}^i\mathbf{x}^i \leq K^i + (K^f - \mathbf{k}^i\mathbf{x}^i - \mathbf{k}^f\mathbf{x}^f) \qquad (r)$$

Endogenous variables

D: Aggregate household consumption demand in the economy

$\mathbf{x}^f, x^i$: Column vector of formal and informal' output

Exogenous variables

e: A unit row vector.

d_h: A scalar of share of hth household's demand in the total (consumption weights).

f: Column vector of household's share of consumption demand for a commodity.

g: Column vector of fixed final demand other than household consumption demand.

$\mathbf{A}^f, \mathbf{A}^i$: Intermediate demand coefficients matrices of the formal and informal activities.

$\boldsymbol{\lambda}^f, \boldsymbol{\lambda}^i$: Row vector of technical coefficients of casual labor in the formal and informal sectors.

$\mathbf{l}^f$: Row vector of technical coefficients of regular labor in the formal sector.

$\boldsymbol{\kappa}^f, \boldsymbol{\kappa}^i$: Row vector of technical coefficients of informal capital in the formal and informal sectors.

$\mathbf{k}^f, \mathbf{k}^i$: Row vector of technical coefficients of formal capital in the formal and informal sectors.

N^f, N^i: Total supply of formal (regular) and informal (casual) labor in the economy.
K^f, K^i: Stock of formal and informal capital.

The first constraint is the commodity constraint; total demand is constrained by the perfectly substitutable formal and informal commodities. The shadow price of it, **p**, reflects the uniform shadow price for both the formal and informal sectors. The two labor constraints reflect the downward mobility of the labor. The casual labor constraint sets the base wage, w, for regular labour in the formal sector. This constraint shows that demand for casual labor is constrained by the sum of its supply and also the unemployed regular laborers. The third constraint is the constraint for regular labor. The shadow price of this constraint gives the wage premium (ω) for regular labour over the casual labor. The fourth constraint is for the demand and supply of informal capital, where demand of informal capital is constrained by the sum of its supply and the surplus of formal capital. Its shadow price sets the competitive rent (R) for the informal capital. The final constraint generates the formal capital premium, ρ.

National income and hence the household income and consumption on the frontier are evaluated at shadow prices. The equilibrating mechanism involves maintaining the propensity to consume at competitive prices with respect to the observed level for each household group with the adjustment of household consumption weights. In the equilibrium, the ratio of new propensity to consume to observed one should be the same for each household group. This is because, if the household's propensity to consume at the optimum exceeds the benchmark propensity to consume more than the other household, then the general equilibrium welfare maximization requires that the former household should be assigned with higher consumption share than the later. This is compatible with the welfare maximization program that shows that a competitive equilibrium can be represented through a welfare optimum with non-zero welfare weights (consumption weights) such that all consumers satisfy their budget constraints (Negishi, 1960).

The optimum incomes of formal and informal households are written as $Y_f = r\gamma_K^i K^i + (r+\rho)\gamma_K^f K^f + w\gamma_N^i N^i + (w+\pi)\gamma_N^f N^f$ and $Y_i = r\gamma_K^{ih} K^i + (r+\rho)\gamma_K^f K^f + w\gamma_N^i N^i$ given household groups' shares γ_K^f

and γ_K^i of formal and informal capital, and γ_N^f and γ_N^i of regular and casual labour. The new propensity to consume at competitive prices is $m_h^1(d) = \mathbf{pf}d_hD/Y_h^1$, where the subscript h stands for both formal and informal household groups ($h = 1, \ldots, 8$). The observed propensities to consume, $m_h^0(d)$, valued at competitive prices are similar, but with the optimal consumption baskets $\mathbf{f}_h d_h D$ replaced by the observed baskets. Now the equilibrating mechanism is $m_h^N(d)/m_h^0 = m_{h+1}^N(d)/m_{h+1}^0$, where $h = 1, \ldots, 7$. The maximization program is iteratively recomputed with adjusted consumption weights resulting in final optimum values for the endogenous variables.

We thus find the optimum pattern of formal and informal production along with the supporting shadow prices of commodities and factors of production. We use shadow prices to compute the productivity index for each activity in the observed economy. Given below are the productivity indices based on the value-added concept.

$$\Pi^f = \frac{(\mathbf{X}_0^f - \mathbf{A}^f\mathbf{X}_0^f)\mathbf{p}}{(r+\rho)\mathbf{k}^f\mathbf{X}_0^f + \mathbf{rk}^f\mathbf{X}_0^f + (\mathrm{w}+\omega)\mathbf{l}^f\mathbf{X}_0^f + \mathbf{w}\boldsymbol{\lambda}^f\mathbf{X}_0^f}$$

$$= \frac{(\boldsymbol{I} - \mathbf{A}^f)\mathbf{p}}{(r+\rho)\mathbf{k}^f + r\mathbf{K}^f + (\mathrm{w}+\omega)\mathbf{l}^f + \mathbf{w}\boldsymbol{\lambda}^f}$$

$$\Pi^i = \frac{(\mathbf{X}_0^i - \mathbf{A}^i\mathbf{X}_0^i)\mathbf{p}}{(r+\rho)\mathbf{k}^i\mathbf{X}_0^i + \mathrm{r}\mathbf{k}^i\mathbf{X}_0^i + \mathbf{w}\boldsymbol{\lambda}^f\mathbf{X}_0^i} = \frac{(\boldsymbol{I} - \mathbf{A}^i)\mathbf{p}}{(r+\rho)\mathbf{k}^i + r\mathbf{K}^i + \mathrm{w}\boldsymbol{\lambda}^f}$$

where $\mathbf{X}_0^f$ and $\mathbf{X}_0^i$ are observed formal and informal production respectively. Our dual program, where factor costs are minimized subject to price constraints, besides normalizing the prices, defines the shadow prices in the following constraints.

$$\mathbf{p}(\mathbf{I} - \mathbf{A}^f) \leq (r+\rho)\mathbf{k}^f + r\boldsymbol{\kappa}^f + (w+\omega)\mathbf{l}^f + w\boldsymbol{\lambda}^f$$

$$\mathbf{p}(\mathbf{I} - \mathbf{A}^i) \leq (r+\rho)\mathbf{k}^i + r\boldsymbol{\kappa}^i + w\boldsymbol{\lambda}^f$$

This shows that value added of an activity must be less than or equal to factor costs. Equality holds for the active sectors due to complementary slackness (see ten Raa, 2005). This establishes that our productivity indices take the value between 0 and 1. The inefficient production activity is marked by the index less than 1. If we use gross output instead of the value-added, the productivity indices will become

$$\Pi^f = \frac{\mathbf{p}}{(r+\rho)\mathbf{k}^f + r\mathbf{k}^f + (w+\omega)\mathbf{l}^f + w\boldsymbol{\lambda}^f + \mathbf{A}^f\mathbf{p}}$$

$$\Pi^i = \frac{\mathbf{p}}{(r+\rho)\mathbf{k}^i + r\mathbf{k}^i + w\boldsymbol{\lambda}^f + \mathbf{A}^i\mathbf{p}}$$

We can also notice from our dual program that the values of these indices vary between 0 and 1.

The maximization of final consumption demand in the primal program gives us the expansion factor, $c = D^*/D_0$, which is considered as an inverse measure of efficiency, which compares the potential of the economy against the actual performance. The D^* is the value of total consumption demand, D, at the optimum while D_0 is the observed value. We could also see from the objective values of primal and dual that the productivity level (ratio of total final demand to the total factor cost evaluated at shadow prices) of overall economy is the inverse of the optimal expansion factor (see ten Raa, 2006).

Given the difference in technology between formal and informal activities to produce homogeneous commodities and services, the pattern of specialization at the frontier will depend on our substitutability and mobility assumptions for factors of production. The gain in production efficiency is achieved through better production and allocation of resources. However, if there exists an observed underutilization of resources, the full utilization of them at the frontier results in an additional gain in efficiency.[7] The varying degree of utilization rates among different factors of production affects the competitive factor prices and, hence the productivity differentials. This also additionally decides the pattern of sectoral productivity and specialization.[8]

[7]This can be defined as X-efficiency (ten Raa, 2006).

[8]Besides the degree of underutilization, alternative assumptions regarding the mobility and substitutability of factor of production would generate different patterns of specialization at the frontier.

5. Model Results

Our productivity level, i.e. the ratio of value added to factor cost at competitive prices, ranges from 0 to 1. A unit productivity level implies that given the competitive prices, the particular technology is efficient and hence is able to recover the factor costs as value added. Productivity level less than one suggest that it is costly to produce that commodity or service by that technology (formal or informal). The formal and the informal activities could be equally efficient in producing any goods and services if both have productive level of unit ratio. Table 3 shows that formal activities producing all goods and services are more productive than the informal activities. Only in the production of 'other services', the informal sector is as productive as its formal counterpart. Shadow prices for the factor of production that the model generates reflect the factor productivities at the frontier. Table 3 shows that both formal and informal capitals are the economically scarcest primary inputs, having highest competitive rewards, and the casual labor is the least.

It is also observed that optimum allocation yields no competitive premium for formal capital over informal capital, indicating that they

Table 3. Productivity levels and shadow prices.

Activities	Productivity		Shadow prices				
	Informal	Formal	Output	Casual labor	Regular labor	Informal capital	Formal capital
Agriculture	1.00	X	0.93	1.69	5.80	11.05	11.05
Agro Processing	0.93	1.00	1.05	1.69	5.80	11.05	11.05
Readymade Garments	0.97	1.00	1.00	1.69	5.80	11.05	11.05
Rice Milling	0.96	1.00	1.05	1.69	5.80	11.05	11.05
Other manufacturing	0.97	1.00	0.75	1.69	5.80	11.05	11.05
Capital	X	1.00	0.58	1.69	5.80	11.05	11.05
Construction	1.00	X	0.63	1.69	5.80	11.05	11.05
Other Services	1.00	1.00	1.12	1.69	5.80	11.05	11.05
Government	X	1.00	0.62	1.69	5.80	11.05	11.05
Expansion Factor		1.38					

Note: 'X' stands for a commodity not at all produced by either of the sectors.

are equally productive, while regular labor is more productive than casual labor. We see from Table 2 that almost 94% of formal capital, 43% of informal capital and all regular labor are used by formal activities. Hence, it is expected that the overall formal sector would be more productive than the informal. We could also notice that the observed economy is operating at an efficiency level of 0.88, which is the inverse of the expansion factor, 1.38. This implies that there would be a potential gain in efficiency for the economy by 22% if factors were reallocated to productive sectors.

6. Conclusion

We use shadow prices instead of observed inefficient prices to evaluate productivity differences between the formal and informal activities in the Indian economy. Our model synthesizes the frontier analysis with the general equilibrium approach to generate shadow prices. Our major finding is that formal sector activities are strictly more productive than the informal ones. However, there is an exception for the 'service sector', where the formal and the informal production technologies are equally efficient. Capitals are scarcer factors than labors, indicating higher competitive rents than wages. Formal capital is as productive as informal capital and formal labor is more productive than informal labor. If factors were efficiently allocated to the productive activities, there would be a potential productive gain of 22% for the economy. We admit that the results can be refined with the help of a more disaggregated classification of production sectors.

References

Bruno, M. (1978). Duality, intermediate inputs and value-added. In *Production Economics: A Dual Approach to Theory and Applications*, Eds. Fuss, M. and D. McFadden, Amsterdam: North-Holland, Vol. 2.

Diewert, E. W. (1978). Hicks' aggregation theorem and existence of real value-added function. In *Production Economics: A Dual Approach to Theory and Applications*, Eds. Fuss, M. and D. McFadden, Amsterdam: North-Holland, Vol. 2.

Esfahani, H. S. and D. Salehi-Isfahani (1989). Effort observability and worker productivity: Towards an explanation of economic dualism. *Economic Journal*, **99**, 818–836.

Farrell, D. (2004). Boost growth by reducing the informal economy. *The Asian Wall Street Journal*, October 18.

Fare, R., S. Grosskopf and C. A. K. Lovell. (1985). *The Measurement of Efficiency of Production*, Boston: Kluwer Academic Publishers.

Fare, R., S. Grosskopf, M. Norris and Z. Zhang. (1994). Productivity growth, technical progress, and efficiency change in industrialized countries. *American Economic Review*, **84**, 66–83.

Fortin, B., N. Marceau and L. Savard. (1997). Taxation, wage controls and the informal Sector. *Journal of Public Economics*, **66**, 293–312.

Gereffi, G. (1994). The organization of buyer-driven global commodity chains: How U.S. retailers shape overseas production networks. In *Commodity Chains and Global Capitalism*, Eds. Gereffi, G. and M. Korzeniewicz, Westport, CT: Praeger.

Gerxhani, K. (2004). The informal sector in developed and less developed countries: A literature survey. *Public Choice*, **120**, 267–300.

Gibson, B., N. Lustig and L. Taylor. (1986). Terms of trade and class conflict in a computable general equilibrium model for Mexico. *Journal of Development Studies*, **23**, 40–59.

Gibson, B. and D. van Seventer. (1995). Toward a growth strategy for the South African economy. Working Paper, Pretoria, South Africa, Development Bank of South Africa.

Gordon, J. and P. Gupta. (2003). Understanding India's services revolution. Paper Prepared for IMF-NCAER Conference, A Tale of Two Giants: India's and China's Experience with Reform, 14–16 November.

Government of India. (2000). Employment and unemployment in India 1999–2000. NSS 55th round, National Sample Survey Organization, Ministry of Statistics and Program Implementation, New Delhi.

Hashim, D. A. (2005). Cost and productivity in Indian textiles: Post MFA implication. Working Paper, Indian Council for Research on International Economic Relations (ICRIER), New Delhi.

IBEF. (2006). Food Processing. Indian Brand Equity Foundation, presented in Davos, 25–29 January.

Kearney, A. T. (2006). *Emerging Market Priorities for Global Retailers: The 2006 Global Retail Development Index*, Chicago: A.T. Kearney, Inc.

Kelley, B. (1994). The informal sector and the macro-economy: A computable general equilibrium approach for Peru. *World Development*, **22**, 1393–1411.

Kenyon, T. and E. Kapaz. (2005). The Informal Trap. Public Policy for the Private Sector. The World Bank group Private Sector Development Vice Presidency, December, Washington, DC, World Bank.

Loayza, N. V. (1996). The economics of the informal sector: A simple model and some evidence from Latin America. *Cambridge-Rochester Conference Series on Public Policy*, **45**, 129–162.

Meagher, K. (1995). Crisis, informalization and the urban informal sector in sub-Saharan Africa. *Development and Change*, **26**, 259–284.

Morrisson, C. (1995). What institutional framework for the informal sector? Policy Brief No. 10, OECD Development Centre, Paris.

Negishi, T. (1960). Welfare economics and existence of an equilibrium for a competitive economy. *Metroeconomica*, **12**, 92–97.

Rogers, C. A. and K. A. Swinnerton. (2004). A model of informal sector labour markets. Northeast University Development Consortium Conference, 1–3 October, HEC Montreal, Canada.

Schaefer, K. K. (2002). Capacity utilization, income distribution and the urban informal sector: An open-economy model. Working Paper Series, No. 35, Political Economy Research Institute, University of Massachusetts Amherst.

Schneider, F. and D. H. Enste. (2000). Shadow economies: Sizes, causes and consequences. *Journal of Economic Perspectives*, **38**, 77–114.

Sinha, A., K. A. Siddiqui and N. Sangeeta. (2003). The Impact of Alternative Economic Policies on the Informal Sector, National Council of Applied Economic Research, New Delhi.

Sinha, A., K. A. Siddiqui and P. Munjal. (2004). The Indian Informal Economy within a SAM Framework, National Council of Applied Economic Research, New Delhi.

Stark, E. (1982). On modeling the informal sector. *World Development*, **10**, 413–416.

Stifel, D. C. and E. Thorbecke. (2003). A dual-dual CGE model of an archetype African economy: Trade reform, migration and poverty. *Journal of Policy Modeling*, **25**, 207–235.

ten Raa, T. (2005). *The Economics of Input–Output Analysis*, New York: Cambridge University Press.

ten Raa, T. (2006). Benchmarking and Industry Performance. Department of Econometrics and Operations Research, Tilburg University, The Netherlands.

ten Raa, T. and P. Mohnen. (2001). The location of comparative advantages on the basis of fundamentals only. *Economic Systems Research*, **13**, 93–108.

ten Raa, T. and P. Mohnen. (2002). Neoclassical growth accounting and frontier analysis: A synthesis. *Journal of Productivity Analysis*, **18**, 111–128.

ten Raa, T. and V. Shestalova. (2006). Alternative measures of total factor productivity growth. Working Paper, Department of Econometrics and Operations Research, Tilburg University, The Netherlands.

Webster, L. and P. Fidler. (1996). The informal sector and microfinance institutions in West Africa. Technical Paper No. 342F, World Bank, Washington, DC.

Chapter 15

Wage-Productivity Differentials and Indian Economic Efficiency*

Amarendra Sahoo[†,¶] and Thijs ten Raa[‡]

[†]*Researcher, Institute for environmental Science (CML)*
Leiden University, P.O. Box 9518, 2300 RA
Leiden, The Netherlands
amar_sahoo@hotmail.com
Correspondence address: Sabelhof 2,
5044 JR Tilburg, Netherlands

[‡]*Department of Economics, Tilburg University,*
Tilburg, The Netherlands
tenraa@uvt.nl

Abstract. A frontier-general equilibrium analysis with skill transformation evaluates the productivities of skilled and unskilled labour and potential of the Indian economy. We compare the wages of skilled and unskilled labour between 1994 and 2002 with their respective productivities over this period. Education is considered to be responsible for the skill formation over this period: the change in skilled labour supply is endogenous in the model. Compared to its productivity, skilled labour is underpaid in the initial period and overpaid in the second period. Unskilled labour is underpaid in both periods. A decomposition exercise shows that skilled labour gains from free trade, and stands to lose due to education and domestic competition in the second period.

*Reprinted from *Journal of Economic Modelling*, **29**, 341–348, 2012, with permission from Elsevier Science Publishers B.V.

¶Author is responsible for proofs and correspondence.

The annualized rate of return to education is between 7 and 10%. The economy operates below its potential in both periods, particularly in the second — due to trade limitations and the failure to capture the return to education. Service sectors are found to have potential to grow significantly.

Keywords: Competitive Pressure, Wage and Productivity Inequality, Efficiency, Returns to Education, Frontier-general Equilibrium Analysis, Multiplicative Decomposition, Skill Formation, Trade Efficiency

JEL-codes: D24, D41, D57, D58, I20, J24, J31, O53

1. Introduction

Do wage differentials follow productivity differentials and which economic inefficiencies cause distortions? For long, Indian industries were characterized by inefficiency, high costs and uneconomical means of production with pervasive government control. With a view to improving efficiency and global competitiveness, liberalization policy and economic reforms were introduced at the outset of 1990s. Post liberalization period is marked by much higher productivity growth and increased contributions from the service sector and the skilled-based manufacturing industries (Virmani, 2005; Bosworth *et al.*, 2006), which have possibly increased the wage premium for higher education. It is believed that India still needs a higher pace of reforms towards competitive markets (Bajpai and Sachs, 1997; Fischer, 2002). The resulting competitive factor prices that reflect the factor productivities would determine the returns to education. Our study compares the wages of skilled and unskilled labour between 1994 and 2002, over the decade of strong reform, with the respective productivities and also measures the potential of the economy in these two periods. We conduct a decomposition exercise in order to track the factors responsible for the wage-productivity differentials and observed-potential gap in the economy. Our observations of the study can be indications for the performance of Indian economy in the later periods.

Tinbergen (1975) argued that opposing effects of technology (skilled labour demand) and education (skilled labour supply)

determine the relative wage. Between 1987 and 1993, the returns to education in India increased significantly for middle and secondary levels, but not for primary and higher education (Bargain *et al.*, 2006). The returns to middle and secondary level education fell over the next period 1993–2004, while the returns to higher education (college) grew (Asian Development Bank, 2007). Prior to 1993 (the pre-liberalization period) lack of demand for basic education could have been the reason for the high middle and secondary education premiums. Pradhan and Subramanian (2000), based on the MIMAP-India Survey (Pradhan and Roy, 2003) for 1994–95, argue demand for education was low due to dim expected future earnings. Incomplete markets for higher education depress returns to higher education during this period.

Sectoral skilled-unskilled wage differentials in India depict no clear pattern over time (see Table 1). The gap increased in 'agriculture', 'heavy industries', 'transports and storage', and 'wholesale and retailed trade', but decreased in the other sectors. From 1994 to 2002 the supply of skilled labour increased in all sectors relative to unskilled except in 'construction'. Supply and demand of 'education' increased over this period. The relative wage of skilled to unskilled labour declined marginally from 2.95 in 1994 to 2.91 in 2002. We compare the relative wage with the relative productivity. The relative productivity signals the potentials differential between skilled and unskilled labour.

The productivity and efficiency aspects of growth have attracted attention in the real business cycle (Kydland and Prescott, 1996 and Prescott, 1986) and endogenous growth (Romer, 1986 and Lucas, 1988) literatures. Our model is a dynamic extension of ten Raa and Mohnen's (2002), bringing in dynamic physical capital inefficiency and education inefficiencies. Following Negishi (1960), the efficiency frontier is determined subject to commodity, factor and trade constraints. The distance of the economy towards its frontier determines inefficiency. We make the frontier approach dynamic by incorporating human and physical capital formation. Education process in our model determines the returns to education, skill transformation and productivity of skilled labour. A dynamic framework seems a natural response to the inconclusive literature.

Table 1. Skilled-unskilled wages and labour supply, real output and final demand between 1994 and 2002.

	Ratio of skill to unskilled wages		Ratio of skilled to unskilled labour		Ratio of 2002 to 1994	
Sectors	1994	2002	1994	2002	Real Output	Real final demand
1. Agriculture and allied	1.30	1.58	0.19	0.39	1,19	1,12
2. Mining and quarrying	2.03	1.91	0.33	0.57	1,52	3,43
3. Light manufacturing	1.98	1.84	0.37	0.69	1,67	2,42
4. Heavy manufacturing	2.26	2.44	0.92	1.40	1,94	1,15
5. Construction	1.58	1.46	0.31	0.55	1,79	2,01
6. Electricity, gas and water	1.72	1.64	1.75	4.42	1,46	1,97
7. Transports, storage	1.69	1.84	0.81	1.40	1,67	2,40
8. Wholesale, ret. trade	1.78	1.83	0.81	1.31	1,77	2,07
9. Finance, insurance, real est.	3.39	2.97	10.19	11.70	2,60	2,85
10. Services	3.70	2.92	1.17	2.18	2,28	2,19
11. Education	3.70	2.92	1.17	2.18	5,65	5,75
All Sectors	2.95	2.91	0.38	0.64		

Sources: Pradhan *et al.* (1999) and Pradhan *et al.* (2006).

Trade liberalization increased the skilled-unskilled wage gap in Latin America (Hanson and Harrison, 1999), but reduced it in East Asia (Wood, 1994; 1999). Wage differentials between skilled and unskilled labour have been analyzed for both developed and developing countries (Wood, 1999; Katz and Autor, 1999; Williamson, 1999). The explanations include skilled-biased technological change, international trade, and supply-demand factors (Katz and Murphy, 1992; Learner, 1996; Krusell *et al.*, 1997; Berman *et al.*, 1998; Kiley, 1999; Machin, 2002). In the Indian context, studies have shown that trade openness has an exacerbating effect on the skilled-unskilled wage gap (Pradhan, 2002; Marjit and Acharya, 2003; Beladi and Chakraborty, 2004; Dutta, 2004), but no clear picture has emerged as regards the effect of education on the skill premium during the period of liberalization. Pradhan (2002), with the help of a general equilibrium model, observed that even large increases in the access to education preserve the wage inequality, but an econometric study by Dutta (2005) found that despite the increase in the skill premium education helped reduce the wage gap.

We will assess the contributions of various factors to the productivity-wage differentials. Productivity is determined at the frontier, which is beyond actual output due to four reasons: static inefficiency from domestic allocative inefficiency, i.e. domestic competition, static trade inefficiency, dynamic inefficiency from human capital formation and dynamic inefficiency from physical capital formation. The decomposition is based on an extended Fisher Index approach, to ensure path independence (which is an issue due to the non-linearity of our model). As the elasticity of substitution between skilled and unskilled labour is expected to influence wage differentials, we simulate with different values for this parameter.

The rest of the paper is divided into four sections. The theoretical model is presented in the Section 2. Section 3 analyses the basic data set and calibrates. The model results are discussed in the Section 4, while Section 5 concludes.

2. The Model

We determine the frontier of the economy by maximizing the vector of total final demand excluding the investment demand and net export (which will be endogenous) subject to commodity, factor and trade deficit constraints. There are three types of factors, viz. Capital, skilled labour and unskilled labour. We consider a small open economy, where producers of tradable products take the world prices as given, with Leontief preferences. The endogenous pattern of trade is constrained by the observed deficit on the balance of payment. The model computes the economy's production frontier and the competitive factor and commodity prices. The gap between the frontier and the observed total final demands (observed total economic activities) measures inefficiency. The economy is classified into 11 economic activities including education sector (see Table 1).

Human and physical capital formations are modelled as forward-looking processes without adjustment costs. The initial supply of capital and education is fixed by past investments. Households are modelled by means of a forward-looking intertemporal utility-maximizing representative consumer. A commonly used additively separable intertemporal preference function is assumed, where the second period's utility is added with a discount factor, $\beta(0 \leq \beta \leq 1)$. The implicit discount rate is $\mu = (1-\beta)/\beta$. We maximize the additive intertemporal utility, $D^0 + \beta D^1$, subject to constraints on demand, resources, trade, capital formation and education process. Here D^t is the value of aggregate final demand at the optimum for period t. This model is a finite horizon Ramsey model, where a fictitious planning authority splits production between consumption and capital accumulation.

The expansion factor is defined as $c^t = D^t/D_0^t$, where D_0^t is the observed value of aggregate final demand. The inverse of the expansion factor measures the efficiency of the economy in period t and the residual $1 - 1/c^t$ the inefficiency.

In each period producers face a nested production function. A Leontief production function of intermediate inputs and a factor-input aggregate forms the first rung of the nested structure. The aggregate is a Cobb-Douglas function of capital and a labour composite, a CES function of skilled and unskilled labour. Capital is sector specific, in the Ricardo-Viner spirit, but skilled and unskilled labour may move freely between sectors. We assume "downward mobility" of skilled labour, the ability to join the unskilled pool if unsuccessful in the skilled labour search[1]. Here is the model:

$$Max \quad D^0 + \beta D^1 \quad w.r.t. \quad D^t, X_i^t, T_i^t, I^0, K_i^t, L_{s_i}^t, L_{u_i}^t, \sigma^0, \Delta S \geq 0$$

$$t = 0, 1\, s.t.$$

$$\sum_j a_{ij}^t X_i^t + f_i^t D^t + \tau_i^t I^t + T_i^t \leq X_i^t$$

$$(i, j = 1, \ldots, 11;\ 11 = \text{education}) \tag{1}$$

$$X_i^t \leq \theta_i^t (K_i^t)^{(1-\phi_i^t)} [\alpha_i^t (L_{s_i}^t)^{\rho_i} + (1 - \alpha_i^t)(L_{u_i}^t)^{\rho_i}]^{\phi_i^t/\rho_i} \tag{2}$$

$$\sum_i L_{u_i}^t \leq N^t - \sum_i L_{s_i}^t - \sigma^t \tag{3}$$

$$\sum_i L_{s_i}^0 \leq S^0, \quad \sum_i L_{s_i}^1 \leq S^0 + \Delta S \tag{4}$$

[1]This ensures that the competitive skilled wage is at least as big as the unskilled.

$$K_i^0 \leq \overline{K_i^0}, \quad K_i^1 \leq K_i^0 + \delta_i I^0 \tag{5}$$

$$-\sum_i \pi_i^t T_i^t \leq B^t \tag{6}$$

$$\Delta S = \xi(\sigma^0), \quad \sigma^0 = \lambda^0 X_{11}^0 \tag{7}$$

Endogenous variables:

D^t: Aggregate final demand excluding investment and net export in period t

I^0: Aggregate investment demand in the initial period

X_i^t: Output of ith sector in period t

T_i^t: Net exports of tradable sector in period t; $i \neq 5$, 6 and 10

ΔS: Addition to stock of skilled labour in the end period over the initial period

σ^0: Stock of unskilled labour force going for education in the initial period

$L_{u_i}^t$: Demand for unskilled labour for period t respectively by i^{th} sector

$L_{s_i}^t$: Demand for skilled labour for period t respectively by i^{th} sector

K_i^t: Demand for capital in period t respectively by i^{th} sector

$\overline{K_i^1}$: Stock of capital in the end period

Exogenous variables:

β: Inter-temporal time-discount factor, takes value between 0 and 1

a_{ij}^t: Intermediate demand in period t

f_i^t: Share of total demand for i^{th} sector in period t

I^1: Aggregate investment demand in the end period

τ_i^t: Share of total investment demand coming from i^{th} sector in period t

B^t: Observed trade deficient for period t

π_i^t: Terms of trade in period t

λ^t: Coefficients of unskilled labour joining education with respect to educational output in initial period

ξ: Coefficient of additional skilled labour stock in the end period with respect to labour joining education in the initial period

δ_i: Sector-wise rate of increase in investment in the end period, 1, over the initial period 0

σ^1: Stock of unskilled labour force going for education in the end period

$\overline{K_i^0}$: Stock of capital in the initial period

N^t: Total population of labour force in period t

S^t: Supply of skilled labour in period t

C_i^t: Supply of capital stock in period t

θ_i^t: Cobb-Douglas shift parameters for period t

ϕ_i^t: Cobb-Douglas share parameters for composite labour for period t

α_i^t: Share parameters of skilled and unskilled labour for period t

ρ_i: Substitution parameters between skilled labour and unskilled labour[2]

The first constraint of each period is the commodity constraint, i.e. the material balance for the tradable and non-tradable products, while the second constraint represents the CES nested production function. The next three constraints are for unskilled and skilled labour, and capital, respectively. The skilled labour demand in the initial period is constrained by an exogenously given skilled labour

[2] ρ_i is substitution parameter between skilled and unskilled labour, which is defined as $(\delta - 1)/\delta$, where δ is the elasticity of substitution.

supply, and in the second period by the number of initial period skilled labour plus the additional skill supplies; see constraint (4). In (3) N^1 is the given labour force in period 1. Part σ goes to school and the residual determines the supply of unskilled labour. Unemployed skilled labour may join the unskilled labour pool in both periods; see the second right hand side term of the unskilled constraints (3). Basically, competitive unskilled wages sets the minimum wages for the skilled labour in constraint (3), while the shadow prices from constraints (4) are the competitive skill premiums; the competitive skilled wage will thus be the competitive unskilled wage plus the competitive skill premium. The capital demand constraints are (5). Constraint (6) states that net exports valued at world prices cannot exceed the existing trade deficit for each period. Shadow prices associated with each constraint, i.e. commodity, production function, unskilled labour, skilled labour, capital and trade, P_i^t, $P_{v_i}^t$, w_u^t, $P_{S_i^t}$, r_i^t and ε^t, represent the competitive prices of output, value added, unskilled wage, skill premium, rent to capital, and purchasing power parity for both periods.

Capital in the second period, 2002, depends on the initial period capital stock plus a fixed rate of increase in initial endogenous investment, δ_i; see constraint (5). Investment in the terminal period is exogenous. Constraint (7) captures the process of skill formation with the help of education. Every of the eight years between 1994 and 2002, a portion of the potential work force joins the school or training. Education or training does not necessarily take one year to transform the unskilled to skilled labour. However, every year there is a net turnover of skilled labour. In the initial period (1994), number of unskilled labour goes for education is proportional to educational output, λ^1. We assume that educational output grows at a fixed rate between 1994 and 2002, hence also the number of unskilled labour enrolled in education. Considering education sector's output as number of educated students, net of enrolments and dropouts, the change in the stock of skilled labour in the next sub-period is assumed to be proportional to the number of labour joining education in the previous period, ξ.[3] The shadow prices of constraints (7) determine

[3]This is similar to a Poisson process where the distribution of intervals between successive occurrences is exponential, implying a fixed rate of occurrence.

the cost of skill formation between 1994 and 2002 (χ_c), as well as the opportunity cost of tending education (χ_e). In our fixed duration scenario, education stops playing any role in transforming the labour into skilled for periods afterward 2002. Hence we consider the amount of workforce (σ^2) going to education in the end period an exogenous 'reserve army' for the future.

The first order conditions of the model are reported in Appendix 1. The shadow prices of the skilled labour constraint (A6) give the static and dynamic competitive premiums for 1994 and 2002 respectively: $P_s^0 = w_s^0 - w_u^0$ and $P_s^1 = w_s^1 - w_u^1$. Conditions A9 and A8 show the equivalence of the competitive skill premium in the second period with the cost of skill transformation, which is the competitive unskilled wage forgone by tending education plus the cost of education: $P_s^1 = \chi_c, \chi_c\xi = w_u^0 + \chi_e$. The competitive consumer price of education at the optimum consists not only of the cost of producing it, but also the unskilled wage forgone in the first period net of the competitive skill premium the student expects, see A3, A8 and A9: $P_{11}^0 = \sum_j A_{11,j}^0 P_{11}^0 + P_{v_{11}}^0 + w_u^0 - P_s^1\xi$. The competitive skill premium also measures the premium on skill productivity. Returns to education are the benefit accrued to labour going for education to become skilled instead of remaining as unskilled, i.e. the ratio of the competitive premium to the competitive unskilled wage, P_s^1/w_u^1.

Conditions A4 and A5 show that the equilibrium rental price for capital is equal to its marginal product for each industry, and it also equilibrates the demand for capital with the stock. The price of the initial period capital is the sum of initial period value of the marginal product of capital and the second period price of capital with long run growth rate. In the dynamic equilibrium, the price of capital for each sector in the second period equals the price of investment in the initial period with a constant long run growth rate (see A10): $r_i^{t+1} = P_i^t(\tau_i^t/\delta_i)$.

Equation A1 establishes price normalization condition for the general equilibrium model and also implicitly establishes that equilibrium prices and wages are discounted value of the future prices and earnings: $\sum_i f_i^0 P_i^0 = 1, \sum_i f_i^1 P_i^1 = \beta$. We decompose the efficiency of the economy, i.e. performance of the economy relative to its potential, and the productivity over the wage ratio into the contributions of the following factors: (a) static allocative efficiency, (b) trade efficiency, (c) dynamic efficiency from physical capital formation, and (d) dynamic efficiency from human capital formation (education process). Due to nonlinearities, the sequence of the decomposition may influence the decomposition. Often in computable general equilibrium models (CGE) there is an interest to split the total effect of a package of shocks into individual or group effects. Harrison *et al.* (2000) propounded a method of decomposing the endogenous changes from a general equilibrium simulation into sources attributable to each of the exogenous shocks by using an arbitrarily accurate approximation to the linear path. Shorrocks (1999) proposed a decomposition method for sources and causes of poverty and inequality, based on the Shapley value; the contribution of any given source of income to overall change in indicator can be interpreted as the expected marginal impact of the factor when such an expectation is made over all possible sequences of elimination. The last two methodologies decompose additively, absolute differences. Since our outputs are analysed in relative differences, e.g. productivity-wage ratios and efficiency, we follow the modification of Ang *et al.* (2004). They extend the Fisher index to an *n-factor* model by taking the geometric average of all the combinations of the Laspeyres and Paasche indices, which satisfies the factor reversal test as well the perfect decomposition. Suppose the model is $V = f(X_1, \ldots, X_n)$ and the set $N = \{1, 2, 3, 4\}$. Aggregate value changes from V^0, the observed value to V^*, the optimum. The multiplicative decomposition is represented by $V^*/V^0 = D_T D_E D_I D_F$, where D_T, D_E, D_I and D_F represent the decomposed individual effect of trade efficiency, human capital formation, physical capital formation, and static allocative efficiency. Let us define the function $V(S) = f(X^*_{l \in S}, X^0_{m \in N/S})$. Individual factor's contribution can be represented by $D_i = \prod_{S \subset N, i \in S} [V(S)/V(S/\{i\})]^{(s-1)!(n-s)!/n!}$ where S are subsets of N and s is the cardinality of S[4]. If the individual effect is less than one, then that factor is responsible for V^0 to exceed V^* (a negative impact), and if an individual effect is above one, then factor is responsible for V^* to be above V^0 (a positive effect). In order to place a weight on individual impact we use a simple method. We take the log on both sides of the equation and normalize the impacts,

[4]The mathematical description is close to Ang *et al.* (2004). Appendix II gives detailed formulae for all the components.

in absolute term, to 100, expressing the weight of individual impact in percentage.

3. Data and Calibration

The data on inter-industry flows, final demand, investment, net-exports, output and value-added of capital and labour for the years 1994 and 2002 are based on the social accounting matrices (SAM) from Pradhan *et al.* (1999) and Pradhan *et al.* (2006). The economy is classified into 11 major production sectors, including education. The original SAMs do not categorize labour by type of education. The unskilled labour is defined as labour having primary education or less, while the skilled ones are above the primary level of education[5]. To calculate industry average wage rates and employment we used the National Sample Survey Organisation (NSSO) 50th employment survey for the year July 1993–June 1994, their 55th for the year 1999–2000 and the 58th for 2002. For the labour force we take the number of persons engaged for a longer time in work related economic activities (principal and subsidiary status). The working age of the labour force is cut off at age 14, following the Government of India. We admit that we overlook child labour. On the basis of the above-mentioned NSS data the total labour force is split into working population, attending school and seeking for job (unemployed).

The values of industry output, net exports, intermediate demand, final consumption, and investment demands net of indirect taxes are computed in real terms for 1994 and 2002 by using GDP price deflators calculated from information provided in the National Accounts Statistics (Government of India, 2004, 2006). The terms of trade reflect the value of Indian tradable commodities in the world market. We use the Global Trade Analysis Project (GTAP) database, which provides fairly detailed value of imports by industry at the levels of India and the world to get the terms of trade for the years 1995

[5]Primary education is essential for good quality unskilled work in modern manufacturing and services, low levels of education in the labour force result in low quality of service and mass consumer goods while secondary education ensured that labour was gradually able to undertake the semi-skilled jobs that opened up as the economy moved to middle income level (Virmani, 2006).

and 2001; see www.gtap.agecon.purdue.edu/databases. Choosing a discount rate, for β, is a difficult issue, particularly for a developing country. We take the annualised real interest rate, using lending rates and wholesale price indices (WPI) to capture the real interest rate[6]. The real interest rate is lowest in 1994 (2.40) due to high inflation and highest in 1996 (10.14). It is stable until 2002. We use the geometric average of the real interest rates over the period between 1994 and 2002 for our time discount rate, 8.6 percent[7]. Applying this annualised rate over the years from 1994 till 2002, discount factor β becomes around 0.5.

To get parameter values for the CES production function, we calibrate as in applied general equilibrium modelling[8]. The elasticity of substitution parameters plays a crucial role in calibration exercises; usually these are acquired through estimation or with some estimates (prior knowledge or outside information). We vary the elasticity parameters between a low value of 0.5 and a high 2.5, across the industries, and assume that these parameters do not change over time[9].

The nested production function can be split into Cobb-Douglas function of capital and composite labour, and a CES labour composite of skilled and unskilled labour:

$$X_i^b = \theta_i(K_i^b)^{(1-\phi_i)}(L_i^b)^{\phi_i} \quad i = 1, \ldots, 11 \tag{8}$$

$$L_i^b = [\alpha_i(L_{s_i}^b)^{\rho_i} + (1-\alpha_i)(L_{u_i}^b)^{\rho_i}]^{\frac{1}{\rho_i}} \quad i = 1, \ldots, 11 \tag{9}$$

The profit maximizing behavior of the producer in a Cobb Douglas production function yields the share parameters ϕ. Given the information on the sector-wise output, capital, total labour, skilled and

[6]Morgan (2006) explains the reason for considering lending rate and WPI for the estimation.

[7]A study by Shanmugam (2006) on the rate of time preference in India estimated that real discount rate ranges from 7.6 to 9.7 percent.

[8]For details on calibration, see Shoven and Whalley (1984), Howitt (1995), Sims (1996), Hansen and Heckman (1996), Kydland and Prescott (1996) and Dawkins, *et al.* (2001).

[9]The low elasticity of substitution between skilled and unskilled labour is a plausible assumption for a country like India. Jung and Thorbecke (2003) have taken similar number for some African countries.

unskilled labour, at the observed period, we calibrate parameters θ, and α for both the beginning and end years.

4. Results

We run two scenarios, with the elasticity of substitution between skilled and unskilled labour low or high. In case of a lower elasticity of substitution, the analysis shows that the Indian economy operated at 88 and 49 percent of its potential in the respective years of 1994 and 2002 (see Table 2). In case of a higher elasticity of substitution, the economy operated at 90 and 47 percent in 1994 and 2002, respectively. It is worth mentioning here that in our model 1994 is considered to be static efficiency and 2002 dynamic. Possibility of education and investment process creates substantial potential for the economy in 2002. Introduction of perfectly competitive market would push the economy to its potential by doubling the economic activities in the long run.

The competitive wages of skilled and unskilled labour determine their respective productivities. The competitive skill premium

Table 2. Efficiency, wages and productivities in 1994 and 2002.

	Elasticity of substitutions between skilled and unskilled: 0.5*		Elasticity of substitutions between skilled and unskilled: 2.5*	
	1994	2002	1994	2002
Efficiency	0.88	0.49	0.90	0.47
Productivity ratio	6.93	1.76	3.50	2.19
Productivity ratio/observed wage ratio	2.35	0.60	1.19	0.75
Skilled productivity/observed skilled wage	2.42	0.79	2.12	0.84
Unskilled productivity/ observed unskilled wage	1.03	1.30	1.79	1.12

*Returns to education, $P_s^1/w_u^1 = w_s^1/w_u^1 - 1$, are 0.76 and 1.19 respectively for the low and high elasticity of substitutions respectively. Considering 8 periods of gap, the annualised returns turn out to be around 7.3 % and 10 % respectively.

accounts for the cost of education including the wage forgone, all evaluated at competitive prices. We define the returns to education as the ratio of the competitive skill premium to the competitive unskilled wage, i.e. the premium over unskilled productivity. The annualised rate of returns to education between 1994 and 2002 are found to be 7.3 and 10 percents for the lower and the higher elasticity of substitutions respectively[10]. We report the wage (and productivity) differentials as skilled/unskilled wages (and productivities). Table 2 shows that skilled productivity is significantly higher than the unskilled and this differential declines in the end period. With a lower elasticity of substitution, the productivity differential remains as high as 6.93 in 1994 and drops significantly to 1.76 in 2002; it declines significantly in 1994 with the increase in the elasticity of substitution. Productivity differential remains above the wage differential in the initial period and below it in the end period irrespective in both the scenarios. We have already noticed from Table 1 that wage ratio between skilled and unskilled labour has already started declining, from 2.95 in 1994 to 2001 in 2002. Government of India (2010a) report on Employment and Unemployment Situation in India has indicated even a lower wage ratio in 2005–2006, 2.54.

Table 2 shows that in 1994 the skilled labour productivity is more than double the observed wage but it is below the wage in 2002. A higher elasticity of substitution between skilled and unskilled labour reduces the productivity-wage differential. The unskilled wage is below its productivity in either period. We notice that in case of lower elasticity of substitution between skilled and unskilled labour, unskilled labour is paid only marginally less than its productivity in the initial period and much lower than productivity in the second period. However, in case of higher elasticity of substitution, the unskilled wage lies substantially lower than its productivity in the initial period; this wage still lies below the productivity in second period, but not as much below as initial period. Under the lower elasticity of substitution scenario, the unskilled productivity lies much above the wage in the end period as compared to the initial and in

[10]Asian Development Bank (2007) reported returns to education for 2004 based on Mincerian equation, which are 6.3 and 12.3 (middle level education) for midcarrier and senior workers respectively.

Table 3. Sector-wise ratio of optimal to observed output.

	Elasticity of substitution between skilled and unskilled: 0.5		Elasticity of substitution between skilled and unskilled: 2.5	
	1994	2002	1994	2002
1. Agriculture and allied	0.45	0.14	0.37	0.17
2. Mining and quarrying	1.11	1.02	1.06	1.02
3. Light manufacturing	0.15	0.75	0.13	0.89
4. Heavy manufacturing	0.38	0.99	0.37	1.14
5. Construction	1.63	1.12	1.99	1.13
6. Electricity, gas and water	0.71	1.47	0.71	1.57
7. Transports, storage	0.71	0.54	0.74	0.61
8. Wholesale, retail trade	1.00	1.76	1.02	1.95
9. Finance, insurance, real est.	1.02	1.40	1.06	1.49
10. Other Services	3.96	7.00	4.29	7.06
11. Education	2.58	2.03	2.60	2.14

case of higher elasticity of substitution, it is just the opposite. On the other hand, skilled productivity declines relative to wage in the end period in both scenarios.

Table 3 shows that the service sector in general, in which 'other services', 'wholesale, retail trade', 'finance, insurance, real estate' and 'education' in particular have more potential for growth, while potential levels of 'agriculture', 'light manufacturing', 'heavy manufacturing' (particularly in the first period, 1994), and 'transport and storage' sectors lie below their observed outputs. 'Other service' sector has the highest potential to grow, almost over seven times of the observed in the end period, 2002. It is worth mentioning here that information technology services, outsourcing and business services have been major contributors to the performance of the 'other services' these days.

A cursory look at the changes in the composition of sector-wise gross domestic products (GDP) and their growth rates from 2003 till 2009 clearly displays the growing importance of service sectors in the economy (see Table 4). The 'agriculture' sector has recently shown increasing growth rates; however, its share in GDP has been continuously declining. Share of 'manufacturing' sector in total GDP

Table 4. Sector-wise composition and growth rates of observed GDP at factor cost from 2002 to 2009.

	2002	2003	2004	2005	2006	2007	2008	2009
Percentage shares								
Agriculture	22.52	22.83	19.03	18.82	18.29	18.26	17.59	17.76
Mining	2.75	2.51	2.86	2.79	2.70	2.72	2.62	2.52
Manufacturing	15.60	15.59	15.25	15.39	16.06	15.99	15.45	14.76
Electricity, gas, water	2.21	2.15	2.11	2.04	1.93	1.83	1.59	1.51
Construction	6.20	6.18	7.70	7.93	8.16	8.49	8.55	8.18
Wholesale, retail trade	14.75	14.94	16.06	16.70	17.07	17.09	16.93	16.31
Transports, storage	7.69	8.02	8.43	8.25	8.17	8.00	7.84	7.78
Finance, insurance, real estate	13.75	13.50	14.71	14.55	14.84	15.09	16.08	16.75
Other Services	14.52	14.27	13.84	13.55	12.78	12.52	13.34	14.44
Growth rates								
Agriculture		13.28	−1.71	12.79	13.36	15.70	11.05	17.26
Mining		2.00	34.20	11.10	13.05	16.88	11.09	11.27
Manufacturing		11.68	15.35	15.10	21.69	15.42	11.40	10.90
Electricity, gas, water		8.48	15.82	10.26	10.20	10.08	0.40	10.11
Construction		11.51	46.86	17.38	20.03	20.62	16.07	11.14
Wholesale, retail trade		13.20	26.77	18.62	19.15	16.03	14.28	11.84
Transports, storage		16.52	23.92	11.63	15.46	13.59	12.96	15.18
Finance, insurance, real estate		9.68	28.54	12.79	18.96	17.88	22.81	20.96
Other services		9.85	14.40	11.62	10.01	13.59	22.84	25.62

Source: Government of India (2010b).

has also shown declining trend with almost stagnant growth rates. Government of India (2010b) rightly observes that the technological breakthrough in agriculture achieved in 1960s is gradually waning and there is need for a second green revolution. The Survey also claims that lack of capacity utilization in core sectors and infrastructure bottlenecks are responsible for the slow growth in manufacturing sectors. The challenges India faces to retain the already acclaimed competitiveness in the IT services and India is yet to tap its full potential in international market for its trade services, education, financial services and other business services.

Trade efficiency, human capital formation, physical capital formation, and static allocative efficiency are the four factors contributing to the performance of the economy and to the productivities of skilled and unskilled labour relative to their wages. We make decompositions for both the initial and the final period. In case of efficiency, factor that causes performance of the economy less than its potential indicates a decomposition value less than one (negative impact). It is other way around if the value is more than one. In case of productivity-wage ratio, if the factor causes productivity to be higher than the wage, decomposition value will be higher than one; it is the opposite if the value is less than one. The value in the bracket suggests the importance of a factor relative to the other in terms of percentage.

Main reasons for the Indian economy to perform under its potential are declining efficiency from free trade (see Table 5). It is the static allocative efficiency, which has contributed to the performance of the economy. However, the contribution of allocative efficiency is not strong enough to bring the economy to its potential. Lack of human capital formation is also responsible for decreasing the performance of the economy in the end period.

Table 5 clearly shows that trade efficiency is the main source of skilled productivity in both periods, 1994 and 2002. However, the contribution of free trade to the skilled productivity declines drastically in 2002. The principal cause of skilled productivity to be lower than the wage is due to lower human capital formation. Failure to capture the higher rate of returns to education has created a large number of undereducated labour force in 2002. Shortage of skilled labour in 2002 prompts in excessive skilled wage relative to its productivity.

Contrary to skilled productivity, unskilled productivity is sensitive to the degree of elasticity of substitution assumed between skilled and unskilled labour. In case of lower elasticity of substitution, free trade is responsible in lowering the productivity of unskilled labour relative to its wage. Static allocative efficiency contributes significantly to the unskilled productivity in 1994. On other hand, human capital formation is the sole factor that has caused unskilled productivity to be much higher than the wage in 2002. In case of higher elasticity of substitution, free trade and the human capital formation contribute significantly to the increase in unskilled productivity above its wage.

Table 5. Multiplicative decomposition of efficiency and productivity-wage ratios.

	Efficiency		Productivity of skilled labour/skilled wage		Productivity of unskilled labour/unskilled wages	
	1994	2002	1994	2002	1994	2002
Low elasticity of substitution						
Trade efficiency	0.83	0.61	3.11	1.65	0.63	0.82
	(59.34)	(63.34)	(78.48)	(40.31)	(48.59)	(15.94)
Human capital	1.03	0.84	1.03	0.67	1.17	2.13
	(9.41)	(22.34)	(2.04)	(32.24)	(16.51)	(60.75)
Physical capital	0.97	0.93	0.98	0.9	1.04	0.87
	(9.70)	(9.30)	(1.40)	(8.48)	(4.12)	(11.19)
Static allocative efficiency	1.07	1.04	0.77	0.79	1.34	0.86
	(21.55)	(5.03)	(18.08)	(18.97)	(30.78)	(12.12)
Total	**0.89**	**0.49**	**2.42**	**0.79**	**1.03**	**1.30**
High elasticity of substitution						
Trade efficiency	0.82	0.57	2.58	1.61	1.27	1.23
	(67.12)	(62.62)	(79.76)	(42.58)	(41.32)	(28.05)
Human capital	1.03	0.85	1.02	0.74	1.15	1.25
	(10.00)	(18.10)	(1.67)	(26.92)	(24.16)	(30.23)
Physical capital	1.00	0.90	0.99	0.90	1.11	0.98
	(0.00)	(11.74)	(0.85)	(9.42)	(18.04)	(2.74)
Static allocative efficiency	1.07	1.07	0.81	0.79	1.1	0.75
	(22.88)	(7.54)	(17.73)	(21.08)	(16.48)	(38.98)
Total	**0.90**	**0.47**	**2.12**	**0.84**	**1.79**	**1.12**

Note: Figure in parenthesis indicates the absolute weight of the individual impact in percentage.

5. Conclusion

Given the earlier past, the 1994 Indian economy operated at 90 percent of its potential. The performance in 2002 dropped to 50 percent, taking into account the missed investment and education opportunities. Service sectors including education have significant potential to achieve higher growth.

Both openness and education would push the productivity differential more than the observed wage differential in the first period and would reduce it in the end period. The intensity of the pressure would be greater under the low elasticity of substitution between skilled and unskilled labour. The data shows that the observed wage inequalities (skilled-unskilled wage ratio) for the two periods are 2.95 and 2.91. However, productivity inequalities (skilled-unskilled competitive wage ratio) are 6.93 and 1.76 in 1994 and 2002 respectively for the lower elasticity of substitution between skilled and unskilled labour, and 3.50 and 2.19 for the higher elasticity of substitution.

Compared to its productivity, skilled labour is significantly underpaid in the initial period and overpaid in the end period. However unskilled labour is underpaid in both periods compared to its productivity. This indicates the existence of still large pool of undereducated Indians. The pattern of change in productivity relative to the wage for unskilled labour is sensitive to degree of elasticity of substitution. Human capital formation through education process is an important component for productivity-wage disparity. The optimum returns to education are 7.3 % and 10 % for a lower and higher degree elasticity of substitutions respectively.

We conduct a decomposition exercise to capture the importance of various factors that influence the efficiency of the economy and the productivity-wage differential. Skilled labour benefits from free trade, but stands to lose from education and domestic competition. On the other hand, unskilled labour gains from domestic competition and human capital formation. However, wage-productivity differential for unskilled labour is sensitive to degree of elasticity of substitution. Unskilled labour loses from free trade under a lower elasticity of substitution, while gains in the case higher elasticity of substitution.

The static allocative efficiency, i.e. the domestic competition is the only factor that contributes to the efficiency gain of the Indian economy. However, the main reasons for India to under-perform are its deviation from free trade potential, followed by failure to capture returns to education (human capital formation) and investment potential (physical capital formation) in the end period. We have already observed that there exists a higher potential returns to education. Failure to capture it has led to shortage of skilled labour and excessive wage inequality in the economy.

References

Abrego, L. and J. Whalley. (2000). The choices of structural modeling trade-wages decompositions. *Review of International Economics*, **8**(3), 462–477.

Ang, B. W., F. L. Liu and H.-S. Chung. (2004). A generalized Fisher index approach to energy decomposition analysis. *Energy Economics*, **26**, 757–763.

Asian Development Bank. (2007). Returns to Education. *Asian Development Outlook*.

Bajpai, N. and J. D. Sachs. (1997). India's economic reforms: Some lessons from East Asia. *Journal of International Trade and Economic Development*, **6**(2), 135–164.

Bargain, O., S. K. Bhaumik, M. Chakrabarty and Z. Zhao. (2006). Returns to education in Chinese and Indian formal sectors: Implications for skill shortages. Employment and Development Conference. IZA and World Bank.

Beladi, H. and A. Chakraborty. (2004). Trade, wage inequality in developing countries. *Economic Enquiry*, **42**(2), 295–303.

Berman, E., J. Bound and S. Machin. (1998). Implications of skilled-biased technological change: International evidence. *Quarterly Journal of Economics*, **113**(4), 1245–1279 (November).

Bosworth, Barry, Collins, Susan, M., Virmani, Arvind (2007). Sources of growth in the Indian economy. NBER Working Paper No. 12901, National Bureau of Economic Research, Cambridge, Massachusetts.

Dawkins, C., T. N. Srinivasan and J. Whalley. (2001). Calibration. In *Handbook of Econometrics*, Eds. Heckman, J. J. and E. Learner, New York: Elsevier, Vol. 5, Chapter 58, pp. 3653–3703.

Dutta, P. V. (2004). Trade protection and inter-industry wages in India. Working Paper no.27, Poverty Research Unit at Sussex, Department of Economics, University of Sussex.

Dutta, P. V. (2005). Accounting for wage inequality in India. Working Paper no. 29, Poverty Research Unit at Sussex, Department of Economics, University of Sussex.

Fischer, S. (2002). Breaking out of the third world: India's economic imperative. A speech prepared for delivery at the India Today Conclave, New Delhi, January 22.

Hansen, L. P. and J. J. Heckman. (1996). The empirical foundations of calibration. *Journal of Economic Perspectives*, **10**, 87–89.

Hanson, G. H. and Harrison, A. (1999). Trade liberalisation and wage inequality in Mexico. *Industrial and labor Relations Review*, **52**, 271–288.

Harrison, J., Horridge, M. and Pearson, K. R. (2000). Decomposing simulation results with respect to exogenous shocks. *Computational Economics* **15**(3), 227–249.

Howitt, R. A. (1995). Positive mathematical programming. *American Journal of Agricultural Economics*, **77**(2), 329–342.

Government of India. (2004, 2006). *National Accounts Statistics.* Ministry of Statistics and Programme Implementation, New Delhi.

Government of India. (2010a), NSSO Report No.522: Employment and unemployment situation in India, July, 2005–June, 2006, National Sample Survey Office, Ministry of Statistics and Programme Implementation, New Delhi.

Government of India (2010b). Economic Survey of India. Ministry of Statistics and Programme Implementation, New Delhi.

Government of India. (2011). *National Accounts Statistics.* Ministry of Statistics and Programme Implementation, New Delhi.

Jung, S. E. and E. Thorbecke. (2003). The impact of public education expenditure on human capital, growth and poverty in Tanzania and Zambia: A general equilibrium approach. IMF Working Paper No. 01/106, August.

Katz, L. F. and Autor, D. (1999). Changes in wage structure and earnings inequality. In: Ashenfelter, O., Card, D. (Eds.), *Handbook of Labour Economics*, Elsevier, North Holland Publishing Co., Amsterdam.

Katz, L. F., Murphy, Kevin M. (1992). Changes in relative wages, 1963–1987: supply and demand factors. *Quarterly Journal of Economics* **107**(1), 35–78.

Kiley, M. T. (1999). The Supply of skilled-biased technological progress. *Economic Journal*, **109**, 708–724.

Krusell, P., L. E. Ohanian, J. Rios-Rull and G. L. Violante. (1997). Capital-skill complementarities: A macroeconomic analysis. Federal Bank of Minneapolis Research Department Staff Report, No. 236.

Kydland, F. E. and E. C. Prescott. (1996). The computational experiment: An econometric tool. *Journal of Economic Perspectives*, **10**, 69–71.

Learner, E. E. (1996). Wage inequality from international competition and technological change: Theory and country evidence. *American Economic Review, Papers and Proceedings*, **86**(2), 309–314.

Lucas, R. E. B. (1988). On the mechanics of economic development. *Journal of Monetary Economics*, **22**, 3–42.

Machin, S. (2002). Labour market inequality and change in the relative demand for skills. Paper Prepared for the Royal Statistical Society "Explanations of Rising Economic Inequality" Conference.

Marjit, S. and R. Acharyya. (2003). *International Trade, Wage Inequality and the Developing Economy: A General Equilibrium Approach*, Heidelberg, New York: Physica-Verlag.

Morgan, J. P. (2006). India focus: real interest rates. Economics Research: India Focus. (September 7).

Negishi, T. (1960). Welfare economics and existence of an equilibrium for a competitive economy. *Metrorconomica* **12**, 92–97.

Pradhan, B. K., A. Sahoo and M. R. Saluja. (1999). A social accounting matrix for India, 1994–95. *Economic and Political Weekly*, November 27.

Pradhan, B. (2002). The role of education in wage inequality change in India: 1988–97. DFID project paper, department for International Development, UK.

Pradhan, B. K. and P. K. Roy. (2003). *The Well-Being of Indian Households: MIMAP-India Survey Report*. New Delhi: Tata McGraw-Hill Publishing Company Limited.

Pradhan, B. K. and A. Subramanian. (2000). Education, openness and the poor: Analysis of an all-India sample of households. NCAER Discussion Paper No. 14, New Delhi.

Pradhan, B. K. M. R. Saluja and S. Sing. (2006). *Social Accounting Matrix for India: Concepts, Construction and Applications*. New Delhi: Sage Publications.

Prescott, E. C. (1986). Theory ahead of business-cycle measurement. *Carnegie-Rochester Conference Series on Public Policy*, **25**, 11–14.

Romer, P. M. (1986). Increasing returns and long-run growth. *Journal of Political Economy*, **94**(5), 1002–1037.

Shanmugam, K. R. (2006). Rate of time preference and the quantity adjusted value of life in India. *Environment and Development Economics*, **11**, 569–583.

Shoven, J. B. and J. Whalley. (1984). Applied general equilibrium models of taxation and international trade: An introduction and survey. *Journal of Economic Literature*, **22**, 1007–1051.

Shorrocks, A. F. (1999). Decomposition procedures for distributional analysis a unified framework based on the shapely value. University of Essex mimeo.

Sims, C. A. (1996). Macroeconomics and methodology. *Journal of Economic Perspectives*, **10**, 105–107.

ten Raa, Th. and P. Mohnen. (2002). Neoclassical growth accounting and frontier analysis: A synthesis. *Journal of Productivity Analysis*, **18**, 111–128.

Tinbergen, J. (1975). *Income Distribution: Analysis and Policies*. Amsterdam: North Holland.

Virmani, A. (2006). Sustaining employment and equitable growth: Policies for structural transformation of the Indian economy. Working Paper, No. 3//2003 PC, Planning Commission, New Delhi.

Wood, A. (1994). *North-South Trade, Employment and Inequality, Changing Fortunes in Skill-Driven World.* Oxford: Clarendon Press.

Wood, A. (1999). Openness and wage inequality in developing countries: The Latin American challenge to East Asian conventional wisdom. In *Market Integration, Regionalism and the Global Economy*, Eds. Baldwin, R. E. *et al.*, Cambridge University Press, Cambridge.

Appendix I

$$D^t: \sum_i f_i^t P_i^t = (\beta)^t \quad t = 0, 1 \tag{A1}$$

$$X_i^t: P_i^t = \sum_j A_{ij}^t P_i^t + P_{v_i}^t \quad \begin{cases} i = 1, \ldots, 10 & t = 0 \\ i = 1, \ldots, 11 & t = 1 \end{cases} \tag{A2}$$

$$X_{11}^0: P_{11}^0 = \sum_j A_{11,j}^0 P_{11}^0 + P_{v_{11}}^0 - \chi_e \lambda^0 \tag{A3}$$

$$K_i^t: P_{v_i}^t \theta_i^t (1 - \phi_i^t)(K_i^t)^{-\phi_i^t} [\alpha_i^t (L_{s_i}^t)^{\rho_i} + (1 - \alpha_i^t)(L_{u_i}^t)^{\rho_i}]^{\frac{\phi_i^t}{\rho_i}}$$

$$= r_i^t - r_i^{t+1} \left(\frac{1}{\delta_i}\right) \qquad t = 0 \tag{A4}$$

$$K_i^{t+1}: P_{v_i}^{t+1} \theta_i^{t+1} (1 - \phi_i^{t+1})(K_i^{t+1})^{-\phi_i^{t+1}}$$

$$\times [\alpha_i^{t+1} (L_{s_i}^{t+1})^{\rho_i} + (1 - \alpha_i^{t+1})(L_{u_i}^{t+1})^{\rho_i}]^{\frac{\phi_i^{t+1}}{\rho_i}} = r_i^{t+1} \left(\frac{1}{\delta_i}\right) \tag{A5}$$

$$L_{s_i}^t: P_{v_i}^t \theta_i^t (K_i^t)^{1-\phi_i^t} \phi_i^t [\alpha_i^t (L_{s_i}^t)^{\rho_i} + (1 - \alpha_i^t)(L_{u_i}^t)^{\rho_i}]^{\frac{\phi_i^t}{\rho_i} - 1}$$

$$\alpha_i^t (L_{s_i}^t)^{\rho_i - 1} = w_u^t + P_s^t \tag{A6}$$

$$L_{u_i}^t: P_{v_i}^t \theta_i^t (K_i^t)^{1-\phi_i^t} \phi_i^t [\alpha_i^t (L_{s_i}^t)^{\rho_i} + (1 - \alpha_i^t)(L_{u_i}^t)^{\rho_i}]^{\frac{\phi_i^t}{\rho_i} - 1}$$

$$(1 - \alpha_i^t)(L_{u_i}^t)^{\rho_i - 1} = w_u^t \tag{A7}$$

$$\sigma^0: \chi_c \xi = w_u^0 + \chi_e \tag{A8}$$

$$\Delta S: P_s^1 = \chi_c \tag{A9}$$

$$I^t: r_i^{t+1} = P_i^t \left(\frac{\tau_i^t}{\delta_i}\right) \qquad t = 0 \tag{A10}$$

$$T_i^t: \pi_i^t \varepsilon^t = P_i^t \qquad \text{(for tradables)} \tag{A11}$$

Appendix II

The multiplicative decomposition is written as $\frac{V^*}{V^0} = D_T D_E D_I D_F$.

$$D_T = \left[\frac{T^*E^0I^0F^0}{T^0E^0I^0F^0}\right]^{\frac{1}{4}} \quad when\ S = \{1\}$$

$$\cdot\left[\frac{T^*E^*I^0F^0}{T^0E^*I^0F^0}\right]^{\frac{1}{12}} \quad when\ S = \{1,2\}$$

$$\cdot\left[\frac{T^*E^0I^*F^0}{T^0E^0I^*F^0}\right]^{\frac{1}{12}} \quad when\ S = \{1,3\}$$

$$\cdot\left[\frac{T^*E^0I^0F^*}{T^0E^0I^0F^*}\right]^{\frac{1}{12}} \quad when\ S = \{1,4\}$$

$$\cdot\left[\frac{T^*E^*I^*F^0}{T^0E^*I^*F^0}\right]^{\frac{1}{12}} \quad when\ S = \{1,2,3\}$$

$$\cdot\left[\frac{T^*E^*I^0F^*}{T^0E^*I^0F^*}\right]^{\frac{1}{12}} \quad when\ S = \{1,2,4\}$$

$$\cdot\left[\frac{T^*E^0I^*F^*}{T^0E^0I^*F^*}\right]^{\frac{1}{12}} \quad when\ S = \{1,3,4\}$$

$$\cdot\left[\frac{T^*E^*I^*F^*}{T^0E^*I^*F^*}\right]^{\frac{1}{4}} \quad when\ S = \{1,2,3,4\}$$

Similarly, we can derive for D_E, D_I and D_F respectively.

$$D_E = \left[\frac{T^0E^*I^0F^0}{T^0E^0I^0F^0}\right]^{\frac{1}{4}} \cdot \left[\frac{T^*E^*I^0F^0}{T^*E^0I^0F^0} \cdot \frac{T^0E^*I^*F^0}{T^0E^0I^*F^0} \cdot \frac{T^0E^*I^0F^*}{T^0E^0I^0F^*}\right]^{\frac{1}{12}}$$

$$\cdot\left[\frac{T^*E^*I^*F^0}{T^0E^0I^*F^*} \cdot \frac{T^0E^*I^*F^*}{T^*E^0I^0F^*} \cdot \frac{T^*E^*I^0F^*}{T^*E^0I^*F^0}\right]^{\frac{1}{12}} \cdot \left[\frac{T^*E^*I^*F^0}{T^*E^0I^*F^*}\right]^{\frac{1}{4}}$$

$$D_I = \left[\frac{T^0E^0I^*F^0}{T^0E^0I^0F^0}\right]^{\frac{1}{4}} \cdot \left[\frac{T^*E^0I^*F^0}{T^*E^0I^0F^0} \cdot \frac{T^0E^*I^*F^0}{T^0E^*I^0F^0} \cdot \frac{T^0E^0I^*F^*}{T^0E^0I^0F^*}\right]^{\frac{1}{12}}$$

$$\cdot \left[\frac{T^*E^*I^*F^0}{T^*E^*I^0F^0} \cdot \frac{T^0E^*I^*F^*}{T^*E^0I^0F^*} \cdot \frac{T^*E^*I^0F^*}{T^0E^*I^0F^*}\right]^{\frac{1}{12}} \cdot \left[\frac{T^*E^*I^*F^*}{T^*E^*I^0F^*}\right]^{\frac{1}{4}}$$

$$D_F = \left[\frac{T^0E^0I^0F^*}{T^0E^0I^0F^0}\right]^{\frac{1}{4}} \cdot \left[\frac{T^*E^0I^0F^*}{T^*E^0I^0F^0} \cdot \frac{T^0E^*I^0F^*}{T^0E^*I^0F^0} \cdot \frac{T^0E^0I^*F^*}{T^0E^0I^*F^0}\right]^{\frac{1}{12}}$$

$$\cdot \left[\frac{T^*E^*I^0F^*}{T^*E^*I^0F^0} \cdot \frac{T^0E^*I^*F^*}{T^0E^*I^*F^0} \cdot \frac{T^*E^0I^*F^*}{T^*E^0I^*F^0}\right]^{\frac{1}{12}} \cdot \left[\frac{T^*E^*I^*F^*}{T^*E^*I^*F^0}\right]^{\frac{1}{4}}$$

Chapter 16

The Choice of Model in the Construction of Industry Coefficients Matrices*

José M. Rueda-Cantuche† and Thijs ten Raa‡

†*European Commission — DG, Joint Research Center, IPTS — Institute for Prospective Technological Studies, Edificio EXPO, C/Inca Garcilaso s/n, 41092 and Pablo de Olavide University at Seville, Spain*
jose.rueda-cantuche@ec.europa.eu

‡*Department of Economics, Tilburg University, Tilburg, The Netherlands*
tenraa@uvt.nl

Abstract. Kop Jansen and ten Raa's (1990) characterization of input-output product tables were adopted by the United Nations (1993) but recent frequent OECD publications and several EU funded projects in input-output analysis pitch product against industry tables and raise the issue of construction for the latter. We show how the main models are instances of the transfer principle, with alternative assumptions on the variation of input-output coefficients across product markets. We augment the theory by formulating desirable properties for industry tables and investigate the so-called fixed product and fixed industry sales structure models, which are used by statistical institutes. The fixed industry sales structure model is shown to be superior from an axiomatic point of view.

Keywords: Input-Output Tables

JEL-codes: C67, D57

*Reprinted from *Economic Systems Research*, **21**, 363–376, 2009, with permission from Taylor & Francis.

1. Introduction

The conflict between products and industries in input-output analysis manifests itself at two, independent levels, i.e. the dimension of the table and the method of construction. As regard the type of table, *product tables* describe the technological relations between products, how to produce products in terms of the others, independently of the producing industry. In contrast, *industry tables* depict inter-industry relations, showing for the industries the use of each other's produce. See Eurostat (2008). The choice between product and industry tables seems to us a matter of scope of applications rather than axioms or tests. For instance, the Leontief type model may be appropriate for backward impact studies using product tables (derived from assumptions on input structures), while the Ghosh type model may be suitable for forward impact analyses using industry tables (derived from assumptions on sales structures).

Most countries construct and use product tables and do so on the basis of the so-called product technology model, which indeed has nice properties (Kop Jansen and ten Raa, 1990, and ten Raa and Rueda Cantuche, 2003) and has been endorsed by the United Nations (1993). The alternative construction method in the realm of product tables is the so-called industry technology model (which is not plagued by the problem of negative coefficients). A few (but hard to neglect) countries — Canada, Denmark, Finland, the Netherlands, and Norway — construct and use industry tables, most frequently on the basis of the fixed product sales structure assumption (which is also free of the problem of negatives). Here the alternative is the fixed industry sales structure model. Industry tables have not been scrutinized yet from an axiomatic point of view.

In what follows, $\mathbf{e}$ will denote a column vector with all entries equal to one, ^{T} will denote transposition and $^{-1}$ inversion of a matrix. Since the latter two operations commute, their composition may be denoted $^{-\mathrm{T}}$. Also, $^\wedge$ will denote diagonalization, whether by suppression of the off-diagonal elements of a square matrix or by placement of the elements of a vector. $^\sim$ will denote a matrix with all the diagonal elements set null. A use matrix $\mathbf{U} = (u_{ij})$ comprises commodities $i\ (= 1, \ldots, n)$ consumed by sectors $j\ (= 1, \ldots, n)$ and a make matrix $\mathbf{V} = (v_{ji})$ shows the produce of commodities i in terms of industries j; it is the transposed of a supply matrix (Eurostat, 2008).

The next section presents the established constructs currently used for industry tables. Section 3 shows a general framework based on transfers over columns and over rows that encompasses them. Subsequent sections sort the input-output constructs axiomatically and single out one method through characterization. The final section concludes.

2. Industry Coefficients

The assumption of a *fixed industry sales* structure postulates that each industry has its own specific sales structure, irrespective of its product mix. Eurostat (2008) shows that the corresponding matrix of industry input-output coefficients is given by:

$$\mathbf{A}_{\mathrm{FI}}(\mathbf{U},\mathbf{V}) = (\widehat{\mathbf{Ve}})\mathbf{V}^{-\mathrm{T}}\mathbf{U}(\widehat{\mathbf{Ve}})^{-1}. \tag{1}$$

The alternative assumption of a *fixed product sales* structure postulates that each product has its own specific market shares (deliveries to industries) independent of the industry where it is produced. Here market shares refer to the shares of the total output of a product delivered to the various intermediate and final users. Eurostat (2008) shows that the consequent matrix of industry input-output coefficients is given by:

$$\mathbf{A}_{\mathrm{FP}}(\mathbf{U},\mathbf{V}) = \mathbf{V}(\widehat{\mathbf{V}^{\mathrm{T}}\mathbf{e}})^{-1}\mathbf{U}(\widehat{\mathbf{Ve}})^{-1}. \tag{2}$$

It seems more reasonable to assume that secondary outputs have different destinations than the primary outputs. This is the reason why the fixed product sales structure assumption catches more attention in the literature; see Thage and ten Raa (2006) or Yamano and Ahmad (2006). Moreover, equation (2) has no negative elements, unlike equation (1), because of the inversion of the output table. Denmark, the Netherlands, Finland, Norway, Canada, the US and the OECD fully or partially adopt equation (2) to compile industry tables (Yamano and Ahmad, 2006).

3. General Framework

In the construction of a *product symmetric input-output table* (*SIOT*), secondary outputs are transferred out to the industries where they are primary outputs (Figure 1).

In the construction of an *industry SIOT*, secondary products are transferred in to the primary output of the industry (Figure 2).

The transfers are mirrored on the input side. Here the principle is the following. *When outputs are transferred, the corresponding inputs must be transferred along.* There are alternative ways to decide how much input corresponds with output. Ten Raa and Rueda-Cantuche (2007) use a flexible framework to address this issue, indexing input-output coefficients by *three* subscripts. The first subscript indexes the *input*, the second the *observation* unit, and the third the *output*. Hence a *product coefficient* is defined as the amount of product i used by industry j to make one unit of product k. Similarly, we define an *industry coefficient*, a_{jik}, as the delivery by industry j in product market i per unit of output of industry k.

The point of departure for the construction of a product SIOT is the amount of product i used by industry j (to produce products k): intermediate use u_{ij}. For industry tables this will be viewed as a product i contribution of industry j to industry k. Schematically,

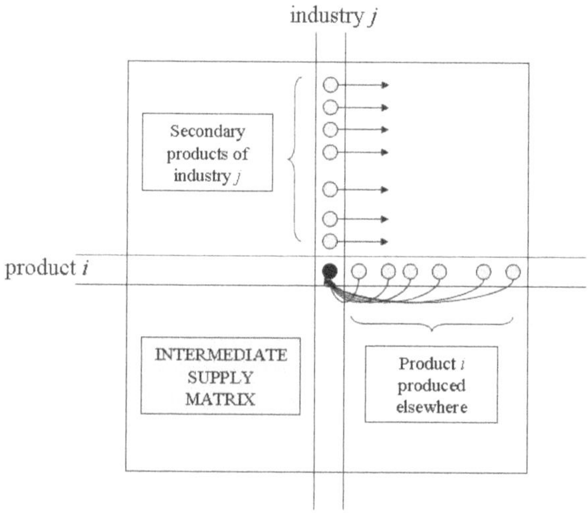

Fig. 1. Transfers for a product table.

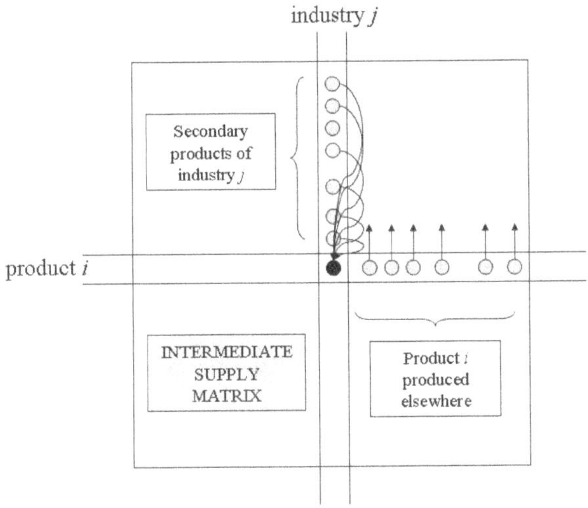

Fig. 2. Transfers for an industry table.

the transformation underlying product tables,

$$\text{product } i \to \text{industry } j \to \text{product } k,$$

is reconsidered for industry tables as:

$$\text{industry } j \to \text{product } i \to \text{industry } k.$$

In the construction of *product* tables secondary products (of industry j), and their input requirements are transferred out from industry j to industry k; the flipside of the coin is that products produced elsewhere as secondary and their input requirements are transferred in from industries k. Ten Raa and Rueda Cantuche (2007) use this principle to show how both the commodity technology and the industry technology models for product tables can be derived in a unifying framework, under alternative assumptions of the variation of coefficients across industries. The reasoning extends to industry tables as follows. In the construction of *industry* tables the intermediate supply does not originate exclusively from the main supplier of product i. Secondary supplies v_{ji}, $j \neq i$, and their product deliveries to industries k, $a_{jik}v_{ji}$, are transferred out from market i to industry j. The flipside of the coin is that amounts $a_{ijk}v_{ij}$ are transferred in from markets j, $j \neq i$. Hence, the amount delivered by industry i to industry k becomes:

$$u_{ik} - \sum_{j \neq i} a_{jik} v_{ji} + \sum_{j \neq i} a_{ijk} v_{ji}. \tag{3}$$

To construct an industry table, inputs and outputs should be transferred over the rows and not over the columns as in the product tables. In other words, the rows of the use table are shifted from a product classification to an industry classification while the columns still remain as industries and therefore, no column-based transfers will be needed. However, figures 1 and 2 jointly show that by using the transposition of **U** and **V**, the column-based transfers approach might still be valid and thus its mathematical expressions.

3.1. *The fixed industry sales structure model*

Industry SIOTs consist of *input-output coefficients* a_{ik}, which measure the unitary supplies of industry i to industry k. Now the total delivery of industry i to industry k is given by (3) and the total output of industry i is $\sum_j v_{ij}$. Simple division yields the industry input-output coefficient:

$$a_{ik} = (u_{ik} - \sum_{j \neq i} a_{jik} v_{ji} + \sum_{j \neq i} a_{ijk} v_{ij}) / \sum_j v_{ij}. \tag{4}$$

We will show that if we postulate that all industries have unique input delivery structures, irrespective the product market, then (4) becomes (1). In other words, industry j's unitary deliveries to industry k must be independent of the product i sold. Indeed, under this postulate the second subscript may be removed by defining fixed industry sales coefficients b_{jk}. Formally, the *fixed industry sales* assumption is defined by condition (FI):

$$a_{jik} = b_{jk} \text{ for all } i. \tag{FI}$$

In assumption (FI) inter-industry sales coefficients b_{jk} are the deliveries from industry j to industry k per unit of sales of industry j. These deliveries consist of products i. In fact, v_{ji} is the amount of product i supplied by industry j. The share delivered to industry k is $b_{jk} v_{ji}$. Summing over supplier industries j, product i is delivered to industry k in a total amount of $\sum_j b_{jk} v_{ji}$. This must match the observed quantity,

$$u_{ik} = \sum_j b_{jk} v_{ji} \tag{5}$$

Theorem 1. *Under assumption* (FI) *the input-output coefficients* (4) *reduced to fixed industry sales structure coefficients* (1).

Proof: Under assumption (FI), equation (4) reads:

$$a_{ik} = (u_{ik} - \sum_{j \neq i} b_{jk} v_{ji} + \sum_{j \neq i} b_{ik} v_{ij}) / \sum_j v_{ij}$$

and:

$$\begin{aligned}
\mathbf{A}(\mathbf{U}, \mathbf{V}) &= (\mathbf{U} - \widetilde{\mathbf{V}^{\mathrm{T}}}\mathbf{B}(\mathbf{U}, \mathbf{V}) + (\widehat{\widetilde{\mathbf{V}}\mathbf{e}})\mathbf{B}(\mathbf{U}, \mathbf{V}))\,(\widehat{\mathbf{Ve}})^{-1} \\
&= (\mathbf{U} - (\mathbf{V}^{\mathrm{T}} - \hat{\mathbf{V}})\mathbf{B}(\mathbf{U}, \mathbf{V}) + (\widehat{\mathbf{Ve}})\mathbf{B}(\mathbf{U}, \mathbf{V}) \\
&\qquad - \hat{\mathbf{V}}\mathbf{B}(\mathbf{U}, \mathbf{V}))(\widehat{\mathbf{Ve}})^{-1} \qquad (6) \\
&= (\mathbf{U} - \mathbf{V}^{\mathrm{T}}\mathbf{B}(\mathbf{U}, \mathbf{V}) + (\widehat{\mathbf{Ve}})\mathbf{B}(\mathbf{U}, \mathbf{V}))(\widehat{\mathbf{Ve}})^{-1} \\
&= \mathbf{U}(\widehat{\mathbf{Ve}})^{-1} - \mathbf{V}^{\mathrm{T}}\mathbf{B}(\mathbf{U}, \mathbf{V})(\widehat{\mathbf{Ve}})^{-1} \\
&\quad + (\widehat{\mathbf{Ve}})\mathbf{B}(\mathbf{U}, \mathbf{V})(\widehat{\mathbf{Ve}})^{-1}.
\end{aligned}$$

Next, by substituting (5), i.e. $\mathbf{U} = \mathbf{V}^{\mathrm{T}}\mathbf{B}(\mathbf{U}, \mathbf{V})$, equation (6) becomes equation (1) indeed:

(1) $\mathbf{U}(\widehat{\mathbf{Ve}})^{-1} - \mathbf{V}^{\mathrm{T}}\mathbf{V}^{-\mathrm{T}}\mathbf{U}(\widehat{\mathbf{Ve}})^{-1} + (\widehat{\mathbf{Ve}})\mathbf{V}^{-\mathrm{T}}\mathbf{U}(\widehat{\mathbf{Ve}})^{-1} = \mathbf{A}_{\mathrm{FI}}(\mathbf{U}, \mathbf{V})$.

The supply table needs to be square to compute its inverse, and negatives may emerge from this operation. This completes the proof.

3.2. *The fixed product sales structure model*

Industry coefficients can also be derived from an alternative assumption. If we postulate that all products require unique industry deliveries, irrespective the industry of fabrication, then (4) becomes (2). In other words, product i's unitary deliveries to industry k must be independent of the supplier industry (j). Hence the first subscript may be removed by defining fixed product sales coefficients c_{ik}. Formally, the *fixed product sales* assumption is:

$$a_{jik} = c_{ik} \text{ for all } j. \tag{FP}$$

In assumption (FP) product-by-industry sales coefficients (market shares) c_{ik} are the deliveries of product i to industry k per unit of output of product i. These deliveries are supplied by industry j. Actually, v_{ji} is the amount of product i supplied by industry j.

The share delivered to industry k is $c_{ik}v_{ji}$. Summing over supplier industries j, product i is delivered to industry k in a total amount of $\sum_j c_{ik}v_{ji}$. This must match again the observed, quantity u_{ik}. Briefly speaking, intermediate uses are now proportional to total commodity outputs.

$$u_{ik} = \sum_j c_{ik}v_{ji}. \tag{7}$$

Theorem 2. *Under assumption* (FP) *the input-output coefficients* (4) *reduced to fixed product sales structure coefficients* (2).

Proof: Equation (4) turns out to be:

$$a_{ik} = \Big(u_{ik} - \sum_{j\neq i} c_{ik}v_{ji} + \sum_{j\neq i} c_{jk}v_{ij}\Big)/\sum_j v_{ij}$$

where $c_{ik} = u_{ik}/\sum_j v_{ji}$ or $\mathbf{C}(\mathbf{U},\mathbf{V}) = (\widehat{\mathbf{V}^{\mathrm{T}}\mathbf{e}})^{-1}\mathbf{U}$. Therefore:

$$\begin{aligned}
\mathbf{A}(\mathbf{U},\mathbf{V}) &= (\mathbf{U} - (\widehat{\widetilde{\mathbf{V}^{\mathrm{T}}}\mathbf{e}})\mathbf{C}(\mathbf{U},\mathbf{V}) + \tilde{\mathbf{V}}\mathbf{C}(\mathbf{U},\mathbf{V}))\,(\widehat{\mathbf{V}\mathbf{e}})^{-1} \\
&= (\mathbf{U} - (\widehat{\mathbf{V}^{\mathrm{T}}\mathbf{e}})\mathbf{C}(\mathbf{U},\mathbf{V}) + \hat{\mathbf{V}}\mathbf{C}(\mathbf{U},\mathbf{V}) \\
&\qquad\qquad + (\mathbf{V} - \hat{\mathbf{V}})\mathbf{C}(\mathbf{U},\mathbf{V}))(\widehat{\mathbf{V}\mathbf{e}})^{-1} \qquad (8) \\
&= (\mathbf{U} - (\widehat{\mathbf{V}^{\mathrm{T}}\mathbf{e}})\mathbf{C}(\mathbf{U},\mathbf{V}) + \mathbf{V}\mathbf{C}(\mathbf{U},\mathbf{V}))(\widehat{\mathbf{V}\mathbf{e}})^{-1} \\
&= \mathbf{U}(\widehat{\mathbf{V}\mathbf{e}})^{-1} - (\widehat{\mathbf{V}^{\mathrm{T}}\mathbf{e}})\mathbf{C}(\mathbf{U},\mathbf{V})(\widehat{\mathbf{V}\mathbf{e}})^{-1} + \mathbf{V}\mathbf{C}(\mathbf{U},\mathbf{V})(\widehat{\mathbf{V}\mathbf{e}})^{-1}.
\end{aligned}$$

Then, by substituting (7), i.e. $\mathbf{U} = (\widehat{\mathbf{V}^{\mathrm{T}}\mathbf{e}})\mathbf{C}(\mathbf{U},\mathbf{V})$, (8) becomes (2) indeed:

$$\begin{aligned}
&\mathbf{U}(\widehat{\mathbf{V}\mathbf{e}})^{-1} - (\widehat{\mathbf{V}^{\mathrm{T}}\mathbf{e}})(\widehat{\mathbf{V}^{\mathrm{T}}\mathbf{e}})^{-1}\mathbf{U}(\widehat{\mathbf{V}\mathbf{e}})^{-1} \\
&\qquad\qquad + \mathbf{V}(\widehat{\mathbf{V}^{\mathrm{T}}\mathbf{e}})^{-1}\mathbf{U}(\widehat{\mathbf{V}\mathbf{e}})^{-1} = \mathbf{A}_{\mathrm{FP}}(\mathbf{U},\mathbf{V}).
\end{aligned}$$

The supply table does not need to be square and negatives do not emerge. □

4. An Axiomatic Context for Industry Tables

The four axioms described by Kop Jansen and ten Raa (1990) for product tables can be respecified for industry tables.

Let a_{jk} be the delivery of industry j (of products i) per unit of output of industry k and v_k the total output of industry k. Then, $a_{jk}v_k$ are the total deliveries of industry j to industry k for making its primary and secondary production. In addition, the amount of product i supplied by industry j is only part (secondary) of its total output, v_{ji}/v_j. Therefore, summing over the supplier industries j, we obtain that:

$$u_{ik} = \sum_j (v_{ji}/v_j)a_{jk}v_k \quad \text{or } \mathbf{U} = \mathbf{V}^{\mathrm{T}}(\widehat{\mathbf{Ve}})^{-1}\mathbf{A}(\mathbf{U},\mathbf{V})(\widehat{\mathbf{Ve}}). \tag{9}$$

Equation (9) presumes that the outputs of industry j are supplied in given proportions. This should not lead to the conclusion that since (9) can be reduced to (1) we could not expect anything else then that the assumption to satisfy the axioms subsequently derived.

Axiom M. Based on equation (9), we can define the *material balance* as the equality of supply and demand of products in the following way:

$$\mathbf{V}^{T}(\widehat{\mathbf{Ve}})^{-1}\mathbf{A}(\mathbf{U},\mathbf{V})(\widehat{\mathbf{Ve}})\mathbf{e} = \mathbf{Ue}. \tag{M}$$

Axiom F. Dual to the material balance is the financial balance, where supply and demand for all industries must be coincident. Notice that axiom M is defined by the equivalence of the row sums of both sides of equation (9) while the axiom F will be defined by the column sums instead. The *financial balance* equates revenues and costs for all sectors and reads:

$$\mathbf{e}^{\mathrm{T}}\mathbf{V}^{\mathrm{T}}(\widehat{\mathbf{Ve}})^{-1}\mathbf{A}(\mathbf{U},\mathbf{V})(\widehat{\mathbf{Ve}}) = \mathbf{e}^{\mathrm{T}}\mathbf{U}. \tag{F}$$

Axiom P. In the spirit of Kop Jansen and ten Raa (1990), price invariance avoids the possibility that a change in the base year prices could affect industry coefficients. Equation (9) becomes for industry j:

$$a_{jk}(\mathbf{U},\mathbf{V}) = \frac{v_j}{v_{ji}}\frac{u_{ik}}{v_k} = \frac{\sum_i v_{ji}}{v_{ji}}\frac{u_{ik}}{\sum_i v_{ki}} = \frac{v_{j\bullet}\mathbf{e}}{v_{ji}}\frac{u_{ik}}{v_{k\bullet}\mathbf{e}}$$

where $v_{j\bullet}\mathbf{e}$ is the row vector of product outputs of industry j and $v_{k\bullet}\mathbf{e}$ the same but for industry k. Revaluating intermediate uses by $p_i u_{ik}$ and commodity outputs by $p_i v_{ji}$, we can write:

$$a_{jk}(\hat{\mathbf{p}}\mathbf{U}, \mathbf{V}\hat{\mathbf{p}}) = \frac{\sum_i p_i v_{ji}}{p_i v_{ji}} \frac{p_i u_{ik}}{\sum_i p_i v_{ki}} = \frac{v_{j\bullet}\mathbf{p}}{v_{ji}} \frac{u_{ik}}{v_{k\bullet}\mathbf{p}}$$

$$= \frac{v_{j\bullet}\mathbf{e}}{v_{j\bullet}\mathbf{e}} \frac{v_{j\bullet}\mathbf{p}}{v_{ji}} \frac{u_{ik}}{v_{k\bullet}\mathbf{p}} \frac{v_{k\bullet}\mathbf{e}}{v_{k\bullet}\mathbf{e}} = \frac{v_{j\bullet}\mathbf{p}}{v_{j\bullet}\mathbf{e}} a_{jk}(\mathbf{U}, \mathbf{V}) \frac{v_{k\bullet}\mathbf{e}}{v_{k\bullet}\mathbf{p}}.$$

Now, since $v_{j\bullet}\mathbf{e}$ is the j-th element of the main diagonal of $(\widehat{\mathbf{Ve}})$ and likewise for industry k, $v_{j\bullet}\mathbf{p}$ can also be considered to be the j-th element of the main diagonal of $(\widehat{\mathbf{Vp}})$. The same applies for industry k, $v_{k\bullet}\mathbf{p}$. Hence, in matrix terms, the *price invariance* is given by:

$$\mathbf{A}(\hat{\mathbf{p}}\mathbf{U}, \mathbf{V}\hat{\mathbf{p}}) = (\widehat{\mathbf{Vp}})(\widehat{\mathbf{Ve}})^{-1}\mathbf{A}(\mathbf{U}, \mathbf{V})(\widehat{\mathbf{Ve}})(\widehat{\mathbf{Vp}})^{-1} \quad \text{for all } \mathbf{p} > 0. \quad \text{(P)}$$

Axiom S. The *scale invariance* considers multiplication of inputs and outputs of industries by factors. So, we multiply all product requirements and outputs of industry 1 by a common scale factor, say s_1, and likewise for other industries. From equation (9):

$$a_{jk}(\mathbf{U}, \mathbf{V}) = \frac{\sum_i v_{ji}}{v_{ji}} \frac{u_{ik}}{\sum_i v_{ki}}$$

and by re-scaling, we obtain:

$$a_{jk}(\mathbf{U}\hat{\mathbf{s}}, \hat{\mathbf{s}}\mathbf{V}) = \frac{\sum_i v_{ji} s_j}{v_{ji} s_j} \frac{u_{ik} s_k}{\sum_i v_{ki} s_k} = \frac{s_j \sum_i v_{ji}}{s_j v_{ji}} \frac{s_k u_{ik}}{s_k \sum_i v_{ki}} = a_{jk}(\mathbf{U}, \mathbf{V}).$$

Axiom S postulates that industry coefficients should not change when input requirements and product outputs vary proportionally. So, for all industries, it must be that:

$$\mathbf{A}(\mathbf{U}\hat{\mathbf{s}}, \hat{\mathbf{s}}\mathbf{V}) = \mathbf{A}(\mathbf{U}, \mathbf{V}) \text{ for all } \mathbf{s} > 0. \quad \text{(S)}$$

The axiom is not a constant returns to scale assumption, but merely postulates that *if* industry coefficients are constant for each product, *then* industry coefficients must be fixed (Kop Jansen and ten Raa, 1990).

5. Performance

Table 1 summarizes the results of the performance of models (1) and (2). The fixed industry sales structure model (1) fulfils all the four axioms while the fixed product sales structure model (2) only fulfils the financial balance. This is not surprising since the financial balance accounts for the equality between supply and demand of industry outputs and the industry by industry input-output tables are balanced. Proofs of the latter are relegated to the Appendix.

Theorem 3. *The input-output industry coefficients derived from the fixed industry sales structure model are industrial and financially balanced; and price and scale invariant.*

Proof: From (1), we obtain for Axiom M that:

$$\mathbf{V}^{\mathrm{T}}(\widehat{\mathbf{Ve}})^{-1}\mathbf{A}_{\mathrm{FI}}(\mathbf{U},\mathbf{V})(\widehat{\mathbf{Ve}})\mathbf{e} = \mathbf{V}^{\mathrm{T}}(\widehat{\mathbf{Ve}})^{-1}(\widehat{\mathbf{Ve}})\mathbf{V}^{-\mathrm{T}}\mathbf{U}(\widehat{\mathbf{Ve}})^{-1}(\widehat{\mathbf{Ve}})\mathbf{e}$$
$$= V^{\mathrm{T}}\mathbf{V}^{-\mathrm{T}}\mathbf{Ue} = \mathbf{Ue}.$$

For the financial balance,

$$\mathbf{e}^{\mathrm{T}}\mathbf{V}^{\mathrm{T}}(\widehat{\mathbf{Ve}})^{-1}\mathbf{A}_{\mathrm{FI}}(\mathbf{U},\mathbf{V})(\widehat{\mathbf{Ve}})$$
$$= \mathbf{e}^{\mathrm{T}}\mathbf{V}^{\mathrm{T}}(\widehat{\mathbf{Ve}})^{-1}(\widehat{\mathbf{Ve}})\mathbf{V}^{-\mathrm{T}}\mathbf{U}(\widehat{\mathbf{Ve}})^{-1}(\widehat{\mathbf{Ve}})$$
$$= \mathbf{e}^{\mathrm{T}}\mathbf{V}^{\mathrm{T}}\mathbf{V}^{-\mathrm{T}}\mathbf{U} = \mathbf{e}^{\mathrm{T}}\mathbf{U}.$$

For the price invariance axiom,

$$\mathbf{A}_{\mathrm{FI}}(\hat{\mathbf{p}}\mathbf{U},\mathbf{V}\hat{\mathbf{p}}) = (\widehat{(\mathbf{V}\hat{\mathbf{p}})\mathbf{e}})(\mathbf{V}\hat{\mathbf{p}})^{-\mathrm{T}}\hat{\mathbf{p}}\mathbf{U}(\widehat{(\mathbf{V}\hat{\mathbf{p}})\mathbf{e}})^{-1}$$
$$= (\widehat{\mathbf{V}\hat{\mathbf{p}}\mathbf{e}})\mathbf{V}^{-\mathrm{T}}\hat{\mathbf{p}}^{-1}\hat{\mathbf{p}}\mathbf{U}(\widehat{\mathbf{V}\hat{\mathbf{p}}\mathbf{e}})^{-1}$$
$$= (\widehat{\mathbf{Vp}})\mathbf{V}^{-\mathrm{T}}\mathbf{U}(\widehat{\mathbf{Vp}})^{-1}$$
$$= (\widehat{\mathbf{Vp}})(\widehat{\mathbf{Ve}})^{-1}(\widehat{\mathbf{Ve}})\mathbf{V}^{-\mathrm{T}}\mathbf{U}(\widehat{\mathbf{Ve}})^{-1}(\widehat{\mathbf{Ve}})(\widehat{\mathbf{Vp}})^{-1}$$
$$= (\widehat{\mathbf{Vp}})(\widehat{\mathbf{Ve}})^{-1}\mathbf{A}_{\mathrm{FI}}(\mathbf{U},\mathbf{V})(\widehat{\mathbf{Ve}})(\widehat{\mathbf{Vp}})^{-1}.$$

Table 1. Performance of IO constructs for industry tables.

Model	Material balance	Financial balance	Price invariance	Scale invariance
Fixed industry sales structure	√	√	√	√
Fixed product sales structure		√		

And for axiom S,

$$\begin{aligned}\mathbf{A}_{\mathrm{FI}}(\mathbf{U}\hat{\mathbf{s}}, \hat{\mathbf{s}}\mathbf{V}) &= (\widehat{(\hat{\mathbf{s}}\mathbf{V})\mathbf{e}})(\hat{\mathbf{s}}\mathbf{V})^{-\mathrm{T}}\mathbf{U}\hat{\mathbf{s}}(\widehat{(\hat{\mathbf{s}}\mathbf{V})\mathbf{e}})^{-1} \\ &= (\widehat{\mathbf{V}\mathbf{e}})\hat{\mathbf{s}}\hat{\mathbf{s}}^{-1}\mathbf{V}^{-\mathrm{T}}\mathbf{U}\hat{\mathbf{s}}\hat{\mathbf{s}}^{-1}(\widehat{\mathbf{V}\mathbf{e}})^{-1} \\ &= (\widehat{\mathbf{V}\mathbf{e}})\mathbf{V}^{-\mathrm{T}}\mathbf{U}(\widehat{\mathbf{V}\mathbf{e}})^{-1} = \mathbf{A}_{\mathrm{FI}}(\mathbf{U}, \mathbf{V})\end{aligned}$$

since $\widehat{(\hat{\mathbf{s}}\mathbf{V})\mathbf{e}} = \mathbf{e}^{\mathrm{T}}\widehat{(\mathbf{V}^{\mathrm{T}}\hat{\mathbf{s}})} = (\widehat{\mathbf{V}\mathbf{e}})\hat{\mathbf{s}}$.

We may conclude that the fixed industry sales structure model is axiomatically the best one to construct industry coefficients. Furthermore, since the fixed industry sales structure assumption depends on the inverse of the supply matrix, it also must be square and may cause negatives as well as the product technology model for product tables. Conversely, the fixed product sales structure model has the advantage of coming out without negatives. □

6. Characterization

Following the first work providing a characterization result concerning the construction of input-output coefficients for product tables (Kop Jansen and ten Raa, 1990), this paper provides the other side of the coin, i.e. two characterization theorems for the construction of industry tables. This section shows the main results. They determine the fixed industry sales structure model as the single method that fulfils the desirable properties listed in the fourth section. As a matter of fact, if we accept one balance and one invariance axiom, then we must impose the fixed industry sales structure model.

Theorem 4. (*Real sphere*) *The material balance and scale invariance axioms characterize the fixed industry sales structure model.*

Proof: The fixed industry sales structure model implies that the material balance and scale invariance axioms hold by Theorem 3. Conversely, let us assume that the material balance and scale invariance are met. By axiom M,

$$\mathbf{V}^{\mathrm{T}}(\widehat{\mathbf{V}\mathbf{e}})^{-1}\mathbf{A}(\mathbf{U}, \mathbf{V})(\widehat{\mathbf{V}\mathbf{e}})\mathbf{e} = \mathbf{U}\mathbf{e}$$

for all $\mathbf{A}(\mathbf{U},\mathbf{V})$. Replace $\mathbf{A}(\mathbf{U}\hat{\mathbf{s}},\hat{\mathbf{s}}\mathbf{V})$. Then

$$(\hat{\mathbf{s}}\mathbf{V})^{\mathrm{T}}(\widehat{(\hat{\mathbf{s}}\mathbf{V})\mathbf{e}})^{-1}\mathbf{A}(\mathbf{U}\hat{\mathbf{s}},\hat{\mathbf{s}}\mathbf{V})(\widehat{(\hat{\mathbf{s}}\mathbf{V})\mathbf{e}})\mathbf{e}=\mathbf{U}\hat{\mathbf{s}}\mathbf{e}.$$

By axiom S and since $(\widehat{(\hat{\mathbf{s}}\mathbf{V})\mathbf{e}})=(\widehat{\mathbf{V}\mathbf{e}})\hat{\mathbf{s}}$ and $\hat{\mathbf{s}}\mathbf{e}=\mathbf{s}$,

$$\mathbf{V}^{\mathrm{T}}\hat{\mathbf{s}}((\widehat{\mathbf{Ve}})\hat{s})^{-1}\mathbf{A}(\mathbf{U},\mathbf{V})(\widehat{\mathbf{Ve}})\mathbf{s}=\mathbf{U}\mathbf{s}$$

being:

$$\mathbf{V}^{\mathrm{T}}\hat{\mathbf{s}}\hat{\mathbf{s}}^{-1}\widehat{(\mathbf{Ve})}^{-1}\mathbf{A}(\mathbf{U},\mathbf{V})\widehat{(\mathbf{Ve})}\mathbf{s}=\mathbf{V}^{\mathrm{T}}\widehat{(\mathbf{Ve})}^{-1}\mathbf{A}(\mathbf{U},\mathbf{V})\widehat{(\mathbf{Ve})}\mathbf{s}=\mathbf{U}\mathbf{s}.$$

Since this holds for all positive $\mathbf{s}$ and thus for a basis, the matrices acting on them must be equal:

$$\mathbf{V}^{\mathrm{T}}\widehat{(\mathbf{Ve})}^{-1}\mathbf{A}(\mathbf{U},\mathbf{V})\widehat{(\mathbf{Ve})}=\mathbf{U}$$

Therefore,

$$\mathbf{A}(\mathbf{U},\mathbf{V})=\widehat{(\mathbf{Ve})}\mathbf{V}^{-\mathrm{T}}\mathbf{U}\widehat{(\mathbf{Ve})}^{-1}.$$

This completes the proof.

Theorem 5. (*Nominal sphere*) *The financial balance and price invariance axioms characterize the fixed industry sales structure model.*

Proof: Necessity has already been proved in Theorem 3. For the sufficiency proof, let us assume that the financial balance and price invariance axioms hold. By axiom F,

$$\mathbf{e}^{\mathrm{T}}\mathbf{V}^{\mathrm{T}}(\widehat{\mathbf{Ve}})^{-1}\mathbf{A}(\mathbf{U},\mathbf{V})(\widehat{\mathbf{Ve}})=\mathbf{e}^{\mathrm{T}}\mathbf{U}$$

for all $\mathbf{A}(\mathbf{U},\mathbf{V})$. Substitute $\mathbf{A}(\hat{\mathbf{p}}\mathbf{U},\mathbf{V}\hat{\mathbf{p}})$. Then:

$$\mathbf{e}^{\mathrm{T}}(\mathbf{V}\hat{\mathbf{p}})^{\mathrm{T}}(\widehat{(\mathbf{V}\hat{\mathbf{p}})\mathbf{e}})^{-1}\mathbf{A}(\hat{\mathbf{p}}\mathbf{U},\mathbf{V}\hat{\mathbf{p}})(\widehat{(\mathbf{V}\hat{\mathbf{p}})\mathbf{e}})=\mathbf{e}^{\mathrm{T}}\hat{\mathbf{p}}\mathbf{U}$$

for which the LHS, since $\mathbf{e}^{\mathrm{T}}\hat{\mathbf{p}}\mathbf{V}^{\mathrm{T}} = \mathbf{p}^{\mathrm{T}}\mathbf{V}^{\mathrm{T}}$, is:

$$\begin{aligned}
&\mathbf{p}^{\mathrm{T}}\mathbf{V}^{\mathrm{T}}(\widehat{\mathbf{V}\hat{\mathbf{p}}\mathbf{e}})^{-1}\mathbf{A}(\hat{\mathbf{p}}\mathbf{U}, \mathbf{V}\hat{\mathbf{p}})(\widehat{\mathbf{V}\hat{\mathbf{p}}\mathbf{e}}) \\
&\quad = \mathbf{p}^{\mathrm{T}}\mathbf{V}^{\mathrm{T}}(\widehat{\mathbf{V}\mathbf{p}})^{-1}\mathbf{A}(\hat{\mathbf{p}}\mathbf{U}, \mathbf{V}\hat{\mathbf{p}})(\widehat{\mathbf{V}\mathbf{p}}) \\
&\quad = \mathbf{p}^{\mathrm{T}}\mathbf{V}^{\mathrm{T}}(\widehat{\mathbf{V}\mathbf{p}})^{-1}(\widehat{\mathbf{V}\mathbf{p}})(\widehat{\mathbf{V}\mathbf{e}})^{-1}\mathbf{A}(\mathbf{U}, \mathbf{V})(\widehat{\mathbf{V}\mathbf{e}})(\widehat{\mathbf{V}\mathbf{p}})^{-1}(\widehat{\mathbf{V}\mathbf{p}}) \\
&\quad = \mathbf{p}^{\mathrm{T}}\mathbf{V}^{\mathrm{T}}(\widehat{\mathbf{V}\mathbf{e}})^{-1}\mathbf{A}(\mathbf{U}, \mathbf{V})(\widehat{\mathbf{V}\mathbf{e}})
\end{aligned}$$

and then, since $\mathbf{e}^{\mathrm{T}}\hat{\mathbf{p}}\mathbf{U} = \mathbf{p}^{\mathrm{T}}\mathbf{U}$:

$$\mathbf{p}^{\mathrm{T}}\mathbf{V}^{\mathrm{T}}(\widehat{\mathbf{V}\mathbf{e}})^{-1}\mathbf{A}(\mathbf{U}, \mathbf{V})(\widehat{\mathbf{V}\mathbf{e}}) = \mathbf{p}^{\mathrm{T}}\mathbf{U}.$$

Since this is true for all $\mathbf{p} > 0$, we may proceed to conclude that:

$$\mathbf{V}^{\mathrm{T}}(\widehat{\mathbf{V}\mathbf{e}})^{-1}\mathbf{A}(\mathbf{U}, \mathbf{V})(\widehat{\mathbf{V}\mathbf{e}}) = \mathbf{U}$$

and hence (1).

7. Conclusions

Product tables and industry tables coexist and each type can be constructed in accordance with a product or an industry based model. For product tables, it is well accepted that the *product* (technology) *model* is superior to the *industry* (technology) *model*, on the basis of the axiomatic analysis of Kop Jansen and ten Raa (1990). This paper brings in two characterization theorems for industry tables and argues that the *fixed industry sales structure model* emerges as the best one to construct industry tables in comparison with the fixed product sales structure model. The fact that industry tables can be brought in, in accordance with an axiomatic approach, provides a justification for the current statistical practices in Canada, Denmark, Finland, the Netherlands and Norway. From this axiomatic approach, the frequent use of the fixed product sales structure assumption to arrive at industry tables is not superior, but it avoids the undesirable emergence of negatives.

Acknowledgments

The authors wish to thank Luc Avonds for his helpful comments on a first draft of this paper. The views expressed in this paper belong to the authors and should not be attributed to the European Commission or its services.

References

Eurostat. (2008). *Eurostat Manual of Supply, Use and Input-Output Tables*, Luxembourg: Eurostat.

Konijn, P. J. A. (1994). *The Make and Use of Commodities by Industries*, Enschede: Universiteit Twente.

Kop Jansen, P. and T. ten Raa. (1990). The choice of model in the construction of input-output coefficients matrices. *International Economic Review*, **31**, 213–227.

ten Raa, T. and J. M. Rueda-Cantuche. (2003). The construction of input-output coefficients matrices in an axiomatic context: Some further considerations. *Economic Systems Research*, **15**, 439–455.

ten Raa, T. and J. M. Rueda-Cantuche. (2007). A generalized expression for the commodity and the industry technology models in input-output analysis. *Economic Systems Research*, **19**, 99–104.

Thage, B. and T. ten Raa. (2006). Streamlining the SNA 1993 chapter on supply and use tables and input-output. Paper presented at the 29th General Conference of the International Association for Research in Income and Wealth, Joensuu, Finland.

United Nations. (1993). *Revised System of National Accounts*, Studies in Methods, Series F, No. 2, rev.4, New York: United Nations.

Yamano, N. and N. Ahmad. (2006/8). The OECD Input-Output Database: 2006 Edition. OECD Science, Technology and Industry Working Papers, OECD Publishing doi:10.1787/308077407044.

Appendix

This Appendix details the performance of the fixed product sales structure model for industry tables. It fulfils only the financial balance axiom. By using the same fictitious use and supply matrices (originally make matrix) as in Kop Jansen and ten Raa (1990), we will present counterexamples that violate some of the balance axioms.

Axiom F

Since equation (2) provides the formulation of the fixed product sales structure model and (F) the financial balance, by substitution in the LHS of (F):

$$\mathbf{e}^{\mathrm{T}}\mathbf{V}^{\mathrm{T}}(\widehat{\mathbf{Ve}})^{-1}\mathbf{V}(\widehat{\mathbf{V}^{\mathrm{T}}\mathbf{e}})^{-1}\mathbf{U}(\widehat{\mathbf{Ve}})^{-1}(\widehat{\mathbf{Ve}}) = \mathbf{e}^{\mathrm{T}}\mathbf{V}(\widehat{\mathbf{V}^{\mathrm{T}}\mathbf{e}})^{-1}\mathbf{U}.$$

Therefore, since $\mathbf{e}^{\mathrm{T}}\mathbf{V}^{\mathrm{T}} = \mathbf{e}^{\mathrm{T}}(\widehat{\mathbf{Ve}})$ and $\mathbf{e}^{\mathrm{T}}\mathbf{V} = \mathbf{e}^{\mathrm{T}}(\widehat{\mathbf{V}^{\mathrm{T}}\mathbf{e}})$, then:

$$\mathbf{e}^{\mathrm{T}}(\widehat{\mathbf{V}^{\mathrm{T}}\mathbf{e}})(\widehat{\mathbf{V}^{\mathrm{T}}\mathbf{e}})^{-1}\mathbf{U} = \mathbf{e}^{\mathrm{T}}\mathbf{U}.$$

Axiom M

Let us define the following use and make tables:

$$\mathbf{U} = \begin{pmatrix} 1/2 & 0 \\ 1 & 1/2 \end{pmatrix}; \quad \mathbf{V} = \begin{pmatrix} 1 & 1 \\ 0 & 1 \end{pmatrix}; \quad \mathbf{p} = \mathbf{s} = \begin{pmatrix} 2 \\ 1 \end{pmatrix}.$$

A straightforward computation shows that:

$$\widehat{\mathbf{Ve}} = \begin{pmatrix} 2 & 0 \\ 0 & 1 \end{pmatrix}; \quad \mathbf{Ve} = \begin{pmatrix} 2 \\ 1 \end{pmatrix}; \quad \widehat{\mathbf{V}^{\mathrm{T}}\mathbf{e}} = \begin{pmatrix} 1 & 0 \\ 0 & 2 \end{pmatrix}; \quad \mathbf{V}^{\mathrm{T}}\mathbf{e} = \begin{pmatrix} 1 \\ 2 \end{pmatrix}$$

and therefore, equation (2):

$$\begin{aligned} \mathbf{A}_{\mathrm{FP}}(\mathbf{U},\mathbf{V}) &= \mathbf{V}(\widehat{\mathbf{V}^{\mathrm{T}}\mathbf{e}})^{-1}\mathbf{U}(\widehat{\mathbf{Ve}})^{-1} \\ &= \begin{pmatrix} 1 & 1 \\ 0 & 1 \end{pmatrix}\begin{pmatrix} 1 & 1 \\ 0 & 1/2 \end{pmatrix}\begin{pmatrix} 1/2 & 0 \\ 1 & 1/2 \end{pmatrix}\begin{pmatrix} 1/2 & 0 \\ 0 & 1 \end{pmatrix} = \begin{pmatrix} 1/2 & 1/4 \\ 1/4 & 1/4 \end{pmatrix} \end{aligned}$$

being the material balance (M),

$$\begin{aligned} &\mathbf{V}^{\mathrm{T}}(\widehat{\mathbf{Ve}})^{-1}\mathbf{A}_{\mathrm{FP}}(\mathbf{U},\mathbf{V})(\widehat{\mathbf{Ve}})\mathbf{e} \\ &= \begin{pmatrix} 1 & 0 \\ 1 & 1 \end{pmatrix}\begin{pmatrix} 1/2 & 0 \\ 0 & 1 \end{pmatrix}\begin{pmatrix} 1/2 & 1/4 \\ 1/4 & 1/4 \end{pmatrix}\begin{pmatrix} 2 & 0 \\ 0 & 1 \end{pmatrix}\begin{pmatrix} 1 \\ 1 \end{pmatrix} = \begin{pmatrix} 5/8 \\ 11/8 \end{pmatrix} \end{aligned}$$

which is not equal to: $\mathbf{Ue} = \begin{pmatrix} 1/2 & 0 \\ 1 & 1/2 \end{pmatrix}\begin{pmatrix} 1 \\ 1 \end{pmatrix} = \begin{pmatrix} 1/2 \\ 3/2 \end{pmatrix}.$

Axiom P

The price invariance axiom (P) is violated since for:

$$\hat{\mathbf{p}}\mathbf{U} = \begin{pmatrix} 2 & 0 \\ 0 & 1 \end{pmatrix} \begin{pmatrix} 1/2 & 0 \\ 1 & 1/2 \end{pmatrix} = \begin{pmatrix} 1 & 0 \\ 1 & 1/2 \end{pmatrix};$$

$$\mathbf{V}\hat{\mathbf{p}} = \begin{pmatrix} 1 & 1 \\ 0 & 1 \end{pmatrix} \begin{pmatrix} 2 & 0 \\ 0 & 1 \end{pmatrix} = \begin{pmatrix} 2 & 1 \\ 0 & 1 \end{pmatrix}$$

$$\begin{aligned}
\mathbf{A}_{\mathrm{FP}}(\hat{\mathbf{p}}\mathbf{U}, \mathbf{V}\hat{\mathbf{p}}) &= (\mathbf{V}\hat{\mathbf{p}})(\widehat{(\mathbf{V}\hat{\mathbf{p}})^{\mathrm{T}}\mathbf{e}})^{-1}\hat{\mathbf{p}}\mathbf{U}(\widehat{(\mathbf{V}\hat{\mathbf{p}})\mathbf{e}})^{-1} \\
&= \begin{pmatrix} 2 & 1 \\ 0 & 1 \end{pmatrix} \begin{pmatrix} 1/2 & 0 \\ 0 & 1/2 \end{pmatrix} \begin{pmatrix} 1 & 0 \\ 1 & 1/2 \end{pmatrix} \begin{pmatrix} 1/3 & 0 \\ 0 & 1 \end{pmatrix} \\
&= \begin{pmatrix} 1/2 & 1/4 \\ 1/6 & 1/4 \end{pmatrix}
\end{aligned}$$

being:

$$\begin{aligned}
&(\widehat{\mathbf{Vp}})(\widehat{\mathbf{Ve}})^{-1}\mathbf{A}_{\mathrm{FP}}(\mathbf{U}, \mathbf{V})(\widehat{\mathbf{Ve}})(\widehat{\mathbf{Vp}})^{-1} \\
&= \begin{pmatrix} 3 & 0 \\ 0 & 1 \end{pmatrix} \begin{pmatrix} 1/2 & 0 \\ 0 & 1 \end{pmatrix} \begin{pmatrix} 1/2 & 1/4 \\ 1/4 & 1/4 \end{pmatrix} \begin{pmatrix} 2 & 0 \\ 0 & 1 \end{pmatrix} \begin{pmatrix} 1/3 & 0 \\ 0 & 1 \end{pmatrix} \\
&= \begin{pmatrix} 1/2 & 3/8 \\ 1/6 & 1/4 \end{pmatrix}.
\end{aligned}$$

Axiom S

For the scale invariance axiom (S),

$$\begin{aligned}
\mathbf{A}_{\mathrm{FP}}(\mathbf{U}\hat{\mathbf{s}}, \hat{\mathbf{s}}\mathbf{V}) &= (\hat{\mathbf{s}}\mathbf{V})(\widehat{(\hat{\mathbf{s}}\mathbf{V})^{\mathrm{T}}\mathbf{e}})^{-1}\mathbf{U}\hat{\mathbf{s}}(\widehat{(\hat{\mathbf{s}}\mathbf{V})\mathbf{e}})^{-1} \\
&= \begin{pmatrix} 2 & 2 \\ 0 & 1 \end{pmatrix} \begin{pmatrix} 1/2 & 0 \\ 0 & 1/3 \end{pmatrix} \begin{pmatrix} 1 & 0 \\ 2 & 1/2 \end{pmatrix} \begin{pmatrix} 1/4 & 0 \\ 0 & 1 \end{pmatrix} \\
&= \begin{pmatrix} 7/12 & 1/3 \\ 1/6 & 1/6 \end{pmatrix}
\end{aligned}$$

and

$$\mathbf{A}_{\mathrm{FP}}(\mathbf{U}, \mathbf{V}) = \begin{pmatrix} 1/2 & 1/4 \\ 1/4 & 1/4 \end{pmatrix},$$

are different and hence, (S) does not hold.

Chapter 17

Testing Assumptions Made in the Construction of Input-Output Tables*

José M. Rueda-Cantuche[†] and Thijs ten Raa[‡]

[†]*European Commission — DG, Joint Research Center, IPTS — Institute for Prospective Technological Studies, Edificio EXPO, C/Inca Garcilaso s/n, 41092 and Pablo de Olavide University at Seville, Spain*

jose.rueda-cantuche@ec.europa.eu

[‡]*Department of Economics, Tilburg University, Tilburg, The Netherlands*

tenraa@uvt.nl

Abstract. Product input-output (IO) tables are mainly constructed on the basis of product and/or industry technology assumptions. The choice is not trivial and deserves empirical analysis using input and output data at the level of establishments. This paper offers input-output compilers econometric tests to facilitate the construction of tailored hybrid technology based product IO tables. We provide weighted likelihood ratios of the product and industry technology assumptions. Although the proposed econometric tests are aimed to be used ex-ante, we construct four variants of hybrid technology based product IO tables using establishment data from Andalusia (Spain) and contrast them to the official product

*Reprinted from *Economic Systems Research*, **25**, 170 189, 2013, with permission from Taylor & Francis.

IO table and the pure product and industry technology based tables. Our econometric tests are not valid for industry IO tables.

Keywords: Input-Output Tables, Econometric Tests

1. Introduction

There are two types of input-output (I-O) tables and each type has two main methods of construction. *Product IO tables* are conceptually clean and their construction has nice theoretical foundations, but *industry IO tables* make a comeback (Yamano and Ahmad, 2006). Product IO tables are constructed chiefly according to the product technology assumption (the favorite of theorists, Kop Jansen and ten Raa, 1990, and ten Raa and Rueda-Cantuche, 2003, and of statistical offices) or the industry technology assumption (which yield no negative coefficients and have been adopted by the US Bureau of Economic Analysis and other offices). Industry IO tables are constructed chiefly according to the fixed product sales structure assumption (Canada, Denmark, Finland, the Netherlands and Norway) or the fixed industry sales structure model (criticized as unrealistic by Eurostat, 2008, but defended on theoretical grounds by Rueda-Cantuche and ten Raa, 2009). In this paper we take a pragmatic look at product IO tables, letting the data decide which of the two competing assumptions is better for each product. We thus construct a hybrid technology based IO table. We also explain why this approach is not applicable to industry IO tables.

Most statistical offices already use hybrid product and industry technology assumptions to construct product IO tables (and also hybrid fixed product and fixed industry sales structure assumptions to construct industry tables), but on the basis of expert judgments. Our purpose is to supplement the judgment with econometric analysis of establishment data, which are unlikely to become publicly available, but can be used in-house.

The product and industry technology assumptions are the main competitors (albeit not the only ones). One of the two assumptions is not the alternative to the other in the sense of hypothesis testing. The assumptions are not even nested. Our strategy, therefore, is to determine the level of confidence of each assumption and then to select one of them accordingly, on a product by product basis.

2. Testing the Assumptions in Product Input-Output Tables

2.1. *The tests*

Product IO tables[1] describe the technological relations between products: how to produce products by means of products. In contrast, industry IO tables[2] depict inter-industry relations, displaying the industries' use of each other's products.

To construct a product IO table, secondary outputs must be transferred out to the industries for which they are primary outputs, along with the associated inputs. (And to construct an industry IO table, secondary products must be transferred in to the primary output of the industry, see Rueda-Cantuche and ten Raa, 2009.) The question is how to associate inputs with the transferred outputs. This can be handled in different ways and these distinguish the competing construction models.

Primes denote transposition, $^{-1}$ inversion of a matrix and $^{\wedge}$ diagonalization, whether by suppression of the off-diagonal elements of a square matrix or by placement of the elements of a vector. A use matrix $\mathbf{U} = (u_{ij})$ comprises commodities i $(= 1, \ldots, n)$ consumed by industries j $(= 1, \ldots, n)$ and a make matrix $\mathbf{V} = (v_{ji})$ shows the produce of commodities i in terms of industries j; it is the transposed of a supply matrix (Eurostat, 2008). Following Rueda-Cantuche and ten Raa (2009), product input-output coefficients can be defined generically by:

$$a_{ij} = \frac{u_{ij} - \sum_{\substack{k=1 \\ k \neq j}}^{n} a_{ijk} v_{jk} + \sum_{\substack{k=1 \\ k \neq j}}^{n} a_{ikj} v_{kj}}{\sum_{k=1}^{n} v_{kj}} \tag{1}$$

where product coefficient a_{ijk} is the amount of product i used by industry j to make one unit of product k. The product technology assumption postulates that all products have unique input structures

[1]Hereafter, product IO tables will refer to "product by product symmetric input-output tables".

[2]Hereafter, industry IO tables will refer to "industry by industry symmetric input-output tables".

irrespective the industry of fabrication (removal of the second subscript) and can be written as:

$$a_{ijk} = a_{ik}^{PT} \quad \text{for all } j \tag{2}$$

Substitution of (2) into (1) confirms the well-known product technology formula (Rueda-Cantuche and ten Raa, 2009):

$$u_{ij} = \sum_k a_{ik}^{PT} v_{jk}. \tag{3}$$

The industry technology assumption postulates that every industry has its own specific input structure irrespective of the product-mix of that industry (removal of the third subscript) and can be written as:

$$a_{ijk} = a_{ij}^{IT} \quad \text{for all } k. \tag{4}$$

Substitution of (4) into (1) confirms the well-known industry technology formula (Rueda-Cantuche and ten Raa, 2009):

$$u_{ij} = a_{ij}^{IT} \sum_k v_{jk}. \tag{5}$$

The idea of this paper is to add error terms to equations (3) and (5) and thus to consider the input-output coefficients as regression coefficients (Mattey and ten Raa, 1997). The regressions of the inputs on outputs are performed at the level of establishments. If this is done for the subsets of establishments which constitute the industries, the product technology assumption is confirmed if the input coefficients are the same across subsets. The imposition of this equality will increase the residual sums of squares and the increase is measured by the F-statistic. A modification of this procedure is used to test the industry technology assumption.

To explain the basic idea, imagine 100 establishments produce cheese, of which 25 in agriculture, 15 in the meat industry and 60 in the cheese industry. All establishments are supposed to use milk as input in their production process. Therefore, if cheese is supposed to be produced with the same input structure irrespective the industry of production (the product technology assumption) the input share of milk across the hundred establishments must be similar. However, if we admit different cheese technologies, the input shares will differ between industries.

To test the industry technology assumption, imagine 100 establishments which main business is the production of meat and meat products. Some establishments also feature livestock activities and production of animal fats. All establishments use plastic materials. If the industry technology holds for livestock and animal fats the input ratio of plastic materials to the total output of the meat industry (including primary and secondary activities) across all establishments must be similar to the input ratio accounting only for the primary output (meat production). The larger the difference between these two input shares, the more likely it is that the industry technology assumption is rejected.

Let $m(> c)$[3] be the total number of establishments, m_1 the number of establishments populating industry 1, m_2 establishments populate industry 2, ..., so that $m = m_1 + m_2 + \cdots + m_n$. We propose the following null hypothesis, being $a_{ik}^{PT}(j)$ the technical coefficient a_{ik}^{PT} of the j-th component of (3):

$$H_0 : a_{ik}^{PT}(j) = a_{ik}^{PT}, \quad \text{for } j = 1, 2, \ldots, n \tag{H1}$$

under which the product technology assumption is fulfilled. Running the corresponding regressions for the product and industry technology assumptions yield estimations of the associated inputs (left-hand side of equations), which by difference with respect to their actual values lead to the so called residuals. They are subsequently made square and summed over all observations, i.e. the residual sum of squares (RSS). Next, we will use the RSS of two different models to construct a standard F-statistic that would allow us for testing (H1). On the one hand, we will take for granted (H1) and assume that for all industries, we have the same input structures and consequently one single regression shall be run using all the considered observations, namely r (or establishments). This is the so called restricted model. On the other hand, the so called unrestricted model consists of regressions with n restrictions or equations, all of which must be estimated independently with a subset of m_j observations in each case (only

[3]Notice that m should be greater than c (number of products) to get positive degrees of freedom in the econometric regression. Besides, m might be also referred to a more detailed breakdown of n industries and not necessarily to establishment micro data, which would be the highest detail level. We also assume that firms of the same industry operate with the same technology.

those establishments producing effectively product k). By using the F-test[4] based on the residual sum of squares of the restricted (RSS_C) and unrestricted (RSS) models,

$$F_{(n-1),m-n} = \frac{(RSS_C - (RSS_1 + RSS_2 + \cdots + RSS_n))\,/(n-1)}{(RSS_1 + RSS_2 + \cdots + RSS_n)\,/(r-n)}$$

we will be able to test the statistical significance of the product technology assumption for each of the inputs. As long as we accept the null hypothesis in most of them, we may eventually accept the product technology assumption on the basis of a weighted ratio of the number of accepted inputs over the total number of inputs used. The weights would correspond to the input structure of those surveyed establishments that produce product k independently of the industry to which they belong. The so-called probability values (usually abbreviated as p-values) provide the minimum significance levels to reject the null hypothesis. For example, if a p-value equals 0.05, then the imposition of the product-technology model pushes the error terms in the tail with 5% mass, i.e. we shall accept (H1).

For the industry technology assumption, the following null hypothesis can be proposed, for $a_{ij}^{IT}(k)$ the technical coefficient in the k-th component of (5):

$$H_0 : a_{ij}^{IT}(k) = a_{ij}^{IT}, \quad \text{for } k = 1, 2, \ldots, m_s \tag{H2}$$

under which the industry technology model is fulfilled. Next, we regress input i's use of industry j's establishments on their primary and secondary outputs. In standard econometrics, the F-test[5] is frequently used to test the equality of regression coefficients in a flexible manner. With $q = (m_s - 1)$ independent equations in (H2), m_j number of observations (number of establishments populating industry j) and m_s explanatory variables (number of different secondary outputs), we may define the F-statistic as:

$$F_{(m_s-1),m_j-m_s} = \frac{(\mathbf{R}\hat{\boldsymbol{\beta}} - \mathbf{r})'[\mathbf{R}(\mathbf{X}'\mathbf{X})^{-1}\mathbf{R}']^{-1}(\mathbf{R}\hat{\boldsymbol{\beta}} - \mathbf{r})/(m_s - 1)}{RSS/(m_j - m_s)}$$

[4]This F-test is a modified version of the Chow test for structural change (Gujarati, 2003, pp. 275–279).

[5]Johnston, J. and Di Nardo, J. (1997) *Econometric methods*, New York: McGraw-Hill (pp. 92–93).

where $\mathbf{X}$ is a matrix of explanatory variables (industry j's output by product type in columns), RSS to the sum of the (ordinary least squares) squared residuals and $\mathbf{R}$, $\mathbf{r}$ and $\boldsymbol{\beta}$ as follows:

$$\mathbf{R} = \begin{pmatrix} 1 & -1 & 0 & \cdots & 0 \\ 0 & 1 & -1 & \cdots & 0 \\ \vdots & \vdots & \vdots & \ddots & \vdots \\ 0 & 0 & \cdots & 1 & -1 \end{pmatrix}_{(m_s-1)\times m_s} \quad \mathbf{r} = \begin{pmatrix} 0 \\ \vdots \\ 0 \end{pmatrix} \quad \boldsymbol{\beta} = \begin{pmatrix} a_{ij}^{IT}(1) \\ \vdots \\ a_{ij}^{IT}(m_s) \end{pmatrix}.$$

By means of this F-test the reader may test the equality of the regression coefficients and therefore, whether the input requirement of product i is independent of the commodity produced in industry j. For instance, if we have a p-value equal to 0.3, the imposition of the industry-technology model pushes the error terms less, in the tail with 30% mass. In general, a greater p-value indicates a better fit of the technology assumption to the data. The analysis can be extended to all the other inputs and as long as we accept (H2) in most of them, we may accept eventually the industry technology model on the basis of a weighted ratio of the number of accepted inputs over the total number of inputs used. In this case, the weights correspond to the product input structures of the surveyed establishments of industry j.

2.2. *Data sources and preparation*

The Andalusian Input-Output Framework, MIOAN-95 (IEA, 1999) was one of the first Spanish regional input-output tables based on the new European System of Accounts (ESA-95) published by Eurostat (1996). The Institute of Statistics of Andalusia (IEA) provided the authors with the cross-section inputs and outputs establishment data used for the construction of the MIOAN-95. The data provided by the IEA had been completed and edited to obtain a full specification of inputs and outputs, e.g. including adjustments accounting for changes in inventories, computing trade outputs as a difference between sales and purchases of goods that are neither processed nor transformed; estimating net premiums in insurance services; FISIM as intermediate consumption, etc. These adjustments led in some cases to consolidate input and output structures into single overall structures depending on the data availability. Evidently, those industries for which there was eventually one single input and output structure were not taken into account for the econometric analyses (e.g. public administration, finance, insurance services, agriculture, public hospital services, public social services, etc.). Redefinitions implemented in the course of the actual input-output compilation were not carried back to the establishment data used for our analysis. They were made at the aggregated level during the compilation process.

The conversion from purchasers' prices into basic prices is reported in ten Raa and Rueda-Cantuche (2007, pp. 332–334). We used the same trade, transport and net taxes on products rates that were reported by the valuation matrices used in the compilation of the use table at basic prices in the IEA. We assumed equality of margins and net product taxes across establishments in industry j producing product k. Once trade and transport margins and net taxes on products were subtracted from the use flow data, we reallocate the subtracted total trade and domestic transport margins to trade and transport industries, respectively. We received the technical support of the IEA to carry out this task.

The surveys collected the information on inputs at the level of 89 products requiring a full specification of inputs used for the production process. At this point, there were also different ad-hoc industry-specific designs for the surveys conveyed to wholesale trade, retail trade, construction, (simplified surveys for) small and medium enterprises in the manufacturing industries, fisheries and services.

The sample used by IEA (1999) in the construction of the supply and use system covered nearly 45% of total domestic output and more than one third of total employment. The IEA completed the initial survey-based data on industries' detailed turnovers and purchases with other statistical sources from the National Statistical Institute (INE), the Central Balance Sheet Office and public institutions (health services, government budget data, education, agriculture, etc.) to achieve such large sample coverage. The final sample size eventually achieved 18,084 observations (ten Raa and Rueda-Cantuche, 2007), which were classified into 89 different industries (see the complete list in the Annex). The availability of establishments' data is not really very common outside statistical offices. Actually, this is the reason why we had to use data from a region and a less recent year. However, we recognize that it would be desirable to extend the analyses presented in this paper to other regions and countries to see their implications for the general applicability of the tests.

2.3. *Discussion of the empirical results*

Following the theoretical approach suggested in the previous section, we have tested the product technology and the industry technology hypotheses using establishments' data from Andalusia (Spain) for 43 products and 47 industries. The base year is 1995. The complete list comprises 89 products and 89 industries. The remaining products and industries were not analyzed for two reasons: (a) there was not enough surveyed information available to run the regressions; and (b) there was not sufficient and/or reliable information on the input structures of those establishments that produce secondarily one product that is produced almost exclusively by its own primary industry.

Tables 1 and 2 depict the parameters of estimation of the tests carried out for the product and industry technology assumptions. For instance, for the product technology test, we made the estimations for $c = 58$ non-zero inputs (number of estimated equations), with $n = 2$ different industry suppliers and a total amount of $r = 168$ establishments producing fish and fishing products; for the industry technology test, we included $m_s = 3$ different types of output (including its primary production) and estimated the regression with $m_j = 168$ establishments populating the fishing activities. Fifty-six regressions were estimated for $m_i = 56$ non-zero inputs. The same applies for the other products and/or activities (see Tables 1 and 2 for details). In total, we run 2,793 regressions for testing the product technology assumption and 2,304 regressions for testing the industry technology assumption.

Table 3 summarizes the outcomes from the estimated regressions. For instance, 82.04% of the input requirements of the fish and fishing activities can be said to be used in the same proportion by other industries to produce fish and fishing products secondarily, but only 24.64% of the input structure might be considered specific from the industries that produce fish and fish products (primarily or secondarily). We might then interpret these two ratios as measurements of the likelihood of the respective technology assumptions. Accordingly, we may postulate that the input requirements used by secondary

Table 1. Parameters of estimation for the product technology test.

Code	Products	c	n	r
6	Fish and fishing products	58	2	168
12	Meat and meat products	70	2	244
13	Canned and preserved fish, fruit and vegetables	67	6	424
14	Fats and oils	59	3	325
15	Milk and dairy products	58	4	123
16	Grain mills, bakery, sugar mills, ...	61	4	626
17	Miscellaneous food products	65	9	601
18	Wines and alcoholic beverages	64	3	173
19	Beer and soft drinks	55	2	66
22	Clothing products	55	3	573
23	Leather tanning, leather products and footwear	50	2	144
24	Cork and wood products	52	2	4,269
25	Paper and allied products	57	5	818
26	Printing, publishing and editing services	73	2	454
27	Petroleum refining products	56	3	64
28	Basic chemical products	60	5	117
29	Other chemical products	63	3	194
30	Rubber and plastic products	62	8	4,227
31	Cement, lime and allied products	55	2	504
32	Ceramics, clay, bricks and other products for building	56	2	230
33	Stone and glass products	58	3	319
34	Primary metal products	53	3	128
35	Fabricated metal products	75	6	1,496
38	Electrical and electronic machinery	56	4	2,386
40	Professional and scientific instruments	71	2	109
41	Motor vehicles transportation equipment	54	2	52
42	Naval transportation and repairing services	52	2	78
43	Miscellaneous transportation equipment	52	2	66
44	Furniture	60	5	757
50	Construction work	78	4	1,237
54	Wholesale trade services	80	24	9,455
55	Retail trade and repair domestic and personal effects	71	7	8,726
56	Hotels services	76	2	51
57	Bars and restaurants services	80	5	596

Table 1. (*Continued*)

Code	Products	c	n	r
62	Allied transportation services	79	3	164
63	Post and communications services	76	4	251
68	Machinery and equipment rental	81	3	45
69	Computer services	69	2	94
71	Accounting and law activity services	76	3	276
73	Marketing services	74	4	63
79	Private education services	77	3	3,618
84	Public drainage and sewerage services	70	2	35
87	Other amusement, cultural, sport and recreation services	79	3	588

Source: Own elaboration.

Notes: c = number of non-zero inputs (estimated equations); n = number of industry suppliers of product i; r = number of establishments producing product i.

suppliers to produce fish and fishing products should be removed according to the input structure of the fishing activities (product technology assumption). The tests might also be used to investigate if individual inputs (rather than entire input structures) are processed in product or industry style.

Our tests are not single tests of one technology against the other, but merely indicate which technology assumption is more likely. Due to the insufficient level of breakdown in the classification used, there are products and industries for which both ratios of acceptance are over 50% (or both under 50%). We simply select the technology assumption with the highest rate of acceptance. However, there were cases with only one available estimated ratio of acceptance; these cases we handled as follows. If the available product technology model ratio was below 50% (e.g. machinery and equipment rental), we opted for the industry technology model (and for the product technology model otherwise). If the available industry technology model ratio was below 50% (e.g. petrol and motor vehicles trade activities), we opted for the product technology model (and for the industry technology model otherwise). Table 3, last column, lists our choices "P" and "I" (product and industry technology assumption, respectively).

Table 2. Parameters of estimation for the industry technology test.

Code	Industries	m_i	m_s	m_j
6	Fishing	56	3	168
12	Meat manufacturing industry	53	11	239
13	Manufacture of canned and preserved fish, fruit and vegetables	56	12	148
14	Fats and oils manufacturing industry	53	11	252
15	Milk and dairy products industry	51	8	34
16	Grain mills, bakery, sugar mills, ... industry	55	9	469
17	Miscellaneous manufactured food industry	56	14	139
18	Wines and alcoholic beverages fabrication	51	9	105
19	Beer and soft drinks industry	46	4	23
22	Clothing	49	6	483
23	Leather tanning, leather products and footwear industry	45	5	135
24	Cork and wood products industry	47	7	299
25	Paper manufacturing	45	6	51
26	Printing, publishing and editing	50	6	447
27	Petroleum refining	43	3	9
28	Basic chemicals industry	51	6	52
29	Other chemical products industry	50	7	96
30	Rubber and plastic industry	47	11	122
31	Cement, lime and allied products industry	50	10	200
32	Ceramics, clay, bricks and other products for building industry	51	3	126
33	Stone and glass manufacturing industry	50	5	282
34	Metallurgy	48	6	58
35	Fabricated metal products industry	51	14	1,087
38	Electrical and electronic machinery industry	48	6	88
40	Professional and scientific instruments industry	47	3	60
41	Motor vehicles transportation equipment industry	44	9	45
42	Naval transportation and repairing	49	8	65
43	Miscellaneous transportation equipment industry	47	4	22
44	Manufacture of furniture	50	6	601
47	Electricity and irrigations services industry	46	7	51
49	Water and sewerage services industry	45	6	67
50	Construction	55	7	1,136
52	Petrol and motor vehicles trade	44	6	380
54	Wholesale trade	50	15	4,535
55	Retail trade and repairing activities	56	12	4,113

Table 2. (*Continued*)

Code	Industries	m_i	m_s	m_j
56	Hotels	60	12	20
57	Bars and restaurants	70	10	352
62	Allied transportation activities	50	7	142
63	Post and communications	42	4	205
69	Computer activities	30	4	84
71	Accounting and law activities	46	10	235
72	Engineering and architecture technical activities	38	4	31
73	Marketing services activities	28	4	8
74	Security services activities	41	4	48
79	Private education	56	5	150
84	Public drainage and sewerage services activities	40	6	15
87	Other amusement, cultural, sport and recreation activities	68	13	538

Source: Own elaboration.

Notes: m_i = number of non-zero inputs (estimated equations); m_s = number of different products produced by establishments populating industry j; m_j = number of establishments populating industry j.

Still the list of industries/products in Table 3 is not complete.[6] Therefore, we must simply assume either the product technology assumption or the industry technology assumption for those not covered by the econometric tests. (See Table A.1 in the Annex for a full list of all 89 products and their equivalent industries)

There are other examples, for which the choice in favor of the product technology assumption might even be clearer, i.e. weighted ratios of acceptance close to hundred percent for the product technology assumption while much less than 50% for the industry technology assumption, namely: clothing; leather tanning, leather products and footwear; professional and scientific instruments; naval transportation; allied transportation services; and other amusement, cultural, sport and recreation services.

[6]Recall that industries with one single representative input and output structure were excluded from the econometric analysis (e.g. public administration, finance, insurance services, agriculture and others mentioned in Section 2.2).

Table 3. Testing the assumptions. Weighted ratios of acceptance.

Code	Products/Industries	PTM	ITM	Dec
6	Fish and fishing products	82.04%	24.64%	P
12	Meat and meat products	4.65%	1.11%	P
13	Canned and preserved fish, fruit and vegetables	19.00%	69.09%	I
14	Fats and oils	39.54%	1.09%	P
15	Milk and dairy products	38.28%	1.85%	P
16	Grain mills, bakery, sugar mills, ...	43.70%	0.75%	P
17	Miscellaneous food products	40.03%	41.41%	I
18	Wines and alcoholic beverages	46.01%	5.14%	P
19	Beer and soft drinks	55.24%	16.54%	P
22	Clothing products	94.55%	0.04%	P
23	Leather tanning, leather products and footwear	100.00%	10.28%	P
24	Cork and wood products	6.30%	1.39%	P
25	Paper and allied products	36.81%	37.11%	I
26	Printing, publishing and editing services	3.36%	1.05%	P
27	Petroleum refining products	94.87%	12.67%	P
28	Basic chemical products	83.29%	7.28%	P
29	Other chemical products	98.37%	23.59%	P
30	Rubber and plastic products	1.43%	21.01%	I
31	Cement, lime and allied products	4.34%	7.30%	I
32	Ceramics, clay, bricks and other products for building	62.40%	40.70%	P
33	Stone and glass products	10.90%	1.95%	P
34	Primary metal products	99.64%	50.89%	P
35	Fabricated metal products	6.45%	3.69%	P
38	Electrical and electronic machinery	0.57%	88.96%	I
40	Professional and scientific instruments	98.83%	3.58%	P
41	Motor vehicles transportation equipment	87.39%	60.52%	P
42	Naval transportation and repairing services	92.68%	7.13%	P
43	Miscellaneous transportation equipment	67.51%	45.36%	P
44	Furniture	3.92%	29.86%	I
47	Electricity and irrigations services	—	0.11%	P
49	Water and sewerage services	—	53.10%	I
50	Constructions	28.92%	0.43%	P
52	Petrol and motor vehicles trade services	—	20.97%	P
54	Wholesale trade	0.25%	2.72%	I
55	Retail trade and repair domestic and personal effects	0.22%	1.03%	I
56	Hotels services	6.13%	30.37%	I
57	Bars and restaurants services	64.20%	0.01%	P

Table 3. (*Continued*)

Code	Products/Industries	PTM	ITM	Dec
62	Allied transportation services	99.95%	12.90%	P
63	Post and communications services	3.24%	1.17%	P
68	Machinery and equipment rental	5.21%	—	I
69	Computer services	18.83%	13.68%	P
71	Accounting and law activity services	84.29%	3.28%	P
72	Engineering and architecture technical services	—	18.07%	P
73	Marketing services	48.77%	4.88%	P
74	Security services	—	52.34%	I
79	Private education services	0.59%	0.02%	P
84	Public drainage and sewerage services	0.06%	38.47%	I
87	Other amusement, cultural, sport and recreation services	96.43%	0.02%	P

Source: Own elaboration.
Notes: PTM = product technology model; ITM = industry technology model; 'Dec' = Decision adopted (P = PTM and I = ITM). Although labels correspond to the product dimension only, they can be interpreted as their equivalent industries for the interpretation of column ITM.

As regards the industry technology assumption, there are only two industries for which it is clearly more likely that the corresponding input structure might be of an industry-specific type, namely: the manufacture of canned and preserved fruit, fish and vegetables and the fabrication of electrical and electronic machinery. The heterogeneity of the mix product classification in both cases definitely play a relevant role in the results obtained, thus being unlikely to find a single input structure common to all industries. Therefore, the industry technology model is likely to be largely supported, as it is shown in Table 3. Nearly 70% of the inputs used in the canned and preserved fruit, fish and vegetables are industry-specific while this amounts to nearly 90% in the case of the fabrication of electrical and electronic machinery.

We believe that the results obtained from these tests might be helpful in the construction of symmetric input-output tables. For the very first time, a new approach uses establishment's data not only for the compilation process but also for the testing of the assumptions in the construction of input-output tables. To illustrate it with an example, let us choose the fishing activities. Fish and fish products are produced almost exclusively by fisheries. Consequently, it can be said that the actual input structure of the fishing industry performs a single product (and industry) technology. But however, nearly a quarter of its total output corresponds to the production of canned and preserved fish, which makes the input structure be largely distorted. Hence, in order to achieve the pure product technology of fishing products, the inputs used for its secondary production should be subtracted from its actual input structure according to its own specific technology (industry technology model). Indeed, Table 3 shows that there is not a likely common product technology for producing canned and preserved fish products throughout the industries. In other words, the industry technology model fitted better the data (69.09%) rather than the product technology model (19%). In the same line, the inputs used by the canned and preserved fish producers to produce fish and fishing products secondarily should be subtracted according to the input structure of the fishing activities (product technology model). However, hybrid technology based product IO table are compiled at the aggregate level, without individual transfers between industries.

As mentioned earlier, the heterogeneity of the mix product classification definitely plays a crucial role in the identification of a single product input structure common to all industries. As long as the classification is not largely broken down into detailed products, it seems that the empirical tests will favor the industry technology assumption against its counterpart. Nonetheless, we must be cautious in the conclusions. This does not mean at all that the product technology assumption might be false or unrealistic in some cases. All it means is that the heterogeneity of the mix product output of industries makes their input structures specific everywhere, thus making really difficult to single out almost any product technology. The power of the tests may be raised by increasing the number of observations and/or the detail breakdown of surveyed establishments' purchases and turnovers.

In the next section we will go one step further and construct a set of hybrid technology input-output tables (only the intermediate use matrix) according to the choices made and depicted in Table 3. We will discuss their similarities with respect to the official product IO table. Pure product and industry technology based product IO tables will also be constructed and compared against the official one. Complementarily, we will also discuss how close the official and the different product IO table estimates are to the use table at basic prices, which is basically the starting point of the IO compilation.

3. Hybrid Technology Product IO Tables

Hybrid product and industry technology methods for the construction of product IO tables date back to the SNA-68 (UN, 1970). The hybrid technology method assumes that subsidiary production fits either the commodity technology or the industry technology assumptions. The hybrid methods require the supply table to be split into two matrices,[7] $\mathbf{V}_1$ and $\mathbf{V}_2$, where the former comprises the outputs for which the product technology assumption is made and the latter, the outputs for which the industry technology assumption holds. One would expect that most commodities have the same input structure wherever they are produced, but that some secondary products are obtained as a result of industrial processes (i.e. by-products). Therefore, secondary outputs are most likely to be included in $\mathbf{V}_1$, and by-products in $\mathbf{V}_2$. We will use the notation and mathematical formulation of ten Raa and Rueda-Cantuche (2003).

Following the SNA-68 (UN, 1970), we assume that the secondary outputs included in $\mathbf{V}_1$ have product outputs ($\mathbf{q}_1$) proportional to the industry outputs ($\mathbf{g}_1$). Similarly, we assume that industries produce by-products ($\mathbf{g}_2$) proportional to their total commodity output ($\mathbf{q}$). This pair of assumptions together implies that the intermediate use matrix is $\mathbf{Z}_{\mathrm{H}}(\mathbf{U}, \mathbf{V})$, specified below.

Alternatively, the secondary outputs may be assumed proportional to their commodity output (assuming fixed market shares) and the production of by-products proportional to their total industry output. Then the intermediate use matrix becomes $\mathbf{Z}_{\mathrm{Y}}(\mathbf{U}, \mathbf{V})$, also specified below:

$$\mathbf{Z}_{\mathrm{H}}(\mathbf{U}, \mathbf{V}) = \mathbf{U}\hat{\mathbf{g}}^{-1}(\hat{\mathbf{g}}_1\mathbf{V}_1^{-\mathrm{T}}(\mathbf{I} - \hat{\mathbf{q}}^{-1}\hat{\mathbf{q}}_2) + \mathbf{V}_2\hat{\mathbf{q}}^{-1})\hat{\mathbf{q}},$$
$$\mathbf{Z}_{\mathrm{Y}}(\mathbf{U}, \mathbf{V}) = \mathbf{U}\hat{\mathbf{g}}^{-1}(\hat{\mathbf{g}}_1\mathbf{V}_1^{-\mathrm{T}}(\mathbf{I} - \mathbf{V}_2^{\mathrm{T}}\hat{\mathbf{g}}^{-1}\mathbf{H}) + \mathbf{V}_2\hat{\mathbf{q}}^{-1})\hat{\mathbf{q}},$$

[7]The interested reader can find numerical examples in ten Raa and Rueda-Cantuche (2003) and in Rueda-Cantuche (2010).

with $\mathbf{H}$ such that $\mathbf{g} = \mathbf{Hq}$ or equivalently:

$$\mathbf{H} = (\hat{\mathbf{q}}_1 \mathbf{V}_1^{-1}(\mathbf{I} - \hat{\mathbf{g}}^{-1}\hat{\mathbf{g}}_2) + \mathbf{V}_2^{\mathrm{T}}\hat{\mathbf{g}}^{-1})^{-1}.$$

As regards notation, $\mathbf{g} = \mathbf{Ve}$ and $\mathbf{q} = \mathbf{V}^{\mathrm{T}}\mathbf{e}$ stand for product and industry outputs, respectively, while $\mathbf{Z}$ corresponds to the intermediate part of the constructed product IO tables. The vector $\mathbf{e}$ denotes a column vector with all entries equal to one. For each one of the hybrid technology variants, we will determine those products following either the product or the industry technology assumption according to the results obtained from the econometric tests (Table 3). For the remainder up to 89 products/industries, we will assume either that all of them follow a product technology assumption or an industry technology assumption. Figure 1 summarizes the different hybrid technology based variants that we have constructed.

As regards the choice between Z_H and Z_Y, there is not a clear statement in the literature to make a choice on this issue. Armstrong (1975) preferred Z_H for his application to the United Kingdom and ten Raa and Rueda-Cantuche (2003) proved that they both perform the same concerning the axiomatic framework proposed by Kop Jansen and ten Raa (1990). Therefore, we would just report on the results obtained from both hybrid technology variants.

In addition, pure product (Z_P) and industry (Z_I) technology based IO tables were also constructed for the sake of comprehensiveness. For comparability purposes, we have used the Mean Average Percentage Error (MAPE), the Weighted Average Percentage Error (WAPE), the Standardized Weighted Absolute Difference (SWAD) and the coefficient of determination as in Temurshoev, Yamano and Webb (2011).

Our analysis of the methods of construction used in the compilation of the official product IO table is ex-post. Ideally, the analysis would be done ex-ante, guiding IO compilers in choosing between the two technology assumptions. Our analysis reveals which method

	Remainder	
	PTM	**ITM**
Z_H	Z_HP	Z_HI
Z_Y	Z_YP	Z_YI

Fig. 1. Hybrid IO constructs.

agrees best with the official IO table, throwing some light on the implicit assumptions made by input-output compilers in Andalusia. We had no access to the compilation method used by Andalusian IO compilers, the manual expert-based adjustments to balance supply and demand. The product technology assumption fits best the transition from the use and make tables to the official IO table and this was confirmed by the IO compilers contacted at the Andalusian Statistical Office. However, the aim of this paper is not the difficult reconstruction of the methods used by IO compilers, but rather to use firms' data on inputs and outputs for splitting the make table and applying the hybrid technology model, to construct a product-by-product IO table.

Similarly, since it is very well known that use table at basic prices are the starting point for the construction of product IO tables, we will also discuss to what extent the former deviates or changes as a result of the compilation processes of the official and the different estimated product IO tables.

Table 4 summarizes the main results. The pure product technology assumption reports the least mean and weighted average errors with respect to the official product IO table. It amounts to 6.14% as a weighted average. In terms of absolute weighted differences, the hybrid Z_HP variant is closest to the official IO table (also mostly product technology based). Conversely, the pure industry technology assumption gives the best fit in terms of linear correlations with respect to the official IO table, probably due to the fact that it is the only method that does not yield negatives and therefore, it might be the most highly correlated matrix with respect to a non-negative official product IO table. The common ranking shows that the product technology assumption (either in its pure or mixed forms) has played an important role in the compilation of the Andalusian official product IO table.

By definition, all the methods discussed for the construction of product IO tables modify the input structures of a use table at basic prices to accommodate column-wise industries into products. By using the same measures of error, we find that the official IO table is the one that changes the use table the least, followed by the industry technology assumption (where the absence of negatives might have played a role again; the negative values amounted on average 1% of the overall total) and the hybrid Z_HI variant (almost

Table 4. Comparison between hybrid and pure technology models.

Comparison between different IO tables vs. official IO table

	MAPE	Rk.	WAPE	Rk.	SWAD	Rk.	R^2	Rk.	**CmR.**
PTM	36.30	1	6.14	1	0.0176	2	0.9944	3	**1**
ITM	73.08	6	6.33	3	0.0322	6	0.9973	1	**5**
Z_HP	50.27	3	6.39	4	0.0172	1	0.9939	5	**2**
Z_HI	58.53	5	6.28	2	0.0245	5	0.9945	2	**3**
Z_YP	45.63	2	6.79	5	0.0181	3	0.9940	4	**4**
Z_YI	56.29	4	7.03	6	0.0215	4	0.9934	6	**6**

Comparison between Use Table at basic prices vs. official IO table and others

	MAPE	Rk.	WAPE	Rk.	SWAD	Rk.	R^2	Rk.	**CmR.**
Use vs. IOT	29.33	2	4.84	1	0.0202	1	0.9981	1	**1**
Use vs. PTM	61.85	6	7.87	5	0.0309	5	0.9933	5	**5**
Use vs. ITM	26.04	1	7.12	2	0.0300	4	0.9978	2	**2**
Use vs. Z_HP	56.01	4	7.19	3	0.0278	2	0.9940	4	**4**
Use vs. Z_HI	44.42	3	7.23	4	0.0294	3	0.9943	3	**3**
Use vs. Z_YP	59.12	5	9.56	6	0.0351	6	0.9922	6	**6**
Use vs. Z_YI	64.00	7	10.24	7	0.0394	7	0.9913	7	**7**

Source: Own elaboration.

Notes: PTM = product technology model; ITM = industry technology model; IOT = actual input-output table; Z_HP, Z_HI, Z_YP and Z_YI = hybrid input-output constructs (see Figure 1); MAPE = mean average percentage error; WAPE = weighted average percentage error; SWAD = standardized weighted absolute difference; R^2 = coefficient of determination; Rk. = ranking; CmR = common ranking.

industry technology based). The same applies in terms of correlations, being the official IO table the one with the highest coefficient of determination with respect to the use table.

4. Limitations of Applicability

4.1. *Detailed data requirements*

The main problem of the applicability of our new approach is that it requires detailed commodity data on inputs and outputs at the level of individual establishments, (perfectly) classified according to the NACE Rev. 1.1 classification and valued in basic prices. These data are not readily available from surveys. Firms report data of goods and services with insufficient specification and mostly in purchasers' prices. Smaller firms are generally less accurate in the description of their inputs. There are many examples of partly-specified inputs, e.g. single aggregates for a mixed bunch of goods (food and drinks in hotels and restaurants; consumed building materials in construction firms; office material in services firms, etc.) and the "other costs" items, which may include a large variety of commodities. It is common practice to complete the full specification of firms' data on inputs and outputs by using assumptions that come close to product or industry technology assumptions. In doing so, the adjustments are not made at the level of the reporting firms but rather at the level of industry groups, which might distort the final outcomes of the tests proposed in this paper.

Fortunately this shortcoming does not plague our study. The Institute of Statistics of Andalusia (IEA) specifies firms' data on inputs and outputs without filling incomplete responses with previously reported product or industry related input-output structures. Instead actual (real) structures of other firms/establishments (with the same economic activity and similar number of workers) are used. We believe that this procedure of filling the incomplete responses affects our test results little, because no prior product or industry input-output structure was imposed when filling the missing input-output data. Moreover, the IEA produces real input-output structures for all firms/establishments with more than 200–300 workers, which may well cover a substantial amount of the total output of each industry (IEA, 1999). This is another reason why we believe that the IEA procedure affects the results of our tests little.

A second limitation stems from the difference between the valuation at basic prices and at purchasers' prices, consisting of trade and transport margins plus taxes less subsidies on products. However, firms report the price paid including trade and transport margins and (if any) net taxes on products (purchasers' prices). In order to circumvent this problem, we have followed ten Raa and Rueda-Cantuche (2007) and have converted firms' input data from purchasers' prices into basic prices using the same procedure as the

Andalusian Statistical Office did for the compilation of its Input-Output Framework (IEA, 1999).

We will briefly describe this procedure, which was carried out at the level of industry and product groups. Letting u^b_{kj} and u^p_{kj} be the total domestic inputs of commodity k by industry j at basic and at purchasers' prices, respectively, we have:

$$u^b_{kj} = u^p_{kj} - T^d_{kj} - T_{kj} - N_{kj} - H_{kj}.$$

Here, for each use of commodity k by industry j, T^d_{kj} and T_{kj} are the total amount of trade and transport margins, respectively, N_{kj} is the total amount of taxes less subsidies on products (excluding not deductible value added tax, VAT) and H_{kj} is the total amount of not deductible VAT. We assume that the trade margins are proportional to the use data at purchasers' prices:

$$T^d_{kj} = t^d_{kj} u^p_{kj}, \quad 0 < t^d_{kj} < 1.$$

We also assume that taxes less subsidies on products (excluding not deductible VAT) and transport margins are proportional to the use data at basic prices:

$$N_{kj} = n_{kj} u^b_{kj}, \quad 0 < n_{kj} < 1;$$

$$T_{kj} = t_{kj} u^b_{kj}, \quad 0 < t_{kj} < 1.$$

With respect to VAT, the assumption is as follows:

$$H_{kj} = h_{kj} \left(\frac{u^p_{kj}}{1 + h_{kj}} \right), \quad 0 < h_{kj} < 1.$$

Then, by substituting T^d_{kj}, T_{kj}, N_{kj} and H_{kj} into u^b_{kj}:

$$u^b_{kj} = u^p_{kj} \left(\frac{1 - t^d_{kj} - \frac{h_{kj}}{1+h_{kj}}}{1 + t_{kj} + n_{kj}} \right),$$

which was used by the IEA to transform use data from purchasers' values to basic values provided some product ratios of trade and transport margins, not deductible VAT and remaining taxes less subsidies on products. Since, as stated before, the information on inputs and outputs are reported at the level of establishments and not at the level of industry groups, we must estimate the unknown u^b_{kji}, that is, the total use of commodity k by an establishment i from industry j at basic prices, with only information on data from industry and product groups. By assuming equality of margins and taxes less subsidies on products ratios across firms in industry j, which consume some commodity k, we use

$$u^b_{kji} = u^p_{kji}\left(\frac{1 - t^d_{kj} - \frac{h_{kj}}{1+h_{kj}}}{1 + t_{kj} + n_{kj}}\right)$$

for converting firms' input data from purchasers' prices into basic prices.

Once trade and transport margins and taxes less subsidies on products were subtracted from use flow data, the last step was to allocate the subtracted total trade and domestic transport margins to the trade and transport industries, respectively. This was done with the help and technical support of IEA.

4.2. *Industry-by-industry input-output tables*

Following Rueda-Cantuche and ten Raa (2009), input-output coefficients b_{ik} in industry IO tables measure the unitary supplies of industry i to industry k. Subsequently, the industry input-output coefficient is given by:

$$b_{ik} = \Big(u_{ik} - \sum_{j\neq i} b_{jik}v_{ji} + \sum_{j\neq i} b_{ijk}v_{ij}\Big)\Big/\sum_{j} v_{ij}.$$

The *fixed industry sales structure assumption* postulates that all industries have unique sales structures, irrespective the product market (removal of the second subscript). Consequently, fixed industry sales coefficients may be defined accordingly:

$$b_{jik} = b^{FI}_{jk} \quad \text{for all } i. \tag{H3}$$

Under the hypothesis (H3), inter-industry sales coefficients b_{jk} are the deliveries from industry j to industry k per unit of sales of industry j. As a consequence, if (H3) holds then it is verified that:

$$u_{ik} = \sum_j b_{jk} v_{ji}. \tag{6}$$

The *fixed product sales structure model* assumes that product i's unitary deliveries to industry k must be independent of the supplier industry (j). Therefore, all products have unique sales structures irrespective of the industry of fabrication (removal of the first subscript):

$$b_{jik} = b_{ik}^{FP} \quad \text{for all } j. \tag{H4}$$

If hypothesis (H4) holds, then product-by-industry sales coefficients (market shares) b_{ik}^{FP} are the deliveries of product i to industry k per unit of output of product i. As a result, it is verified that:

$$u_{ik} = \sum_j b_{ik}^{FP} v_{ji}. \tag{7}$$

With industry tables we proceed as follows. Let $l = 1, \ldots, f(> n)$[8] be the number of firms producing a certain product i while being f_1 the number of those populating industry 1, f_2, those populating industry $2, \ldots$, so that $f = f_1 + f_2 + \cdots + f_n$. Following (6), we may regress industry k's firm consumption of products $i = 1, 2, \ldots, c$ on firm's output of commodity i by industries $j(= 1,2, \ldots ,n)$:

$$u_{ikl} = \sum_{k=1}^{n} b_{jk}^{FI} v_{jil} + \varepsilon_{ikl} = b_{1k}^{FI} v_{1il} + b_{2k}^{FI} v_{2il} + \cdots + b_{nk}^{FI} v_{nil} + \varepsilon_{ikl} \tag{8}$$

where u_{ikl} represents industry k's firm intermediate uses of inputs $i = 1, 2, \ldots, c$ and v_{jil}, product i's firm output of industries $j = 1, 2, \ldots, n$.

But notice, however, that there is no easy way out in (8) to find a proper econometric estimation of the parameters since the dependent

[8]Notice that f shall be greater than n (number of industries) to get positive degrees of freedom. Moreover, f might be regarded as well to be a more detailed breakdown of commodities, remaining the number of industries unchanged. We also assume that firms of the same industry have the same sales structure.

and the independent variables do not correspond with the same units of observation. The units (and number) of observations in the right-hand side of (8) might be different from that of the left-hand side. In other words, the RHS of (8) depicts the number of firms producing product i, which does not need to correspond with the number of firms from industry k using product i. It might be that in the case of product tables, we have information of input uses and product outputs of the same unit of observation (establishment) but however, for industry tables, there is no explicit link between the supplier and the user industry for one certain product i. It seems the necessary data for testing the market share assumptions in industry IO tables depends on the distribution of total output of establishments over the different user categories, which is very unlikely to ever become available. The same applies for the fixed product sales structure assumption (see (7)).

5. Conclusions

The main contribution of this paper refers to the choice of technology assumption for the construction of product IO tables. We provide input-output compilers with two new econometric tests that can be used in the compilation of a product IO table. These tests will enable statistical offices and researchers to apply more tailored hybrid technology assumptions, which can be complemented with expert judgments in order to improve the whole compilation process. Ideally, these tests should lead to statistically significant conclusions on the selection of the most appropriate technology assumption but the power of the tests can be largely affected by the heterogeneity in the product classification, the insufficient detailed breakdown of products and the errors of measurement at the establishment level. We are convinced however that as long as we were able to dispose of a high level of detail in the product classification, the tests presented in this paper can identify more clearly the correct assumption in all products and industries. In the meantime, we can experience sometimes inconclusive results due to the fact that the proposed tests are not single tests of one assumption against the other but rather independent tests, which provide likelihood ratios for each technology assumption separately.

These tests could be definitely used as a guide towards the selection of one of the two technology assumptions in the construction of a hybrid technology based product IO table. Unfortunately, similar econometric tests for industry IO tables are not allowed within this framework.

All in all, we must be cautious. The general applicability of the results obtained for Andalusia is very difficult to justify because each country and/or region may have their own specific economic structures and data availability. Nonetheless, we believe that the proposed tests and this methodology can be used by statistical offices provided that, in a previous stage, reporting firms' input and output data are fully specified and converted into basic prices.

Acknowledgments

The authors thank the two anonymous referees for their helpful comments that served to improve substantially the first version of this article. Also, special thanks to Bart Los for his guidance in the review process and Luc Avonds for earlier comments and suggestions. The authors thank the IO team of the Institute of Statistics of Andalusia, without whom this article would not have been possible. An earlier version of this article was presented at the 17th International Input-Output Conference in 2009 during the Leontief Prize Special Session, being one of the finalists of the award. The views expressed in this paper belong to the authors and should not be attributed to the European Commission or its services.

References

Armstrong, A. G. (1975). Technology assumptions in the construction of United Kingdom input-output tables. In *Estimating and Updating Input-Output Coefficients*, Eds. Allen, R. I. G. and W. F. Gossling, London: Input-Output Pub. Co.

Eurostat. (1996). *European System of Accounts — ESA*, Luxembourg: Office for Official Publications of the European Communities.

Eurostat. (2008). Eurostat manual of supply, use and input-output tables. Methodologies and Working Papers, Luxembourg, Office for Official Publications of the European Communities.

Gujarati, D. N. (2003). *Basic Econometrics*, New York: McGraw-Hill.

IEA. (1999). *System of Economic Accounts of Andalusia. Input-Output Framework* 1995. Seville: Institute of Statistics of Andalusia [in Spanish].

Johnston, J. and J. Di Nardo. (1997). *Econometric Methods*, New York: McGraw-Hill.

Kop Jansen, P. S. M. and T. ten Raa. (1990). The choice of model in the construction of input-output coefficients matrices. *International Economic Review*, **31**, 213–227.

Mattey, J. P. and T. ten Raa. (1997). Primary versus secondary production techniques in US manufacturing. *Review of Income and Wealth*, **43**, 449–464.

Rueda-Cantuche, J. M. and T. ten Raa. (2009). The choice of model in the construction of industry coefficients matrices. *Economic Systems Research*, **21**, 363–376.

Rueda-Cantuche, J. M. (2010). *Stochastic Input-Output Analysis of the Andalusian Economy*, Seville: Institute of Statistics of Andalusia [in Spanish, available in English upon request to the author].

Temurshoev, U., N. Yamano and C. Webb. (2011). Projection of supply and use tables: Methods and empirical assessment. *Economic Systems Research*, **23**, 91–123.

ten Raa, T. and J. M. Rueda-Cantuche. (2003). The construction of input-output coefficients matrices in an axiomatic context: Some further considerations. *Economic Systems Research*, **15**, 439–455.

ten Raa, T. and J. M. Rueda-Cantuche. (2007). Stochastic analysis of input-output multipliers on the basis of use and make tables. *Review of Income and Wealth*, **53**, 318–334.

United Nations. (1970). A System of National Accounts — 1968, Studies in Methods Series F, No. 2, rev. 3, New York, USA, United Nations.

Yamano, N. and N. Ahmad. (2006). The OECD input-output database: 2006 edition. OECD Science, Technology and Industry Working Papers, 2006/8, OECD Publishing, doi:10.1787/308077407044.

Table A.1. NACE Rev.1.1 Classification.

CODE	Description of products
1	Fruits and vegetables
2	Olive and vine
3	Other agriculture and related services
4	Livestock and hunting
5	Forestry and related services
6	Fish and fishing products
7	Coal mining
8	Extraction of crude petroleum and natural gas
9	Mining of uranium and thorium ores
10	Metallic minerals
11	Non-metallic and non-energetic minerals
12	Meat and meat products
13	Canned and preserved fish, fruit and vegetables
14	Fats and oils
15	Milk and dairy products
16	Grain mills, bakery, sugar mills, ...
17	Miscellaneous food products
18	Wines and alcoholic beverages
19	Beer and soft drinks
20	Tobacco products
21	Textile mill products
22	Clothing products
23	Leather tenning, leather products and footwear
24	Cork and wood products
25	Paper and allied products
26	Printing, publishing and editing services
27	Petroleum refining products
28	Basic chemical products
29	Other chemical products
30	Rubber and plastic products
31	Cement, lime and allied products
32	Ceramics, clay, bricks and other products for building
33	Stone and glass products
34	Primary metal products
35	Fabricated metal products
36	Machinery and mechanic equipment
37	Computers and office equipments
38	Electrical and electronic machinery
39	Electronic materials, radio and television equipments
40	Professional and scientific instruments

Table A.1. (*Continued*)

CODE	Description of products
41	Motor vehicles transportation equipment
42	Naval transportation and repairing services
43	Miscellaneous transportation equipment
44	Furniture
45	Miscellaneous manufactured products
46	Recycling products
47	Electricity and irrigations services
48	Gas and water steam and irrigation services
49	Water and sewerage services
50	Construction work
51	Preparing, installation and finishing construction services
52	Petrol and motor vehicles trade services
53	Repair motor vehicles services
54	Wholesale trade activities
55	Retail trade and repair domestic and personal effects
56	Hotels services
57	Bars and restaurants services
58	Railway transportation services
59	Other earthbound transportation services
60	Sea and river transportation services
61	Air transportation services
62	Allied transportation services
63	Post and communications services
64	Finances
65	Insurance
66	Allied financial services
67	Real Estate
68	Machinery and equipment rental
69	Computer services
70	Research and development
71	Accounting and law activity services
72	Engineering and architecture technical services
73	Marketing services
74	Security services
75	Cleaning services
76	Other business services
77	Public Administration
78	Public education services
79	Private education services
80	Public medical and hospitals services

(*Continued*)

Table A.1. (*Continued*)

CODE	Description of products
81	Private medical and hospitals services
82	Public social services
83	Private social services
84	Public drainage and sewerage services
85	Social services
86	Cinema, video, radio and television services
87	Other amusement, cultural, sport and recreation services
88	Personal services
89	Household employers services

Source: NACE Rev.1.1

Chapter 18

The Problem of Negatives Generated by the Commodity Technology Model in Input-Output Analysis: A Review of the Solutions*

Thijs ten Raa† and José M. Rueda-Cantuche‡

†*Department of Economics, Tilburg University, Tilburg, The Netherlands*
tenraa@uvt.nl

‡*European Commission — DG, Joint Research Center, IPTS — Institute for Prospective Technological Studies, Edificio EXPO, C/Inca Garcilaso s/n, 41092 and Pablo de Olavide University at Seville, Spain*
jose.rueda-cantuche@ec.europa.eu

Abstract. Many economic models (e.g. computable general equilibrium models, econometric input-output models) revolve around a matrix of technical coefficients. However, these matrices can be estimated only once every 5 years as long as they are calculated from input-output tables and these are only published on a 5-year basis. Alternatively, use and make (or supply) tables are being regularly published on a yearly basis. However, they need to be converted into input-output tables as a previous step to form the matrix of technical coefficients. In doing so, this paper aims to shed light on the construction process of input-output

*Reprinted from *Journal of Economic Structures*, **2**, Article number: 5, with permission from Springer Nature.

tables and to guide economic modelers in making a decision on the way to make such conversion and how to deal with the subsequent problems, particularly with negative technical coefficients.

Keywords: Input-Output Analysis, Technical Coefficients, Use and Make Tables, Input-Output Modeling

JEL-codes: C67, D57

1. Introduction

Many economic models (e.g. computable and/or applied general equilibrium models, econometric input-output models) revolve around a matrix of technical coefficients, the amounts of commodities i used for the production of units of commodities j.[1] These matrices can be derived directly from input-output tables, which, however, tend to be published every five years only (e.g., Eurostat), or indirectly from annually published use and make (or supply) tables, which describe the use of commodities by industries, households, government and the foreign sector, and the production of commodities by industry, respectively. The indirect construction of a technical coefficients matrix essentially removes secondary activities from industries and this procedure may create negative input coefficients. We review variants of this procedure and the ways negative coefficients are circumvented.

Some farmers produce cheese as a secondary activity; the farmers' input structure of their main activity is distorted by the inputs of cheese. These inputs must be removed somehow, shifted to the cheese industry. There are two removal procedures, employing the input structure of the farmers who produce cheese (admitting that cheese can be produced differently in different industries) or of the cheese manufacturing industry. The former option is denoted as the industry technology assumption, while the latter is denoted as the commodity technology assumption. This paper will give insight in the

[1]We are aware that industry-by-industry input-output tables can also lead to the construction of a matrix of input coefficients but these are not generally conceived as matrices of technical coefficients; therefore, they will not be discussed in this paper.

pros and cons of the two options. The next section introduces a common framework encompassing the commodity and industry technology assumptions and also identifies the former as theoretically superior according to the existent literature. However, section 3 identifies sources of potential negative technical coefficients that plague the commodity technology assumption. In section 4, we provide a comprehensive review of the procedures available in the literature to deal with these negatives, both for square and rectangular use and make tables. We conclude with some guidelines for economic modellers.

2. Background Context

The theoretically superior method for the construction of technical coefficients, the so-called commodity technology model, is plagued by the problem that it generates negative results. This explains the continuing popularity of the main competing method, the industry technology model, also as a basis for modifications of the commodity technology model. Ten Raa and Rueda-Cantuche (2007) presented an encompassing framework[2] for both models, which will be used to review the sources of negative coefficients and the procedures that have been proposed to remove them.

It is a bit surprising that an encompassing formula exists. After all, the industry and commodity technology models are very different. The industry technology model takes weighted averages of industry coefficients, where the latter are defined by dividing inputs by total industry output. The weights are market shares and the consequent commodity input coefficients are simple and nonnegative. The commodity technology model, however, involves an inversion of the output matrix. Commodity input coefficients are postulated and for each industry the implied input demand vector is equated with the observed use vector; a system of equations must be solved.

Following the United Nations System of National Accounts (1968, 1999) consider a *use* matrix $\mathbf{U} = (u_{ij})_{i,j=1,\ldots,n}$ comprising

[2]Later on, Rueda-Cantuche and ten Raa (2009) presented a similar encompassing framework for the two other methods used in the construction of industry-by-industry input-output tables.

commodities i consumed by sectors j, and a *make* matrix $\mathbf{V} = (v_{ij})_{i,j=1,\ldots,n}$ showing the produce of sectors i in terms of commodities j. Notice that we consider square tables, with the same number of commodities as of industries. The issue is the derivation of input coefficients (a_{ij}). In other words, how can we estimate the amount of commodity i used for the production of one unit of commodity j?

Following ten Raa and Rueda-Cantuche (2007), our point of departure is the amount of commodity i used by industry $j(u_{ij})$. The basic idea, common to the main methods of construction, is to subtract from u_{ij} the consumptions of commodity i used by industry j for its secondary products, $k \neq j$. The problem is that secondary outputs of industry j do not necessarily have the same input structure as in the industries where they are primary output. The flip-side of the coin is that to compute the average input requirements of commodity j, we must *add* the secondary output to v_{jj} and the associated inputs to u_{ij}. The total input requirements of commodity i for making commodity j (as a single product) are thus:

$$u_{ij} - \sum_{\substack{k=1 \\ k \neq j}}^{n} a_{ijk} v_{jk} + \sum_{\substack{k=1 \\ k \neq j}}^{n} a_{ikj} v_{kj},$$

where a_{ijk} is the amount of commodity i used by industry j for making a unit of commodity k. Dividing by the total output of commodity j we obtain our general formula for technical coefficients:

$$a_{ij} = \frac{u_{ij} - \sum_{\substack{k=1 \\ k \neq j}}^{n} a_{ijk} v_{jk} + \sum_{\substack{k=1 \\ k \neq j}}^{n} a_{ikj} v_{kj}}{\sum_{k=1}^{n} v_{kj}}. \tag{1}$$

We shall now show how this formula encompasses the main constructs of the literature, namely the commodity technology model and the industry technology model. In what follows, $\mathbf{e}$ will denote a column vector with all entries equal to one, ^{T} will denote transposition and $^{-1}$ inversion of a matrix. Since the latter two operations commute, their composition may be denoted $^{-\mathrm{T}}$. Also, $\hat{}$ will denote diagonalization, whether by suppression of the off-diagonal elements of a square matrix or by placement of the elements of a vector. $\sim$ will denote a matrix with all the diagonal elements set zero.

The *commodity technology model* assumes that all commodities have the same inputs structure irrespective the industry of fabrication:

$$a_{ijk} = a_{ik}, \quad \forall j = 1, 2, \ldots, n.$$

Therefore, (1) becomes:

$$a_{ij} = \frac{u_{ij} - \sum_{\substack{k=1 \\ k \neq j}}^{n} a_{ik} v_{jk} + \sum_{\substack{k=1 \\ k \neq j}}^{n} a_{ij} v_{kj}}{\sum_{k=1}^{n} v_{kj}}, \tag{2}$$

which, in matrix terms, is:

$$\begin{aligned} \mathbf{A} &= \left(\mathbf{U} - \mathbf{A}\tilde{V}^{\mathrm{T}} + \mathbf{A}\left(\widehat{\tilde{\mathbf{V}}^{\mathrm{T}}\mathbf{e}}\right)\right)\left(\widehat{\mathbf{V}^{\mathrm{T}}\mathbf{e}}\right)^{-1} \\ &= \left(\mathbf{U} - \mathbf{A}\tilde{\mathbf{V}}^{\mathrm{T}} + A\left(\widehat{\tilde{\mathbf{V}}^{\mathrm{T}}\mathbf{e}}\right)\right)\left(\widehat{\mathbf{V}\mathbf{e}} + \left(\widehat{\tilde{\mathbf{V}}^{\mathrm{T}}\mathbf{e}}\right) - \widehat{\tilde{\mathbf{V}}\mathbf{e}}\right)^{-1}, \end{aligned} \tag{3}$$

and operating with (3), it yields,

$$\begin{aligned} \mathbf{U} - \mathbf{A}\tilde{\mathbf{V}}^{T} + A\left(\widehat{\tilde{\mathbf{V}}^{\mathrm{T}}\mathbf{e}}\right) &= A\left(\widehat{\mathbf{V}^{\mathrm{T}}\mathbf{e}}\right) \\ = \mathbf{A}\left(\widehat{\mathbf{V}\mathbf{e}} + \left(\widehat{\tilde{\mathbf{V}}^{\mathrm{T}}\mathbf{e}}\right) - \widehat{\tilde{V}\mathbf{e}}\right) &= A\widehat{\mathbf{V}\mathbf{e}} + A\left(\widehat{\tilde{\mathbf{V}}^{\mathrm{T}}\mathbf{e}}\right) - \mathbf{A}\left(\widehat{\tilde{\mathbf{V}}\mathbf{e}}\right), \end{aligned}$$

which is the same as:

$$\begin{aligned} \mathbf{U} - \mathbf{A}\tilde{\mathbf{V}}^{\mathrm{T}} &= \mathbf{A}\widehat{\mathbf{V}\mathbf{e}} - \mathbf{A}\left(\widehat{\tilde{\mathbf{V}}\mathbf{e}}\right) = \mathbf{A}\left(\widehat{\mathbf{V}\mathbf{e}} - \widehat{\tilde{\mathbf{V}}\mathbf{e}}\right) = \mathbf{A}\left(\widehat{\mathbf{V}\mathbf{e} - \tilde{\mathbf{V}}\mathbf{e}}\right) \\ &= \mathbf{A}\left(\widehat{\hat{\mathbf{V}}\mathbf{e}}\right) = \mathbf{A}\hat{\mathbf{V}}^{\mathrm{T}} \end{aligned}$$

and:

$$\mathbf{U} = \mathbf{A}\tilde{\mathbf{V}}^{\mathrm{T}} + \mathbf{A}\hat{\mathbf{V}}^{\mathrm{T}} = \mathbf{A}\left(\tilde{\mathbf{V}}^{\mathrm{T}} + \hat{\mathbf{V}}^{\mathrm{T}}\right) = \mathbf{A}\mathbf{V}^{\mathrm{T}}.$$

Consequently, $\mathbf{A} = \mathbf{U}\mathbf{V}^{-\mathrm{T}}$. Notice that technical coefficients can be negative when the total consumption of input i for the making of secondary outputs of industry j, according to each one of these commodity technologies, is larger than the total use of commodity i by the industry j, either for its primary or secondary products. Following the example in Section 1, a negative coefficient would arise if farmers were producing cheese with their own milk only instead of purchasing it elsewhere. Indeed, the input structure of the manufacturing industry of cheese would use milk as an input while farmers would not; subtraction of the inputs associated with the secondary production of cheese (using the commodity technology assumption) from the current mixed farmers' input structure yields a negative input coefficient.

The *industry technology model* assumes that all industries have the same inputs structure irrespective of the commodities they produce. This means that:

$$a_{ijk} = a_{ij}, \quad \forall k = 1, 2, \ldots, n.$$

Hence, (1) becomes into:

$$a_{ij} = \frac{u_{ij} - \sum_{\substack{k=1 \\ k \neq j}}^{n} a_{ij} v_{jk} + \sum_{\substack{k=1 \\ k \neq j}}^{n} a_{ik} v_{kj}}{\sum_{k=1}^{n} v_{kj}},$$

which, in matrix terms, is:

$$\mathbf{A} = \left(\mathbf{U} - \mathbf{A}\left(\widehat{\widetilde{\mathbf{V}}\mathbf{e}}\right) + \mathbf{A}\widetilde{\mathbf{V}}\right)\left(\widehat{\mathbf{V}^{\mathrm{T}}\mathbf{e}}\right)^{-1}, \tag{4}$$

and operating (4) properly,

$$\mathbf{U} = \mathbf{A}\left(\widehat{\mathbf{V}^{\mathrm{T}}\mathbf{e}}\right) + \mathbf{A}\left(\widehat{\widetilde{\mathbf{V}}\mathbf{e}}\right) - \mathbf{A}\widetilde{\mathbf{V}} = \mathbf{A}\left(\widehat{\mathbf{V}^{\mathrm{T}}\mathbf{e}} + \widehat{\widetilde{\mathbf{V}}\mathbf{e}} - \widetilde{\mathbf{V}}\right),$$

and:

$$\mathbf{A} = \mathbf{U}\left(\widehat{\mathbf{V}^{\mathrm{T}}\mathbf{e}} + \widehat{\widetilde{\mathbf{V}}\mathbf{e}} - \widetilde{\mathbf{V}}\right)^{-1} = \mathbf{U}\left(\widehat{\mathbf{V}^{\mathrm{T}}\mathbf{e}} + \widehat{\mathbf{V}\mathbf{e}} - \mathbf{V}\right)^{-1},$$

since $\widetilde{\mathbf{V}}\mathbf{e} = \mathbf{V}\mathbf{e} - \widehat{\mathbf{V}}\mathbf{e}$ and $\widetilde{\mathbf{V}} = \mathbf{V} - \widehat{\mathbf{V}}$.

Under the industry technology assumption no negative technical coefficient can be obtained in (4).

The commodity technology assumption is considered theoretically superior (Kop Jansen and ten Raa, 1990; Steenge, 1990; Konijn, 1994; Rainer, 1989; Mattey and ten Raa, 1997; ten Raa and

Rueda Cantuche, 2003), but agreement is not uniform. For instance, de Mesnard (2004) stated that the commodity technology hypothesis has to be rejected since it breaks the linkages of commodity flows internal to the industries. No information is available to determine which industry supplies a positive variation in final demand of a particular commodity. Mesnard suggests that the industry technology model may be preferred even though it violates some axioms of Kop Jansen and ten Raa (1990).

3. Sources of Negative Coefficients

Commodity technology model based coefficients may be negative for a number of reasons.

First, some commodities are produced with different technologies (Armstrong, 1975; ten Raa, Chakraborty and Small, 1984; ten Raa and van der Ploeg, 1989; Rainer and Richter, 1992; Konijn, 1994; Mattey and ten Raa, 1997). In this case, the commodity technology assumption is not valid.

Second, production classifications are heterogeneous (ten Raa, Chakraborty and Small, 1984; Rainer, 1989; Konijn, 1991; Rainer and Richter, 1992; Konijn, 1994; Konijn and Steenge, 1995; Mattey and ten Raa, 1997; Avonds and Gilot, 2002).

And third, the use and make data have errors of measurement (Armstrong, 1975; ten Raa, 1988; ten Raa and van der Ploeg, 1989; Rainer, 1989; Steenge, 1990; Mattey, 1993; Konijn, 1994; Konijn and Steenge, 1995; Avonds and Gilot, 2002).

In spite of these complications, the handbook of the compilation of input-output tables (UN, 1993) recommends the use of the commodity technology assumption. Hence, we must review procedures that have been suggested to remove the negative coefficients.

4. Removal Procedures

Since the pioneering work of Edmonston (1952, p. 569) several procedures remove the negatives that come with the commodity technology model.

4.1. *Armstrong procedure* (*Armstrong*, 1975)

Armstrong (1975) applied a hybrid technology assumption based on Gigantes (1970). Secondary products that yield negatives in the input-output table were subjected to the industry technology assumption. Hybrid methods require that the make matrix is split into two matrices, $\mathbf{V}_1$ and $\mathbf{V}_2$, where in this case the first one includes outputs for which the commodity technology assumption is made and the second includes those, which are to be treated on an industry technology assumption. Particularly, in the United Kingdom (UK) Input-Output Tables for 1963, 55% of secondary production was treated on the industry technology assumption and the remaining 45% on the commodity technology hypothesis. However, in some cases this procedure leads to unacceptable situations. For instance, in Armstrong (1975) other food industries have as secondary outputs distribution services, which have large inputs of printing, while other food industries do not use much of them. Application of the industry technology assumption would result in a large amount of agricultural inputs into distribution services. In such cases disaggregation was adopted.

Formally, industry outputs of commodities for which the commodity technology assumption is made, are proportional to the output of each industry:

$$\mathbf{V}_1^{\mathrm{T}} = \mathbf{C}_1(\widehat{\mathbf{V}_1\mathbf{e}}),$$

and the market shares are denoted by:

$$\mathbf{V}_2 = \mathbf{D}_2^*(\widehat{\mathbf{V}_2^{\mathrm{T}}\mathbf{e}}).$$

Armstrong (1975) obtains two variants of technical coefficients matrices, depending on which of the following two assumptions is made. Industry outputs for which an industry technology assumption is made are proportional to the economy-wide outputs of each commodity whatever industry produces them. Commodity outputs for which an industry technology assumption is made are proportional to the economy-wide outputs of the producing industries (Armstrong 1975, pp. 74–76). Mathematically, the former assumption is denoted as:

$$\mathbf{V}_2\mathbf{e} = \mathbf{D}_2\left(\mathbf{V}^{\mathrm{T}}\mathbf{e}\right),$$

whereas the latter is defined by:

$$\mathbf{V}_2^{\mathrm{T}}\mathbf{e} = \mathbf{C}_2\,(\mathbf{V}\mathbf{e}).$$

In the UK Input-Output Tables for 1963, Armstrong (1975) used the first assumption and the resulting technical coefficients matrix was given by:

$$\begin{aligned}\mathbf{A}_{\mathbf{H}}(\mathbf{U},\mathbf{V}) = \mathbf{U}(\widehat{\mathbf{V}\mathbf{e}})^{-1}((\widehat{\mathbf{V}\mathbf{e}_1})\mathbf{V}_1^{-\mathrm{T}}(\mathbf{I} - (\widehat{\mathbf{V}^{\mathrm{T}}\mathbf{e}})^{-1} \\ \times (\widehat{\mathbf{V}_2^{\mathrm{T}}\mathbf{e}})) + \mathbf{V}_2(\widehat{\mathbf{V}^{\mathrm{T}}\mathbf{e}})^{-1}).\end{aligned}$$

Nevertheless, there were some remaining negatives that Armstrong (1975) set manually to zero or to a slightly positive value adjusting other entries of the input-output table so that overall accounting constraints in rows and columns still remain, as one expects when the commodity technology assumption continues to be used for part of the economy.

4.2. *Almon procedure* (*Almon*, 1970)

Almon (2000)[3] devised an iterative method that calculates non-negative technical coefficients matrices through a commodity-technology based algorithm. It is solved by the Seidel iterative process:

$$a_{ij}^{(h+1)}\sum_{k=1}^{n} v_{kj} = u_{ij} - \sum_{\substack{k=1\\k\neq j}}^{n} a_{ik}^{(h)} v_{jk} + \sum_{\substack{k=1\\k\neq j}}^{n} a_{ij}^{(h)} v_{kj}. \tag{5}$$

Convergence is guaranteed if more than half of the production of a product is in its primary industry. Almon (2000) interprets this equation for the use of chocolate (i), in the production of cheese (j). Then, "the first term on the right of (5) tells us to begin with the

[3]Almon first devised this procedure in Almon (1970).

chocolate purchases by the establishments in the cheese industry. The second term directs us to remove the amounts of chocolate needed for making the secondary products of those establishments by using our present estimate of the technology used for making those products, $a_{ik}^{(h)}$. Finally, the last term causes us to add back the chocolate used in making cheese in other industries". However, Almon's claim that the third term is exactly equal to the amount stolen, via second terms, from other industries, is not true. Unless all products are considered and not only cheese, the sum of the two latter terms of the right-hand side of (5) do not necessarily be null. Therefore, only by summing both sides of (5) over j, we will obtain the amount of input i used for the making of all products of the economy and not only for cheese (product j). That is,

$$\sum_{j=1}^{n}\left(a_{ij}^{(h+1)}\sum_{k=1}^{n} v_{kj}\right) = \sum_{j=1}^{n} u_{ij} - \sum_{j=1}^{n}\sum_{\substack{k=1\\k\neq j}}^{n} a_{ik}^{(h)} v_{jk} + \sum_{j=1}^{n}\sum_{\substack{k=1\\k\neq j}}^{n} a_{ij}^{(h)} v_{kj}. \tag{6}$$

It is straightforward that the second and the third term of the right-hand side of (6) are indeed exactly the same with opposite signs. This does not mean of course that for each product j, both terms must coincide.

Proposition 1: *If* $\mathbf{V}$ *is non-singular and non-negative, the technical coefficients matrix* $\mathbf{A}$ *derived from* $\mathbf{U} = \mathbf{A}\mathbf{V}^{\mathrm{T}}$ *will yield negative values if and only if for some product* j,

$$u_{ij} < \sum_{\substack{k=1\\k\neq j}}^{n} a_{ik}^{(h)} v_{jk} - \sum_{\substack{k=1\\k\neq j}}^{n} a_{ij}^{(h)} v_{kj}. \tag{7}$$

In short, when the difference between the amount of chocolate needed for making the secondary products of the cheese industry (j) and the amount of chocolate used by other industries to produce cheese is larger than the total purchases of chocolate by the establishments of the cheese industry (for making either primary or secondary products), negatives arise. The sufficiency proof follows from (5). For the necessity proof, let us assume a given negative technical coefficient,

$a_{ij}^{(h+1)} < 0$, since $\sum_{k=1}^{n} v_{kj} > 0$, then $a_{ij}^{(h+1)} \sum_{k=1}^{n} v_{kj} < 0$, and bearing in mind (5), it follows that:

$$a_{ij}^{(h+1)} \sum_{k=1}^{n} v_{kj} = u_{ij} - \sum_{\substack{k=1 \\ k \neq j}}^{n} a_{ik}^{(h)} v_{jk} + \sum_{\substack{k=1 \\ k \neq j}}^{n} a_{ij}^{(h)} v_{kj} < 0$$

and, consequently,

$$u_{ij} < \sum_{\substack{k=1 \\ k \neq j}}^{n} a_{ik}^{(h)} v_{jk} - \sum_{\substack{k=1 \\ k \neq j}}^{n} a_{ij}^{(h)} v_{kj}.$$

Proposition 2: *A technical coefficients matrix* **A** *calculated on the basis of* $\mathbf{U} = \mathbf{AV}^{\mathrm{T}}$ *will not yield negative values when for a non-singular and non-negative make matrix* **V**,

$$\sum_{\substack{k=1 \\ k \neq j}}^{n} a_{ik}^{(h)} v_{jk} < \sum_{\substack{k=1 \\ k \neq j}}^{n} a_{ij}^{(h)} v_{kj}, \forall j. \tag{8}$$

Since $u_{ij} \geq 0$, and assuming $\sum_{\substack{k=1 \\ k \neq j}}^{n} a_{ik}^{(h)} v_{jk} < \sum_{\substack{k=1 \\ k \neq j}}^{n} a_{ij}^{(h)} v_{kj}$ or $\sum_{\substack{k=1 \\ k \neq j}}^{n} a_{ik}^{(h)} v_{jk} - \sum_{\substack{k=1 \\ k \neq j}}^{n} a_{ij}^{(h)} v_{kj} < 0$, then it always occur that $u_{ij} - \left(\sum_{\substack{k=1 \\ k \neq j}}^{n} a_{ik}^{(h)} v_{jk} - \sum_{\substack{k=1 \\ k \neq j}}^{n} a_{ij}^{(h)} v_{kj}\right) > 0$, which, according to Proposition 1, implies a non-negative value of A. The necessity proof does not hold because $u_{ij} - \left(\sum_{\substack{k=1 \\ k \neq j}}^{n} a_{ik}^{(h)} v_{jk} - \sum_{\substack{k=1 \\ k \neq j}}^{n} a_{ij}^{(h)} v_{kj}\right) > 0$ does not guarantee that (8) will be fulfilled.

As it has been developed so far, negatives still can remain after having solved Almon's algorithm. In fact, the procedure to keep the negatives out of **A** consists of scaling down all components of the removal term, i.e. the second on the right-hand side of (5), to leave a zero balance. Then, the "total-stolen-from-other-industries" term is added gradually and not all at once. This process can be expressed in equations introducing in (5) scale factors, $s_{ij}^{(h)}$, which are defined by:

$$s_{ij}^{(h)} = \begin{cases} \dfrac{u_{ij}}{\sum_{\substack{k=1 \\ k\neq j}}^{n} a_{ij}^{(h)} v_{kj}} & \text{if } u_{ij} < \sum_{\substack{k=1 \\ k\neq j}}^{n} a_{ij}^{(h)} v_{kj} \\ 1 & \text{if } u_{ij} \geq \sum_{\substack{k=1 \\ k\neq j}}^{n} a_{ij}^{(h)} v_{kj} \end{cases} \tag{9}$$

Equation (5) is then replaced by:

$$a_{ij}^{(h+1)} \sum_{k=1}^{n} v_{kj} = u_{ij} - s_{ij}^{(h)} \sum_{\substack{k=1 \\ k\neq j}}^{n} a_{ik}^{(h)} v_{jk} + \sum_{\substack{k=1 \\ k\neq j}}^{n} s_{ik}^{(h)} a_{ij}^{(h)} v_{kj}. \tag{10}$$

However, as described in Almon (2000), only when the removal term is larger than the entry in the use matrix from which it is being removed — that is, when u_{ij} is lower than the negative term on the right-hand side of (5) — scaling down is applied to leave a zero balance. Therefore, scale factors should be redefined replacing in $s_{ij}^{(h)}$, $\sum_{\substack{k=1 \\ k\neq j}}^{n} a_{ij}^{(h)} v_{kj}$ by $\sum_{\substack{k=1 \\ k\neq j}}^{n} a_{ik}^{(h)} v_{jk}$.

Though by summing both sides of (10) over j it is easy to see that the result is the same no matter what scale factor is defined, economic interpretation of the two latter terms of (10) is guaranteed in case we assume the redefined scale factor. Then, substituting in (10)[4], we obtain:

$$a_{ij}^{(h+1)} \sum_{k=1}^{n} v_{kj} = u_{ij} - \left(\frac{u_{ij}}{\sum_{\substack{k=1 \\ k\neq j}}^{n} a_{ik}^{(h)} v_{jk}} \right) \sum_{\substack{k=1 \\ k\neq j}}^{n} a_{ik}^{(h)} v_{jk} + \sum_{\substack{k=1 \\ k\neq j}}^{n} \left(\frac{u_{ik} a_{ij}^{(h)} v_{kj}}{\sum_{\substack{k=1 \\ k\neq j}}^{n} a_{ik}^{(h)} v_{jk}} \right), \tag{11}$$

where it is straightforward that a zero balance is obtained by summing the two former terms of the right-hand side of (11).

[4]Notice that for scale factor equals to one, (10) becomes (5) and it is easy to see that, by summing both sides of (5) over j, the result is given by the total uses of input i by industry j.

Finally, (11) results in:

$$a_{ij}^{(h+1)}\sum_{k=1}^{n}v_{kj}=\sum_{\substack{k=1\\k\neq j}}^{n}\left(u_{ik}\frac{a_{ij}^{(h)}v_{kj}}{\sum_{\substack{p=1\\p\neq k}}^{n}a_{ip}^{(h)}v_{kp}}\right),\tag{12}$$

where $a_{ij}v_{kj}$ represents the total inputs of commodity i used for making the secondary product j of industry k, and $\sum_{\substack{p=1\\p\neq k}}^{n}a_{ip}v_{kp}$, the total inputs of commodity i used for making all secondary products of industry k. Actually, in (12) the total requirements of inputs i needed by industry $k(u_{ik})$ is multiplied by the proportion of inputs i used for making secondary outputs of commodity j by industry k over the total consumption of these inputs for making all secondary products by the same industry. The result is the so-called: "total-stolen-from-other-industries" term (Almon, 2000). Finally, by summing both sides of (12) over j, it yields:

$$\begin{aligned}\sum_{j=1}^{n}\left(a_{ij}^{(h+1)}\sum_{k=1}^{n}v_{kj}\right)&=\sum_{j=1}^{n}\sum_{\substack{k=1\\k\neq j}}^{n}\left(u_{ik}\frac{a_{ij}^{(h)}v_{kj}}{\sum_{\substack{k=1\\k\neq j}}^{n}a_{ik}^{(h)}v_{jk}}\right)\\&=\sum_{j=1}^{n}u_{ij}\left(\frac{\sum_{\substack{j=1\\j\neq k}}^{n}a_{ij}^{(h)}v_{kj}}{\sum_{\substack{p=1\\p\neq k}}^{n}a_{ip}^{(h)}v_{kp}}\right)=\sum_{j=1}^{n}u_{ij}.\end{aligned}$$

As a final result of the iterative process, by the choice of the scalar factors s, it is guaranteed that no negative technical coefficients will be obtained. In fact, this procedure actually converges but it is not clear to what. Ten Raa, Chakraborty and Small (1984) criticize this arithmetic manipulation arguing that it goes without justification, is arbitrary and depends on the choice of **V**-decomposition as well as the iteration scheme. Notwithstanding these arguments, Almon (2000) considers this procedure to be with perfectly reasonable economic interpretation and continues to use it for more than thirty years in the INFORUM model (Almon, 1991, 2000). Almon's approach is generally used when negatives arise because of the inexactness in make and use tables or because of slight differences in the technologies in different industries. Incidentally, the

Belgian input-output tables (Avonds and Gilot, 2002) comprise a commodity-by-commodity input-output table using Almon's procedure to remove the minor negatives that could not be removed manually.

4.3. *Rainer procedure* (*Rainer*, 1989)

Rainer focuses on the fact that different data setups must be constructed since the purpose of making a homogeneous input-output table differs from the objective of making a descriptive make-use system in terms of National Accounts. Rainer (1989) and Rainer and Richter (1992) show for the 1976 Austrian use and make tables that when the commodity technology assumption is applied, some negatives can be removed with data rearrangements but not all of them. The remaining negatives were treated with the industry technology assumption. Basically, in most cases, these data rearrangements consist of giving answer to vertically integrated processes, features underlying classification systems, product mix problems and others mainly specific of the Austrian economy. In conclusion, data arrangement can be an answer to the problem of negatives when the commodity technology hypothesis is assumed.

4.4. *Activity technology model* (*Konijn*, 1994)

Konijn (1994) assumes that industries can produce commodities according to several production processes and that the same production process can be used by other industries. Moreover, production processes may have multiple outputs, as in the by-product technology model described in Kop Jansen and ten Raa (1990). However, the resulting activity-by-activity input-output table is still not free of negatives. Konijn (1994) and Konijn and Steenge (1995) argue that remaining negatives clearly indicate that some classification adjustments must be made or some further research on errors data must be developed. Although the need of further information on the use and make system is required to apply the activity technology model, Statistics Netherlands actually adopted this way of removing negatives. In conclusion, Konijn (1994) proposes that we explicitly look at production processes instead of commodities and that we take the commodity classification of use and make matrices as an instrument rather than a fixed datum.

4.5. *Stahmer procedure* (*Stahmer*, 1985)

Stahmer (1985) established a modified transformation procedure based on the commodity technology model using special transformation matrices for certain rows and columns and using additional data. The procedure firstly defines a "special transformation table" for a particular input k as shown in Table 1.

According to the commodity technology assumption, technical coefficients for making the same product whatever industry produces them are coincident. Therefore, the output totals in each row are multiplied by the same input coefficient. In matrix terms, Stahmer (1985) define a "special transformation matrix" for each input k as shown in Table 1: $\mathbf{S}_k = \hat{\mathbf{A}}_k\mathbf{V}^{\mathrm{T}}$ where $\hat{\mathbf{A}}_k$ represents a diagonal matrix with the elements of the k-th row of the technical coefficients matrix in the diagonal. The column totals of each $\mathbf{S}_k$ show the use data available before the adjusting procedure and the row totals, the result of the transition process.

Stahmer (1985)[5] proposes to use the special transformation matrix $\mathbf{S}_k$ in cases where the commodity technology model generates negatives. With additional available information, $\mathbf{S}_k$ is corrected in such a way that total uses of input k by each industry remain unchanged. However, since during the correction process available

Table 1. Stahmer procedure (1985).

	Industries					Totals
Commodities	$a_{k1}v_{11}$	$\cdots$	$a_{k1}v_{j1}$	$\cdots$	$a_{k1}v_{n1}$	$a_{k1}\sum_{j=1}^{n} v_{j1}$
	$\cdots$	$\cdots$	$\cdots$	$\cdots$	$\cdots$	$\cdots$
	$a_{ki}v_{1i}$	$\cdots$	$a_{ki}v_{ji}$	$\cdots$	$a_{ki}v_{ni}$	$a_{ki}\sum_{j=1}^{n} v_{ji}$
	$\cdots$	$\cdots$	$\cdots$	$\cdots$	$\cdots$	$\cdots$
	$a_{kn}v_{1n}$	$\cdots$	$a_{kn}v_{jn}$	$\cdots$	$a_{kn}v_{nn}$	$a_{kn}\sum_{j=1}^{n} v_{jn}$
Totals	u_{k1}	$\cdots$	u_{kj}	$\cdots$	u_{kn}	

Source: Stahmer (1985).

[5]Stahmer (1982) originally includes also the value-added row into the use matrix.

data about use or inputs requirements remain unchanged for every industry and commodity input, it may occur that several different input structures for one commodity can be established in certain rows and columns of **A**, which in fact introduce some distortion in terms of the commodity technology assumption (Konijn, 1994). Actually, the commodity technology hypothesis would not hold any more.

The German Federal Statistical Office applied this procedure for its 1980 input-output tables.

4.6. *Steenge procedure* (*Steenge*, 1990)

Steenge (1990) locates errors in such a way that minimal changes are needed to obtain a non-negative technical coefficients matrix. Unlike ten Raa (1988) and ten Raa and van der Ploeg (1989) — who use *a priori* estimated errors, Steenge proposes a way to locate errors *a posteriori*.

The United States available information in Steenge (1990) was performed with only 14 industries and commodities for 1977 and illustrates how very few corrections are required to obtain make and use matrices such that the commodity technology produces no negative coefficients. However, the adjustments lack statistical significance.

4.7. *United States procedure* (*Young*, 1986)

The Bureau of Economic Analysis hybrid procedure (Guo, Lawson and Planting, 2002) first applies the commodity technology assumption to those secondary products that are not suitable for the industry technology model. All the resulting transfers of associated inputs and outputs are made at the same time as the use and make matrices are compiled. Hence, the published use and make tables actually includes all these transformations. However, some additional information on inputs structures is also used so that the commodity technology model cannot be applied in a fully mechanical way (redefinition process). The remaining secondary products are then transferred according to the industry technology assumption.

4.8. *Non-negativity conditions and rectangular matrices*

Konijn (1994) and Steenge (1990)[6] gave a mathematical answer to the question of when we can have a non-negative matrix **A** which satisfies the commodity technology assumption, for given rectangular use and make matrices. That is, a non-negative matrix **A** exists, satisfying $\mathbf{U} = \mathbf{A}\mathbf{V}^{\mathrm{T}}$, if and only if for any vector $\mathbf{s} \geq 0$ with $\mathbf{V}^{\mathrm{T}}\mathbf{s} > 0$, we have $\mathbf{U}\mathbf{s} \geq 0$ (*Mangasarian's theorem*). If s is interpreted as a vector of changes in activity levels this theorem states that if for some change in industry activity the output of all commodities is increased, then the use of none of the commodities is decreased. Otherwise, a firm could produce more of everything, while using less of something, which is strange according to Konijn (1994). Steenge (1990) argues that the resulting technical coefficients matrix only would represent imputed commodity specific input proportions, consistent with the overall use and make tables. Further research by industrial experts on empirical data is required to see if columns of the **A** matrix can be interpreted as production functions.

5. Conclusions: A Guiding Procedure

Once we have formalized the problem of how to construct a technical coefficients matrix and once we have discussed the different problems and solutions given to the drawbacks underlying the commodity technology model when the construction of a technical coefficients matrix is the main purpose, we conclude providing a guiding procedure.

Three reasons support the use of the commodity technology model. First, at a micro level data the commodity technology model seems to be a useful working hypothesis according to the tests provided in Mattey and ten Raa (1997) and in Rueda-Cantuche and ten Raa (2013). Hence, disaggregation is commendable. Second, as shown in Steenge (1990) and Konijn (1994), it is theoretically possible to find a non-negative technical coefficients matrix consistent with the

[6]For a full description of all theorems and propositions see Steenge (1990, p. 380) and Konijn (1994, pp. 139–142).

make-use system (even with rectangular use and make matrices), provided some adjustments are made. And third, the commodity technology assumption fulfills the axioms of Kop Jansen and ten Raa (1990).

Therefore, it seems that a commonly and desirable guide to proceed in order to construct technical coefficients matrices would consist in applying the commodity technology assumption, using afterwards location methods for errors of measurement (although these adjustments may be rejected statistically, they are supposed to be accepted by industrial experts) or negatives as indicators of errors of measurement and/or aggregation problems. Once these problems are solved no more negatives should arise. It is desirable to use the industry technology assumption just in the needed cases.

References

Almon, C. (1970). Investment in input-output models and the treatment of secondary products. In *Applications of Input-Output Analysis*, Eds. Carter, A. P. and A. Brôdy, Amsterdam: North-Holland.

Almon, C. (1991). The INFORUM approach to interindustry modelling. *Economic Systems Research*, **3**, 1–8.

Almon, C. (2000). Product-to-product tables via product technology with no negative flows. *Economic Systems Research*, **12**, 27–43.

Armstrong, A. G. (1975). Technology assumptions in the construction of United Kingdom input-output tables. In *Estimating and Updating Input-Output Coefficients*, Eds. Allen, R. I. G. and W. F. Gossling, London: Input-Output Publishing Co.

Avonds, L. and A. Gilot. (2002). The new Belgian input-output table. General principles, paper presented at the Fourteenth International Conference on Input-Output Techniques, Montreal, Canada, 10–15 October. http://www.iioa.org/pdf/14th%20conf/Avonds8.pdf.

de Mesnard, L. (2004). Understanding the shortcomings of commodity-based technology in input-output models. An economic circuit approach. *Journal of Regional Science*, **44**, 125–141.

Edmonston, J. H. (1952). A treatment of multiple-process industries. *Quarterly Journal of Economics*, **66**, 557–571.

Gigantes, T. (1970). The representation of technology in input-output systems. In *Contributions to Input-Output Analysis*, Eds. Carter, A. P. and A. Brôdy, Amsterdam: North-Holland.

Guo, J., A. M. Lawson and M. A. Planting. (2002). From make-use to symmetric I-O tables: An assessment of alternative technology assumptions. Working Paper 2002–03 of the Bureau of Economic Analysis. http://www.bea.gov/papers/pdf/alttechassump.pdf.

Konijn, P. J. A. and A. E. Steenge. (1995). Compilation of input-output data from the National Accounts. *Economic Systems Research*, **7**, 31–45.

Konijn, P. J. A. (1991). Aggregation in the commodity technology model. *Österreichische Zeitschrift für Statistik und Informatik*, **21**, 39–56.

Konijn, P. J. A. (1994). *The Make and Use of Commodities by Industries: On the Compilation of Input-Output Data from the National Accounts.* Enschede: University of Twente.

Kop Jansen, P. S. M. and T. ten Raa. (1990). The choice of model in the construction of input-output coefficients matrices. *International Economic Review*, **31**, 213–227.

Mattey, J. P. (1993). Evidence on input-output technology assumptions from the longitudinal research database. Discussion Paper Centre for Economic Studies 93-8, Washington DC, US Bureau of the Census.

Mattey, J. P. and T. ten Raa. (1997). Primary versus secondary production techniques in US manufacturing. *Review of Income and Wealth*, **43**, 449–464.

Rainer, N. (1989). Descriptive versus analytical make-use systems: Some Austrian experience. In *Frontiers of Input-Output Analysis*, Eds. Miller, R., K. Polenske and A. Z. Rose, New York: Oxford University Press.

Rainer, N. and J. Richter. (1992). Some aspects of the analytical use of descriptive make and absorption tables. *Economic Systems Research*, **4**, 159–172.

Rueda-Cantuche, J. M. and T. ten Raa. (2009). The choice of model in the construction of industry coefficients matrices. *Economic Systems Research*, **21**, 363–376.

Rueda-Cantuche, J. M. and T. ten Raa. (2013). Testing assumptions made in the construction of input-output tables. *Economic Systems Research*, **25**, 2, 170–189. [An earlier version can be downloaded at: http://www.iioa.org/working%20papers/WPs/WPIOX09-011.pdf].

Stahmer, C. (1982). Connecting national accounts and input-output tables in the Federal Republic of Germany. In *Compilation of Input-Output Tables*, Ed. Skolka, J., Berlin: Springer.

Stahmer, C. (1985). Transformation matrices in input-output compilation. In *Input-Output Modelling*, Ed. Smyshlyaev, A., New York: Springer.

Steenge, A. E. (1990). The commodity technology revisited: Theoretical basis and an application to error location in the make-use framework. *Economic Modelling*, **7**, 376–387.

ten Raa, T. (1988). An alternative treatment of secondary products in input-output analysis: Frustration. *Review of Economics and Statistics*, **70**, 535–540.

ten Raa, T., D. Chakraborty and J. A. Small. (1984). An alternative treatment of secondary products in input-output analysis. *Review of Economics and Statistics*, **66**, 88–97.

ten Raa, T. and J. M. Rueda-Cantuche. (2003). The construction of input-output coefficients matrices in an axiomatic context: Some further considerations. *Economic Systems Research*, **15**, 439–455.

ten Raa, T. and J. M. Rueda-Cantuche. (2007). A generalized expression for the commodity and the industry technology models in input-output analysis. *Economic Systems Research*, **19**, 99–104.

ten Raa, T. and R. van der Ploeg. (1989). A statistical approach to the problem of negatives in input-output analysis. *Economic Modelling*, **6**, 2–19.

United Nations. (1968). A system of national accounts. Studies in Methods Series F, No. 2, rev. 3, New York.

United Nations. (1999). Handbook of input-output table compilation and analysis. Studies in Methods Series F, No. 74, New York.

United Nations, EUROSTAT, IMF, OECD and WB. (1993). *A System of National Accounts* 1993, New York, Paris, Washington DC: Brussels-Luxembourg.

Young, P. C. (1986). The US input-output experience — Present status and future prospects. In *Problems of Compilation of Input-Output Tables*, Eds. Franz, A. and N. Rainer, Vienna: Orac.

Chapter 19

The Use-Make Framework and the Derivation of Functional Forms in Production Theory*

Thijs ten Raa

Department of Economics, Tilburg University, Tilburg, The Netherlands

tenraa@uvt.nl

Abstract. The use-make framework is employed to explain functional forms in production theory, including Cobb-Douglas and Leontief. Productivity and efficiency are interrelated by augmenting the framework with a linear program that determines the frontier output.

Keywords: Use-make Framework, Productivity, Efficiency, Functional Forms

1. Introduction

In this paper I present the concepts of productivity and efficiency in the use-make framework of input-output analysis. This framework is very flexible. It accommodates different numbers of inputs, outputs, and production units. Perhaps surprisingly, it even has the capacity to explain parametric production functions, not only Leontief functions, but also functions featuring substitution. The different results,

*Reprinted from *Economic Systems Research*, **31**, 132–141, 2018, with permission from Taylor & Francis.

particularly the derivation of the Cobb-Douglas and Leontief functions and the decomposition of productivity growth in technical change and efficiency, are not new, but are now interrelated in a unifying framework, the use-make framework. This has not only pedagogical appeal, but I hope also stimulates cross fertilization, such as the introduction of efficiency measures in input-output analysis and, vice versa, the use of a general equilibrium input-output framework in productivity analysis.

I have taken a leave of absence from input-output research and studied the concepts of efficiency and productivity in the fundamental framework of Debreu (1951); see ten Raa (2008). This paper is a coming home. I show how the stuff I learned is useful in input-output analysis and, perhaps more significant, how use-make tables are an organizing framework not only for national accounting (Beutel, 2017) but also for economic theory (Rueda-Cantuche, 2017, ten Raa, 2017, and Shestalova, 2017, and the references given there).

The use-make framework is presented in the next section. To connect with traditional input-output analysis I review the case where the number of products is equal to the number of industries. Section 3 determines the frontier output of the economy. To connect with traditional productivity analysis I also consider the case of a small, open economy. In such an economy all products are priced by the international terms of trade and, therefore, all industries are machines transforming factor inputs into value-added. In other words, industries have multiple (factor) inputs, but essentially a single 'output', namely value-added. This single output case facilitates the construction of the Cobb-Douglas production function in section 4. General productivity and efficiency accounting follow in section 5, including the decomposition of the Solow residual in technical change and efficiency change terms. In section 6 I consider the opposite extreme case, an economy with a single 'input', say labor, and multiple products. This case shows emergence of the Leontief function between output and input. The final section concludes.

2. The Use-Make Framework

An economy has endowments, activities, which make products, and consumers. The endowments are used as factor inputs. The activities are called decision making units in operations research, firms in economics, and industries in input-output analysis. In this journal I opt for the latter terminology. The products are used by the industries and the consumers. The industries thus use factor inputs and intermediate (produced) inputs. Products not used by the industries feed the consumers. This is final demand. The economy is a machine that transforms factor inputs into final demand. Productivity is final demand per unit of factor input. The trouble is that both the numerator and the denominator are multidimensional. After presenting the use-make framework the cases with a single output and a single input will be dealt with first.

Presently the main reference for the use-make framework is Beutel (2017). I focus on what is necessary for the development of production functions and productivity measures. I begin with some notation. The economy has l factor inputs, m industries, n products. The factor use table is $l \times m$-dimensional matrix L. The first row depicts the distribution of say labor by industry. The first column depicts the factor inputs of industry 1. And so on for the other rows and columns. The use table is $n \times m$-dimensional matrix U. The first column depicts the intermediate inputs of industry 1. The first row depicts the distribution of the first intermediate input by industry. The make table is $n \times m$-dimensional matrix V. The first column depicts the products of industry 1. The first row depicts the distribution of the first product by industry. In the System of National Accounts the make table is of opposite dimension, but for this paper it is handy to have it as the same dimension as of the use table. The unit vector, with all entries equal to 1, is denoted by e. It acts as summation vector. For example, Ve is the vector of row totals of the make table, i.e. the gross output product vector, denoted x:

$$x = Ve \tag{1}$$

Subtraction of the intermediate input vector, Ue, yields the final demand vector, denoted y:

$$y = (V - U)e \tag{2}$$

The economy is a machine that transforms factor inputs L into final demand y. An economy is more productive if it produces more y for less L. The framework is very general. Activities, of which there are

m, may well be production establishments. Establishments producing the same outputs, even in the same proportions, may have disproportionate inputs. If so, one establishment is more efficient than another. Efficient establishments determine the production possibility frontier of the economy. The further away an establishment is from the frontier, the less efficient it is.

In traditional input-output analysis, however, the number of activities is equal to the number of products. All industries determine the production possibility frontier. None are inefficient. This is why, historically, there is little attention for efficiency analysis in the input-output community. In traditional input-output analysis $m = n$ and, therefore, make table V is square. If it has a dominant diagonal (meaning that the majority of any product is produced in the corresponding industry), then V is invertible and

$$A = UV^{-1} \tag{3}$$

is the matrix of input-output coefficients (following the commodity technology model, Rueda-Cantuche, 2017). Input-output coefficients are inputs divided by outputs. Equations (1), (2) and (3) imply that final demand $y = x - UV^{-1}Ve$ or

$$y = x - Ax. \tag{4}$$

Equation (4) is the basic equation of traditional input-output analysis. It connects final demand to the factor inputs. The vector of factor inputs is obtained by summation of the factor use table over industries: Le. Analogous to equation (3) the matrix of factor input coefficients is

$$B = FV^{-1}. \tag{5}$$

By equations (5) and (1) the vector of factor inputs is $Le = LV^{-1}Ve = Bx$. Substituting the Leontief inverse of equation (4), $x = (I - A)^{-1}y$,

$$Le = \Lambda y \tag{6}$$

where $\Lambda = B(I - A)^{-1}$ is the matrix of factor contents. If products have low factor contents, then the factor inputs produce much net output, the economy is productive.

3. Frontier Output

The economy maps factor inputs Le into net output $(V - U)e$. Could it produce more? Not in the traditional case, with as many industries as products. However, if there are more activities than products, $m > n$, there will be room for improvement by reallocation of factor inputs to the efficient activities. The way to model this is by setting up a linear program that maximizes the level of net output by reallocating activity. The implicit assumption is that the consumers have Leontief preferences. This assumption has been shown to free the analysis from unobserved consumer data and to yield conservative inefficiency estimates (ten Raa, 2008). In the observed situation the activity level vector is e. The reallocation vector will be denoted by s. If, for example, $s_1 = 1.1$, then industry 1 will produce 10% more. The level of final consumption will be denoted by c. If, for example, $c = 1.25$, then the economy will produce 25% more. The actual level of net output, normalized at 1, is lower than potential net output, 1.25. The economy, in this example, is 80% efficient. In general, *efficiency* is measured by $1/c$.

In maximizing the level of final demand by reallocation the economy is constrained by the material balance and the factor endowments. The linear program is as follows:

$$\max_{s,c\geq 0} e' \, yc : (V - U)s \geq yc, Ls \leq Le. \tag{7}$$

The objective function is final demand level c. I have included a multiplicative scalar, $e'y$, the national product. (The prime denote transposition, making summation vector e a row vector.) Program (7) has n product constraints and l factor input constraints. Denote the Lagrange multipliers of the product constraints by p and of the factor input constraints by w. By the theory of linear programming, the Lagrange multipliers equal the marginal products of the constraining entities, $w_i = \frac{\partial yec}{\partial (Le)_i}$, and the total value of the bounds (0 and Le) equals the value of the program: $wLe = yec$. National income equals the national potential product.

If the economy is small and open, net output $(V - U)s$ can be distributed between domestic final demand yc and net exports z. Net exports are constrained below by the balance of payments, $\pi z \geq 0$, where π is the row vector of the world terms of trade. In this case the analysis of the linear program simplifies. This is demonstrated by invoking the dual program. On the suggestion of a referee I present the concepts of primal and dual programs in full (ten Raa, 2005).

A *linear program* is a triplet $(a \;\; b \;\; C)$ where a is an n-dimensional row vector of objective function coefficients, b an m-dimensional column vector of bounds, and C an $m \times n$-dimensional matrix of constraint coefficients. The primal program reads

$$\max_{x} ax : Cx \leq b. \tag{8}$$

In problem (8) x is an n-dimensional column vector of variables. The first order condition of problem (8) is that the gradient of the objective function, a, is proportional to the gradient of the constraint function, $a = \lambda C$, where λ is an m-dimensional row vector of Lagrange multipliers, one for each constraint. The dual program associated with (8) reads

$$\min_{\lambda \geq 0} \lambda b : a = \lambda C. \tag{9}$$

According to the main theorem of linear programming the solution values of programs (8) and (9) match. This means that the value of program (8) is imputed to the binding entities according to the prices given by vector λ. For this reason Lagrange multipliers are also called shadow prices. And, related, program (9) shows that the shadow prices equal the marginal productivities of the binding entities. They reign in perfectly competitive economies.

Let us write frontier program (7) in the general format (8) and bring in net exports z, and the balance of payments, $\pi z \geq 0$. The constraints are the material balance, the factor constraint, the balance of payments, and the nonnegativity of the allocation variable. (The nonnegativity of the consumption level variable, c, is automatic, since $c = 1$ is observed hence feasible.) These are the four rows in the constraint matrix:

$$\max_{s,c,z}(0 \quad e'y \quad 0)\begin{pmatrix} s \\ c \\ z \end{pmatrix} : \begin{pmatrix} U - V & y & I \\ L & 0 & 0 \\ 0 & 0 & -\pi \\ -I & 0 & 0 \end{pmatrix}\begin{pmatrix} s \\ c \\ z \end{pmatrix} \leq \begin{pmatrix} 0 \\ Le \\ 0 \end{pmatrix}. \tag{10}$$

Denote the Lagrange multipliers of the constraints by p, w, ε and σ: the product prices, the factor input prices, an exchange rate, and nonnegativity slack variables, respectively. Then the dual constraint, in (9), reads

$$(0 \quad e'y \quad 0) = (p \quad w \quad \varepsilon \quad \sigma) \begin{pmatrix} U - V & y & I \\ L & 0 & 0 \\ 0 & 0 & -\pi \\ -I & 0 & 0 \end{pmatrix}. \tag{11}$$

The first component of (11) is $p(V - U) = wL - \sigma$: value added equals factor costs minus slack. If a slack component is positive, then the associated constraint, which is a nonnegativity constraint of a component of allocation variable s, is binding and, therefore, industries with greater factor cost than value added are inactive in the allocation supporting frontier output. The second component of (11) is a price normalization constraint, $py = e'y$. The third component, $p = \varepsilon\pi$, dictates the international relative prices and the level $\varepsilon = e'y/\pi y$, so that $p = (e'y/\pi y)\pi$. The dual program minimizes factor costs, wLe, subject to the value constraints $p(V - U) \leq wL$. There are l variables (for the factor prices) and m constraints (for the industries). l constraints will be binding (ten Raa, 2005, p. 48) and locate the active industries. The $m - l$ nonbinding constraints signal positive slack components of σ, hence inactivity.

I will now rewrite this in simplified value added notation, to clarify the structure of the frontier program and to pave the way for the introduction of industry capacity constraints which may preclude the extreme specialization into only l constraints. Denote value added by $v = p(V - U)$, a row vector with m components, one for every activity.

Frontier output is determined by maximizing $e'yc$. By the second component of (11) this pyc. Now we are going to apply the fact that any slack in a constraint is nullified by the Lagrange multiplier to the material balance, the first component of the constraint in (10). Hence $p(U - V)s + pyc + pz = 0$ or, substituting the balance of payments and the definition of value added, $pyc = vs$. In other words, the maximization of the level of final consumption is equivalent to the maximization of value added. A small, open economy can thus be considered a single output producer, of value added, which is derived by valuating product outputs and inputs at world prices and taking the differences, for each industry.

4. Multiple Input-Single Output Production Functions

Identify an activity by its factor input structure per unit of value added. For example, the first activity, with value added $v_1 = p(V_{\cdot 1} - U_{\cdot 1})$, is identified by $L_{\cdot 1}/v_1$. This is a vector of factor intensities. In the traditional case there are two factor inputs, namely capital and labor. Denote the two factor intensities by k and l, respectively, and the total endowments by M and N, respectively. Rescale activity levels such that activity level one corresponds to the use of k and l in the produce of one unit of value added. The primal program selects a pair of activities with minimal factor intensities. And the scales of production are now equal to value added. But now let there be capacity constraints $s(k, l) \leq S(k, l)$. The optimal activities are now bound, will be used to full capacity, and next best activities will also be engaged. Activities with binding capacity constraints pick up a positive shadow price of the capacity constraint (Ricardian rent) and activities run with nonbinding capacity constraints break even, as before the active industries with no capacity constraints.

Subject to the factor constraints $\int\int s(k,l)kdkdl \leq M$ and $\int\int s(k,l)ldkdl \leq N$ we maximize value added $\int\int s(k, l)dkdl$. This is a linear program with a continuum of variables $s(k, l)$. With a slight abuse of notation (previously w was the row vector of all factor input prices) now denote the shadow prices of the two factor constraints by scalars r and w, respectively. By the phenomenon of complementary slackness unprofitable activities, with unit cost $rk+wl > 1$, are not run, $s(k, l) = 0$. By the same argument, profitable activities, with unit cost $rk + wl < 1$, are run at full capacity, $s(k, l) = S(k, l)$. Activities which break even, $rk+wl = 1$, have activity $0 \leq s(k, l) \leq S(k, l)$, but since the set of such activities has measure zero we may set $s(k, l) = S(k, l)$. It follows that inputs and output are $M = \int\int_{rk+wl\leq 1} S(k,l)kdkdl$, $N = \int\int_{rk+wl\leq 1} S(k,l)ldkdl$, and value added $Y = \int\int_{rk+wl\leq 1} S(k,l)kdkdl$, respectively. The implicit assumption is that all factor input can be fully employed. There must be activities with factor intensity k/l below endowment ratio K/L and activities with factor intensity above the endowment ratio.

The three expressions, for inputs K and L and output Y, are interrelated by the two shadow prices r and w. The idea of Houthakker (1955) is to use the first to expressions to solve for r and w in terms of K and L. Substitution of the results in the third expression yields output as function of the inputs. Houthakker (1955) carries out this calculation for the capacity distribution with Pareto density function, $S(k, l) = \mu k^{\kappa-1} l^{\lambda-1}$, where μ, κ and λ are positive constants. The result is $Y = AK^{\alpha}L^{\beta}$ with $\alpha = \kappa(\kappa + \lambda + 1)$, $\beta = \lambda(\kappa + \lambda + 1)$ and A a positive constant depending on μ, κ and λ. In other words, a Pareto capacity distribution yields a Cobb-Douglas production function. This is Houthakker's Theorem.

At the micro level activities have fixed input-output ratios — it takes given amounts of labor to operate given machinery and equipment — but a change in resources, such as the inclusion of the East German labor force in the year 1989, is accommodated by the activation of new activities and the deactivation of some incumbent activities. Reallocations of resources across activities with different factor intensities manifest as substitutions at the macro level of the economy.

Clearly, different capacity distributions for the activity levels will generate different production functions. Houthakker (1955) has generated a stream of theoretical and applied research, to day. The bulk of this literature features a lower dimension, with only one variable input, namely labor, and again one fixed output, which is now capital. In this one fixed-one variable input framework Levhari (1968) found the capital distribution for which total output is a CES function of the total fixed input (capital) and the total variable input (labor) and showed it encompasses the Cobb-Douglas function. Muysken (1983) has consolidated the Cobb-Douglas, CES and VES functions by showing they are all generated by beta distributions, with alternative parametrizations. Two books on the distribution approach to production are Johansen (1972) and Sato (1975). In this literature activities have fixed input-output proportions and capacity constraints explain the existence of inefficient activities. Increases in levels of inputs prompt the activation of less efficient activities, in Ricardian style. The law of one price yields rents to the more efficient activities. The activation of different activities prompts different proportions between the input totals and the output.

5. Productivity and Efficiency

The continuum of activities was a theoretical device to explain the emergence of the Cobb-Douglas function in the use-make framework. Having completed that business, let us return to the case of a finite number of activities, in fact two suffices, with only one factor input. So firm 1 has factor input intensity l_1 and firm 2 l_2. We organize them in row vector l. The (labor) endowments are N_1 and N_2. Let the first industry be more productive than the second: $l_1 < l_2$. (This is an innocent assumption, because we are free to relabel the industries.) Then industry 1 can produce no more than it produces, at least under the assumption that the data represent all conceivable practices of production. Industry 2, however, could perform better by adopting the technique of industry 1.

Frontier output is determined by a maximization program. The program can be applied to a firm (1 or 2) or to the industry (the duopoly) and the results can be combined to determine firm and industry efficiencies (ten Raa, 2011). The simplest program features constant returns to scale and is applied to the economy:

$$\max_{s \geq 0} s_1 + s_2 : l_1 s_1 + l_2 s_2 \leq N_1 + N_2. \tag{12}$$

The dual program minimizes the value of the bound, $w(N_1 + N_2)$, subject to the dual constraint. The matrix of constraint coefficients, including of the nonnegativity constraints, is $\begin{pmatrix} l_1 & l_2 \\ -1 & 0 \\ 0 & -1 \end{pmatrix}$. The dual constraint is $\begin{pmatrix} w & \sigma_1 & \sigma_2 \end{pmatrix} \begin{pmatrix} l_1 & l_2 \\ -1 & 0 \\ 0 & -1 \end{pmatrix} = \begin{pmatrix} 1 & 1 \end{pmatrix}$. As the solution is economy-wide adoption of technique 1, $s_1 > 0$, hence $s_1 \geq 0$ is nonbinding, hence its Lagrange multiplier is zero, $\sigma_1 = 0$, hence the first component of the dual constraint reads $wl_1 = 1$ or $w = 1/l_1$. Since l_1 is the amount of labor per unit of output in the relatively productive industry, the shadow wage equals output per unit of labor, i.e. *productivity*, in the relatively productive industry. If this shadow wage would prevail, industry 1 would break even and industry 2 would be unprofitable. This confirms that shadow prices are perfectly competitive prices, would induce profit maximizers to select the activities that yield frontier output.

The frontier program can also be applied to individual industries. For industry 2 it reads

$$\max_{s \geq 0} s_1 + s_2 : l_1 s_1 + l_2 s_2 \leq N_2. \tag{13}$$

The solution is $s = (N_2/l_1 \ 0)$: industry 2 would adopt the technique of industry 1. Actual output is N_2/l_2 and frontier output is N_2/l_1.

As in section 3, the ratio of actual output to frontier output defines *efficiency*. Here efficiency is equal to $\frac{1/l_2}{1/l_1}$, i.e. the ratio of actual productivity to optimal productivity.

Now we return to the general use-make framework, (7), with the factor input shadow prices arranged in row vector w. Productivity growth of factor input i is $\dot{w}_i$, where the dot stands for the derivative with respect to time. This is sensitive with respect to the unit of measurement. However, aggregating across factor inputs, weighing by the units of inputs, $\sum_i \dot{w}_i L_{i\cdot}e$, the sensitivity gets lost, because $\dot{w}_i L_{i\cdot}e = \frac{\dot{w}_i}{w_i} w_i L_{i\cdot}e$, in which the ratio is a growth rate while the subsequent product is insensitive with respect to the unit of measurement. It is also customary to express the change in the output/input ratio as a growth rate, by dividing by the level, $\sum_i w_i L_{i\cdot}e = wLe$, and to use real wages by subtracting the growth rate of the final demand prices. In short, the output/input ratio grows at the rate

$$TC = \dot{w}Le/wLe - \dot{p}y/py. \tag{14}$$

Expression (14) is called *technical change*. This Lagrange multiplier approach to productivity can be related to the Solow residual approach. Recall that the value of the primal program, (10), is imputed to the bounds by the shadow prices $e'yc = wLe$ or, using the second component of (11), $pyc = wLe$. Differentiating totally, $\dot{w}Le - \dot{p}yc = p\dot{y}c - w\dot{L}e + py\dot{c}$ and, therefore, expression (14) equals $TC = (p\dot{y}c - w\dot{L}e + py\dot{c})/pyc$ or

$$p\dot{y}/py - w\dot{L}e/wLe = TC + EC. \tag{15}$$

The left hand side of expression (15) is the Solow (1957) residual between net output growth and factor input growth. On the right hand side the first term is technical change and the second term is efficiency change $-\dot{c}/c$, indeed the growth rate of efficiency term $1/c$ of section 3.

6. Single Input-Multiple Output Production

In section 4 substitution was considered a symptom of the change in the range of active activities (run with positive intensity), from labor intensive to capital intensive. Not surprisingly, this mechanism disappears when there is only one input. Perhaps surprisingly though, the disappearance of the substitution mechanism holds true even when there are multiple outputs, as the next section will review in detail.

In classical economics labor is the only factor input; all other inputs are produced commodities, also called intermediate inputs. Production output is used to fulfill intermediate demand and final demand, where the latter is defined residually, as the difference between output and intermediate input. Production output is also called gross output; similarly, final demand is also called net output. In standard input-output analysis each output has a single technique to produce it. Assuming constant returns to scale, the input of commodity j, $j = 1, \ldots, n$, per unit of output, is denoted by the input vector $(a_{1j}, \ldots, a_{nj}, l_j)$, of which the components represent the n intermediate inputs and the factor input (labor), respectively. If these unit input requirements are fixed, they are necessarily efficient, because actual and optimal production coincide. If, however, there is a set of input vectors for each product j, there is room to reallocate labor between alternative techniques, which may save labor or, alternatively, increase output. This would increase the output/input ratio from actual productivity to optimal productivity. The ratio of the two would be efficiency. A deep result states that the optimal input vectors, one for each product, are independent of the composition of final demand. This is the substitution theorem, but for obvious reason also called non-substitution theorem, which goes back to Samuelson (1951). The proof of the theorem has a long history, in which details have been worked out and minor flaws eliminated. This culminated in a proof based on the efficiency program of maximizing the expansion factor of some net output vector, determining the optimal input vectors, one for each product, and showing that this combination of input vectors remains optimal when the net output vector is replaced by another one (ten Raa, 1995).

The substitution theorem yields an all purpose frontier technology, featuring one technique for each product. Given any net output vector one can compare the optimal labor input to the actual labor input. The ratio is the efficiency of the economy. The extension of the analysis to multiple factor inputs is the subject of the next section.

7. Conclusion

When the number of products is equal to the number of industries, the use-make framework specializes to traditional input-output analysis. At the reporting level use-make data are not consolidated, but firm specific. The raw use-make tables are rectangular, with more "industries" than products. The consequent scope for reallocations is exploited to determine the frontier output of the economy by linear programming. Moreover, if the economy is small and open, all industries are machines transforming factor inputs into value-added. This essentially single output case facilitates the construction of the Cobb-Douglas and related production functions. The ratio between actual and potential output measures efficiency and productivity may grow due to efficiency and technical changes, as is shown in the general multiple input and multiple output case. In the opposite polar case, an economy with a single 'input', say labor, and multiple products, generates the Leontief function between output and input.

Opposite functional forms of production functions, such as Cobb-Douglas and Leontief, are thus generated by the general use-make framework, which is the basis of modern input-output analysis. In this sense nonparametric analysis, including input-output and linear programming, is more fundamental than parametric analysis.

References

Beutel, J. (2017). The supply and use framework of national accounts. In *Handbook of Input-Output Analysis*, Ed. ten Raa, Th., Cheltenham: Edward Elgar.

Debreu, G. (1951). The coefficient of resource utilization. *Econometrica*, **19**(3), 273–292.

Houthakker, H. S. (1955). The Pareto distribution and the Cobb-Douglas production function in activity analysis. *The Review of Economic Studies*, **23**(1), 27–31.

Johansen, L. (1972). *Production Functions: An Integration of Micro and Macro, Short Run and Long Run Aspects*, Amsterdam: North-Holland.

Levhari, D. (1968). A note on Houthakker's aggregate production function in a multifirm industry. *Econometrica*, **36**(1), 151–154.

Muysken, J. (1983). Transformed beta-capacity distributions of production units. *Economics Letters*, **11**(3), 217–221.

Samuelson, P. A. (1951). Abstract of a theorem concerning substitutability in open Leontief models. *Activity Analysis of Production and Allocation*, **13**, 142–146.

Sato, K. (1975). *Production Functions and Aggregation*, Amsterdam: North-Holland.

Solow, R. M. (1957). Technical change and the aggregate production function. *The Review of Economics and Statistics*, **39**(3), 312–320.

ten Raa, Th. (1995). The substitution theorem. *Journal of Economic Theory*, **66**(2), 632–636.

ten Raa, Th. (2005). *The Economics of Input-Output Analysis*, Cambridge: Cambridge University Press.

ten Raa, Th. (2008). Debreu's coefficient of resource utilization, the Solow Residual, and TFP: The connection by Leontief preferences. *Journal of Productivity Analysis*, **30**(3), 191–199.

ten Raa, Th. (2011). Benchmarking and industry performance. *Journal of Productivity Analysis*, **36**(3), 285–292.

ten Raa, Th. (2017). Multipliers, factor contents, and productivity. In *Handbook of input-output analysis*, Ed. ten Raa, Th., Cheltenham: Edward Elgar.

Rueda-Cantuche, J. M. (2017). The construction of input-output coefficients. In *Handbook of Input-Output Analysis*, Ed. ten Raa, Th., Cheltenham: Edward Elgar.

Shestalova, V. (2017). Input-output based general equilibrium analysis of efficiency. In *Handbook of Input-Output Analysis*, Ed. ten Raa, Th., Cheltenham: Edward Elgar.

Chapter 20

Linkages, Fields of Influence and Key Sectors*

Thijs ten Raa
Department of Economics, Tilburg University, Tilburg, The Netherlands
tenraa@uvt.nl

Abstract. Linkages, fields of influence and key sectors are troublesome concepts.

Keywords: Linkages, Fields of Influence, Key Sectors

JEL-codes: C67

1. Introduction

Backward linkages measure the impact of final demand changes on output. Forward linkages measure the impact of value-added changes on price. Backward linkages are given by the column totals of the Leontief inverse and forward linkages by the row totals. Industries with higher linkages have more influence on the economic system and industries with above average backward linkage and above average forward linkage are deemed key sectors. The extensive literature on these concepts is a playground for fanciers of matrix algebra and, not surprisingly, is a flourishing subfield of input-output analysis.

*Reprinted from *Journal of Economic Structures*, **9**, Article number: 29, 2020, with permission from Springer Nature.

With due respect to the practitioners I address the question if all this hard theoretical work is useful. I have three worries.

2. Worry #1

Linkages, influence, and key sectors all have positive connotation. The concepts identify important industries, which impact the economy. Such industries have big multiplier effects, which are supposed to be good to the economy. Big multipliers mean big entries in the Leontief inverse. Now there is an increasing relationship between the Leontief inverse and the underlying intermediate input coefficients (as the Neumann series clearly demonstrates). So having big multipliers is equivalent to having big input coefficients. Frankly, I'd rather live in an economy with small input coefficients. Then industries need little and leave much to the consumers. After all an economy is a machine that transforms resources into household consumption, the objective to be fulfilled. The aforementioned literature ignores that. The fascination with high multipliers is perverse. Industries are important if they contribute directly or indirectly to household consumption; value added is a better indicator than the magnitude of intermediate input coefficients. The standard macroeconomic policy to focus on industries with high input coefficients is simplistic. Moreover, income multipliers boost industrial multipliers, in fact in a uniform way (ten Raa, 2005, Theorem 3.1). Last but not least, in a multiregional economy comparative advantages better be factored in when the importance of industries are assessed (e.g. ten Raa and Pan, 2005).

3. Worry #2

Intermediate input coefficients and multipliers are intermediate constructs in economic analysis and better be commingled with factor input coefficients. This is even true in disequilibrium analysis where, for example, an industry is targeted to boost labor employment. The labor employment multipliers are given by the product of the (row vector of) labor coefficients and the Leontief inverse. It is not enough that a target industry has big output multipliers. Actually, it is not relevant. The product of the (row vector of) labor coefficients and the target industry column of the Leontief inverse must be big.

4. Worry #3

Column totals of the Leontief inverse (backward linkages) and row totals (forward linkages) are suspicious from a measurement perspective. Apples and oranges are added. This is particularly true of column totals, where different products are added (backward linkages). However, even row totals (forward linkages) have this defect.

A simple example illustrates my discussion. Consider the matrix of intermediate input coefficients $\begin{pmatrix} 0 & 1 & 0 \\ 0 & 0 & 1 \\ 0 & 0 & 0 \end{pmatrix}$. Its Leontief inverse is $\begin{pmatrix} 1 & 1 & 1 \\ 0 & 1 & 1 \\ 0 & 0 & 1 \end{pmatrix}$. The row totals are $\begin{pmatrix} 3 \\ 2 \\ 1 \end{pmatrix}$ and the column totals $(1\ 2\ 3)$. Sonis, Hewings and Guo (1997, 2000) consolidate multipliers, influences and linkages by taking the product matrix of the two: $\begin{pmatrix} 3 & 6 & 9 \\ 2 & 4 & 6 \\ 1 & 2 & 3 \end{pmatrix}$.

Two findings are the following. The industry hierarchy in terms of forward linkages (row totals) is: (i) industry 1, (ii) industry 2, (iii) industry 3. The multipliers product matrix shows that industries 1 and 3 have equal influence: the products of their own multipliers are equal (the first and the third diagonal entries), as are their fields of influence (1, 2, 6, 9 in the first row and column, as well as in the third row and column).

I claim the findings are not invariant with respect to the units of measurement. To prove this, I measure product 2 in a different unit. For example, the old unit was kilogram and the new unit is metric pound (which is 500 grams). The input-output matrix becomes $\begin{pmatrix} 0 & 1/2 & 0 \\ 0 & 0 & 2 \\ 0 & 0 & 0 \end{pmatrix}$. The Leontief inverse becomes $\begin{pmatrix} 1 & 1/2 & 1 \\ 0 & 1 & 2 \\ 0 & 0 & 1 \end{pmatrix}$. The row multipliers become $\begin{pmatrix} 2.5 \\ 3 \\ 1 \end{pmatrix}$ and the column multipliers become $(1\ 1.5\ 4)$. The multipliers product matrix becomes $\begin{pmatrix} 2.5 & 3.75 & 10 \\ 3 & 4.5 & 12 \\ 1 & 1.5 & 4 \end{pmatrix}$.

Let me check the two findings. The industry hierarchy in terms of forward linkages (row totals) is now: (i) industry 2, (ii) industry 1, (iii) industry 3. That is different than before I changed the unit of measurement. And industries 1 and 3 now have unequal influence: The products of their row and column multipliers are now 2.5 and 4, respectively. And their cross effects are 1, 3, 3.75 and 10 for industry

1 and 1, 1.5, 12 and 10 for industry 3. So industry 3 now has more influence than industry 1. That is also different.

5. Conclusion

I have changed the importance of industries in terms of linkages and fields of influence just by measuring the output of an industry in metric pounds instead of kilograms. The concepts of linkages and fields of influence are not invariant with respect to the units of measurement. Key sectors are a derived concept and, therefore, have the same defect, as have the concepts of construction importance (Jensen and West, 1980) and social accounting based impacts (Pyatt and Round, 1979).

All this is reminiscent of ten Raa, Chakraborty and Small's (1984) finding that some methods of constructing input coefficients are not invariant with respect to the units of measurement. That spurred a lot of theory, which eventually solved the problem (Rueda-Cantuche, 2017). I hope some readers take up the challenge to rethink linkages, fields of influence and key sectors.

References

Jensen, R. C. and G. R. West. (1980). The effect of relative coefficient size on input-output multipliers. *Environment and Planning A*, **12**(6), 659–670.

Pyatt, G. and J. I. Round. (1979). Accounting and fixed price multipliers in a social accounting matrix framework. *Economic Journal*, **89**(356), 850–873.

Rueda-Cantuche, J. M. (2017). The construction of input-output coefficients. In *Handbook of Input-Output Analysis*, Ed. ten Raa, T., Cheltenham: Edward Elgar, pp. 133–174.

Sonis, M., G. J. D. Hewings and J. Guo. (1997). Comparative analysis of China's metropolitan economies: An input-output perspective. In *Regional Science in Developing Countries*, Eds. Chatterji, M. and Y. Kaizhong, Basingstoke: Macmillan Press, pp. 147–162.

Sonis, M., G. J. D. Hewings and J. Guo. (2000). A new image of classical key sector analysis: Minimum information decomposition of the leontief inverse. *Economic Systems Research*, **12**(3), 401–423.

ten Raa, T. (2005). *The Economics of Input-Output Analysis*, Cambridge: Cambridge University Press.

ten Raa, T., D. Chakraborty and J. A. Small. (1984). An alternative treatment of secondary products in input-output analysis. *Review of Economics and Statistics*, **66**(1), 88–97.

ten Raa, T. and H. Pan. (2005). Competitive pressures on China: Income inequality and migration. *Regional Science and Urban Economics*, **35**(6), 671–699.

Chapter 21

Professor Jones' Re-Appraisal of Heckscher–Ohlin Trade Flows*

Thijs ten Raa
Department of Economics, Tilburg University, Tilburg, The Netherlands
tenraa@uvt.nl

Abstract. Jones (2008) questions Leontief's procedure to test if a country's trade pattern is according to the Heckscher–Ohlin theory of factor abundance. In a Heckscher–Ohlin framework he shows that the country with the higher capital/labor endowment ratio may export a relatively labor-intensive commodity whereas its import-competing sector is more capital-intensive. In this paper I argue that imports which drive domestic producers out of the market should enter the calculation. This observation is shown to resurrect Leontief's procedure. Finally, I shed some light on his paradox that American exports are more labor intensive than its imports.

Keywords: Leontief Paradox, Factor Intensities, Cycling Behavior, Relative Factor Endowment Ranking

JEL-codes: F10, F11

In the paper that inaugurated Trade and Development Review, Jones (2008) discusses the famous Leontief paradox. Leontief (1953) found that the American exports were produced by more labor-intensive

*Reprinted from *Trade and Development Review*, **1**, 144–147, 2008, with permission from Jadavpur University.

techniques than those used in American production activities that competed with imports. This finding contradicted the Heckscher–Ohlin Theorem, according to which a country exports products which are intensive in the relatively abundant resource. The United States is well endowed with capital rather than labor. The paradox proved a fountain of articles, both theoretical and empirical. The theoretical ones, including earlier ones by Jones, pointed out that there are conditions which violate the Heckscher–Ohlin Theorem assumptions. The two such conditions Jones mentions are factor-intensity reversal and demand asymmetry. The amazing feature of Jones' present paper is that he seems to reconcile Leontief's finding with Heckscher–Ohlin theory without invoking these peculiarities. In his own words (Jones 2008, p. 4), "Here I have explicitly avoided that technological reversal phenomenon" and "Here demand conditions could be the same between countries and balanced among commodities (say equal shares in a Cobb-Douglas setting)".

Jones illustrates his point with a pair of countries producing four commodities. As the factor endowment ratio of a country changes — say towards relatively more capital — it switches to the production of a more capital intensive product. At the switch any weighted combination of the two products is possible. Ordering products by increasing capital/labor intensity, he considers a pair of countries where the country with the lowest capital/labor endowment ratio ("Home," think of India) switches from product 1 to product 2 and the other country ("Foreign,") switches from product 3 to product 4. The locations of either country on the switch (the shares of the two products) are determined by demand and the endowments and are manipulable indeed. Jones (2008) assumes this is fixed such that Home is near the end of the switch between products 1 and 2, producing much of 2, exporting it, but little of 1, importing it to meet domestic demand. Similarly, he assumes Foreign is at the beginning of the switch between products 3 and 4, exporting 3 and importing 4. In technical language the two countries are in different "cones of diversification" and that is a known upsetter of the Heckscher–Ohlin Theorem.

Jones rightly observes that in Foreign (think of the U.S.) the exports sector (which produces commodity 3) is labor intensive relative to the import-competing sector (which produces commodity 4). This would resolve the Leontief paradox in a non-anomalous two-country framework with a common technology (reversal-free), but different factor endowment properties. Or, to put it more sharply, it "invalidates" the Leontief procedure.

I doubt it. More precisely, I question if the representation of Leontief's procedure is accurate. In other words, would Leontief compare the factor contents of exports to the factor contents of competing imports? A case in point is that Leontief (1953) calculated the factor contents of American imports using U.S. input-output coefficients. The latter are known only if the imports are produced domestically as well, i.e. are competing imports. The crucial distinction between competing and noncompeting imports, however, is not that noncompeting imports are not produced domestically, but cannot be produced domestically. In Jones' model technology is common to the different countries and, therefore, any import is competitive import. Some commodities may not be produced domestically, but that is because it would incur a loss. Moreover, even in this case it is very well possible to calculate the factor contents of such imports, at least under constant returns to scale, namely at the optimal point where the marginal rate of substitution equals the factor price ratio. It seems to me that correct application of the Leontief procedure would include the factor contents of all imports.

This correction unravels Jones' finding that the country endowed with relatively more capital may export relatively labor intensive products. My point is made forcefully if the (universal) technology is a Leontief technology, i.e. with fixed input-output coefficients. Then factor contents calculations do not depend on the country and the four commodities can be represented as packages of labor and capital, of which the quantities are determined by the product of the direct factor input coefficients and the Leontief inverse of the matrix of intermediate input coefficients. Now Jones (2008) assumption of demand symmetry equalizes the commodity proportions of consumption between the countries and, therefore, the factor proportions of consumption. By the material balance these common factor proportions must be equal to the proportions of the total or world endowments of labor and capital. It follows that the country with the low capital/labor endowment, Home, has a consumption package with a greater capital/labor intensity (than its endowment) and vice versa for Foreign. Now the calculation that consumption equals output (net of intermediate demand) minus net exports is true not only in terms of commodities, but also in terms of labor and capital contents. Since Home's output "package" is equal to its endowment package — which is more labor intensive than the world endowments — it must be that its net exports are also more labor intensive. The final point is to conclude that its exports are more labor intensive than its imports. Leontief was not explicit about this theoretical step and Leamer (1980) made a big fuss of this, but the conclusion remains valid if there is no trade deficit.

If technology is not Leontief, some extra work has to be done. Even though technology is assumed to be the same in Home and Foreign, the factor contents can now be different, since the countries may substitute factor inputs to accommodate their endowments. However, under the assumption that capital/labor ratios of the different commodities do not overlap (the aforementioned ordering of commodities is uniform with respect to factor input prices) Jones (1956) has shown that there is a uniform ordering of commodities in terms of relative production costs, in the sense that if Home's price of a product is lower than of Foreign's, the same will be true for the more labor intensive products. There can be no reversals and the result that Home's exports are relatively labor intensive — proved for fixed input-output coefficients — stands firm.

Jones not only shows that the better capital endowed country may have an exports sector which is more labor intensive than the import-competing sector, but also the export sector cycles relative to its import-competing sector, as a country's relative capital endowment rises. I find this intriguing. However, this is not true relative to total imports.

There have been numerous attempts to solve Leontief's paradox. I mentioned the role of the balance of payments and now the focus is on the different cones of diversification. When I was his research assistant, I asked Wassily Leontief what he thought explained his result that American exports are relatively labor intensive. He replied that in the U.S. it takes one worker to operate a tractor. In India, he said with a twinkle, in his eyes, it takes two workers, one to drive and one to chat. (This conversation was before the liberalization of the Indian economy was in full swing.) In his view, the Achilles heel of Heckscher–Ohlin theory is its assumption of a common technology. This assumption can be dropped, by adjusting a reference technology, the U.S. (Trefler, 1993), or by working directly with independent input-output tables. Factor abundance remains a source of comparative advantage — that can be assessed using Leontief's procedure — along with the other sources, namely asymmetries in technologies and demand (ten Raa and Mohnen, 2001).

References

Jones, R. W. (1956). Factor proportions and the Heckscher–Ohlin theorem. *Review of Economic Studies*, **24**(1), 1–10.

Jones, R. W. (2008). Heckscher–Ohlin trade flows: A re-appraisal. *Trade and Development Review*, **1**(1), 1–6.

Leamer, E. E. (1980). The Leontief Paradox, reconsidered. *Journal of Political Economy*, **88**(3), 495–503.

Leontief, W. W. (1953). Domestic production and foreign trade: The American capital position re-examined. *Proceedings of the American Philosophical Society*, **97**, 332–349.

ten Raa, Th. and P. Mohnen. (2001). The location of comparative advantages on the basis of fundamentals only. *Economic Systems Research*, **13**(1), 93–108.

Trefler, D. (1993). International factor price differences: Leontief was right! *Journal of Political Economy*, **101**(6), 961–987.

Chapter 22

Facets of Innovation and Stages of Development*

Thijs ten Raa†

Department of Economics, Tilburg University, Tilburg, The Netherlands

tenraa@uvt.nl

Abstract. Innovation has been redefined as the implementation of a new product, process or organization. Adoption from a developed economy is considered innovation. The mirror image is that productivity growth accounts not only for technical change, but also efficiency change. The latter component is more important to developing economies. R&D pertains more to technical change and competition and free trade to efficiency change. Empirical studies confirm that R&D is more potent in developed economies and that competition and free trade spur development.

Keywords: Innovation, Productivity Growth, Development, Competition, Free Trade

JEL-codes: F10, O10, O20, O30

*Reprinted from *Trade and Development Review*, **2**, 28–33, 2009, with permission from Jadavpur University.

†This paper is based on an invited presentation at the OECD Global Forum on Trade, 15–16 October 2007, La Defense, Paris. Input and feedback from Osamu Onodera, OECD, is gratefully acknowledged. The paper has also been presented at the Young Economist Students' Meet, Jadavpur University, 4th January, 2008.

1. Introduction

It seems a natural idea to connect the distinction between technical change and efficiency change in the literature on innovation and productivity growth with the distinction between developed and developing economies. Since the two facets of innovation have different sources — with R&D driving technical change and competition and free trade driving efficiency change — developing and developed economies have different stakes in the latter. The purpose of this paper is to interrelate the two facets of innovation with the two stages of development.

This paper proceeds as follows. In the next section I discuss the recent redefinition of innovation, which accounts for other elements than technical improvements. The components of technical change and efficiency change are related to the distance to the production possibility frontier and, in turn, to competition in section 3. The relationship with free trade is discussed in section 4 and implications for developing economies are drawn in section 5. Section 6 corroborates the role of free trade for development and section 7 concludes.

2. Innovation, Broadly Speaking

Innovation is a fad that has reached development economics. If taken in the narrow sense, the act of pushing out the technology frontier, this creates some mixed feelings. When I was invited to lecture in South Africa about R&D, spillovers and technical progress, my instinct was that this subject would be less relevant to my hosts. I mean, what is the point of engaging a developing economy in the costly process of R&D in new products and processes? I must admit, however, that OECD (2005) redefines innovation broadly as "the implementation of a new or significantly improved product (good or service), or process, a new marketing method, or a new organizational method in business practices, workplace organization or external relations". In other words, a new product, process or organization may be adopted from a developed economy and *be implemented*, and we are still in the ball game of innovation.

In a sense, recent productivity analysis accommodates this broad perspective. While in the old days economic growth was understood to be the outcome of the combination of size effects (demographics and investment driving labor and capital growth) and productivity growth (the Solow residual between output and input growth, representing technological change), nowadays organizational improvements are accounted for in the measurement of factor productivity growth. More precisely, the fruits of innovation are measured by total factor productivity growth but the latter consists of two components, namely technical change *plus* efficiency change. An economy may grow by shifting the production possibility frontier or by *catching up* with the frontier. Clearly, it matters where an economy stands relative to the frontier. This observation takes us to the recent literature on competition and performance.

3. Distance to the World Frontier and Virtues of Competition

What is the role of competition in the latter two components of productivity growth? The traditional, neoclassical point of view is that competition is good, because it eliminates slack and allocates resources where they are most productive. This view has been countered by Schumpeter, who argued that monopoly power, a departure from competition, is the source of profit, and profit is indeed the main funding for R&D. Both mechanisms seem to be at work and the overall effect of competition is mixed indeed. ten Raa and Mohnen (2008) studied the panel of Canadian industries and found that it matters who benefits from prices in excess of competitive costs: labor or capital. If it is capital Schumpeter's argument flies and competition may thwart innovation indeed, but if it is labor — such as managerial rents — the neoclassical argument gets some support.

A comparison of competition effects on innovation between developed and developing economies is facilitated by a disentanglement of the effects on the technical change and efficiency change components of productivity growth. It seems to me that the Schumpeterian argument pertains more to the technical change component of productivity growth and the neoclassical argument to the efficiency change component. Not surprisingly, Acemoglu, Aghion and Zilibotti (2006) document that R&D is more important in industries or countries closer to the world technology frontier. But surprisingly, they also find that competition becomes more important close to the frontier. However, in my view their latter finding is a consequence of their model design — they define competition as cost proximity between the leader and the fringe in an industry. One would expect that when there is cost proximity that the stakes of innovation would increase in a competitive game between profit maximizing players. The model is full with assumptions. On the other hand, its partial equilibrium nature precludes an important source of inefficiency, other than the use of out-of-date technology, namely the wrong mix of production in countries, in violation of the international trade theoretic principle of comparative advantage.

4. The Role of Free Trade

ten Raa and Mohnen (1994, 2002) decompose the efficiency change component of productivity growth further into three components: the elimination of waste (X-inefficiency, the use of excessive inputs), reallocations of resources to the better companies, and comparative advantage gains. Free trade obviously helps to capture the third gains, but may also be helpful in checking the first two inefficiencies. An effect of free trade is that it puts competitive pressure on local producers. It forces weak domestic companies out of business and frees resources to more efficient ones. This competitive role is particularly important to inefficient economies, i.e. the ones remote from the frontier, the developing economies. The harmful effect of competition on the appropriability of the returns to innovation pertains to frontier economies.

Aggregate productivity can be decomposed in company productivities and market share effects. Company innovations boost aggregate productivity, but so do market share gains of the better companies. Companies can be innovative in the narrow sense of technical change or they can catch-up (company efficiency change), while the market share effect reflects competition between companies (market efficiency change). At least in principle, trade orientation may impact all these components. The overall correlation between export intensity and productivity is strong, 80 percent for the UK; non-exporters show 1 percent productivity change between 2000–2001 and exporters 4.5 percent. Rizov and Walsh (2007) also find that the decompositions differ. For non-exporters it is company change, while for exporters the bulk (some two-thirds) is the market share effect. Since the non-exporters happen to be the followers, I ascribe their productivity growth to company efficiency change. The exporters show technical change, but the bulk of their performance is a result of the competitive selection of winners. Indeed, they must overcome obstacles to penetrate foreign markets. Only the best succeed.

5. Implications for Developing Economies

What do these results imply for developing countries? I do acknowledge that the neoclassical recipe of competition is not always effective. In fact, our research of the Canadian economy lends some support to the Schumpeterian point of view. Capital rents driven technical change shifts the world production possibility frontier. This mechanism is important in the OECD economies. But remember, there is more to innovation and growth than technical change. In fact, the *other* components of productivity growth are important to developing countries: Company catch-up with modern technology and the market share effect — the weeding out of less productive companies. Both are forms of efficiency change and, therefore, benefit from an open, competitive climate.

Indeed, developing economies have much to gain from free international trade and much opposition comes from the EU and the US, be it in agriculture, clothing, or light manufacturing. At least in principle, this policy division could be rationalized by the appropriability problem of innovation — which affects primarily the OECD economies. I am afraid, however, that short-sighted protection considerations weigh more. Impediments to free trade not only harm consumers — who buy unnecessarily expensive home produce — but also reduce the pressure on developing countries companies to compete and thus to reduce inefficiency. Though efficiency improvements are the less spectacular component of innovation, they are the important ones, particularly to developing countries.

6. Trade and Growth

There is an astounding relationship between international trade and economic growth. In fact, Lewer and Van den Berg (2003) have shown that a one percentage point increase in the growth of exports is associated with a one-fifth percentage point increase in economic growth. The average coefficient on export growth for high income countries is 0.43, 0.15 for upper-middle, 0.22 for lower-middle, and 0.21 for low income. The seemingly smallness of the trade effect for developing economies reflects dramatic trade differences between open and closed economies. On average, during the 1980s all East Asian economies, most of which would be classified as "open", increased exports by 11.1 percent per year, while Sub-Saharan Africa and its mostly "closed" economies increased its exports by just 2.4 percent per year. It just takes a lot of trade to grow.

Schneider (2005) conducts an empirical investigation of the role of trade in determining the rate of innovation and economic growth in developed and developing countries, and investigates the importance of intellectual property rights and foreign direct investment in these processes. Confirming my observation that company catch-up and competitive pressure are more important than technical change to developing countries, she finds that domestic innovation in the narrow technological sense is a significant source of growth *for developed countries only.* Not surprisingly, the main source of growth is physical capital accumulation (per capita). The second strongest impact comes from the growth of high-technology imports (also per capita). Intellectual property rights have distinct effects on developed versus developing countries; again the positive effects are confined to the developed countries. Once more this confirms an earlier observation, namely that technical change and the appropriability of the returns is a frontier economy issue and less of a concern to developing countries. Even the other traditional sources of innovation — human capital and R&D — are less pronounced in the developing world, especially when infrastructure is included in the regression equation. This final point suggests that infrastructure plays an important role in the innovative capacity of developing countries. Stiglitz (2007) even argues that India may use part of its foreign exchange reserve to finance infrastructure.

Greenwald and Stiglitz (2006) argue that trade restrictions may help infant economies to spur productivity growth. Their argument is that industry drives technology, even in agriculture. This spillover structure is embedded by assumption in their two sector model, which they "could easily extend". In fact, ten Raa and Wolff (2000) have solved the intersectoral spillover structure of the U.S. economy and identified the key sectors with spillover effects, including computers, communications and automotive. This finding seems to underscore the role of infrastructure.

7. Conclusion

Innovation is the engine of long run growth and free markets may not be the best way to promote innovation in all cases. Restrictive policies have been suggested: import substitution, infant industry support, royalties, and government supply of infrastructure. Not surprisingly, a closer inspection of the literature shows that market failures plague the eye catching facet of innovation — the pushing out of the technological frontier — but not the other facets — corporate catch-up and the market share effect. The latter reflect efficiency improvements and benefit from access to markets and competitive pressure. By their very nature, developing countries innovate more through the latter channels and, therefore, stand to gain from free trade.

The literature also reveals another asymmetry. Traditional sources of innovation seem less potent in developing countries, overwhelmed by the role of infrastructure. This is a key sector indeed and its development deserves full attention. One of the impediments has been the lack of public funding. Luckily this problem is partly being overcome by computer based technologies, which facilitate direct payments by users of the infrastructure. For example, quite a few developing countries now build highways with electronic tolls.

References

Acemoglu, D., Ph. Aghion and F. Zilibotti. (2006). Distance to frontier, selection, and economic growth. *Journal of the European Economic Association*, **4**(1), 37–74.

Greenwald, B. and J. E. Stiglitz. (2006). Helping infant economies grow: Foundations of trade policies for developing countries. *American Economic Review Papers and Proceedings*, **96**(2), 141–146.

Lewer, J. and H. Van den Berg. (2003). How large is international trade's effect on economic growth? *Journal of Economic Surveys*, **17**(3), 363–396.

OECD. (2005). *Oslo Manual*, Paris: OECD.

Rizov, M. and P. P. Walsh. (2007). Productivity and trade orientation in UK manufacturing. Discussion Paper 2808, IZA, Bonn.

Schneider, P. H. (2005). International trade, economic growth and intellectual property rights: A panel data study of developed and developing countries. *Journal of Development Economics*, **78**(2), 529–547.

Stiglitz, J. E. (2007). Use forex reserves for infrastructure. *The Hindu*, January 5.

ten Raa, T. and P. Mohnen. (1994). Neoclassical input-output analysis. *Regional Science and Urban Economics*, **24**(1), 135–158.

ten Raa, T. and P. Mohnen. (2002). Neoclassical growth accounting and frontier analysis: A synthesis. *Journal of Productivity Analysis*, **18**(2), 111–128.

ten Raa, T. and P. Mohnen. (2008). Competition and performance: The different roles of capital and labor. *Journal of Economic Behavior and Organization*, **65**(3–4), 573–584.

ten Raa, T. and E. N. Wolff. (2000). Engines of growth in the U.S. economy. *Structural Change and Economic Dynamics*, **11**(4), 473–489.

Chapter 23

Leontief's Legacy*

Thijs ten Raa
*Department of Economics, Tilburg University,
Tilburg, The Netherlands*
tenraa@uvt.nl

Wassily Leontief, lived the good, old-fashioned, life — impeccably dressed and with a keen eye for beauty in all domains. In economic science he was the general. The Bolsheviks did not know how to handle him, threw him in and out of jail. The U.S. was not amused by his progressive political leanings, but Leontief silenced the administration in court.

As any general Leontief believed in planning. At the beginning of World War II the U.S. economy had to be redirected, to produce military hardware instead of household consumption goods, and Leontief's input-output model was used to guide the transition. In theory the Americans could have relied on the market mechanism, with excess demand for aircraft and other military equipment driving up their prices and making large-scale production profitable, but they did not and for good reasons, according to Leontief.

Firms which do not operate at or near minimal average cost are competed out of the market and as a result the economy features

*Reprinted from *Newsletter International Input-Output Association*, **1**, 191–199, 2009, with permission from International Input–Output Association.

constant returns to the scale. The rate of profit is equalized irrespective the level of output and, therefore, market prices do not suffice to determine the quantities that must be supplied to fulfill demand. Planning is a useful supplement.

Leontief regretted that his ideas became out of fashion during the Cold War, when input-output analysis was perceived as a Soviet tool, as well as during the more recent transition to a market economy in Russia in the 1990s, perhaps for the same reason. However, the first decade after his death we witness a remarkable resurgence of input-output analysis.

I discern at least three developments. First, in the theory of international trade the neoclassical paradigm — with relative factor abundance explaining the comparative advantages — is augmented. Technology differences are factored in and input-output analysis is needed for the modeling. Second, and related, technology spillovers and patents top the world trade negotiations agenda and are analyzed with the same tool. Last but not least, global warming — the most pressing political issue — brought Leontief's environmental model back in action.

Our last conference, in Seville, relaunched the environmental issue and the theme of our next conference, 11–17 July 2009 in Sao Paulo, is "The World in an Ever Changing Environment". Many young scientists — economists and others — contribute to these events and other activities of the IIOA.

Leontief would have loved the liveliness of these meetings. At an NYU seminar a distinguished MIT Professor once asked trivial questions for the sake of a pedagogic presentation. Leontief would answer them quickly, not once but each time. The situation became embarrassing and Professor Bever said: "Of course your answer is right, Professor, but the question was meant for the students". Leontief rebuked: "Here we are all students".

Chapter 24

Wassily Leontief: In Appreciation*

William J. Baumol[†,¶] and Thijs ten Raa[‡,§]

[†]*Berkley Center for Entrepreneurial Studies,*
Stern School of Business, 44 West Fourth Street,
New York, NY 10012-1126, USA
william.baumol@nyu.edu

[‡]*Department of Economics, Tilburg University,*
Tilburg, The Netherlands
tenraa@uvt.nl

Abstract. In this paper we briefly review the work of Wassily Leontief, in respect for his memory and appreciation of his accomplishment. His work encompasses and redirects the entire field of economics, including pure theory.

Keyword: Leontief

1. Introduction

His date and place of death are not controversial: Wassily Leontief died on 5 February, 1999 at the New York University Medical Center.

---

*Reprinted from *The European Journal of the History of Economic Thought*, **16**, 511–522, 2009, with permission from Taylor & Francis.

¶Baumol is Professor of Economics at New York University and Professor Emeritus at Princeton University.

§Corresponding author ten Raa is Associate Professor of Economics at Tilburg University, the Netherlands.

His date of birth was presumed to be 5 August, 1906, but after the collapse of the Soviet Union Leontief apparently first found out, and reported with much amusement, that it was precisely one year earlier, in 1905. Hence he was 93. His gravestone in Connecticut (next to that of Schumpeter) states that Wassily was born in St. Petersburg, while his birth certificate, issued by the municipality of Munich, states correctly that he was born in Munich.[1] Leontief not only spanned the twentieth century, he was also one of its most creative economists. He was the first to put to use the concept of the economic system as a working aggregation of interrelated parts, in which all the parts have their place. His model of the economy is a fine instrument that enabled him to hold it in his hand, to examine it, and understand its workings. He emphasized that micro- and macroeconomics are different depictions of the same system, different parts of which are studied in fields of specialization such as economic growth, spatial and environmental economics, and monetary economics. His representation of the economy as a complex system with many dimensions enables us to interrelate all this, to unite pure theory with policy issues and to connect micro data with national statistics. Leontief's invention of input-output analysis has facilitated both national accounting and applied equilibrium analysis.

Although Leontief, entirely by himself, constructed an operational framework that is now used throughout the discipline and all over the world, his work fits in with that of a chain of predecessors, as will be reviewed in section 2. Section 3 describes some of Leontief's earlier work, which was preponderantly theoretical. This enabled him to pursue the lines of inquiry that he deemed of primary importance. Section 4 describes the revolutionary advance of his basic analysis over that of his predecessors. Section 5 outlines his later work, which was influential, but also controversial, for his relationship with mainstream economists had not been easy.

[1]For more on Leontief's life and further discussion of his work see the special issue of *Economic Systems Research*(18:4, 2006). His birth certificate is posted on the web: http://www.wassily.leontief.net/docum/certifG.jpg. His father was a Munich graduate (Kaliadina and Pavlova, 2006).

2. Leontief and the Chain of Historical Predecessors

Wassily Leontief's work can be seen as the culmination of a sequence that runs from the beginnings of a systematic economic literature to the end of the twentieth century. One way of looking at the antecedents of input-output analysis is to take it as an end point of the strand that began with Léon Walras and continued through the writings on general equilibrium up until the onset of the Great Depression, for in Walras and in Leontief the different sectors of the economy and their interrelations play a central role. Leontief (1937: 111, 1944: 299 and 1949: 275) expressed this point of view,[2] but he (1936B) and others also linked him with a much earlier contribution, the physiocratic *Tableau Économique* (1758–1759), the work of that early economist physician, François Quesnay. (Actually, Quesnay was not the first medical doctor to make a major contribution to the economic literature. Both William Petty and Bernard de Mandeville were physicians. See Kuczinsky and Meek (1972) for an authoritative compilation of the various editions of the *Tableau.* See Phillips (1955) for an early analysis of the relationship between the Tableau and Input-Output.) And here there is a linkage considerably more continuous than is generally recognized.

The *Tableau* is often taken to have more or less disappeared from the economic literature half a century after Du Pont de Nemours left France for the United States,[3] until it was rediscovered by Marx; see his noted letter to Engels, 6 July, 1863 and his characterization of the

[2]He wrote "This is the same type of relation which was originally used by Walras in his first formulation of the general equilibrium theory," "An attempt to approach the empirical analysis of the American national economy from the point of view of general equilibrium, i.e. treating it as a completely determined system, is presented in my Structure of the American Economy, 1919–1929, Cambridge, 1941" and "This is the relationship that Walras describes in terms of his production function, his coefficients of production, each coefficient describing the amount of any particular input necessary to produce one unit of the final output," respectively.

[3]However, an anonymous reviewer draws our attention to the relevant writings of Isnard to Lang and Buquoy. For more on this see Kurz and Salvadori (2000, 2006).

Tableau as "incontestably the most brilliant idea of which political economy had hitherto been guilty," as cited in Sweezy (1942: 75). Marx translated the logic of the Tableau into his structure of "simple reproduction" under capitalism, and then used it in attempting to solve what he called "the transformation problem," (derivation of the numerical relationships between his two concepts, value and surplus value, and the price and profit variables of standard economic analysis).

Marx himself suggested that his solution was imperfect (*Capital* Vol. 3 Chapter IX) and the task of providing the first fully defensible way of dealing with the problem was left to Ladislaus von Bortkiewicz (1868–1931), a distinguished Polish mathematical statistician who was born in St. Petersburg and went on to teach at the University of Berlin; see von Bortkiewicz (1907).

Bortkiewicz is relevant here for two reasons. First, the logic of his solution of the transformation problem rested directly on the Marxian model of simple reproduction, based, as Marx indicated and as we have just seen, on Quesnay. Second, when Leontief came to the University of Berlin as a postgraduate student, since his primary thesis advisor admitted that he could not follow Leontief's (1928) mathematics, it was Bortkiewicz who was appointed as Leontief's second advisor as Leontief recounted with some delight to one of the present authors (in that conversation the name of Werner Sombart as his other adviser did not come up, see Kaliadina and Pavlova, 2006: footnote 17). Thus, the chain was complete — Quesnay to Marx to Bortkiewicz to Leontief.

The story is delightful, but as we will argue later, it is rather misleading, because it puts Leontief in the position of a writer who merely carried previous traditions one step further. This grossly undervalues his revolutionary contribution which, though he himself noted that it was built upon such distinguished predecessors, took him a giant step further, well beyond anything that the previous links in the historic chain had provided.

3. Early Work: Pure Theory and the Closed Model

If one were to ask a student of economics whether the national product should include all outputs of all sectors of activity he would probably answer "yes". The first publication of Leontief (1925) shows that this is erroneous, and that the Soviet statistical office made this mistake. It is now called "the problem of double counting (an issue not new to the literature)". Outputs are distributed between intermediate demand (industries) and final demand (such as households) and Leontief argued that only the latter should be included. This paper is considered the first input-output study, particularly by the Soviets after Stalin, when input-output analysis was no longer viewed as a "bourgeois" tool but — by somewhat creative extension — as a Russian invention. Leontief always kept his distance from such petty matters; his closest approach was in Leontief (1960). Dobb (1965: 200) assesses the status of the "first input-output study" as follows. "From this seminal idea [the dissolution of double counting], simple and unarresting it may appear when one first meets it, the whole system of input-output analysis evidently derives". Thus Leontief (1925) can reasonably be interpreted as the predecessor to input-output analysis.

The year 1925, when this first publication appeared, was also the year that Leontief moved to Berlin, then the center of academic life. During the next ten years Leontief was a prolific source of valuable papers, all highly theoretical, and none of them dealing with input-output analysis, such as his papers on elasticities and indifference curves in foreign trade (Leontief, 1932 and 1933). In hindsight he regarded this period as an antebellum that was a necessary step in establishing himself, playing down his contributions. Modern price index theory, however, still makes use of his first publication in *Econometrica*, (Leontief, 1936). And modern macroeconomics — with its emphasis on dynamics — has reflected Leontief's (1936A) critique of Keynes. In particular, Leontief emphasized that Keynes underplayed the importance of the role of investment, and that it should be viewed as a productive input, and not just as a component of demand.

His purely theoretical work continued after the appearance of his first true input-output study (Leontief, 1936B). Modern macroeconomists use of game theory has roots in his model of wage bargaining (Leontief, 1946). His deepest theoretical work, however, deals with the structure of functional relationships (Leontief, 1947). Leontief was motivated here by production analysis. The economy is a system that transforms resources into final goods and services, in which he considered whether it is possible to distinguish stages of a production process. In other words, can distinct sectors of activity be identified? And, if so, what principles should guide the classification?

Let us denote capital, labor and mineral resources by K, L and M, and the final goods and services by Y, all scalars, for simplicity of exposition. Let the transformation be given by

$$Y = G[F(K, L), M]. \tag{1}$$

Obviously, there are two stages of production: first K and L are combined and then their combination is commingled with M. Leontief noted that the marginal rate of substitution between K and L is independent of M. The demonstration is straightforward. Partial differentiation of (1) with respect to K and L, respectively, yields their marginal products:

$$Y_K = G_F \cdot F_K, \quad Y_L = G_F \cdot F_L. \tag{2}$$

Here we use subscripts to denote partial derivatives by subscripting, without inserting primes. The ratio of the two marginal products yields the marginal rate of substitution between K and L. By equation (2),

$$MRS^{K,L} = Y_K/Y_L = F_K/F_L. \tag{3}$$

This, by equation (1), is a function of K and L only. In other words, the marginal rate of substitution between the inputs used in a stage of production is independent of the other inputs (M). Then he *proved* that this condition is not only necessary but also sufficient for the determination of the internal structure of the overall function, as given by (1), without making any assumption. This theoretical result is strikingly general and continues to be used extensively in modern utility theory. Thus, the widely employed "separability conditions" all go back to Leontief's theory.

Leontief's first input-output study presented what is called the *closed model* (Leontief, 1936B). All outputs are also used as inputs. Industries produce commodities using commodities as well as factor inputs. Households produce these factor inputs using commodities. This, of course, is very much in the spirit of the contemporaneous work of von Neumann (1945). Leontief's *tour de force* was his breakthrough in relating general equilibrium theory to the data for an economy. The input-output matrix encompasses the data for all branches of the economy, including consumption coefficients.

This model was also used to analyze pricing. Assuming perfect competition, the zero-profit condition determines the prices as a row eigenvector of the matrix. However, since this vector is determined only up to a scaling vector, it is only relative prices that are thereby determined.

The weak element in the closed model is its treatment of investment. It is represented in a manner similar to household consumption — which can indeed be treated appropriately as an instantaneous activity. Von Neumann circumvented the problem by assuming balanced growth, but Leontief was not content to proceed in this way. His solution was to assume fixed and given capital coefficients. Changes in output, in this approach imply rigidly predetermined changes in the quantities of capital required and, hence, determinate quantities of investment. The model of the economy thus becomes a system of differential equations. Another more pragmatic solution was to separate out the matters that engendered problems. Leontief felt at ease modeling production sectors by means of equations using intermediate input coefficients. The difficult final demand sector could then be left exogenous.

4. Later Work: The Open Model and Applications

Though he obviously felt deeply about the contribution of input-output analysis and, as we will note, used its logic imaginatively and creatively in a variety of applications that were far from obvious, he might perhaps have emphasized more explicitly its consistency with the principle that guided his views about his discipline. Though a strong believer in the essential role that must be played by theory, as who among us is not, he was passionate about the trap into which, he believed, much of the work in the arena had fallen. His ire was aroused by the types of abstract theoretical work that he considered to have no foundation in reality, to lack applicability and that provided no handle for empirical testing. In his view such endeavors followed a dead end path onto which standard teaching in the graduate schools was determinedly leading the next generation of economists. (See his Presidential Address to the American Economic Association,

Leontief, 1971.) This was a position he held passionately and it was, arguably, the source of his one failure, for it did not discernibly move either the journals or the graduate schools in the direction for which he called. Yet he has left heirs in this endeavor, some who had made major contributions of a sort that may have induced other colleagues to avoid the directions Leontief deplored.

But the bulk of his contributions were successful and influential. As is true of any creative scholar's work there is no comfortable way to classify his contributions and place them into neat boxes. Yet, it is possible to argue that these are, roughly speaking, of three main types, all interconnected. First, there is, of course, the theory of input-output analysis, which is, in itself, a major leap forward from the work of the predecessors who led up to Leontief's analysis (as summed up in Leontief, 1966, particularly chapter 7). The advance here was formulation of the structure of the interdependencies of an economy in a way that was less abstract and far more operational than anything that had appeared before. Second, he was able to quantify the models with the aid of empirical data for an economy, enabling the model to serve as a guide to concrete policy decisions as well as contributing to pure understanding. (The open input-output model appears in *The Structure of the American Economy*, see Leontief, 1941, but only in the second edition. The model was launched in Leontief 1944 and studied in Leontief, 1977.) In dealing with a substantial set of such simultaneous economic interrelationships, nothing like that had ever been done before. Third, while some of the areas of application of the quantified input-output models are obvious as, for example, their use as a guide to central planning, Leontief took the applications far beyond that, sometimes in totally unexpected directions. Thus, Leontief's (1970) application to environmental issues was, surely, far from obvious, though once it had been carried out, it does seem an evident and natural way to go about analysis of its subject. Perhaps his most striking and unexpected application was that to international trade (Leontief, 1953), where "the Leontief paradox" has, for evident reasons, generated a stream of literature seeking to shed light on the puzzling result and to draw out its implications for the field. Again, none of the predecessor works offered anything like this degree of flexibility and rich diversity of application.

It should be added that one of the most significant features of this last accomplishment is that, in addition to the applications that

Leontief himself was able to provide, the analysis left the way open for others to find unexpected applications of the analysis, taking off in still other and very different directions. There evidently can be no clearer demonstration of the power and value of a scholarly contribution such as this.

5. Input-Output Analysis: The Great Step Beyond Predecessors

We have already noted the historic roots of input-output theory. But what input-output added to the work of any predecessor was truly revolutionary. The directly pertinent work of Quesnay, Marx and Bortkiewicz in each case had its limited and specific purpose, and none had any empirical connection. Quesnay used his table largely to support the view that manufacturing is a sterile activity and that only agriculture offers a surplus. Marx explicitly translated Quesnay's work into a static two-sector model, his "simple reproduction" concept (of course, he does offer some unsystematic remarks on a more dynamic [expanded reproduction] construct; see the last chapter of *Capital*, Volume 2). The static analysis provides one immediate conclusion: that in a balanced and stationary economy divided into a sector that produces consumption goods and one that supplies producers' goods, the producers' goods used by the consumption sector must be equal in value to the consumption goods that go to the capital goods sector. Finally, as we have seen, Bortkiewicz used the Marxian reproduction scheme just to solve Marx's transformation problem. The solution was the last stage in the pre-Leontief story. Each step in this pre-Leontief saga, it will be noted, pursued its author's immediate objective, *and was not designed to lead to applications distant from the initial topic of discussion.*

In contrast, input-output offers us a tool with a vast array of uses. The techniques, as just noted, have been applied to subjects as heterogeneous as international trade, economics of the environment, and productivity. It is not merely *capable* of using data; rather, it is designed for the purpose. Just to make the point — how such theory of our century permits both application and use of facts — we provide a single illustration selected because it is so far afield from the topics to which input-output is commonly applied. The topic is energy conservation and the various projects intended to be energy-saving, among them public transportation by rail (subways), recycling of oil, and the use of solar energy and other new energy sources, see Baumol and Wolff (1981). As advocacy of such measures grew in intensity in the 1970s, dispassionate observers noted that these processes all *used up* energy resources, as well as providing or saving energy. For example, the agricultural products that are employed to produce biomass may be transported in trucks that use up gasoline, and the digging of subway tunnels also consumes enormous amounts of power. Seeking to analyze the issue systematically, engineers invented the concept of "net energy" in which the energy used up by a proposed activity is subtracted from the energy it is expected to contribute. But it soon became clear that the engineers' calculations had at least one major shortcoming. No account was taken of the fact that it requires inputs to make inputs — that the trucks carrying the biomass themselves had to be built and used energy in the process of their construction, and that the same was true of the assembly line used to build the trucks, and so on *ad infinitum*. Clearly, there was a Leontief process at work. In the usual notation, if we let D represent the vector of energy consumed per unit of output, and A is the Leontief matrix, then the proper measure of energy consumed is

$$D + DA + DA^2 + \cdots + DA^n + \cdots . \quad (4)$$

But most of the engineers carrying out the net energy studies were considering only D as the measure of energy use. Some studies were more sophisticated and used $D + DA$ as their energy consumption measure. A small number of net energy studies even subtracted DA^2, but none went beyond that, thereby in effect assuming $DA^3 + \cdots = 0$. A full input-output calculation, using the standard data on the U.S. economy offered rather startling conclusions. The usual approach that takes into account only the energy of the directly used input overlooks, on average, over 60 percent of the true quantity of energy used. Even if a second round — the inputs used to make the direct inputs — is taken into account, some 28 percent of the total energy consumption is omitted. Thus, investments in what are deemed to be energy-saving measures that project, say, a 20 percent net energy yield were shown by the input-output calculation as more likely in fact to use up more energy than they provide.

6. Enfant Terrible in the Neoclassical Mainstream

Surely Leontief's work placed him in the mainstream of economic research. However, he found himself increasingly isolated from that mainstream.

His career in the universities of the U.S. reached its apex when Schumpeter invited him to Harvard University, where Leontief became *the* mathematical economist and a primary influence on neoclassical economists such as Paul Samuelson and Robert Solow. But he was dissatisfied with the directions in which his students and others were taking the field. In his view, they were providing theory without measurement and he considered that to be mere speculation at worst and applied mathematics at best.

Leontief was sceptical not only about contemporary theoretical work, but about that in econometrics as well. He was a fervent detractor of much of time-series analysis. In his opinion, the bulk of that work would be unhampered "if you feed it weather reports instead of economic statistics". He considered it measurement without theory. And, unlike physics, the time span in which the results of economic investigation retain their validity is very short. His favorite example was the lack of constancy of input-output coefficients. His attitude toward structural econometrics was, however, milder.

Another attribute that helps to explain his drift from the neoclassical mainstream is his style. He did not choose to ally himself closely with any mainstream group, enjoying his independence and resenting authority that he did not consider intellectual. Radical economists naturally evinced some sympathy for his ideas and positions, but the relationship was no more than a marriage of opportunity.

Many neoclassical economists criticized input-output analysis as excessively mechanical. The open input-output model comprises a system entailing both physical quantities (interrelating final demands and gross outputs) and a value system (interrelating prices and factor rewards). But this raised the question whether interdependence of these two sides of the workings of the economy should not be dealt with more explicitly. Some neoclassical economists took the position that their analysis explains the interaction between prices and quantities and that Leontief's does not.

We will argue that this is a misunderstanding. Leontief (1937: 116–17) did begin to provide an explanation of the determination of prices and quantities that deals with them simultaneously, using his closed model. He deliberately truncated the connection to free himself from assumptions such as the zero-profit condition that restricted application of the model. But the framework is still there and remains effective.

Neoclassical economists use the market values of labor and capital to assess their productivities and to commingle them in total factor expressions. In a sense, they take at face value what they are supposed to measure. This approach is legitimate for perfectly competitive economies, but Leontief believed that such economies inhabit textbooks rather than the real world. Input-output analysis can resolve this problem.[4]

7. Conclusion

The main implication of the preceding discussion is clear. Leontief possessed a strikingly creative mind that was guided by a desire for relevance. His work opened up entirely new and highly fruitful directions to the practitioners of our discipline. We have also shown that there is no basis for the occasionally voiced perception that Leontief was a narrow-minded proponent of an unexciting planning tool. His contributions are far wider than input-output analysis and, moreover, his techniques can be used to analyze problems of value determination, including those that evade standard neoclassical tools.

Because of his contributions the literature of economics has been affected profoundly and is far more illuminating and useful as a result. We economists are indeed all deeply indebted to him.

[4]In ten Raa and Mohnen (2002) productivity growth is measured without recourse to observed factor-values, by disaggregating output and calculating the production prices that would emerge under perfect competition — but do not necessarily prevail in our more complex economy. Leontief's apparatus is thus used simultaneously to account for input and output component growth rates and their valuations. This example underscores the general equilibrium nature of input-output analysis.

Acknowledgments

We are grateful to two anonymous referees for insightful feedback and to the Utrecht School of Economics for hospitality — the paper was completed in their garden.

References

Baumol, W. J. and E. N. Wolff. (1981). Subsidies to new energy sources: Do they add to energy stocks? *Journal of Political Economy*, **89**(5), 891–913.

von Bortkiewicz, L. (1907). On correction of Marx's fundamental theoretical construction in the third volume of capital. *Jahrbűcher főr Nationalőkonomie und Statistik*, Trans. Sweezy, P. M., In *Karl Marx and the Close of his System*, New York: Augustus M. Kelley, 1949, pp. 199–221.

Dobb, M. (1965). The discussions of the twenties on planning and economic growth. *Soviet Studies*, **17**(2): 198–208.

Kaliadina, S. A. and N. Iu. Pavlova. (2006). The family of W.W. Leontief in Russia (edited and annotated by Claus Wittich). *Economic Systems Research*, **18**(4), 335–345.

Kurz, H. D. and N. Salvadori. (2000). 'Classical' roots of input-output analysis: A short account of its long prehistory. *Economic Systems Research*, **12**(2), 153–179.

Kurz, H. D. and N. Salvadori. (2006). Input-output analysis from a wider perspective: A comparison of the early works of Leontief and Sraffa. *Economic Systems Research*, **18**(4), 373–390.

Kuczinsky, M. and R. L. Meek. (1972). *Quesnay's Tableau Économique*, London: Macmillan.

Leontief, W. (1925). Die Bilanz der Russischen Volkswirtschaft — Eine methodologische Untersuchung. *Weltwirtschaftliches Archiv*, **22**(2), 338–344, and (1925) *Weltwirtschaftliches Archiv — Chronik und Archivalien*, **22**(II), 265–269. Russian translation (1925): Balans naradnogo khoziaistva SSSR — Metodologicheskii razbor rabotii TSSU. *Planovoe Khoziaistvo*, **12**, 254–258. English translation (1964): The balance of the economy of the USSR. In *Foundations of Soviet Strategy for Economic Growth, Selected Short Soviet Essays 1924–1930*, Ed. Spulber, N., Bloomington, IN: Indiana University Press, pp. 88–94.

Leontief, W. (1928). Die Wirtschaft als Kreislauf. *Archiv fuer Sozialwissenschaft und Sozialpolitik*, **60**(3), 577–623. Translation: Leontief, W.

(1991). The economy as a circular flow. *Structural Change and Economic Dynamics*, **2**(1), 181–212.

Leontief, W. (1932). Studien ueber die Elastizitaet des Angebots. *Weltwirtschaftliches Archiv*, **35**(1), 66–115.

Leontief, W. (1933). The use of indifference curves in the analysis of foreign trade. *Quarterly Journal of Economics*, **47**(3), 493–503.

Leontief, W. (1936). Composite commodities and the problem of index numbers. *Econometrica*, **4**(1), 39–59.

Leontief, W. (1936A). The fundamental assumptions of Mr. Keynes' monetary theory of unemployment, *Quarterly Journal of Economics*, **51**(1), 192–197.

Leontief, W. (1936B). Quantitative input and output relations in the economic system of the United States. *Review of Economics and Statistics*, **18**(3), 105–125.

Leontief, W. (1937). Interrelation of prices, output, savings, and investment. *Review of Economics and Statistics*, **19**(3), 109–132.

Leontief, W. (1941). *The Structure of the American Economy, 1919–1929*, Cambridge: Harvard University Press.

Leontief, W. (1944). Output, employment, consumption, and investment. *Quarterly Journal of Economics,* **58**(2), 290–314.

Leontief, W. (1946). The pure theory of the guaranteed annual wage contract. *Journal of Political Economy,* **54**(1), 76–69.

Leontief, W. (1947). A note on the interrelation of subsets of independent variables of a continuous function with continuous first derivatives. *Bulletin of the American Mathematical Society*, **53**(4), 343–350.

Leontief, W. (1949). Structural matrices of national economies. *Econometrica*, **17**(Supplement), 273–282.

Leontief, W. (1953). Domestic production and foreign trade: The American capital position re-examined. *Proceedings of the American Philosophical Society*, **97**(4), 332–349.

Leontief, W. (1960). The decline and rise of soviet economic science. *Foreign Affairs*, **38**, 261–272.

Leontief, W. (1966). *Input-Output Economics*, New York: Oxford University Press.

Leontief, W. (1970). Environmental repercussions and the economic structure — An input-output approach. *Review of Economics and Statistics*, **52**(3), 262–270.

Leontief, W. (1971). Theoretical assumptions and nonobserved facts. *American Economic Review*, **61**(1), 1–7. Presidential address delivered at the eighty-third meeting of The American Economic Association, Detroit, Michigan, December 29, 1970.

Leontief, W. (1977). *Studies in the Structure of the American Economy*, White Plains NY: International Arts and Sciences Press (now M.E. Sharpe, Inc.).
von Neumann, J. (1945). A model of general economic equilibrium. *Review of Economic Studies*, **13**(1), 1–9.
Phillips, A. (1955). The Tableau Économique as a simple Leontief Model. *Quarterly Journal of Economics*, **69**(1), 137–144.
ten Raa, Th. and P. Mohnen. (2002). Neoclassical growth accounting and frontier analysis: A synthesis. *Journal of Productivity Analysis*, **18**, 111–128.
Sweezy, P. M. (1942). *The Theory of Capitalist Development*, New York: Oxford University Press.

Chapter 25

Anne Carter and Input-Output: Technology, Trade, and Pollution*

Thijs ten Raa[†] and William J. Baumol[‡,¶]

[†]*Department of Economics, Tilburg University, Tilburg, The Netherlands*
tenraa@uvt.nl

[‡]*Henry Kaufman Management Center, New York University, 44 West Fourth Street, Suite 7-91, New York, NY 10012, USA*
wbaumol@stern.nyu.edu

Abstract. We pay tribute to Anne Carter's contributions to economic analysis. Mainstream economic models, including input-output studies, consider technology as given and do not question the co-existence of different national economic techniques. Carter, however, addresses this key question. Her book, *Structural Change in the American Economy* (1970), was well ahead of its time. The techniques Carter compared were differentiated by time, but the comparative analysis is equally applicable

*Reprinted from *Œconomia*, **1**, 59–72, 2011, with permission from Association Œconomia.

¶Harold Price Professor of Entrepreneurship and Academic Director, Berkley Center for Entrepreneurship and Innovation, New York University; Senior Economist and Professor Emeritus, Princeton University; and Academic Advisor to the Ewing Marion Kauffman Foundation.

to a comparison of techniques that are differentiated by location, such as those of the E.U.-15 member states. We apply Carter's method for the determination of the optimal choice of technique to the problem of allocating production among different countries, so as to make use of their comparative advantages in producing commodities and in meeting environmental constraints. We also draw attention to Carter's recent work on ever deeper questions regarding variations in technology.

Keywords: Carter, Technical Change, Environmental Constraints

JEL-codes: B31, O30, Q51

The essence of the discussion that follows is the contention that the writings of Anne Carter are the most recent, though by no means the least significant, in a two and a half century series of related and deeply illuminating contributions on economic interdependencies. In a recent article devoted to the accomplishments of Wassily Leontief, the present authors stressed the sequence of ever richer contributions beginning with the work of Quesnay, then Marx, followed by his interpreter, Bortkiewicz. As we wrote there, Leontief's work can be seen as the culmination of a sequence that runs from the beginnings of a systematic economic literature to the end of the twentieth century. Indeed, Leontief himself repeatedly linked his work[1] with the much earlier contribution, *Tableau Économique* (1758–1759), by François Quesnay, doctor to Louis XVI. The *Tableau* is probably the earliest known writing that centers on what may be deemed a primitive general equilibrium analysis. It contains a remarkable graph that recognizes the double role of products as both inputs and outputs and traces the resulting sales, purchases, and income flows from agriculture to other main economic sectors — indisputably, a forerunner of a modern input-output table. See Phillips (1955).

The *Tableau* is often taken to have more or less disappeared from the economic literature half a century after Du Pont de Nemours

[1]See, in particular, Leontief, W. (1928). Die Wirtschaft als Kreislauf. *Archiv fuer Sozialwissenschaft und Sozialpolitik*, 60 (3): 577–623. English translation: Leontief, W. (1991). The Economy as a Circular Flow. *Structural Change and Economic Dynamics*, 2 (1): 181–212.

left France for the United States, until it was rediscovered by Marx.[2] Marx translated the logic of the *Tableau* into his structure of "simple reproduction" under capitalism and then used it in attempting to solve what he called "the transformation problem" — derivation of the numerical relationships between his two concepts, value and surplus value, and the price and profit variables of standard economic analysis.

Marx himself suggested that his solution was imperfect (*Capital*, Vol. 3, chapter IX), and the task of providing the first fully defensible way of dealing with the problem was left to Ladislaus von Bortkiewicz (1868–1931), a distinguished Polish mathematical statistician who was born in St. Petersburg and went on to teach at the University of Berlin (Bortkiewicz, 1907(1949)).

Bortkiewicz is relevant here for two reasons. First, the logic of his solution to the transformation problem rested directly on the Marxian model of simple reproduction — based, as Marx indicated and as we have just seen, on Quesnay. Second, as Leontief once enthusiastically recounted to one of the present authors, when he came to the University of Berlin as a postgraduate student, Bortkiewicz was appointed as his second advisor after Leontief's primary thesis advisor admitted that he could not follow his mathematics. Thus, the chain was complete: Quesnay to Marx to Bortkiewicz to Leontief.

However, we maintain that this story is incomplete, for it excludes the most recent step, provided when Leontief handed the torch on to Anne Carter. We know from personal experience how highly Leontief valued her knowledge and her creativity. In particular, soon after he moved from Harvard to New York University, there was an opportunity to hire a new member of the Department of Economics, and Leontief would hear of no candidate other than Carter. Unfortunately, urgent needs in a particular subfield and limited funds prevented her from receiving an offer. We are certain that Leontief never forgot his disappointment over this outcome.

[2]See Marx's noted letter of 6 July, 1863 to Engels, in which he characterizes the *Tableau* as "incontestably the most brilliant idea of which political economy had hitherto been guilty," as cited in Sweezy (1942), p. 75.

1. A Key Leontief Contribution: Application of Input-Output to Other Arenas

It is arguable that, as the input-output torch was passed on from one contributor to the next, substance was added at each stage. This is particularly true of Leontief himself, who expanded and deepened the underlying mathematics, showed the relevance of the analysis to economic planning, and broke through the limited role of the analysis as a fuller and deeper depiction of the interrelations of the flows that make up the activities of economies and the vessels by which these flows are carried. Arguably, however, his most creative contribution was in showing how the input-output analysis could be applied effectively to topics entailing practical applications to policy, for which it had never been used before. This observation is particularly pertinent here, as it is in this arena that some of Anne Carter's most illuminating contributions are found.

While some of the areas of application of the quantified input-output models are obvious as, for example, their use as a guide to central planning, Leontief took the applications far beyond that in sometimes unexpected directions. The application to environmental issues (Leontief, 1970), for instance, was, surely, far from obvious — though once it had been carried out, it does seem an evident and natural way to go about analyzing its subject. However, perhaps his most striking and unexpected application of input-output models was that involving international trade (Leontief, 1953), where "the Leontief paradox" has, for evident reasons, generated a stream of literature seeking to shed light on the puzzling result and draw out its implications for the field. No preceding work offered anything like the degree of flexibility and rich diversity of application present in Leontief's analysis.

Perhaps most significantly, in addition to the applications that Leontief himself was able to provide, his analysis left the way open for others to apply it in unexpected ways — taking off in still other and very different directions. There can be no clearer demonstration of the power and value of a scholarly contribution.

Input-output offers us a tool with a vast array of uses. The techniques, as noted, have been applied to subjects as heterogeneous as international trade, economics of the environment, and productivity. As such, input-output is not merely *capable* of using data; rather, it is designed for the purpose. In order to make the point that such theory of our century permits both application and use of facts, we provide a single illustration selected, in part, because it is so far afield from the topics to which input-output is commonly applied. It is also relevant here because it lies close to an area in which Anne Carter also made some of her important contributions.

The topic is energy conservation and the various projects intended to be energy-saving, among them public transportation by rail (subways), recycling of oil, and the use of solar energy and other new energy sources (Baumol and Wolff, 1981). As advocacy of such measures grew in intensity in the 1970s, dispassionate observers noted that, in addition to providing or saving energy, these processes all *used up* energy resources. For example, the agricultural products that are employed to produce biomass may be transported in trucks that use up gasoline, and the digging of subway tunnels consumes enormous amounts of power. Seeking to analyze the issue systematically, engineers invented the concept of "net energy", in which the energy used up by a proposed activity is subtracted from the energy it is expected to contribute. However, it soon became clear that engineers' calculations had at least one major shortcoming: no account was taken of the fact that it requires inputs to make inputs — that the trucks carrying the biomass themselves had to be built and used energy in the process of their construction, and that the same was true of the assembly line used to build the trucks, and so on *ad infinitum*. Clearly, there was a Leontief process at work. In the usual notation, if D represents the vector of energy consumed per unit of output, and A is the Leontief matrix, then the proper measure of energy consumed is

$$D + DA + DA^2 + \cdots + DA^n + \cdots . \tag{1}$$

Most of the engineers carrying out the net energy studies were considering only D as the measure of energy use. Some studies were more sophisticated and used $D + DA$ as their energy consumption measure. A still smaller number of net energy studies even subtracted DA^2, but none went beyond that, thereby in effect assuming away the portion of the energy usage represented by $DA^3 + \cdots$. To provide an estimate of the magnitude of this omission, a full input-output calculation using the standard data on the U.S. economy offered rather startling conclusions: the usual approach that takes into account only the energy of the directly used input overlooks, on average, more than 60 percent of the true quantity of energy used. Even if a second round — the inputs used to make the direct inputs — is taken into account, some 28 percent of the total energy consumption was shown to be omitted. As such, investments in what are deemed to be energy-saving measures that claim to offer, for example, a 20-percent net energy yield, in fact, use up more energy than they provide, according to the input-output calculation. This result, which surely holds enormous importance for resource conservation policy, was derived completely using the input-output approach.

It is surely important that energy consumption be reduced, not only because it saves resources for the future, but also because doing so will diminish its most threatening side-effect — the resulting carbon dioxide emissions. The U.S, China, and the E.U.-15 countries are severe polluters. The latter group, alone, emitted 350 tons of carbon dioxide per million euro gross value added in 2000 (Luksch, Steinbach, and Markosova, 2006). In North America, Asia, and Europe, the energy industry is probably a major cause of global warming. A two-way breakdown by E.U. member state and industry brings out the role of the energy industry in carbon dioxide emissions. Figure 1 (below) shows the carbon dioxide emissions for the

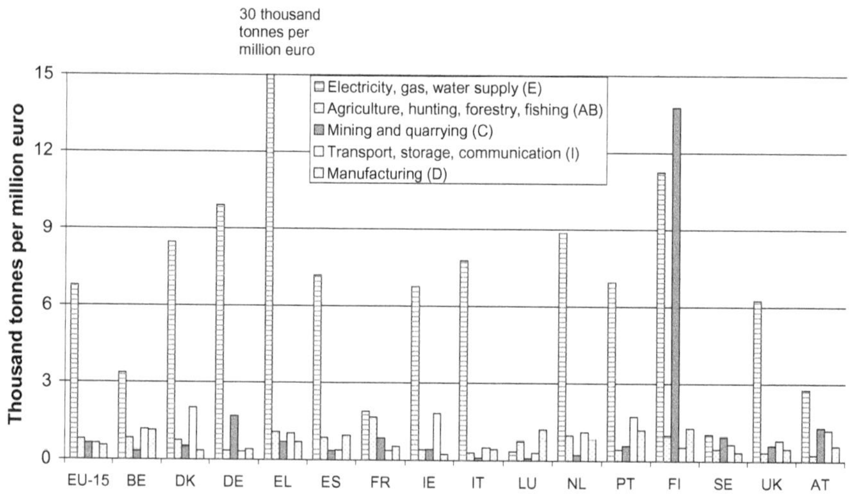

Fig. 1. Ratio of CO_2 emissions and GVA by Member States (MS) and by industry in 2000, in thousand tonnes per million euro.

E.U.-15 member states: Belgium (BE), Denmark (DK), Germany (DE), Greece (EL), Spain (ES), France (FR), Ireland (IE), Italy (IT), Luxemburg (LU), Netherlands (NL), Portugal (PT), Finland (FI), Sweden (SE), United Kingdom (UK), and Austria (AT). For each member state, five bars are displayed, each representing industries that emit carbon dioxide. From left to right these industries are: electricity, gas, water supply (E), agriculture, hunting, forestry, fishing (AB), mining and quarrying (C), transport, storage, communication (I), and manufacturing (D). Except for in Finland, the electricity, gas, and water supply industry (E) is always the greatest emitter.

Greece (EL), Germany (DE), Italy (IT), and Ireland (IE) have the greatest carbon emissions, relative to GDP. Much can be gained by acting on the recognition that world performance can be improved materially by inter-country specialization in energy production. For example, France is a clean producer of energy (41 percent of its output is nuclear) and might well improve matters by supplying energy to Germany.

2. A Key Carter Contribution: The Choice of Technique

It is in this arena that we encounter some of the most significant insights and contributions of Anne Carter. In standard input-output studies, technology is considered to be a given, as in all mainstream economic models, and the co-existence of different national economic techniques is not questioned. Indeed, in the models, even noncompetitive technologies are preserved via assumptions, such as fixed import coefficients or Armington variants. Carter, however, faces up to the key question — why do the differences in technology occur and persist? — using a subtle and interesting approach to deal with those differences, in the manner described below.

The adoption of more similar techniques, as substitutes for those that now differentiate French and German power generation, need not entail replacement of one mode of production by another one, but can be achieved by trade. The analysis of this option is not different from Ricardo's theory of comparative advantage, according to which, products can be produced by common techniques without necessarily adopting them at the national level. International trade is a vehicle that serves to select efficient modes of production — an old idea that has been lost in the pertinent portions of mainstream international trade theory, where endowment differences drive individual countries' choices of technique. Here, we assume that all countries have access to the same set of blueprints for techniques, as in the work of Heckscher and Ohlin. In reality, however, there are more intrinsic technology differences between countries, and this variation can be exploited to raise the standard of living in Ricardian fashion, as well as to satisfy whatever constraints are adopted to protect the environment. Reduction of global warming does not necessarily require technological advances. Much can be achieved by exploiting technical differences that already are extant, through changes in trade patterns.

Before we describe how this intuitive observation can be put to analytical use, we must have an operational understanding of the formulation that can be used explicitly to describe the varying choices of technique among countries. This task is carried out in Carter's *Structural Change in the American Economy* (Carter, 1970), a valuable work that was well ahead of its time. The book contains an ingenious calculation, in which Carter compares an old input-output table of the U.S. with a more recent one by constructing a hybrid model involving a choice between two techniques in each industry — one technique deemed old and the other new. The techniques Carter compared were differentiated by time, but the comparative analysis is equally applicable to a comparison of techniques that are differentiated by location, such as those of the E.U.-15 member states. In Carter's setting, the number of possible input-output matrices is 2 to the power equal to the number of industries, a large number. One might expect that the most efficient way to determine the changes in a bill of final demands would entail use of the information describing the technology represented by the new input-output matrix. However, Carter found an exception in the technique utilized in mining. In general, the most economical technology (that specified by the mixed input-output table) is defined by the new coefficients. Carter used these, along with the old mining coefficients, explaining that the increase of mining input coefficients did not signal technical regress, but a deterioration of the ore quality — much as in the Ricardian theory of value, where agricultural expansion necessitates the use of less fertile land. These ideas called attention to the importance of factoring in quality corrections — a new approach that became especially useful in the mining and computer industries, where traditional accounting undervalues productivity growth. In mining, this is due to input quality decreases that reduce output-input ratios, even though there has been no deterioration in technology; in computers, it is due to output quality increases and the resulting expansion in the value of output that also are not taken into account in the standard productivity calculation. Thus, modern corrections, involving hedonic pricing, can be traced back, via Carter's empirical finding, to Ricardo. More generally, her finding throws light on the productivity puzzle that quite a few industry-level Solow residuals tend to be negative, an outcome that conflicts with the dictum that increasing knowledge pushes out the production possibility frontier.

Carter's invention of an effective way to deal with issues such as construction of a huge family of input-output matrices and use of a linear program to determine the choice of technique has found its way into international trade studies that locate comparative advantages in the presence of technology differences between countries. See, for example, ten Raa and Mohnen (ten Raa and Mohnen, 2001).

3. A Model of Technology, Trade, and Pollution: Origins

Throughout her career, Carter has been far ahead of her peers. Indeed, it is only recently that the choice of technique has been recognized as an essential ingredient of applied input-output models. However, Carter's analyses in this area have long addressed the question of choice of technique.

Input-output analysis has a long tradition of assessing the role of international trade by considering export and import baskets as packages of factor contents. This goes back to the Leontief paradox (Leontief, 1953), where the U.S. export basket was shown to be more labor intensive than the import basket. The factor content calculations of both baskets were based on a single input-output coefficients matrix for the United States.

This methodological practice also has been dominant in environmental economics (Wiedmann *et al.*, 2007), where the factor pollution is imputed to domestic consumption and net exports. This is exemplified by an influential paper by De Haan (De Haan, 2002), in which he finds that the Netherlands' emissions exceed the contents of the country's domestic consumption. De Haan also determines that the Netherlands' main trading partner is the rest of the European Union and, moreover, that the use of Dutch input-output coefficients to assess the emission contents of imports is not too distortionary.

Different techniques are best analyzed in bilateral models. Hayami and Kiji analyze the environmental problem faced by Japan and China (Hayami and Kiji, 1997), using the different input-output coefficients. This approach has been extended to multi-regional models, culminating in the ongoing work of Lenzen, *et al.* (Lenzen, Pade, and Munksgaard, 2004). These models can be used to determine carbon footprints (and others) and to allocate the responsibility for emissions between final users.

While all of this work is very much in the spirit of Carter's analysis of coexisting techniques, her ideas remain ahead of the literature because she addresses the question of choice of technique. Indeed, most input-output models, including the recent multi-regional ones, duck the question entirely by assuming that economies have their own techniques *and* that these are maintained, even in the face of international competition, by imposing fixed import coefficients.

4. A Model of Technology, Trade, and Pollution: Application

In order to demonstrate this, we now apply Carter's method for the determination of the optimal choice of technique to the problem of allocating production among different countries, so as to make use of their comparative advantages in producing commodities, while meeting environmental constraints.

In our setting, the number of conceivable input-output matrices is 15 to the power equal to the number of industries, a number beyond imagination. However, Carter's trick is to reduce the magnitude of the problem of optimal choice of technique (in our setting, the optimal pattern of specialization between member states) by means of a linear program. The idea is best illustrated for a two-country world, since extension to 15 or even more countries entails no additional conceptual or computational complications.

Here, we will use Roman bloc letters for symbols that refer to one country and italics for the other country. The input-output coefficients matrices are denoted A and A, respectively. Similarly, the labor coefficients are denoted by row vectors, l and l. If there are different types of labor, vectors l and l become matrices. These matrices can also accommodate other factor input services — for example, that of capital. The gross output vectors are x and x, and the net output vectors (that is, the nets of intermediate demands, Ax and Ax) are y and y. In this constant-returns-to-scale economy, the standard welfare theorems hold, and therefore, the Walrasian economic equilibrium can be determined by finding the optimal solution for the model (Arrow, 1951; Debreu, 1959).

In principle, one needs information regarding consumer preferences to carry out this procedure, but a conservative criterion can be satisfied by assuming an expansion of the levels of all final demands, without changing their proportions (ten Raa, 2008). Hence, to describe the process, we will consider final demands, cy and cy, where c and c are expansion factors to be maximized. It is always possible to expand one economy at the expense of the other by shipping products, so the question is what the proportion between the expansion factors ideally should be. Let $c = \gamma$ c. This equation leaves us with a single criterion, c. The proportion, γ, will be determined by the balance of payments between the two economies, with outputs constrained by the quantities of resources available. At this point, these constraining resource quantities are the sizes of the labor forces, L and L. The model that encompasses the calculations of the optimal assignment of production tasks reads

$$\max_{\mathrm{x}\geq 0, x\geq 0, \mathrm{c}} \quad \mathrm{c} \text{ subject to}$$

$$\mathrm{x} + x \geq \mathrm{Ax} + \mathrm{cy} + Ax + \gamma \mathrm{c}y, \ \ \mathrm{lx} \leq \mathrm{L}, \ \ lx \leq L. \tag{2}$$

We denote the shadow prices of the constraints by row vector, p, and scalars, w and w. The vector of quantities traded is implicit. As such, Country 1's net exports are x − Ax − cy. If this is valued in terms of the commodity shadow prices, the balance of payments is expressed by, p(x − Ax − cy). If gamma is zero, the balance is negative (i.e. the other economy produces only to help the first economy). If the opposite is true, and gamma is infinity, the balance is positive. Using the intermediate value theorem, we find that gamma is zero for some value of gamma — the general equilibrium. The model will allocate the production of any product to one country or the other. This is indicated by the sign patterns of the components of the optimal gross output vectors, x and x.

Next, we bring in emissions coefficients row vectors, b and b.

$$\max_{\mathrm{x}\geq 0, x\geq 0, \mathrm{c}} \quad \mathrm{c} \text{ subject to}$$

$$\mathrm{x} + x \geq \mathrm{Ax} + \mathrm{cy} + Ax + \gamma cy, \; \mathrm{lx} \leq \mathrm{L}, \; lx \leq L, \; \mathrm{bx} \leq \mathrm{B}, \; bx \leq B. \tag{3}$$

Here, B and B are emission ceilings set by some decision process, such as that underlying the Kyoto treaty. Note that this is formally equivalent to bringing in a second constraining scarce resource (such as capital). The shadow price of an emissions constraint is equivalent to a capital rental rate, but now its role is assumed by a Pigovian tax or, equivalently, an emissions rights fee. As usual, the price serves to limit the social damage caused by the emissions by making such undesirable behavior expensive for the emitter. By finding the prices implicit in the solution of the linear programming problem (3), one obtains the incentive that leads to the optimal balance between the reduction of the emissions in question and the cost of attaining that reduction.

This charge affects all commodity prices in a general equilibrium way, with the new prices revealed by the dual conditions associated with linear program (3). Apart from an uninteresting normalization constraint, these price conditions are given by equation (4).

$$\mathrm{p} \leq \mathrm{pA} + \mathrm{wl} + \mathrm{rb}, \; \mathrm{p} \leq \mathrm{p}A + wl + rb. \tag{4}$$

Wage rates w and w are country specific, but the commodity prices, given by vector p, are not. The emissions rights fees, r and r, are specific, so long as the constraints are country specific. Even in the latter situation, the model shows that international trade is a vehicle that enables environmental constraints to be met. If an emissions coefficient is high in one country, while the other coefficients are similar, then linear program (3) will allocate production to the other country. *The straightforward logic of this result mirrors the Ricardian principle of specialization according to comparative advantage.* Both are effective ways to reduce emissions. In effect, this benefit is the form taken by the gains from trade in the analysis here. However, for the market mechanism to achieve this result, emissions rights must be priced and reflected in the costs of production, as seen in equation (4). We say equation, rather than inequality, because the complementary slackness of the theory of linear programming tells us that a strict inequality requires the activity variable in question (a gross output component) to be zero. As such, only the binding constraints in (4) are relevant.

It is also interesting to observe that we may pool the emission constraints, $\mathrm{bx} + bx \leq \mathrm{B} + B$, which is the equivalent of adopting tradable emission rights. This will raise the standard of living even further and is equivalent to the satisfaction of pollution constraints via a tradable license arrangement that enables the reduction of emissions to be carried out by those polluters who can do so most efficiently — that is, at lowest resources cost. In sum, much can be said for this mechanism, which effectively exploits the room provided by technology variation in order to reduce emissions at minimum real cost.

5. A Tribute to Anne Carter

To summarize, this market mechanism allocates production among countries efficiently and in a manner consistent with environmental constraints. The essence of this allocation is described and effectively analyzed by a linear program that models the choice among techniques — a powerful construct first devised and used by Anne Carter in her study of structural change. That contribution, alone, demonstrates Carter's outstanding ability to undertake pure analysis, as well as to design policy that promises to improve to the general welfare. Leontief's material balances are consistent with the Walrasian idea of general equilibrium, in the sense that supply equals demand as physical quantities, but not yet in the sense of consistent behavior between maximizing producers and consumers. Carter broke the chain of analyses of the role of economic interdependencies that extends from the contribution of Quesnay to those of Leontief by opening it up to Walras and taking it to applications involving choice.[3]

---

[3]The authors are grateful to our editor, Amanar Akhabbar, for the suggestion that we add this observation about the relevance of Carter's work to that of Walras.

Moreover, Carter's book on change (Carter, 1970) has been influential and continues to guide us in our research. However, she has moved on from analyzing the choice of technique to address ever deeper questions. The implementation of a new technique, *even when it is available elsewhere*, requires knowhow. In turn, the acquisition of knowhow is complex, and Carter (Carter, 1989) analyzes how this process differs from that of obtaining ordinary capital, in terms of accounting, and co-determines the diffusion of technological knowledge. Carter also addresses the mind-boggling economic measurement issues that emerge when technical change — in the broader sense of not only new processes, but also new products — affects product and industry classifications (Carter, 1998). In this way, Carter continues to set the research agenda.

References

Arrow, K. J. (1951). An extension of the basic theorems of classical welfare economics. *Proceedings of the Second Berkley Symposium on Mathematical Statistics and Probability*, Berkley, California: University of California Press.

Baumol, W. J. and E. N. Wolff. (1981). Subsidies to new energy sources: Do they add to energy stocks? *Journal of Political Economy*, **89**(5), 891–913.

von Bortkiewicz, L. (1907 [1949]). On correction of Marx's fundamental theoretical construction in the third volume of capital. In *Jahrbűcher fűr Nationalőkonomie und Statistik*, Trans. Sweezy, P. M., In: *Karl Marx and the Close of his System*, New York: Augustus M. Kelley, pp. 199–221.

Carter, A. (1970). *Structural Change in the American Economy*, Cambridge: Harvard University Press.

Carter, A. (1989). Knowhow trading as economic exchange. *Research Policy*, **18**(3), 155–163.

Carter, A. (1998). Measuring the performance of a knowledge-based economy. In *The Economic Impact of Knowledge*, Eds. Neef, D., G. Anthony Siesfeld and J. Cefola, Boston: Butterworth-Heinemann, pp. 203–211.

Debreu, G. (1959). *Theory of Value*, New York: Wiley.

De Haan, M. (2002). Disclosing international trade dependencies in environmental pressure indicators: The domestic consumption perspective. Paper presented at *Fourteenth International Conference on Input-Output Techniques, Montréal, Canada.*

Hayami, H. and T. Kiji. (1997). An input-output analysis on Japan-China environmental problem: Compilation of the input-output table for the analysis of energy and air pollutants. *Journal of Applied Input-Output Analysis*, **4**, 23–47.

Lenzen, M., L.-L. Pade and J. Munksgaard. (2004). CO_2 multipliers in multi-region input-output models. *Economic Systems Research*, **16**, 391–412.

Leontief, W. (1953). Domestic production and foreign trade: The American capital position re-examined. *Proceedings of the American Philosophical Society*, **97**(4), 332–349.

Leontief, W. (1970). Environmental repercussions and the economic structure — An input-output approach. *Review of Economics and Statistics*, **52**(3), 262–270.

Luksch, U., N. Steinbach and K. Markosova. (2006). Economic activities and their pressure on the environment 1995–2000, *Eurostat Statistics in Focus*, Environment and Energy, **2**, 1–11.

Phillips, A. (1955). The Tableau Économique as a simple Leontief Model. *Quarterly Journal of Economics*, **69**(1), 137–144.

ten Raa, Th. and P. Mohnen. (2001). The location of comparative advantages on the basis of fundamentals only. *Economic Systems Research*, **13**(1), 93–108.

ten Raa, Th. (2008). Debreu's coefficient of resource utilization, the Solow residual, and TFP: The connection by Leontief preferences. *Journal of Productivity Analysis*, **30**, 191–199.

Sweezy, P. M. (1942). *The Theory of Capitalist Development*. New York: Oxford University Press.

Wiedmann, T., M. Lenzen, K. Turner and J. Barrett. (2007). Examining the global environmental impact of regional consumption activities — Part 2: Review of input-output models for the assessment of environmental impacts embodied in trade. *Ecological Economics*, **61**(1), 15–26.

Index

www.ingramcontent.com/pod-product-compliance
Lightning Source LLC
LaVergne TN
LVHW011659200926
848484LV00004B/1001